POVERTY AND UNDERNUTRITION

POVERTY
AND
UNDERNUTRITION

*Theory, Measurement,
and Policy*

PETER SVEDBERG

*A study prepared for the World Institute for
Development Economics Research
of the
United Nations University (UNU/WIDER)*

OXFORD

UNIVERSITY PRESS

OXFORD

UNIVERSITY PRESS

Great Clarendon Street, Oxford OX2 6DP

Oxford University Press is a department of the University of Oxford.
It furthers the University's objective of excellence in research, scholarship,
and education by publishing worldwide in

Oxford New York

Athens Auckland Bangkok Bogotá Buenos Aires Calcutta
Cape Town Chennai Dar es Salaam Delhi Florence Hong Kong Istanbul
Karachi Kuala Lumpur Madrid Melbourne Mexico City Mumbai
Nairobi Paris São Paulo Shanghai Singapore Taipei Tokyo Toronto Warsaw

and associated companies in Berlin Ibadan

Oxford is a registered trade mark of Oxford University Press
in the UK and in certain other countries

Published in the United States
by Oxford University Press Inc., New York

© The United Nations University 2000

UNU/WIDER: World Institute for Development
Economics Research of the United Nations University,
Katajanokanlaituri 6B, 00160 Helsinki, Finland

The moral rights of the author have been asserted

Database right Oxford University Press (maker)

First published 2000

British Library Cataloguing Publication Data

Data available

Library of Congress Cataloging in Publication Data
Svedberg, Peter.
Poverty and undernutrition: theory, measurement, and policy/
Peter Svedberg.
p. cm.—(Studies in development economics)
Includes bibliographical references (p.).
1. Malnutrition—Africa, Sub-Saharan. 2. Poor—Africa,
Sub-Saharan—Nutrition. I. Title. II. Series.
RA645.N87S837 2000 363.8'0967—dc21 98–45930

ISBN 0–19–829268–6

1 3 5 7 9 10 8 6 4 2

Typeset in Plantin
by Alliance Phototypesetters, Pondicherry, India
Printed in Great Britain
on acid-free paper by
T. J. International Ltd.,
Padstow, Cornwall

FOREWORD

While famines kill millions of people with dramatic suddenness, chronic undernutrition is responsible for terminating many more lives. Endemic hunger works quietly, on a perennial basis, through increasing mortality rates from standard ailments, and it afflicts a much larger population than is affected by famines. Persistent undernourishment also blights the existence of people who may not die as a result of it but whose ability to lead secure, productive and happy lives is severely afflicted by debilitation and morbidity. All this happens without the climactic swiftness of famines, and tends not to arouse the kind of visual empathy and sympathetic outbursts that famines can generate, with the help of the public media. Indeed, even the exact magnitudes and intensities of undernutrition in different countries in the world remain obscured from public view. A lack of hard data as well as the absence of clear analyses makes this possible. While there is evidence enough to indicate that more people die from undernutrition than from famines (and also that many more people lead severely constrained lives as a result of it), nevertheless it is very difficult to derive definitive estimates of the exact magnitudes of people affected by this endemic deprivation.

Undernutrition is, in this sense, both a bigger and a harder problem to deal with than the more sensational phenomenon of famines. It is not easy to think of any social problem in the contemporary world that deserves greater attention than the foggy adversity of chronic and widespread undernutrition. In this book, Peter Svedberg has taken on the challenge of investigating this difficult problem, which is clearly one of the principal tribulations in the contemporary world.

I should, incidentally, mention here that Peter Svedberg's research was initially done for the World Institute of Development Economics Research (WIDER), located in Helsinki, Finland. The institute is affiliated with the United Nations University. Svedberg's work was done for the project on 'hunger and poverty' at WIDER, which I had the privilege to direct for many years. Clearly, I should declare an interest here, but I believe I am not influenced by this connection at all in commending Svedberg's book as a major achievement in this field.

Svedberg's remarkable book addresses the extraordinary difficulties that make progress in this area of study so very exacting. The difficulties are both conceptual and empirical. There are two main methods that have been used to assess the extent of undernutrition in different parts of the world. The Food and Agriculture Organization of the United Nations—more commonly known by its acronym FAO—approaches the problem through food availability statistics. In contrast, the World Health Organization, also of the United Nations, and more commonly known by its acronym WHO, proceeds to study undernutrition through observed conditions of the human body and basic functionings—the so-called 'anthropometric' measures.

Svedberg rejects the FAO approach very firmly, and comparatively favours the WHO procedures, but proposes ways and means of making better use of the anthropometric approach. Indeed, he goes on to make enhanced use of the approach, utilizing information both from the WHO and from elsewhere, and constructs on that basis a picture of the state of undernutrition in the world, especially focusing on two particularly problematic regions, viz. South Asia and Sub-Saharan Africa. I shall come to that picture presently, but the methodological issues themselves are of considerable interest.

Take the FAO method first. The FAO tends to concentrate on the information it has on national food supply, and proceeds to estimate the food consumption per family and per head in different parts of the population through the use of certain distributional presumptions. The total food supply figure is, in this way, converted into food intake estimates for groups of families. The numbers tell us something about what the problem may look like from one end (that of available supply) with articulated explanation of how that supply is assumed to be distributed. But this approach suffers, Svedberg argues, from several limitations.

Perhaps the most basic problem arises from the fact that food consumption is only one influence among many on nutrition. For example, prevalence of disease and variations of metabolic rates are among other variables with obvious influence on the state of a person's nutrition. The basic difficulty here is that commodity supply or consumption cannot be readily identified with what human beings *get out* of that consumption. A simple example of the problem is illustrated by the possibility that a person with a parasitic intestinal disease may consume a good deal of food and still remain very undernourished, thanks to low bodily absorption. There are other—more complex —problems as well. The FAO has tried to deal with these difficulties through specific assumptions that relate food consumption to bodily functioning. But the approach of relying primarily on 'intake data', rather than on observations of bodily conditions, limits this approach to undernutrition at a very basic level.

In addition to this foundational problem, there are also empirical difficulties with the FAO's estimates. The distributional presumptions of the total food supply are not closely linked with analyses of incomes and purchasing powers of different consumers, so that the linkage with economic causation remains rather loose. This problem can, of course, be avoided by directly observing actual intakes of food by the persons involved. This is not done either. The empirical observations remain rather confined to aggregate levels, and are supplemented by distributional assumptions. In fact, given the difficulty in getting hard data on actual intakes of food by different families and the even greater difficulty of securing reliable statistics on the distribution of food within the family, the informational basis of the food-supply approach to undernutrition remains deeply problematic (quite aside from the further difficulty of translating food intake figures into nutrition achieved, given interpersonal variations in converting ingested ingredients into achieved nourishment).

On the basis of these—and other—criticisms, Svedberg emerges as deeply sceptical of the entire FAO approach. As it happens, the FAO has been increasingly engaged in recent years in re-examining its established methods, and there is evidence of considerable self-criticism at this time. Svedberg's critique and suggestions may, thus, have much constructive value even in the in-house scrutiny in which the FAO is engaged. Given the division of responsibility within the United Nations family, FAO will continue to have a big voice in the investigation of undernutrition in the world, and this makes it all the more important to examine Peter Svedberg's criticisms and suggestions with the attention they deserve.

Svedberg sees more merit in the anthropometric method, which the WHO uses in one form. Even though Svedberg has some detailed criticisms of WHO practice, his own approach is reasonably in line with what WHO aims to do. While the FAO approach is firmly rejected, Svedberg proceeds to use a strategy of conceptual analysis and empirical use that is broadly in alliance with WHO's attempts. Indeed, Svedberg argues the case for collecting these—and related—data much more comprehensively, and also for making much greater systematic use of such data.

Svedberg's application of his own procedure leads to a radically different view of the pattern of undernutrition in the world. While the FAO finds the problem to be severest in Sub-Saharan Africa, Svedberg identifies South Asia (including India) as the area of most widespread undernutrition. Armed with his diagnostic approach, he comments on the nature, configuration and causation of undernutrition in the world, and investigates the extremely grave consequences of the observed pattern on the lives and well-being of the afflicted population.

The diagnostic method used by Svedberg is, as he himself notes, more effective in some cases than in others. For example, his anthropometric method works much better for young children than for adults, and rather better for women of reproductive age than for men of the same age (or for older people of either sex). One of the many attractive features of Svedberg's work is his constant focus on distinguishing between what conclusions emerge very clearly and what remain surrounded by doubts. He also identifies some questions that cannot, at this time, be answered in any satisfactory way at all, given the information that we have and the techniques of analysis that have so far been developed.

This is indeed a major contribution to the understanding of undernutrition in the world, especially for areas most afflicted by this scourge. The reach of the book is very wide indeed. There is methodological scrutiny as well as empirical analysis. There is criticism—often stingingly strong—of established practice as well as constructive development of alternative procedures. There is identification of areas and populations which suffer most from the predicament of undernutrition as well as investigation of the adverse consequences of such undernutrition. There is causal analysis of what may have led to the problems being so serious in particular regions in the world as well as scrutiny of policies for reducing the burden of undernutrition and even constructive speculation on the possible ways and means of eliminating this terrible phenomenon.

We may not yet be able to banish altogether the nasty presence of undernutrition in the troubled world in which we live. But Svedberg's work helps us to understand the challenge with much greater clarity. This in turn can substantially facilitate the making of policies to end the widespread phenomenon of famished lives and reduced living. For these important contributions, we have reason to be grateful to Peter Svedberg.

Amartya Sen

PREFACE

Heads of state and representatives of government from 186 nations have recently signed a resolution to reduce the number of undernourished people in the world by half before the year 2015. If the 'international community' should be able to monitor progress towards this worthy objective, agreed to in Rome at the World Food Summit in late 1996, a necessary precondition is that (i) the initial number of undernourished is reasonably well known and (ii) that changes over time can be observed. Moreover, if this objective is to be accomplished through new policy initiatives, directing and designing these policies require that we know (iii) *where* the undernourished are found, (iv) *who* they are, and (v) *why* they are undernourished.

When addressing the above questions there are only two data sets that can be consulted. One is from the Food and Agricultural Organization (FAO) and relies on national per-capita food 'availabilities' for estimating the proportion of the population that is undernourished in different countries. The other data set is from the World Health Organization (WHO) and is based on the anthropometric approach, the essence of which is to assess the nutritional status of individuals by their weight and height. The disturbing fact is that these two methods give different, or conflicting, answers to the above questions, or no answer at all.

(i) According to the FAO, 20 per cent of all households in the developing countries (or 841 million people) are undernourished. The WHO data suggest that in these countries, when judged by weight for age, 34 per cent of all children below the age of five (179 million) are undernourished; when judged by height for age 41 per cent (215 million); and by being thin for their height, 9 per cent (48 million). If the number of undernourished are to be halved, we must choose between these (or other) numbers in order to establish a bench-mark of the initial level of undernutrition.

(ii) If the monitoring of progress towards the 2015 objective is to be carried out with the present version of the FAO method, it will—in effect—be like monitoring changes in national food supplies. This is because food supplies is the only variable that the FAO is able to measure in terms of changes over time. As of today, the FAO has no data from any country on changes in the *distributions* of calorie intakes and in calorie requirements across households, the other two main parameters in its estimation model. On the other hand, if progress is to be monitored with the anthropometric approach, its coverage has to be extended to all age/gender categories, and measurements have to be obtained more frequently than at present.

(iii) The two methods give diametrically opposite answers to the question of *where* the undernourished are found. The FAO method finds undernutrition to be the most prevalent in the Sub-Saharan African countries (43 per cent on average) and much higher than in South Asia (22 per cent). In sharp contrast, according to all anthropometric measurements, undernutrition is heavily concentrated to the South Asian countries. These indicators suggest that undernutrition among children in the latter region is about twice as common as in Sub-Saharan Africa. The anthropometric measurements of women aged 15–49 provide the same picture. Where undernutrition is concentrated at the *subnational* levels cannot be answered by either method. In the case of the FAO method, based on *national* food supplies, this limitation is non-rectifiable. In the case of anthropometrics, the main problem is the incomplete statistical coverage.

(iv) The FAO approach is designed for estimating the *proportion* of a population that is undernourished; it cannot be used for *identifying* the undernourished households or individuals. The question *who* the undernourished are can thus not be answered with the FAO method. This means that it cannot be relied upon for targeting interventions to undernourished people, estimating intra-household allocation of nutrients, or assessing the nutritional consequences of changes in economic policy, for example structural adjustment programmes. The anthropometric method can in principle answer the *who* question, but so far, only young children have been measured on a large scale; women of reproductive age to some extent, but adolescents, male adults, and old people have yet to be systematically measured. We thus lack empirically based data for targeting interventions along age and gender lines.

(v) The answer to the question *why* part of the population in a country is undernourished is built into the FAO method: the national supply of food is insufficient. (It is notable that the meeting in Rome, convened by the FAO, was called the World *Food* Summit rather than, say, the World *Hunger* Summit.) The anthropometric method, in itself, does not give answers to the question why children (and other cohorts) are underweight, stunted, or wasted. At a superficial level, the answer may seem straightforward: they eat too little. When children are underweight this may well be because they have insufficient access to (suitable) food, but it can equally well be that untreated disease makes it impossible for them to fully utilize the nutrients given to them. When children are stunted, the reasons are often a combination of 'assaults', the details of which are yet not well understood.

The overall objective of this book is to contribute a more detailed and—hopefully—convincing analysis than has been offered so far of the *relative* merits and demerits of the two main approaches for estimating undernutrition. Also their relevance for answering the different policy questions for which we need nutritional indicators is analysed. The possibilities for improving on the two methods will also be taken up extensively. It will be argued that if *no* better data on undernutrition are produced, and a deeper understanding of the causes and consequences is not gained, future interventions will be ineffective and misdirected. Designing policy in the absence of relevant and reliable data is inevitably to fumble in the dark and one may even go as far as saying that to ignore the measurement problems is to ignore the undernutrition problem.

There is no perfect way, and never will be, of defining and measuring undernutrition. It is a phenomenon that spans a multitude of aspects: body size and composition, physical activity, health, cognitive and motoric capacity, and many other capabilities, on all of which it is difficult to put numbers. No single measure can ever capture all these dimensions. For those who are neither altogether sceptical about governments' and the international community's determination to take action against undernutrition, nor inclined to emotional calls for 'immediate action' without prior analysis, the measurement problems nevertheless have to be taken seriously. The main choice is between two imperfect measurement approaches and the challenge is to sort out the least unreliable one, and to improve it. More refined and relevant measurements than those presently advanced by the FAO and WHO, respectively, are required to direct policy, and better indicators of undernutrition are *possible* to derive. To substantiate these claims, as well as the others made above, is the aim of this book.

P. S.

ACKNOWLEDGEMENTS

This book has taken a long time to complete and during the process, a large number of colleagues and friends have contributed in various ways. I will single out one in particular, without whose support the book may not have been finalized: Amartya Sen. When, at times, my faith in being able to finish the manuscript wobbled, he repeatedly encouraged me to make an additional effort. He is also the only person who has read and commented on the whole manuscript. My sincere thanks.

Others who have commented on parts of the book and/or provided advice, constructive critique, and encouragement at one or more occasions are: Harold Alderman, Alok Bhargava, Christoffer Bliss, Howarth Bouis, Angus Deaton, Jean Drèze, Carl Eicher, Wayne Ferris, Jeffery Fine, Nils Gottfries, Lawrence Haddad, Hartwig de Haen, Gerry Helleiner, Henrik and Mia Horn, Nurul Islam, Bo Jerlström, Nanak Kakwani, Ravi Kanbur, Eileen Kennedy, Michael Lipton, John Mellor, Mike Moore, Logan Naiken, Benno Ndulu, Marteen Nube, Siddiq Osmani, Per Pinstrup-Andersen, Shlomo Reutlinger, Hans Rosling, David Sahn, T. N. Srinivasan, Caroline Svedberg Wibling, Peter Timmer, Alberto Valdes, Theresa Wardlaw, John Waterlow, Patrick Webb, and Rolf Åkesson.

Many thanks also to the support staff and the research assistants who have facilitated the technical progress of the manuscript at various stages: Mårten Blix, Sholeh Blom, Thomas Eisensee, Maria Gil, Juhani Holm, Hedvig Jarn, Christina Lönnblad, Helena Matheou, Jesper Roine, Marcus Salomonsson, and Judit Weibull. Finally, but not least, financial support from WIDER and Sida (the Swedish International Development Cooperation Agency) is gratefully acknowledged.

CONTENTS

PART IV

LIST OF TABLES

APPENDIX TABLES

LIST OF FIGURES

APPENDIX FIGURE

ABBREVIATIONS

2SLS	two-stage least squares
AA	adjustment and adaptation (paradigm of undernutrition)
ACC/SCN	Administrative Committee on Coordination/Sub-Committee on Nutrition
ALR	adult literacy rate
BMI	body mass index
BMR	basal metabolic rate
CCOP	calorie cut-off point
CES	constant elasticity of substitution (production function)
CIAF	composite index of anthropometric failure
CMR	child mortality rate
CV	coefficient of variation
DALY	disability-adjusted live years
DES	daily energy supply
DHS	Demographic and Health Survey
DLW	Doubly Labelled Water (method)
EA/P	East Asia and the Pacific
FAO	Food and Agricultural Organization
FAO/ESN	Nutrition planning, assessment and evaluation-service division at FAO
FBS	food balance sheet
FCS	food consumption survey
FLR	female literacy rate
GDPc	gross domestic product per capita ·
Gini	Gini coefficient (of income distribution)
GNPc	gross national product per capita
GP	genetic-potential (paradigm of undernutrition)
H/A	height for age
HIV/AIDS	human immunodeficiency virus/acquired immunodeficiency syndrome
HES	household expenditure survey
HPCCA	household per-capita calorie availability
HPCCR	household per-capita calorie requirements
IBRD	International Bank for Reconstruction and Development
IDRC	International Development Research Centre (Canada)
IFPRI	International Food Policy Research Institute
IFI	International financial institution
IMF	International Monetary Fund
IMR	infant mortality rate
LA/C	Latin America and the Caribbean

LBW	low birth weight
LCE	long-term calorie expenditure (function)
LEB	life expectancy at birth
ME	Middle East
NA	North Africa
NCHS	National Center for Health Statistics (USA)
NGO	non-governmental organisation
NPCCA	national per-capita calorie availability
OECD	Organisation for Economic Co-operation and Development
OLS	ordinary least squares
ORT	oral rehydration therapy
PAL	physical activity level
PEM	protein–energy malnutrition
POU	prevalence of undernutrition
PPP	purchasing power parity
RDI	recommended daily (calorie) intake
REV	(calorie) revenue (function)
RHS	right-hand side (variable)
SA	South Asia
SCE	short-term calorie expenditure (function)
SD	standard deviation
SEA	South-East Asia
SSA	Sub-Saharan Africa(n)
TB	tuberculosis
TFP	total factory productivity
U5MR	under-fives mortality rate
UN	United Nations
UNCTAD	United Nations Conference for Trade and Development
UNDP	United Nations Development Programme
UNICEF	United Nations Children's Foundation
UNU	United Nations University
USDA	United States Department of Agriculture
W/A	weight for age
W/H	weight for height
WAF	weight-for-age failure
WHO	World Health Organization

LBW — low birth weight
LCE — long-term care expenditure (function)
LEB — life expectancy at birth
NMR — ... Post
NA — North Africa
NCHS — National Center for Health Statistics (USA)
NGO — non-governmental organization
NPHCA — national primary health care ability
OECD — Organisation for Economic Co-operation and Development
OLS — ordinary least squares
ORT — oral rehydration therapy
PAL — physical activity level
PDM — ...
POL — promotion of ...
PPP — purchasing power parity
RDI — recommended daily (calorie) intake
RIV — relative income variation
RHS — right-hand side (variable)
SA — South Asia
SER — diet-excess calorie expenditure (function)
SD — standard deviation
SEA — South-East Asia
SSA — Sub-Saharan Africa
TB — tuberculosis
TFP — total factor productivity
U5MR — under-five mortality rate
UN — United Nations
UNCTAD — United Nations Conference on Trade and Development
UNDP — United Nations Development Programme
UNICEF — United Nations Children's Fund
UNU — United Nations University
USDA — United States Department of Agriculture
W — weight for age
WIR — World Investment Report
WRI — World Resources Institute
WHO — World Health Organization

PART I

1

Background and Introduction

1.1. BACKGROUND

According to recent assessment by the Food and Agricultural Organization (FAO) of the UN, almost one billion people in the developing countries are suffering from undernutrition (FAO*a* 1996). On the basis of its estimates of per capita 'food availability' at the level of countries, and of how the food is distributed across households, the FAO asserts that, more specifically, 841 million people do not get enough calories to be able to pursue light manual work for normal hours while at the same time maintaining a body weight that is consonant with health. The FAO estimates further suggest that the incidence of undernutrition in Sub-Saharan Africa (SSA) is now about twice as high as that in South Asia. Furthermore, the FAO estimates purport that SSA is the only region where there has not been a decline in the prevalence of undernutrition (POU) since the early 1970s.[1]

However, there are other nutritional indicators which give a different global picture. The main alternative estimates come from the World Health Organization (WHO) and are also used intensively by the United Nations Children's Foundation (UNICEF). These estimates are based on anthropometric assessment of children, particularly of their weight for age, below the age of five. By this indicator, the prevalence of undernutrition among children is twice as high in South Asia as in SSA, quite the reverse of the picture given by the FAO estimates. Moreover, the weight-for-age indicator further suggests that the prevalence of undernutrition worldwide is almost double that purported by the FAO estimates (Fig. 1.1). With other anthropometric indicators from WHO, still further pictures emerge. The height-for-age indicator, gives a higher overall prevalence of undernutrition worldwide than does the weight-for-age indicator; according to the the weight-for-height indicator, 'only' 7 per cent in SSA and 17 per cent in South Asia are undernourished (WHO 1995).

Also, across individual countries, there is little consistency in the ranking of the prevalence of undernutrition by different indicators. In Fig. 1.2, the share of children being underweight for their age, as estimated by the WHO, is regressed against the FAO estimates of the prevalence of undernourished households. The sample comprises 79 developing countries, and the observations are from the first half of the 1990s. There is a positive association between the two (most widely used) indicators, which is statistically significant,

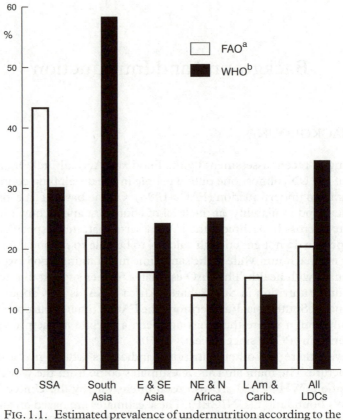

FIG. 1.1. Estimated prevalence of undernutrition according to the FAO and WHO, by major geographical regions, 1990–2

Sources: FAO 1996: table 14 and WHO (1995).

[a] Estimated share of households with inadequate access to calories.
[b] Estimated share of children with inadequate weight for age. Averages based on surveys from mainly 1988–94.

but weak (the R^2-adjusted is only 0.26). The rank correlation coefficient, at 0.31, is also statistically significant, but reveals that most countries are ranked quite differently, depending on the choice of indicator of undernutrition.

1.2. THE CHALLENGES: THE FIVE Ws

The brief summary of key statistics from the international organizations in the preceding section reveals conflicting indications of the seriousness of the nutrition problem worldwide. It also gives conflicting information on where the problems are the most acute, in Africa or in South Asia. The different

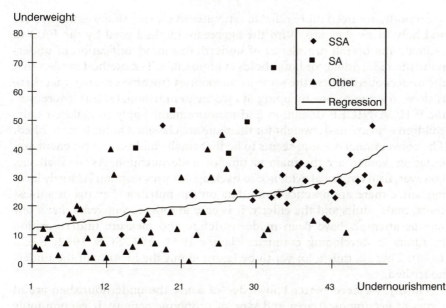

FIG. 1.2. Statistical association between share of underweight children and share of undernourished households across 79 developing countries, 1990s

indicators further suggest that in some regions, the incidence of undernutrition in children is considerably higher than in other age groups. This is so especially in Asia, but not in SSA. All these conflicting indications are not easily reconcilable, as the analysis in this book will demonstrate. The challenges to be tackled have at least five dimensions, which I will call 'the five Ws'.

First of all, we need a better characterization of *what* undernutrition is. The contemporary literature abounds with different definitions: some equate undernutrition with low energy intake; others with retarded growth in stature or low weight; and others still with risk of impaired health or disturbance of mental development and capabilities. As we shall see, the differences in definitions and measurements in use are so large that anything between 7 and 80 per cent of the population in Africa may be classified as undernourished. Undernutrition is by no means an easily defined concept that lends itself readily to empirical assessment. It is a phenomenon that spans a multitude of aspects: body size and composition, physical activity, health, cognitive and psychomotoric development, and many other capabilities which can all be measured by degree of 'severity'. It is therefore not possible ever to arrive at a unidimensional index (or definition) of undernutrition that is universally accepted for all purposes. However, by being more explicit about what different indicators really indicate, one can accomplish a better understanding of the relationship between the various nutritional indicators and the different underlying purposes for which they are used.

Secondly, we need more reliable estimates of *who* the undernourished are
and how many they are. With the aggregate method used by the FAO to
estimate the overall prevalence of undernutrition, identification of undernourished individuals or households is impossible. The method implies that
the undernourished are the same as the poorest (income groups), that there
is close to a one-to-one mapping of income to nutritional status. Moreover,
the WHO/UNICEF definition and measurements apply to children only:
children who are underweight for their age are classified as undernourished.
The conventional wisdom seems to be that small children and pregnant and
lactating women are the main victims of undernutrition. As we shall see,
however, firm empirical evidence to back up this presumption is largely lacking, since there are practically no data on the nutritional status of adolescents, male adults and the elderly. It is only in most recent years that a few
serious attempts have been made to define and measure undernutrition
in adults in developing countries (James 1994, ACC/SCN 1992, FAO*a*
1996). There is thus a lot yet to be learnt about the identity of the undernourished.

Thirdly, we need better knowledge of *where* the undernourished are in
terms of geographical area and type of economic activity. It is commonly
claimed that the most severe nutritional problems are found in rural communities with low levels of productivity. There is a fair amount of evidence
to support this hypothesis, but the picture needs to be sharpened if well-
targeted interventions are to be feasible. Even in the poorest rural districts,
not all poor people (or children) are undernourished by conventional standards, and there are indications of undernutrition in many urban areas too.
Moreover, there are also large differences across the 50 SSA countries, and
between these countries and South Asia, which need more analysis.

Fourthly, there is the question of *when* people are undernourished. Do the
people who are observed to be undernourished by some indicator at one
point in time constitute a stable population, or does its composition change?
Are women especially undernourished when they are pregnant and/or lactating? Is there a large element of seasonality in undernutrition? Is widespread
undernutrition concentrated in years with particularly bad weather and other
adverse natural external conditions, as the repeated outbursts of drought-
related famine in parts of the African region may suggest? Does undernutrition increase during periods of economic decline, as in the 1980s and 1990s?
All these questions call for longitudinal studies that so far have been carried
out only sporadically.

Fifthly, we need to know *why* the people who are found to be undernourished are in this state. Almost tautological—they are undernourished
because they expend too little energy (calories) in relation to what they ought
to expend—the question is why so? General poverty, low household productivity and income, maldistribution of food within the household, lack of
education, or diseases that affect the individual's intake and/or expenditure

of energy are all possible reasons. As we shall see, it has proved difficult to delineate the various reasons for undernutrition and to establish what is cause and what is consequence.

1.3. MAIN OBJECTIVES AND PLAN OF THE BOOK

The book comprises 18 chapters organized into five sections, each with a distinct theme.

Part I comprises this introduction and Chapter 2, in which an analytical description of the main paradigms of how to define and measure undernutrition is provided. Also, the main controversies in these matters and the areas of consensus are highlighted. These two chapters are intended to set the stage; more detailed analyses of the various issues are provided in subsequent chapters.

In Part II, the questions of how calorie intake/expenditure, work effort, body weight, and income are inter-related at the level of individuals are discussed. A model of how these four variables are determined endogenously is presented in Chapter 3. The model can be seen as an attempt to bridge the economists' and the nutritionists' ways of modelling these inter-relationships. In Chapter 4, the predictions of the model are contrasted to the correlations (associations) between calorie intake and income found in the empirical literature on the basis of cross-sectional data.

Part III of the book is aimed at an assessment of the method of defining and measuring undernutrition based on estimates of gaps between calorie intake and calorie requirements for households. This is the method used by the FAO to estimate the prevalence of undernutrition in the world, its distribution across countries, and development over time. Chapter 5 provides a description of this model and the main results reported by the FAO, and also a preliminary test of the robustness of the results for the SSA countries. In the four subsequent chapters (6–9), each of the four building blocks that make up the FAO model are scrutinized.

In Chapter 6, the per-capita estimates of calories 'available' for human consumption in the SSA countries are assessed. The reasons for focusing on these countries are that the statistics for the SSA region are considerably more unreliable than in most other places and that they contain systematic biases. In Chapter 7, the method used by the FAO to estimate the distribution of the nationally 'available' calories across households is the focal point. In Chapter 8, the FAO way of estimating minimum individual calorie expenditure requirements is scrutinized. Chapter 9 takes a critical view of the procedure by which FAO aggregates individual calorie requirement to the per-capita calorie cut-off points, which are subsequently used to delineate the undernourished households. In all these chapters, estimation biases are revealed and margins of error in the estimates are identified. Chapter 10, which closes Part III, provides a discussion of improvements of the FAO model that could be accomplished in the short- and long-term.

In Part IV, a parallel analysis of the main alternative approach to define and measure undernutrition, based on anthropometric assessment of—predominantly—young children, is conducted. Also, here we start out with a presentation of the 'model' and a brief account of the main results reported by WHO and UNICEF, the chief providers of such estimates (Chapter 11). In the two subsequent chapters, the robustness of these results are assessed from various angles. In Chapter 12, measurement and selection biases, as well as the representativeness of the samples from which the national estimates are derived, are analysed. The more conceptual question of how well anthropometric measurements indicate primary undernutrition—as opposed to other genotypic and phenotypic deficiencies—is addressed in Chapter 13. A new 'composite' index of anthropometric failure is also introduced and discussed in this chapter.

In Part V of the study, the consequences and causes of anthropometric failure are analysed. Chapter 14 dwells on the question how well anthropometric measurements indicate the risk of subsequent death for small children. In Chapter 15, the reasons for anthropometric failure and child mortality in mainly SSA and South Asia are analysed. What role do low real incomes (economic poverty) play in comparison to parental literacy, public provision of various services and several other variables which vary across countries world-wide and are statistically (albeit imperfectly) quantifiable? In this chapter, more long-term adverse consequences of anthropometric failure, such as increased life-long morbidity, educationability, and various impairments in adulthood, are analysed. Chapter 16 attempts to resolve the apparent puzzle that child mortality is considerably higher in SSA than it is in South Asia, while the situation is quite the opposite when it comes to the anthropometric status of the children. Can the explanation be differences in the quality and distribution of the public health and sanitation services? Is the pronounced economic decline in most of SSA a major explanation?

In Chapter 17, the policy implications that follow from the previous analysis are discussed, focusing mainly on SSA. What are the lessons from other parts of the world, both positive and negative? Can improvements in anthropometric status and in life expectancy at birth be achieved through public-sector reform, or is overall economic growth a necessary precondition? What are the main constraints on public sector reform and on accomplishing growth? Finally, Chapter 18 contains a summary and the main conclusions and recommendations for how to improve measurements and how to alleviate undernutrition. These questions bear directly on the resolutions adopted at the *World Food Summit* in late 1996, and the possibilities of reaching the overall objective of the Summit as agreed by the governments of 186 countries, *viz.* to halve the number of the undernourished before the year 2015.

1.4. THE FOCUS ON SUB-SAHARAN AFRICA—IN INTERNATIONAL COMPARISON

In the late 1980s and early 1990s, there was a strong sentiment in the international research community and in the international organizations that the world's food and nutrition problems were increasingly concentrated in Africa. This was the single most important reason why this book was initiated. At the time there was not enough statistical evidence available to allow a direct test of this hypothesis; now, as we shall see, a few years later, there are enough data to give a relatively affirmative answer to the question of where the world's food problems are concentrated and what the trends over time are.

The concern in the late 1980s that the nutrition situation in the African countries was deteriorating followed mainly from the unprecedented economic and political setbacks in Africa during that decade. Most of the SSA countries had no doubt experienced what can only be called an accelerating economic and political crisis. The annual per-capita growth of GDP in the region as a whole went down from about 2 per cent in the 1960s to 0.1 per cent in the 1970s; over the 1980s and 1990s, it was in the negative (UNCTAD 1995, see also Table 16.1). Agricultural and food production also declined (FAO*b* 1996). The share of SSA in world exports fell dramatically and the real export earnings of many of the countries in the region had dropped significantly during the 1980s (Svedberg 1991*b*, 1993). Although there are few reliable indicators, poverty most probably increased (Ravallion *et al.* 1991, Chen *et al.* 1994). The negative growth rates have continued in the bulk of the SSA countries during the first half of the 1990s (even though preliminary data for 1996–7 indicate a slight upturn, IBRD*a* 1999).

In recent years, however, several governments in Africa have recognized that the economic problems in their countries may have something to do with their own policies; that all problems can not be blamed on deteriorating terms of trade, high real interest on foreign loans, and other external adversaries. Many governments have also accepted that there has to be a drastic change in economic policy over the 1990s. More than two dozen SSA countries with previously highly overvalued real exchange rates have devalued substantially and have also initiated, or are in the process of initiating, reform in a great number of areas (Killick *et al.* 1992*a*, 1992*b*, IMF 1993, IBRD 1994, 1997). However, the structural adjustment process in Africa is far from completed. During the first decade of the new millennium, many additional policy changes have to be made before an era of sustained growth might be achieved.

During the adjustment period, food consumption and nutrition issues will enter the policy process both as objectives in themselves and as constraints on the achievement of other aims. That improved nutrition should be an explicit policy may seem self-evident. Food is, after all, one of the most basic of all economically constrained human needs and the situation in Africa, even if not as precarious as claimed by the most alarmist analysts (e.g. FAO), is sufficiently serious for nutrition to be a priority issue in its own right.

In a policy perspective it seems imperative to get the numbers right. If more than 40 per cent of the population in SSA is undernourished, and the main reason is faltering aggregate food supplies, as implied by the estimation techniques used by the FAO, the most promising remedy seems to be increased food production or overall economic growth that produces the financial means to import more food. These are long-term policies: to improve the overall productivity in the economy may take several decades. On the other hand, if 'only' some 10 per cent are at nutritional risk, and lack of education, untreated but curable diseases and underprovision of public services are the main reasons, there may be scope for substantial improvement in anthropometric status and mortality rates even in the medium term. In this case, (well-) targeted public health, education, and feeding interventions may be workable.

However, better nutrition is not only an end; nutrition will also come in as a constraint on the short- and medium-term structural adjustment programmes that will dominate the African scene during the coming years. New economic policies will induce shifts in relative prices and real income distribution. This will have different effects on the food entitlements of different groups. If something like 10 per cent of the population in a country is undernourished, the governments will have much more leeway in the pursuit of new macroeconomic and stabilization policies than if it is 30–60 per cent. Moreover, one needs to know who the most undernourished are, otherwise it will be impossible to assure that they are compensated in cases where they suffer from negative side-effects of new economic policies; that is, to accomplish 'adjustment with a human face'.[2]

An improvement in the nutrition and health status of the population in Africa—and South Asia—may be warranted not only on humanitarian grounds. In recent years, a small but growing number of studies at the micro-level suggest that improved human nutrition has positive economic effects through increased productivity of labour in poor countries (IBRD 1993, Behrman 1993, see also Chapter 4). There is also growing evidence at the macro-level that a well-nourished and healthy population (as proxied by life expectancy at birth) has a positive impact on economic growth in subsequent periods (Barro and Sala-i-Martin 1995, Sachs and Werner 1997; more on these new findings are provided in Chapter 17).

Improved nutrition may also have favourable political impacts. Over the years, some SSA governments have been toppled in the wake of policies that have hurt the food interests of relatively strong and well-organized (urban) groups. (Or more frequently, governments have avoided this fate by discontinuing 'unpopular' food policies.) Political stability is desirable in itself, given that governments are dedicated to development, but stability is also conducive to economic progress (*cet par*). It is so by providing stable economic incentives which enhance credibility, and so investment, as emphasized by the so-called 'new growth theory' (Barro and Sala-i-Martin 1995, Sala-i-Martin 1997).[3]

Although this study started out with the intention to understand better and to quantify the nutrition situation in the SSA countries, it soon became obvious that a broader approach and perspective was warranted. While the African countries stand out in some dimensions (e.g. the lack of economic growth for about three decades, a high frequency of civil wars, and weak and unstable governments), there are many similarities with other countries, not least in South Asia. There are no doubt lessons to be learnt for Africa from the latter as well as countries in other parts of the world. In this final version of the study, the focus on the SSA countries is retained, but the study contains much more comparative analysis than was originally planned (which to some extent explains the long time it has taken to complete). Special emphasis has been given to understanding and explaining differences between SSA and South Asia, the two regions with the highest incidence of human deprivation, irrespective of the indicators used. These differences may help us find out which policies may work and which will not work in the respective regions.

1.5. LIMITATIONS OF THE STUDY

Most of the shortcomings of the study will become only too evident to the reader as he or she proceeds, but some of the limitations are deliberate and need to be pointed out from the outset.

1.5.1. Limited Coverage of Food-security Issues

Some aspects of the broad 'food security' complex will not be covered in this monograph.[4] For instance, we will not discuss the roles of (internal and external) trade and food grain stocks as alternative (or complementary) ways of ensuring stable food supplies. Nor will we dwell on the problems with setting up appropriate early-warning systems. Food production self-sufficiency versus free trade as a means for accomplishing increased food supplies and affecting food prices is yet another problem that is left untouched. The reason why these and some other issues (see below) in the food security area are not analysed in the present study is not that they have been considered unimportant. The only reasons are that the author has felt that he has little to add on these issues and that some limitations have to be imposed on every study. Some readers will most likely find that this book has already tried to cover too much.

1.5.2. *Undernutrition versus Malnutrition*

The study deals exclusively with what is here defined as undernutrition; that is, the outcomes of deficiency of the energy component in food over a long period. Food also contains many non-calorific components which are crucial for the sustainment and reproduction of human life, most notably minerals and vitamins, with fats and proteins both performing these latter roles and providing energy. In the nutrition literature, there is no universally accepted terminology to distinguish between various nutritional deficiencies. Many nutritionists do not make the distinction between under- and malnutrition that will be used throughout this study. They speak of malnutrition when obviously referring to energy inadequacy. Still others use the term malnutrition to cover all types of nutritional deficiencies. Others use the term protein–energy malnutrition (PEM) to indicate that lack of energy and of proteins normally go hand in hand; that is, when energy is lacking in the diet, proteins are usually also deficient, and conversely, when energy is adequate, so is protein. This has for some time between the conventionally accepted view, but a few recent studies have contested this notion.[5] Whatever the substance of this new insight, in this study, when the terms undernutrition and undernourishment are used, they refer to energy insufficiency only. The term protein–calorie malnutrition is used only when the combined inadequacy of protein and energy is the focal point. The term malnutrition will be used to describe deficiency of minerals and vitamins.

The main reason for focusing the analysis on undernutrition and—by and large—leaving out the problems related to micronutrients is that undernutrition is clearly an economic 'macro' issue related to food entitlements, poverty, and the socio-economic structure of societies throughout the Third World. Malnutrition also has economic causes and consequences, but it is still more of a 'technical' medical problem, on which an economist has little analytical competence. It also seems that various forms of malnutrition are more local problems that are technically related to location-specific characteristics, such as the chemical composition of soils (e.g. iodine), the vitamin content of the local staple food, etc. It is probably true that under-and malnutrition often go hand in hand, i.e. that several nutritional-element insufficiencies are found in a population simultaneously, and that the consequences are interactive. The basic question in this study is nevertheless the role of 'lack of calories' in explaining poor health and inorderly body composition. The malnutrition aspects will thus only be considered when it is clear that they are important co-factors in the undernutrition complex.

The focus on undernutrition is in no way intended to imply that malnutrition has been ascertained to be a less important problem than the lack of energy in most parts of the Third World. Although this was widely thought to be the case in the 1970s and 1980s, recent research has shown certain forms of malnutrition to be a much more serious problem than previously understood, at least locally. (For recent summaries of new findings about malnutrition, see Gillespie and Mason 1994, Gillespie *et al*. 1991, 1996, Beaton *et al*. 1993, Behrman 1995, Calloway 1995, Haddad *et al*. 1997.) Fortunately, however, it seems as if the progress made in the 1990s in combating the most common and serious facets of malnutrition worldwide, i.e. iodine, vitamin A, and iron deficiencies, has been dramatic and much more pronounced than that of alleviating undernutrition (ACC/SCN 1997*a, c*).

1.5.3. Chronic Undernutrition versus Famine

A conceptual distinction is usually made between chronic undernutrition and famine.[6] The main difference between severe undernutrition and famine is in the intensity of the consequences of lack of food entitlements and concomitant disease. Even under non-famine conditions some people die of undernutrition, or much more frequently, of a disease that is related to undernutrition. What happens in a famine is that the mortality rate for all age groups rises notably in the wake of a decline in food consumption in the afflicted households. This normally happens only within a fairly well-defined *geographical area* (it could be a whole country, but this is rare except in the smallest countries) and *time span*. However, there are no clear demarcations of what exact increase in mortality, within what type of geographical area and time span, defines a famine.[7] 'Normal' fluctuations in the prevalence of undernutrition in a country and famine are very blurred concepts, and in this study no explicit operational distinction is made.

The 'normal' state of undernourishment in the African populations has intensified into what has been widely referred to as famine on several occasions during the post-war period. In South Asia, there has only been one famine—Bangladesh 1974—since 1943 (Sen 1981*a*, Ravallion 1988), even though famine has been impending in parts of India several times: 1966, 1967, 1974, and 1988 (Drèze 1990*a*). The normal food situation in most of Africa—where famine is frequent—is probably somewhat better than in India (Chapters 6 and 11), where no famine occurs. The Indian example shows that famine can be controlled even in countries where hundreds of millions of people are chronically undernourished (by some definitions). The most likely reason for this is that India has built up a formal 'insurance' system (formalized in *The Famine Codes*). The insurance mechanisms, both formal and informal, seem to be severely underdeveloped in most of Africa, although a few countries like Botswana, Kenya, and Zimbabwe have been able to avert rather serious situations on several occasions through apt interventions of governments and international organizations (Drèze 1990*b*, Drèze and Sen 1990*b*).

Famine and famine prevention will not be given a lot of attention in the present study.[8] This is not because famine (no matter the exact definition) is thought to be less important than the more permanent nutrition problems.

The simple reason is that the author believes that he has something to contribute to the understanding of the latter problem, and that a fair treatment of famine would not be possible in one and the same volume. It should be emphasized, however, that in terms of human suffering, there is no reason to think that normal undernutrition in Africa is a smaller problem than the acute outbursts of famine. It is possible that as many as 10 million people in Africa have died in what has generally been called famine during the post-war period (Svedberg 1987). However, each year about two-and-a-half million children between the ages of 0 and 5 die in SSA. Even if only a minor part of these die from undernutrition and nutrition-related disease (a question to be assessed in Chapter 14), their numbers are probably in excess of the famine victims.[9]

1.5.4. Intra-household Allocation of Nutrients

The relative incidence of undernutrition across broad regions of the world, such as SSA and South Asia, will be examined in detail in this study. We will also highlight the relative prevalence of undernutrition across individual countries and, to a lesser extent, across states or districts within countries. Comparisons will also be made along age and gender lines. The one 'distribution' dimension which, unfortunately, will not be covered is that of intra-household allocation of nutrients. There are interesting theoretical analyses of this problem (e.g. Haddad and Kanbur 1990, 1995, Behrman 1992, Farmer and Tiefenthaler 1995, Kanbur 1995, Kanbur and Hadded 1995) and a growing empirical literature (Rosenzweig and Schultz 1982, Pitt *et al.* 1990, Haddad *et al.* 1995, 1997). Some limitations in coverage have to be imposed, and this is one. However, a short list of suggestions for the use of extended anthropometrics to estimate intra-household distribution of calories is offered in Chapter 18.

1.5.5. On Reasons for Poverty

A fifth limitation of the present study is related to the depth in which we will analyse the reasons for the undernutrition that exists in the SSA and South Asian regions. Economic poverty is found to constitute the major reason for undernutrition, although other, partly independent, explanations apply as well (see Chapters 15–17). Poverty means low average income, which follows from low economic productivity. Why many people in the agricultural and service sectors, employing between 80 and 95 per cent of the labour force in most African countries, as well as in South Asia, have low productivity is easily answered at a superficial level. This relates to historical factors and the dismal post-colonial development process in these regions; large sections of the population have very little human capital (education), few material factors of production, inappropriate technology, and—not least—they work in economies with very little infrastructure that have been extremely badly governed for a long time. While the question of why this has occurred is fundamental, it is merely touched upon in Chapter 17. But even though the main focus of this monograph is on other issues, the analysis presented here would have relevance in supplementing and consolidating the already rich literature on the overall failure of the SSA and South Asian countries to develop faster than they actually have.

NOTES

1. The absolute number of people who are undernourished has increased between 1969/71 and 1990/92 in South Asia and Latin America (by 7 and 21 per cent, respectively) according to the FAO*a* (1996: table 14). The FAO maintains that in SSA, the absolute number of undernourished more than doubled during the same period (more details are given in Chapter 5).
2. Of course, even with the best of intentions, better knowledge is not *sufficient* to improve the nutritional situation.
3. A study by Fuso (1992) finds that the 'stable' countries in SSA had a 1.5 percentage higher growth rate per capita than the 'unstable' ones.
4. See for instance Maxwell (1990) for a broad review of issues dealt with in the food security literature. Also see Haddad *et al.* 1997, which is focused on Southern Africa.
5. Since the so-called 'great protein fiasco' of the seventies (see McLaren 1974), very few nutritionists have argued that lack of protein is a significant problem in populations where calories are adequate. The problem was though to be confined to certain areas where the main staples are low in protein, for example, staples such as plantains in some East African countries (Rwanda, Burundi, and Uganda) and cassava and other roots and tubers, which dominate the diet in Zaire and neighbouring countries in western Central Africa. Recently, however, the role of certain proteins has been reassessed and found to be very important for infant and child growth and for the prevention of several diseases in the short as well as the very long term, i.e. in adulthood (see Chapter 14).
6. Hunger' is another term that has been used to describe nutritional inadequacy. Hunger is most commonly thought of as the body's signals (which everyone knows better than words can describe) that it wants food at regular intervals. Hunger in this sense is thus a more short-term phenomenon than undernutrition. They may or may not overlap. A person weighing 400 pounds may be hungry more intensively and more often than someone who is undernourished by conventional weight norms. An undernourished person may not be hungry at all; in fact, the hunger signals tend to disappear after a few days without food, as one is told by people who fast. In an experiment, Wadden *et al.* (1987) found that individuals on a very low daily calorie intake (400 kcal) experienced less hunger than others with an intake of 1,200. However, it is probably true that most people who are undernourished often experience painful hunger feelings. Without in any way implying that hunger is a negligible problem, it will not be within the scope of the present study. The

term hunger has also been used in another meaning, i.e. to encompass all the various disabilities and dysfunctions that are related to a poor or inadequate diet (e.g. Drèze and Sen 1989). Hunger used in that sense is thus a broader concept than undernutrition, as the latter term is used in this study.

7. There have been situations that have been called famines in which the estimated number of victims has been in the 20–30 people range; normally, however, the term is only used when the victims within a region of a country (say the Wollo province in Ethiopia) are numbered in the thousands (see Svedberg 1987).

8. A number of relatively recent studies on this topic are found in Drèze and Sen (1990b). See also the review article by Ravallion (1997a).

9. The historical evidence is strongly in support of this conjecture. For a long time it was widely thought that frequent and severe famine was a major cause of the high mortality rates in Europe during the eighteenth and nineteenth centuries (at least as high as in contemporary Africa). As recently demonstrated by Fogel and others (Fogel 1992), however, famine-related mortality accounted for a relatively minor share, less than 10 per cent, of overall 'excess' mortality in France and England, two of the best-studied countries.

2

Characterization and Measurement of Undernutrition: Controversies and Consensus

2.1. INTRODUCTION

The human being, like all species, needs a range of nutritional elements in order to sustain and reproduce life. Many people, especially in the so-called developing countries, have a habitual diet that is nutritionally inadequate. It is only a slight exaggeration to say that these two generalizations concerning nutrition in developing countries are about as exact as one can be without invoking controversy. There is no consensus among biologists and nutritionists on the basic question of how undernutrition should be defined and by what standard it should be measured. There is no widely accepted theory of, or evidence on, how personal characteristics, genetic heritage, environmental factors and work activity interact with nutritional requirements across individuals (or households). Consequently, there is no agreement on the prevalence of undernutrition in Africa (or any other region for that matter). Only when reading glossy coffee-table publications from some of the international organizations one may get the impression that concepts and measurements are well defined and that estimates are accurate.[1] Likewise, there is little agreement on the causes of the undernutrition that exists in Africa and elsewhere. Many of the controversies are intra-disciplinary as well as inter-disciplinary.

The objective of this chapter is to provide an analytical description of the most common paradigms of how to conceive of and measure undernutrition, while also hinting at the many controversies that exist. The chapter is organized as follows. Section 2.2 contains a brief overview of the two main conflicting paradigms of characterizing undernutrition. In the following two sections, the two main approaches to measuring undernutrition are presented. In section 2.3, I point to some of the problems encountered by those who believe in the possibility of estimating undernutrition directly in terms of the number of calories people actually expend in relation to their energy 'requirement'. Section 2.4 contains a parallel review of the problems involved in measuring undernutrition indirectly, through observations of anthropometric failure. The chapter closes with a brief summary.

2.2. UNDERNUTRITION: OVERVIEW OF PARADIGMS

Although there are many controversies when it comes to defining and measuring undernutrition, there are a few basics that cannot be challenged (even if sometimes forgotten). Among these are the energy identity and the energy balance properties.

2.2.1. The Energy Identity and the Energy Balance

The energy input to the human body's work is always identically equal to the energy expenditure per unit of time; this is the so-called Atwater and Benedict (1899) formula, or the nutritionists' application of the First Law of Thermodynamics (energy cannot be consumed, only transferred to other uses). Being undernourished is therefore not a state where the input of energy falls short of the energy expenditure; this can never be the case for simple physiological reasons. All energy expenditure (E_t) must come from somewhere, and if it is not from current food intake (I_t), the balance is supplied from energy reserves in the body (mainly fat). We thus have the following identity:

$$E_{it} \equiv I_{it} - dW_{it} \qquad (2.1)$$

When an individual's calorie expenditure is equal to his habitual intake, his body weight is stable ($dW_{it} = 0$) he is said to be in energy balance.[2] That he (or she) is in 'balance' is not to not say that he is well-nourished. He is well-nourished only if his energy balance is attained at or above the body weight and physical activity level (PAL) that are consistent with health and functional fitness in all respects. If his habitual intake and expenditure balance at a very low (but constant) body weight and/or PAL, which have negative health or functional consequences, he is undernourished. To be in energy balance below the critical body weight and PAL is usually referred to as *chronic* undernutrition (James *et al.* 1988).

Conversely, that a person is in energy imbalance, i.e. his weight is falling, does not necessarily mean that he is undernourished. This depends on the level of energy balance from which he starts. If he is well-nourished to begin with, it is not until his weight and/or physical activity level falls below the critical 'cut-off' points that he enters the state of undernutrition. The state of being in (negative) energy imbalance below the critical body weight and/or PAL is usually referred to as *acute* undernutrition. A person can thus be in only one of three nutritional statues: (1) well-nourished, (2) chronically undernourished, and (3) chronically and acutely undernourished. He cannot, however, be acutely undernourished while chronically well-nourished (with this terminology).

So far there is consensus (although the terminology differs). The controversies start with how to determine the critical low-energy balance that marks chronical undernutrition and how this balance is best measured. With a little simplification one may claim that there are principally two theoretical approaches to the characterization of undernutrition: the *Genetic-Potential* (GP) and the *Adjustment-and-Adaptation* (AA) paradigms.

2.2.2. The Genetic Potential Paradigm

One of the main controversies in the theoretical nutrition literature is whether well-nourishment is a unique, absolute state of the body, or if there is a whole range (set) of different states in which the individual can be well-nourished. The former notion is the fundament of the GP theory of nutrition. The crucial assumption underlying this paradigm is, as interpreted by Cutler and Payne (1984: p. 1486):

. . . . that the body is a system which is not only self-regulating, but also self-optimising. For each individual there exists a preferred state characterised by a unique set of values of the variables which describe the system components (weight, height, blood levels, etc.). This preferred state is optimal for that individual with respect to all aspects of functions. If there are no constraints on the diet, or continued adverse environmental influences, an individual will always tend to seek out and return to the preferred state.

Interpreted strictly, this view rules out the possibility that different heights and weights are optimal for different objectives and that there may be conflicts of objective. It also assumes that the optimal height and weight are independent of the external environment in which the individual dwells and works. There are few adherents to the GP model in its most unabated form; still, it seems fair to say that the GP model was the conventional, mainstream one until rather recently. It is still widely accepted in the international agencies as well as among independent researchers. There are, as we shall see in later chapters, several issues that are vigorously debated even by people who share the basic assumption about the 'optimality' of a unique, genetically determined state of the body.

2.2.3. The Adjustment and Adaptation Paradigm

Since the early 1980s, the AA paradigm of undernutrition has gained substantial ground. An essential assumption behind this paradigm is that the individual can *adjust* his energy requirements through changes in his body weight and by varying his PAL in accordance with changes in the external environment without any harmful effects on health or functions.

According to the AA paradigm, there is no one state of the body that is optimal in all respects. Both for weight and for physical activity there is a wide range that is compatible with health and capabilities of different kinds, and the optimal weight depends on 'external factors' such as type of work activity.[3] The AA paradigm thus allows for conflicts of objectives and in this theoretical perspective, undernutrition is not an absolute state, but a relative one.

The truly controversial issue, however, is not whether the individual can *adjust* body weight and PAL over a certain range without any harmful effects on health and functions; this is now accepted by most (if not all) scholars. One of the most heatedly debated issues in the nutrition literature in recent years has been whether the individual can *adapt* (permanently) to nutritional stress without any 'cost'. That is, whether children adapt to undernutrition through reduced growth in stature and adults through more efficient metabolism without health or functional impairment. We shall return to this debate and also discuss the empirical evidence in subsequent chapters.

2.3.   DIFFERENT MEASUREMENT APPROACHES

The different approaches to the measurement of undernutrition are illustrated in Fig. 2.1 (and analysed more thoroughly later on). The main sets of reasons why an individual may be undernourished are listed in the leftmost column (1) of the figure. These we leave aside for the moment in order to focus on columns 2–4, where different 'indicators' of undernutrition are listed.

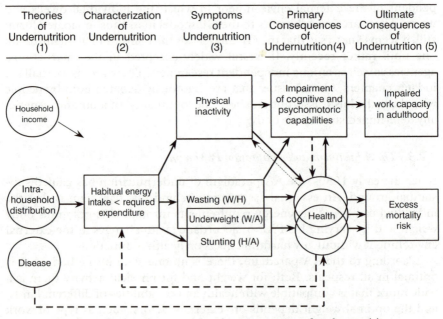

FIG. 2.1. Causes, symptoms, and consequences of undernutrition

In principle, there are three levels at which a person's energy balance can be estimated. One is to estimate energy intake and/or expenditure *directly* (column 2). The second is to look for anthropometric and other symptoms which *indirectly* reflect an inadequate energy balance (column 3). The third is to find measurable indicators of negative *consequences* of an unduly low energy balance (column 4).

In Fig. 2.1, a distinction has been made between 'symptoms' and 'consequences' (and between primary and ultimate consequences) of under-nutrition. Many nutritionists, especially those who favour the GP paradigm, would claim that stunting, wasting, and inactivity are not symptoms, but adverse consequences of undernutrition. This is one of the highly controversial issues; for the time being, the distinction made here is intended to serve an expository purpose only. That is, conceptually one can and should distinguish stunting (and also wasting and inactivity) as a physiological phenomenon from the possible adverse consequences of being short (thin and inactive).

The way Fig. 2.1 is drawn reflects only a few common hypotheses of the causal links in the economics–nutrition–health complex. Several other possible interlinkages (arrows) have been left out in order not to clutter the scheme beyond readability. For instance, most of the adverse outcomes or symptoms of undernutrition in columns (3) to (4) may very well have a (negative) effect on household income and internal distribution. Moreover, the possible reasons for undernutrition listed in column (1) may not be independent, e.g. household income may affect intra-household distribution. These and other links of causality in more than one direction are problematic in all estimations of relationships in the nutrition-cum-economics nexus, as we shall see in subsequent chapters, and can induce simultaneity biases, identification difficulties, and multicollinarity.

2.4.   DIRECT ESTIMATES OF MINIMUM ENERGY BALANCE

The FAO, in collaboration with the WHO and UNU, estimates the prevalence of undernutrition in the world with the direct method. It derives what it finds to be the 'minimum acceptable' energy expenditure on a per-capita basis for households, which is then compared with estimated energy intakes. Their joint definition of undernutrition reads:

undernutrition . . . is defined as describing the extent to which people have *dietary intakes* below certain minimum requirement levels, . . . i.e. that level of energy intake which will balance energy expenditure when the individual has a body size and composition and level of physical activity consistent with long-term good health, and which will allow for the maintenance of economically necessary and socially desirable physical activity (FAO*a* 1985: pp. 18–19, FAO/WHO/UNU 1985: p. 12). (Italics added.)

These international organizations thus define and measure people's (adults') nutritional status by relating their habitual energy intake (= actual expenditure when in balance) to their 'required' expenditure. An abbreviated version of this definition appears in the rectangular box in column (2) of Fig. 2.1.

Direct estimates of the 'acceptable' energy balance can be obtained either from the intake side or from the expenditure side of identity 2.1. The first method amounts to measuring calorie intake in (constant weight) populations with no constraints on basic food supplies. The other is to simulate 'required' expenditures on the basis of a model of energy uses in the body.

2.4.1. Observed Energy Intake

To use estimates of actual calorie intake in nutritionally unconstrained populations as a reference norm has a certain appeal, especially if one favours the GP paradigm. If there exists 'a self-regulating, self-optimizing' mechanism in the human body, the preferred optimal state should be achieved in people who do not face external (e.g. economic) constraints on the basic diet. Their actual energy intake should then reflect this optimal state. Almost all dietary norms that were in use between the middle of the nineteenth century[4] and the early 1970s were based on such observations of actual intake (average for large samples) in the Western countries.

It has later become widely acknowledged that a significant proportion of the population in the developed countries is obese and that the energy balance should be obtained at lower body weights. Moreover, as argued by proponents of the AA paradigm, nor does the actual intake in non-obese populations necessarily reflect what is 'required' in a fundamental sense for health and functional capability (especially not if there is intra-individual adaptation to low intake). It has also been acknowledged that different work activities and environments imply that energy expenditures may differ between people in the temperate North and the tropical South. Finally, since there are wide inter-individual differences in actual intakes in non-constrained (non-obese) populations, there is no *a priori* reason to expect that their average actual intake is equal to the critical low intake. Consequently, the procedure for estimating nutritional requirements for adults from actual average intake in developed countries was largely abolished in the early 1970s.[5] For children under 10 years of age, however, the method is still used, although with some modifications.

2.4.2. Simulated Minimum Energy Expenditures

Since the *Fourth World Food Survey* (FAO*a* 1973), the calorie expenditure norms have been derived on the basis of a model of energy flows in the human body. In order to identify the problems encountered in using this method to simulate the acceptable energy balance, the energy expenditure on the left-hand side of the identity 2.1 must be subdivided into its main components or uses.

First, there is the energy expenditure for maintaining internal body functions during sleep, such as cardiovascular and respiratory activities, the *Basal Metabolic Rate* (BMR), which is determined mainly by body weight. Secondly, there is the energy expended in increased internal body activities during waking hours, such as sustaining increased muscle tone, food digestion and increased heat generation. This latter is labelled 'baseline' expenditure by the FAO/WHO/UNU (1985: p. 73). Thirdly, there is the energy spent in external physical activities, such as manual work and social life. The baseline and the external physical energy expenditures are conventionally expressed as a joint multiple of the BMR, called the *Physical Activity Level* (PAL). We then have that total energy expenditures of a person of category i (i.e. age, sex) during period t is:

$$E_{it} = I_{it} - dW_{it} = PAL_{it} \times BMR_{it} (W_{it}) \tag{2.2}$$

When dW_{it} is zero the individual is in energy balance. Equation 2.2 thus simply tells us that the energy expenditure of an individual (of category i), and thus his intake requirement, depends on his metabolic rate (which is a function of body weight) and the amount of physical activity which he is involved in. Since individuals have different body weights, rates of metabolism, and physical work activities, there will be inter-individual differences in energy expenditures (and required intakes) within any population.

Although most contemporary estimates of energy expenditures in human beings are calculated from a model with the basic properties of equation 2.2, there are two main controversies. One is related to the more exact specification of this equation. The most hotly debated issues are how BMR is related to body weight and whether the BMR is a constant function of body weight or whether it varies with intake (*intra individual* metabolic adaptation to low energy intakes). The other controversial issue is how far an individual can lower his energy expenditures through reduced body weight and physical activity without adverse consequences for health and functional capabilities. These controversies are analysed in more detail in Chapter 8. In Chapter 9, we shall discuss the additional problems encountered when individual minimum energy expenditure requirements are to be aggregated to the calorie cut-off points used by the FAO in order to estimate the prevalence of undernutrition in large populations (countries).

2.5. INDIRECT ESTIMATES OF MINIMUM ENERGY BALANCE

The reason for using anthropometric or other indirect methods to measure undernutrition is not only related to the conceptual and measurement difficulties with the direct method hinted at in the previous section. It is universally agreed that standardized calorie norms cannot be used to identify undernutrition in the individual person, because of genetically inter-individual differences in body size and composition, and also work activity. Moreover, in the Third-World context, to identify undernourished individuals for targeted intervention is a common purpose for which nutritional indicators are used. For this purpose, only indicators of adverse outcome of a low energy balance can be used; the questions are what are the outcomes (symptoms and consequences) that one should look for and at what 'level' or 'degree' is there need for alarm.

So far, work in this area has almost exclusively been focused on pre-school-aged children using anthropometric measurements. Physical (in)activity has been more difficult to get a handle on. Some work has also been done on estimating the consequences of undernutrition; the main concerns are premature deaths, impaired health, and retarded cognitive development.

2.5.1. Anthropometric Failure

A child who spends more energy than he or she habitually ingests inevitably loses weight, which is easily measurable. It is widely believed (see Chapter 14) that when a small child does not receive adequate nutrition for a considerable period, its growth in stature is retarded. Short stature for age (stunting) is thus conventionally held to reflect chronic undernutrition. Low weight for normal height (wasting) is taken to indicate acute undernutrition. If a child is both stunted and wasted, or underweight for its age, he or she is considered to suffer both from acute and chronic undernutrition.

The question in debate is below which weight (for height) and height (for age) a child should be defined as acutely and chronically undernourished, respectively. There are different answers to this question, depending on whether one is apt to lean towards the GP or the AA paradigm and whether one takes a theoretical or an applied view of the problem. Central to the GP paradigm of chronic undernutrition is the optimality of the genetic potential for growth in stature. In this theoretical perspective, the ideal height (for age) norm is the individual-specific genetic potential height. Any deviation from this height is an adverse consequence of undernutrition (or other external adverse factors).

However, with the genetic technology presently available, it is impossible in practice to determine the genetic potential height of a single individual living under imperfect conditions.[6] Only the genetic potential for growth of the average person in a deprived ethnic/social group can be estimated through observations of subsets of individuals for which there is no reason to expect external, environmental constraints. Because there is inter-individual variation in genetic potential for growth, the average for non-constrained subpopulations cannot be used to identify undernourished individuals in Third-World samples.

In practice, when estimating undernutrition in individuals, most nutritionists who lean towards the GP paradigm use anthropometric norms that are derived on the basis of probabilistic reasoning and statistical 'abnormality'. The crucial assumption behind this method is that the average genetic potential for growth in the particular study population, and its distribution across individuals, are the same as in the chosen (Western) reference population. Under these assumptions, if 3 per cent of the reference population have a height below 2 standard deviations (SD) of the median height, there is only a 3 per cent risk that a person from a sample population who is below the 2 SD is erroneously classified as undernourished when the reason is in fact genetic.

The main theoretical feature of the AA paradigm that makes it different from the GP paradigm is the claim that there are 'costless' adjustments in body height and weight to nutritional stress. The slogan 'Small but Healthy' captures this paradigm in a nutshell. However, adherents to the AA paradigm also agree that reduction of body size, and so of BMR, cannot proceed indefinitely without harmful consequences. According to the AA paradigm, it is only when all the possibilities for adjustment and adaptation have been exhausted that the individual is undernourished. This is when the height and weight have fallen to levels that are associated with impaired health and various mental and physiological incapabilities. Thus, from the theoretical perspective, the anthropometric norms that best comply with the AA paradigm should be derived from estimates of health risks and other impairments following low height and weight. In practice, however, risk-associated anthropometric norms have seldom been derived (for reasons discussed in Chapter 14), and most adherents of the *AA* paradigm tend to use the same 'probabilistic' norms as described above.

2.5.2. *Physical-activity Failure*

In the calorie expenditure norms set up by the FAO/WHO/UNU (1985), the allowance for physical activity accounts for more than a third of the total minimum calorie expenditure. The anthropometric norms make no explicit allowance for physical activity. For small children, physical activity means play, exploration, and, for some, also labour. The two first activities have a value in their own right, but they may also be important for the development of cognitive and psychomotoric capabilities. However, the physical activity level of small children is inherently difficult to measure. It has also proved difficult to estimate the minimum required for normal development. Given these difficulties, a key question is how children react to nutritional stress.

If reduced physical activity below the critical level, whatever it may be, is the first line of defence, a child can be 'undernourished' even though his weight and/or height are adequate. In this case, anthropometric indicators cannot be used to say whether physical activity is sufficient or not. On the other hand, if wasting or stunting normally precedes inactivity, the anthropometric measures will capture also those who are unduly inactive. There is no consensus among nutritionists and behaviourists on how small children normally adjust to nutritional stress. However, this issue (to which we shall return in Chapter 13) is of utmost importance for the question of how useful anthropometric measures are as indicators of undernutrition.

2.5.3. Health and Capability Failures

The general hypothesis today is that undernutrition, as manifested in body deformation, impairs the child's immunocompetence, thus increasing morbidity in general, and also that retarded mental and cognitive development may follow. This is to say that health risk is related to wasting and stunting, not to 'undernutrition' in some unobservable dimension.[7] There is by now a relatively large body of literature investigating anthropometric failure and subsequent morbidity and mortality (see Chapter 14). The crucial empirical questions are: (i) what anthropometric measure is the best indicator of subsequent illness or death and (ii) at what degree of anthropometric failure does the increased risk of poor health set in. While it was widely believed for a long time that these 'risks' appear only at 'severe' anthropometric failure, some recent research suggests that there are significant risks associated also with mild-to-moderate undernutrition. This is so not only for risk of subsequent premature deaths (Pelletier 1994), but also for several chronic diseases that appear much later in life (e.g. Schrimshaw 1996). In Chapter 14, we will take a closer look at these new findings.

2.6.   SUMMARY AND CONCLUSIONS

In this chapter we have maintained, broadly in line with the classification suggested by Cutler and Payne (1984), that there are two main schools of thought when it comes to conceptualizing undernutrition: the *Genetic Potential* and the *Adjustment and Adaptation* paradigms.

The claim that the theoretical thinking in this area can be divided into two distinct schools with different constituencies is a simplification, of course. Most nutritionists would probably not be willing to accept either label, at least not without ample qualification. However, there is no doubt one line of thinking that emphasizes the genetic potential for growth in stature as the hallmark of well-nourishment and finds it hard to accept that adjustment and adaptation to nutritional stress can be 'costless'. Leading proponents of this view are Gopalan (1983: p. 1992) and Beaton (1983*a*, *b*, 1989). On the other hand, there are those who strongly argue along the 'small but healthy' line (Sukhatme 1978, Sukhatme and Margen 1982, Seckler 1982, 1984, Margen

1984, Payne 1992). Most other leading nutritionists seem to be somewhere in between, accepting the idea of relatively large adjustment possibilities, but find it hard to accept that adaptation can be completely costless (e.g. James 1989, 1994, Martorell *et al.* 1988, Waterlow 1989*b*, 1990*a*).

When it comes to the measurement of inadequate energy balance, we have hinted at the main problems with the two available methods: the direct estimation (of intakes and requirements) techniques and the indirect estimation (anthropometric) technique. We have seen that some of the issues are the same for both methods, e.g. determination of the minimum weight and height that are compatible with well-nourishment.

The main problem with the direct approach to estimating undernutrition through intakes and requirements is that it entails so many difficult 'steps'. This is well known by most nutritionists, but exactly how many pieces of information are needed to set up a minimum energy expenditure norm and how many assumptions (often without firm empirical support) have to be made in the process are easily forgotten. Some reminders will be provided in Chapters 5–9. It is thus of little surprise that there is so much controversy about the appropriate norms, and that so many different norms have been suggested and used. This is a major reason why the direct method of estimating undernutrition has decreased in importance among nutritionists.[8] The intake/requirement approach today is used mainly by the FAO. In this pursuit, data on actual calorie intakes (or availabilities), as well as their distribution in relation to the distribution of 'requirement' in the population, are needed. As we shall see in Chapters 6 and 7, obtaining accurate estimates of energy availabilities and intakes, and their distributions, in developing countries is no less demanding an endeavour than estimating 'minimum energy expenditure requirements'.

Anthropometric observations as measurements and indicators of undernutrition have come to dominate increasingly since the early 1980s. A major reason is that, nowadays, information about nutrition is often collected with the explicit aim of selecting people for targeted intervention. Then we need to know who is undernourished and who is not, and standardized dietary intake norms cannot be used to detect undernutrition in individuals. For this purpose, anthropometric and related methods have to be applied. They are not conceptually flawless, as indicated above, and some additional problems with empirical measurement and conceptual interpretation will be discussed in Chapters 12 and 13. Nevertheless, most contemporary nutritionists seem to believe that anthropometric measures provide more reliable and useful indications of nutritional status than do intake/requirement measurements. They believe this is so whether the objective is to estimate the overall prevalence of undernutrition in a particular developing country, to make comparisons between countries, to monitor developments over time, or to identify undernourished individuals—the main purposes for which we need nutritional indicators.

NOTES

1. The more technical and scientific publications from the same organizations in recent years often provide a detailed and fair picture of the many conceptual and measurement problems involved in estimating undernutrition.
2. A person's weight tends to vary, not only because of changes in the amount of fat (and lean tissue) he contains, but also because the water content in the body (accounting for about half the body weight) varies over time (James and Schofield 1990: p. 36). This makes complicated the use of weight changes between two points in time as indicators of changes in energy stores (fat).
3. For instance, it is generally an advantage to be small in physical work tasks that involve a lot of body translation, while a big body is more suitable for activities that require great maximum physical strength (lifting heavy burdens).
4. The first calorie requirement norms, or recommended daily intakes (RDI), were established in the middle of the nineteenth century in Holland and the UK. Several additional dietary norms were published during the first decades of the present century by the USDA and the League of Nations, among others. The recommended 'requirement' for the 'moderately active' adult man in all the studies was set at about 3,000 calories (see Miller and Voris 1969, FAO/WHO 1973: pp. 15–19, Harper 1985, Payne 1992: pp. 56–61, for more detailed 'chronologies' of caloric norms).
5. The calorie requirements norms in the *First World Food Survey* in 1946 (FAO*a* 1946) were also derived on the basis of observed intake in Western populations. The first FAO norm was set at 2,600 calories per consumer unit and day worldwide. This per-capita norm implied an increase in requirements for adult men as compared to the norms that were established before and during World War II. In the *Second* and *Third World Food Surveys* (1952 and 1963), the same type of intake-based norms were derived, but the new per-capita requirements for the various African countries were lowered a little. The new estimates took the different population structure in developing countries, where young children make up a much larger share of the population, into consideration. The fact that adults there have a smaller body size was also allowed for.
6. In non-deprived populations, most individuals will attain their genetic potential height; not all will though—some with chronic disease may not.
7. There seem to be no clinical or biochemical signs of impaired health that can be directly and unambiguously related to undernutrition (while there are for malnutrition) that are detectable before signs of anthropometric failure or changes in the level of activity have become apparent (see Waterlow 1992: chapter 7).
8. In the 1970s, nutritionists went out to villages and collected dietary intake data which they related to the FAO/WHO (1973) type of calorie requirement norms (see the surveys in Schofield 1979 and IDRC 1981). On the basis of the average intake and requirement estimates, conclusions about 'general' food standards in the village were drawn. This type of dietary assessment of nutritional standards has all but ceased since the early 1980s. Some economists have continued to rely heavily on dietary data, for example in estimating calorie-expenditure elasticities. The justification for this will be analysed in Chapter 4.

PART II

PART II

3

A Model of Nutrition and Economic Productivity

3.1. INTRODUCTION

Large parts of the labour force in Africa and South Asia are self-employed in agriculture and related sectors. According to the international organizations, it is among these several hundred million people that undernutrition is rampant (FAO*a* 1996, ACC/SCN 1997*a*). The food that supplies the energy they need to work often accounts for between 50 and 80 per cent of their gross income (FAO*d* 1988). Being self-employed, or working for a per-piece wage, they can choose their work intensity and thus how much food (calories) they must indulge in order to sustain the work effort. However, they cannot make independent long-term decisions about how much to work and how much to eat if they are to stay in energy balance. They also have to weigh the cost of the additional food (energy) needed for an extra work effort against the marginal revenue of this effort.

The objective of this chapter is to develop a model of the interactions between the biologically determined need for energy (calories) and the economic activity that the individual must pursue in order to be entitled to food. The plan of the chapter is as follows. The main similarities and dissimilarities to the related nutrition-based efficiency-wage models are summarized in section 3.2; the subtler distinctions are highlighted as we proceed. The basic properties of the model are presented in section 3.3. In section 3.4, the individual's optimal work effort, body weight, calorie intake, and income are derived endogenously. Comparative statics are conducted in section 3.5. The chapter closes with a summary and a few implications for empirical study.

3.2. RELATED THEORY

The links between nutrition and economics have been analysed by economists for a long time. The notion that poverty causes undernutrition dates back at least to Adam Smith and income is still the main explanatory variable in most contemporary attempts to explain poor nutrition. Economists have also suggested the reverse causation: that inadequate nutrition is the reason for low productivity and poverty. This idea, captured in the notion of 'efficiency wages', dates back to Leibenstein (1957) and was subsequently given a stricter formulation by Mirrlees (1975), Stiglitz (1976), and Bliss and Stern (1978a). The backbone in these models is the so-called efficiency-wage function. It is derived on the assumption that the amount of 'efficient' work that can be extracted from labourers by an employer is a function of their pay, which determines the labourers' consumption, including that of food.

The model to be developed below is also based on a notion of a relationship between food, or rather the energy content of food, and work productivity. In addition some other traits are borrowed from Stiglitz and Bliss and Stern (cf. below), but the model to be presented here is different in several respects. First, in the previous literature employers hire labour under *monopsonistic* market conditions. The present model deals with the behaviour of the nutritionally constrained *individual* (referred to as 'he' in the following) working in a market in which he faces given prices and in which he can choose his own workload.[1]

Secondly, while the present model is built on a similar assumption used by Bliss and Stern regarding the biologically determined energy needs, there is one important difference. In the model developed here, a distinction is made between the *biological* production function that converts the energy contained in food into muscular activity and the economical production function that transforms this muscular activity into work which earns an income.

Thirdly, the phenomena that previous models aim to explain differ from those here. The main objective in Mirrlees (1975), Stiglitz (1976), and Dasgupta and Ray (1986, 1987) is to explain involuntary unemployment and how income is distributed under different market structures. In Bliss and Stern (1978a, b), the focus is on the positive theory of *endogenous* wage determination, in which wages are set according to the nutritional status of the labourer as perceived by the employer. In the present model, job-specific wages are *exogenously* determined by aggregate demand and supply in the market in which the individual works (being unrelated to the nutritional status of the individual).[2] Unemployment is not considered here; the central issue is how (poor) individuals' economic and biological behaviour is affected by the fact that food (energy) enters as an input in the labour production function.

The optimal work intensity, body weight, calorie intake/expenditure, and income of the individual are derived endogenously in the model. The model also predicts how the individual's choice of body weight and calorie intake/expenditure is affected by exogenous changes in prices and/or wages. Furthermore, the model explains why there may not be a systematic relationship between income and nutritional variables like body weight and calorie intake across individuals, a relationship which is essential for evaluating the empirical tests that have been conducted in this area (discussed in Chapter 4).

3.3. THE MODEL

The base model is static; it comprises two production functions and one utility function. The first production function traces the biological relationship, in the short as well as the longer term, between the physical activity of the individual and the energy he expends. The second production function describes how this physical activity in the form of manual work is translated into income and consumption. The utility function will be given alternate specifications. The individual has a fixed initial bundle of productive assets such as land, physical capital, human capital, and technology. The only form of savings and credit in the model is the individual's possibility of accumulating and depleting energy stores (fat) in his own body.

3.3.1. The Short-term Calorie Expenditure Function

The human body needs the energy (and other nutrients) contained in food to maintain various processes and activities. As we have seen in Chapter 2, the most basic is the sustainment of internal body functions (respiration, blood circulation, etc.), called the basal metabolic rate (BMR).[3] In addition, the body requires energy in order to be able to pursue external physical activities, such as work. When the current energy intake matches the energy expenditure for all these activities, there is no change in body composition and the person is said to be in energy balance.

The short-term energy expenditure of an adult individual (no index for the individual is used for the time being) depicted in Fig. 3.1 is thus assumed to comprise two parts. The calorie expenditure for BMR is assumed to be a positive function of the individual's body weight (not necessarily linear). For a particular weight (W_j), the calories required for basal metabolism are thus given by the intercept BMR_j on the vertical axis. The short-term energy expenditure function is further assumed to be convex and monotonically increasing in the level of external physical activity that the individual exerts, as measured along the horizontal axis. The physical activity is measured in units such as the number of kilos carried a certain distance per hour. This is the $SCE_j(W_j, A, \mathbf{Z})$ function in Fig. 3.1, where SCE is the short-term calorie expenditure, and where W_j refers to a particular body weight of the individual, A refers to the level of physical activity, and $\mathbf{Z}$ is a vector of personal-specific characteristics, such as age, sex, and height, which are assumed to be fixed. (See Appendix Fig. 3.1 for an empirically based short-term expenditure function with the above properties.)

For each specific body weight and level of external physical activity, the individual expends a certain number of calories (per unit of time). For instance, if he has body weight j and work activity A_a, in Fig. 3.1 his calorie expenditure is C_{ja}. In order to stay in nutritional balance, his calorie intake

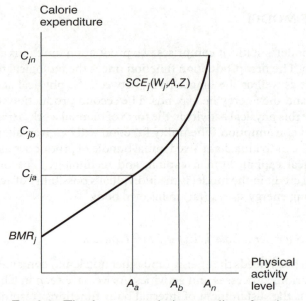

FIG. 3.1. The short-term calorie expenditure function

must also be C_{ja}. If he works more, e.g. has activity level b, he expends more calories (C_{jb}) and must eat correspondingly more to stay in energy balance.

Given his body weight, the individual is further assumed to have a (daily average) maximum physical activity level that he can maintain on a habitual basis (A_n in Fig. 3.1). To attain this maximum activity level, he needs a certain calorie intake, C_{jn}, in order to remain in energy balance. A calorie intake above C_{jn} will not permit increased activity. Per unit of time, the body can only transform a given amount of energy contained in food into muscular activity (Robinson 1968, Spurr 1983). An energy intake above what is expended in physical activity and the BMR will accumulate as fat (and body weight will change; cf. below). All points on the $SCE_j(W_j,A,\mathbf{Z})$ curve represent possible stationary equilibria. That is, at all these points, the individual can be in energy balance (neither gaining nor losing weight), at body weight W_j.

The assumption that the short-term calorie expenditure function is convex (especially in the upper range), may warrant a justification. The function is taken directly from the medical–physiology literature. In their classical survey of this literature, Passmore and Durnin (1955: pp. 806, 819–20), cites several studies which show that 'energy expenditure is linearly proportional to speed [in walking]. . . carrying loads' and several other physical activities over the lower range. However, they also found that in most activities, after a certain activity level, the energy expenditure per unit of physical activity performed (such as increasing the speed of walking by 1 m/min), measured by direct calorimetry as well as by oxygen consumption, increases more than proportionally (see Appendix Fig. 3.1, based on data from the FAO/WHO/ UNU (1985) expert panel's report; and Åstrand and Rodahl 1986: fig. 14.5).[4]

The theoretical explanation of why there are diminishing returns to energy intake in terms of physical (work) performance (per unit of time) at the upper segment of the activity range is the human body's limited capacity to transform energy in food into muscular activity. In the words of medical physiologists, 'this loss of efficiency probably depends on the accumulation of lactate and other anaerobic metabolizes in the muscles, resulting in changes of muscle strength, viscosity, relaxation, and neuromuscular coordination' (Robinson 1968: p. 531). It is also notable that 'a large proportion of the energy released by the working muscle takes the form of heat, and this must be dissipated through the skin' (ibid: p. 520).

3.3.2. The Long-term Calorie Expenditure Function

There are not only an infinite number of combinations of calorie intakes and physical activity levels that leave the individual in energy balance: the individual can also be in energy balance at different body weights. Each weight corresponds to a different BMR and a different short-term calorie expenditure function; there is thus one $SCE_j(W_j, A, Z)$ curve for each body weight ($j = 0, \ldots h, \ldots j, k, \ldots m \ldots$). It is further assumed that there is one specific body weight (W_m) at which the individual can produce a maximum physical activity in absolute terms (for given height, genetic heritage, and other elements in the Z vector). The expenditure function corresponding to this weight is $SCE_m(W_m, A, Z)$ in Fig. 3.2.[5]

At a weight above W_m the individual is overweight and his maximum external activity potential is reduced for the simple reason that he has to move his own excess fat around. A weight lower than W_m means a lower maximum capacity for physical activity. The reason is that changes in 'body fat stores . . . are inevitably linked to some extent with changes of lean tissue as well' (Payne 1992: pp. 79–80), which include the muscles that are used in physical tasks.[6] A lower body weight also means a reduction of energy expenditure for basal metabolism.

A decrease in body weight can be represented by a shift from $SCE_j(W_j, A, Z)$ to $SCE_k(W_k, A, Z)$ in Fig. 3.2, which would reduce the individual's maximum physical activity potential (from A_{jn} to A_{kn}), and lower his calorie requirement for basal metabolism (from BMR_j to BMR_k). This implies that the two functions cross, and so there will be a trade-off between maximum physical activity potential and BMR.

In Fig. 3.2, one could draw a whole 'school' of short-term energy expenditure functions, each one representing a different body weight of the reference individual. The envelope for such a school of curves traces out the combinations of habitual calorie intake, on the one hand, and body weight,

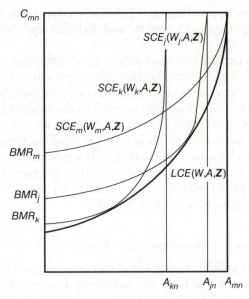

Fig. 3.2. The long-term calorie expenditure function

external activity level, and, thus, energy expenditure, on the other, at which the individual can be in energy balance (the heavy curve). This is what we will call the individual's long-term calorie expenditure (LCE) function and denote $LCE(W,A,Z)$. (Since being overweight causes a reduced work capacity, the $LCE(W,A,Z)$ function will bend 'backwards' above C_{mn}; that portion of the curve is ignored here.) As one moves from the left to the right along $LCE(W,A,Z)$, the different stationary equilibria represent a successively higher external activity level and a higher body weight. The intercept of the $LCE(W,A,Z)$ function is left unexplained for the moment; later on it will be derived endogenously.[7]

3.3.3. The Calorie Revenue Function

As illustrated by Fig. 3.2, from a purely biological point of view, the individual can be in energy balance at an infinite number of combinations of body weight, physical activity level, and calorie intake/expenditure. In a world where food entitlements are based on the economic return to the individual's (or household's) own physical work effort, which requires energy, the number of combinations is restricted.

In the upper panel of Fig. 3.3, the $LCE(.)$ envelope curve is replicated. There is also the $REV(A,K,P)$ curve, which we call the calorie revenue function. It is an ordinary production function that traces out the economic return to the individual's physical work effort (A) for fixed values of the capital-stock vector K (including land), and P is the price of the outputs he produces in relation to the price of calories. The return to the individual's work effort (or gross income) is measured along the vertical axis in how many calories the individual's work output can buy in the market at the prevailing price. His income is thus assumed to be a monotonic and positive function of the physical work activity (number of hours per day multiplied by the intensity).

In the case depicted in Fig. 3.3, the $REV(.)$ function is strictly concave. The underlying assumption is that there are diminishing marginal returns to physical labour effort over the entire range. This is what characterizes the standard production functions used in economic production theory, e.g. the Cobb–Douglas and the constant elasticity of substitution (CES) functions under constant returns to scale.[8] This case can represent a farmer with his own labour, a small piece of land, and some simple tools as the only factors of production, and who faces given prices for his output in the market.

Alternatively, one can think of a person producing a pure labour service that earns a certain fixed return on a per-task or per-piece basis in the market. In such a case it would be more appropriate to depict the revenue function as an upward-sloping, straight line. However, as long as the revenue function does not have a convex portion, its exact shape is not essential for the results to be derived.

In the case shown in Fig. 3.3, the revenue function cuts the expenditure function twice. At A_a the individual's work will pay him exactly the equivalent of the calories he needs for BMR and the work activity itself. At A_d the two curves intersect again, and a higher activity level (and body weight) means that the energy expenditure exceeds the energy revenue. At all work activity levels between A_a and A_d, the individual will produce a 'calorie surplus' that can be transformed into non-calorie consumption goods through market exchange at given prices. The dotted area in Fig. 3.3 thus represents the feasible set of consumption of non-calories that the individual is faced with.[9]

3.4. OPTIMAL WORK EFFORT, BODY WEIGHT, AND CALORIE INTAKE

The feasible set of consumption of non-calories has been reproduced as the area which is upward bounded by the NC curve in the lower panel of Fig. 3.3. Along the vertical axis we have non-calorie consumption; along the horizontal axis, now reading it from the right to the left, we have disutility of work, or leisure. (The maximum leisure he can obtain is thus at A_a, where he can survive in the sense that working this little earns him an income that is just enough to buy the calories needed for metabolism and the work effort.) What particular point in the consumption set he will choose depends on whether his utility function, in addition to non-calories, includes disutility of work effort and health concerns.

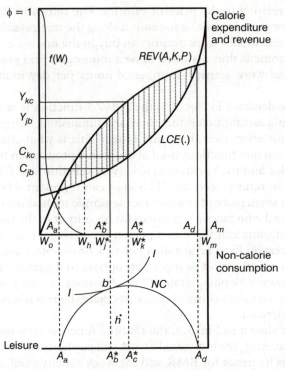

FIG. 3.3. The calorie revenue function and the complete model

The simplest case is when non-calorie consumption is the only argument in the utility function. The optimal activity level in this case is at $A_c^\star$ in the lower panel of Fig. 3.3, where the NC curve reaches a maximum. (In the following, $\star$ is used to indicate optimal states.) In the upper panel of Fig. 3.3, the corresponding point is at the activity level at which the vertical distance is the largest between the energy revenue and expenditure functions, i.e. where the slopes of these two functions are the same. The optimal body weight is $W_k^\star$. At this optimal activity level, the individual earns an income corresponding to Y_{kc}, and he has to have a calorie intake of C_{kc} in order to stay in energy balance.

Consider now the case in which the individual has disutility of labour or, the other way around, a preference for 'leisure'. This means that leisure and non-calorie consumption are substitutes and that the trade-off can be represented by indifference curves. In this case, the individual will choose a lower activity level ($A_b^\star$ in Fig. 3.3), at the point b, where the NC curve touches the highest attainable indifference curve (II). This point also corresponds to a lower body weight than in the previous case without disutility of labour ($W_j^\star < W_k^\star$). His income will in this case be Y_{jb} and his required calorie intake C_{jb}.

The individual may have a third element in his utility function: concern for his health. A person can vary his body weight within a relatively wide range without affecting his probability of getting ill (FAO/WHO/UNU 1985) and thus the mortality risk.[10] However, below a certain body weight (W_h in Fig. 3.3), there is a health risk which increases as weight is further reduced (see Payne 1992). Below some very low body weight (W_o), the probability that the person becomes fatally ill within the period is unity, i.e. the person dies with certainty.[11] Between W_o and W_h, the risk function may take the form depicted by the $\phi(W)$ curve (the exact shape is not essential for the argument here). The intercept of the $SCE_o(A, W_o, \mathbf{Z})$ curve is what determines the intercept of the $LCE(.)$ function, which was left unexplained earlier.

If the person considers health risk (or simply values having a little extra weight) he may choose an interior point in the set bounded by NC, say h in Fig. 3.3. That is, he will forsake some non-calorie consumption in order to eat more so as to maintain a higher body weight.

The above analysis suggests that it does not pay the nutritionally constrained individual to exert his maximum work capacity. This is so because of the convexity of the upper range of the short-term energy expenditure function (irrespective of whether the revenue function is linear or concave). This convexity also means that it is more economical (in terms of calories expended) to pursue a work task at a regular steady pace than to work with alternate intensity.[12] This argument is reinforced if the energy revenue function is concave, as in the case depicted in Fig. 3.3. Moreover, that most individuals of working age in poor countries are thinner than in the rich countries does not necessarily imply that they are undernourished (as long as $W_j^\star > W_h$). A low body weight may be part of an adjustment that is economically motivated. We then have a theoretical case for nutritionally constrained individuals to be 'small and lazy'.[13]

3.5.   COMPARATIVE STATICS

3.5.1. Exogenous Changes in the Revenue Function

The energy expenditure function in the model is assumed to contain no variable that can change exogenously. Two of the variables in this function, A and W, are endogenous and the third, the vector of personal characteristics, $\mathbf{Z}$, is assumed to be given once and for all. All the exogenous variables are contained in the revenue function, i.e. the factor endowment ($\mathbf{K}$) and the price (P). This means that the long-term energy expenditure function cannot shift; changes in the exogenous variables can only induce movements (second-order effects) along it. Only a change in an exogenous variable will induce a shift (a first-order effect) in the revenue function.

Price Change   Let us first examine what happens when an exogenous para-meter changes, i.e. there is an increase in the price of the good or service sup-plied by the individual (which he expects to be permanent), from u to v ($P = (u,v)$). This will induce a multiplicative upward shift in the calorie revenue function (from $REV^u(.)$ to $REV^v(.)$) in Fig. 3.4. The optimizing individual's response would be to increase his work activity and his body weight (from $A^{u\star}$ to $A^{v\star}$ and $W^{u\star}$ to $W^{v,\star}$ respectively). (For simplicity, we disregard dis-utility of work and preferences for 'extra' body weight.) By working more and putting on some extra weight, the individual can now increase his consump-tion of non-calories.

That the new maximum corresponds to a point to the right of the initial location (a) on the revenue function, i.e. at b, is easily seen. The slope of the $REV^u(.)$ curve at a, which is identical to the slope of the $LCE(.)$ curve at c, is less steep than the $REV^v(.)$ curve at d. That is, since the marginal revenue of an additional work effort at the new price exceeds the marginal cost of that effort, the individual has an incentive to increase his work intensity until the marginal revenue and marginal cost are equal again (from $A^{u\star}$ to $A^{v\star}$). A price decline would trigger an opposite response: a lowering of both work activity and body weight. In fact, the lower the economic productivity of the individual (*cet par*), the lower the optimal work effort and body weight.

Income Support   Let us now consider another exogenous change, i.e. the individual receives income support in the form of money or food in kind (aid). Such a gift can be represented by a parallel upward shift of the revenue

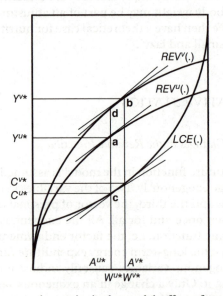

FIG. 3.4. Comparative statics in the model: effect of a price increase

function, from $REV^u(.)$ to $REV^{u+a}(.)$ in Fig. 3.5, where the gift corresponds to the intercept of the $REV^{u+a}(.)$ function. If the individual has no disutility of labour, the gift will not affect his behaviour in terms of work effort, calorie intake/expenditure, or body weight. That is, since a gift shifts the revenue function upwards without changing its slope, the individual still finds his optimum where the slope of the long-term expenditure function is the same as for the initial revenue function (at $A^{u\star}$). In this case, (food) aid will thus lead to *increased* consumption of non-calories (from ab to ac.)

Finally, let us now reintroduce a preference for leisure and see how a gift in the form of (food) aid affects the individual's behaviour. In Fig. 3.6, the gift can be represented by a parallel shift of the upward bound of the non-calorie consumption set, from NC to NC^a (the vertical distance between NC and NC^a is equal to the gift). In this case, the individual will respond to the gift by partly increasing his consumption of non-calories and partly by consuming more leisure (working less).[14] He will reduce his work activity level from $A_b^\star$ to $A_a^\star$. Tracing the effect of reduced work effort back to the new equilibrium position in Fig. 3.5, we find that this will also reduce his (optional) body weight and lower his calorie expenditure/intake—quite the opposite of what is the conventional aim of (food) aid.

3.5.2. Inter-individual Comparison

We have considered above one individual with specific biological characteristics (the fixed Z vector), who works in a specific economic activity with

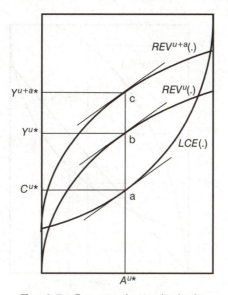

FIG. 3.5. Comparative statics in the model: effect of income support (aid)

given factors of production (the fixed K vector), and who experiences an exogenous change in his revenue function. Let us now examine how income, calorie intake, and body weight relate across individuals whose job activities and biological constitutions are different. Two individuals ($Z = 1,2$) and two job activities ($H = x,y$) will be considered (denoted by superscripts).

Job Activity Differences　　Let us first consider a case with two individuals who have the same biological characteristics, which means that their long-term energy expenditure functions are identical ($LCE(.)$ in Fig. 3.7), while pursuing different job activities. Different work activities mean that they have different revenue functions. The first individual is assumed to have no physical

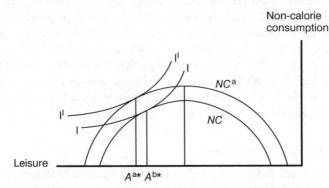

FIG. 3.6.　Effect of (food) aid on work effort with preference for leisure

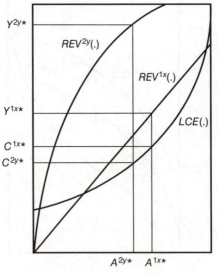

FIG. 3.7.　Comparison of identical
individuals with different jobs

productive assets; he sells his raw labour to, say, a sugar cane plantation. His wage is set on a per-ton-cut basis. Under the assumption that each additional ton requires the same amount of labour effort, his revenue function will assume the property of a straight line ($REV^{1x}(.)$ in Fig. 3.7). The second individual is a small-holder farmer with some land and capital equipment; with decreasing marginal return to physical labour effort, his revenue function is $REV^{2y}(.)$.

The landless labourer will maximize his consumption of non-calories at a work effort corresponding to $A^{1x\star}$. He must then have a daily calorie intake of $C^{1x\star}$ in order to stay in energy balance. His (gross) income is $Y^{1x\star}$. The small-holder farmer's optimal work effort is lower ($A^{2y\star} < A^{1x\star}$) and his energy-balance calorie intake will thus also be lower ($C^{2y\star} < C^{1x\star}$). However, due to the higher productivity of his work effort, his gross (and net) income will exceed that of the sugar-cane cutter ($Y^{2y\star} > Y^{1x\star}$). We thus have here a case where there is a negative association between calorie intake and income across two individuals because of differences in economic productivity. The more productive individual will work and eat less, while still earning a higher income.

Biological Differences   The case depicted in Fig. 3.8 shows two individuals working in the same economic activity (say x) with an identical bundle of capital goods and facing the same exogenously given prices, signifying that they work along the same revenue function ($REV(.)$). The two differ, however, in one dimension: body size. The first man is tall and strong; he thus has a

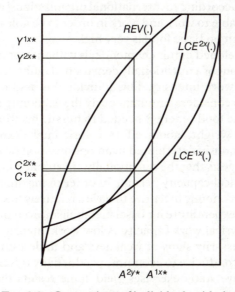

FIG. 3.8. Comparison of individuals with the same job but different biological characteristics

relatively high BMR and maximum capacity for physical work ($LCE^{1x}(.)$ in Fig. 3.8). The second man is smaller and has a lower physical work capacity; his energy expenditure function is $LCE^{2x}(.)$. (The fact that the larger man has both a higher maximum physical work capacity and BMR than the small man means that their two energy expenditure curves intersect at some point.) At their respective optima, the taller man will earn a higher income, while having a lower calorie expenditure than the small man. Again, we have a negative association between calorie expenditure and income; this time due to biological differences across people.

There is no *a priori* reason why the association between incomes and calorie intake should be negative, as just demonstrated in the latter two cases. If other exogenous parameters differ across individuals, such as the wage/price they receive for a given work effort, the association may be positive; in still other cases there may be no association at all. There is, however, reason to expect negative association when there are large inter-individual differences in occupation and in factor endowment (e.g. land, and physical and human capital). This is because low-income jobs on average tend to be physically more energy-demanding than high-income jobs.[15]

3.6. SUMMARY AND CONCLUSIONS

Most people in Africa and South Asia are self-employed in agricultural and related work activities. Many of these are undernourished, or in the risk zone for becoming so, according to international organizations' assessments. They eat in order to be able to work and work in order to be able to eat; the share of gross income spent on basic food is very high.

The model developed in this chapter deals with the optimal economic and biological behaviour of a nutritionally constrained individual who has the option of choosing work intensity. This individual is assumed to be an 'economic man', who considers simultaneously the economic return of his work and the cost of the food (energy) needed to pursue his work. In this setting, his optimal body weight, labour effort, calorie intake/expenditure, and income are endogenously determined in an optimization process.

The model suggests that the nutritionally constrained individual will work less than his physical capacity permits in order to maximize his welfare. He will also have an economic incentive to have a relatively low body weight so as to save on energy expenditure for basal metabolism, even though this reduces his maximum physical work capacity. A low work intensity and body weight are thus not necessarily signs of weakness and undernutrition, but adjustments which are conducive to economic productivity (given his constraints).

The comparative static exercises yield some results that are interesting from the point of view of empirical testing. For an individual engaged in a given work activity, an exogenous increase in his wage (or the price of the product he produces) makes him increase his work activity and body weight and, thus, his calorie intake/expenditure. That is, the expected association between the two endogenous variables income and calorie intake will be positive. This is all in line with the hypotheses in the empirical literature that deal with estimating calorie–income elasticities, or test the possibility that 'better nutrition increases productivity and income', although the positive association does not imply causality, as both income and calorie intake are endogenous variables. The model further suggests that income (or food in kind) support may make the individual reduce his calorie intake if he has disutility of work effort.

The model was also used to predict how income and calorie intake (and body weight) are associated across individuals. It was demonstrated that because of inter-individual differences in the kind of work in which they are engaged (more or less physically demanding) and in biological characteristics (height, age), it may well be that higher incomes are associated with lower calorie intakes (and body weight). The reason is that well-paid jobs are often less physically (energy) demanding than low-paid manual jobs. This may be an explanation for the weak results obtained in the empirical literature which aims at estimating calorie–expenditure elasticities, as well as estimating the effect of nutrition on labour productivity (to be scrutinized in the next chapter).

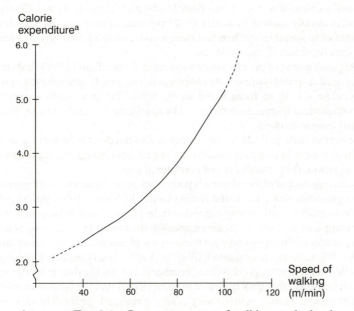

APPENDIX FIG. 3.1. Gross energy cost of walking on the level

Source: FAO/WHO/UNU 1985: annex 3.

ᵃ For a male adult 18–30 years old weighing 60 kg (expressed as a Ratio of BMR).

As with most models, the one developed in this chapter has its obvious shortcomings. The model is static, which means that the dynamic pathways through which the individual adjusts his work effort, calorie intake, and body weight in the face of exogenous shocks cannot be analysed appropriately. This may well conceal important results and insights. Moreover, the model depicts the behaviour of an individual without allowing for the fact that many nutritional decisions are made within households; the determinants of intra-household allocation of food are thus not possible to analyse within this framework. This is to ignore the important question of how food is allocated among adults of different sexes and ages, as well as among members of working age and small children. Furthermore, the only mechanism for savings in the model is the accumulation of fat (body weight changes). This assumption leaves out consumption-smoothing savings in other forms that empirically have been demonstrated to be important (e.g. Anand and Harris 1992). Hopefully, however, these and other shortcomings of the model can be rectified in future work.

NOTES

1. An individual or household is defined as nutritionally constrained when the share of total incomes that goes to buy basic food (calories) is significant. Consumption surveys usually show the poorest 10–25 per cent of the population in developing countries to spend more than half their income on food. See FAO*d* (1986, 1988) for data from Sub-Saharan Africa.

2. In his assessment of the efficiency wage models, Bardhan (1979) finds the theoretical and empirical support for nutrition-based, or efficiency-based, monopsonistic wage setting in India to be weak; rather, he finds more support for the hypothesis that wages are determined by aggregate demand and supply in the different labour markets.

3. During the early periods in life, energy is also needed for internal activity in the form of growth in body size, and women need extra energy during pregnancy and for lactation; these needs are not considered here.

4. The energy cost of physical work is proportional to the amount of oxygen the person consumes above the usual resting value (Robinson 1968: pp. 521–23). The indirect estimates of energy expenditure in physical activities, based on oxygen consumption, also show a linear segment in the low and middle ranges and a convex portion in the upper segment; examples of oxygen-activity elasticities of the order 2.8 have been estimated (ibid: p. 530). Passmore and Durning (1955: p. 806) found that 'so good is the agreement between the data from these five laboratory studies [that they reviewed in some detail] that the tabulation of the many other results seems unnecessary'. The empirical generalizations made by Passmore and Durning are found in many textbooks on medical physiology (e.g. Robinson 1968: p. 522, Åstrand and Rodahl 1986: fig. 14.5).

5. In some of the recent nutrition literature it has been postulated that the body has a built-in mechanism which sees to it that the energy consumed is more

efficiently used during prolonged periods of nutritional stress, i.e. there is intra-individual adaptation to a low calorie intake. This notion is readily represented in the model, simply meaning that the calorie expenditure function has a smaller intercept and lies at a lower level than if such a mechanism is considered not to exist.

6. The proportion in which fat and lean body mass is reduced when a person loses weight varies from one individual to another, with a median value of 85/15 (Dugdale and Payne 1977).

7. It should be noted that the $LCE(.)$ curve is *not* the same as the efficiency–wage-function (EWF) in previous models, although they may look similar. The EWF traces the economic *contribution of labourers* working at a farm (Stiglitz 1976) or a factory (Mirrlees 1975), as a (positive) function of the economic compensation (wage) which they receive. The $LCE(.)$ function derived here depicts the biological relationship between energy expenditure and the external physical activity that the individual undertakes. Labour productivity and economics have yet to be introduced into the model (in subsection 3.3.3).

8. The technical property of this function may look similar to the production function in the particular efficiency wage model developed by Stiglitz (1976: fig. 4). His production function is that of the farm at which the labourers are employed, but not that of the individual, as here. Also note that we have assumed wages to be given, i.e. to be determined by aggregate demand and supply in the economy in which the individual is working, not by a monopsonistic or egalitarian employer. A further notable difference is that Stiglitz is not concerned with the individual, his calorie needs, body weight, and undernutrition. However, as he points out, all his results hinge on the assumption that his efficiency wage requirement function has a convex segment, which he refrains from explaining (ibid: p. 187). In the case of the individual, such a convexity is conveniently represented by an intercept corresponding to the calorie needs for BMR, the assumption used here and in Bliss and Stern (1978*b*).

9. Food is thus assumed to be a good with several characteristics that enter the individual's utility function separately, such as taste, texture, and social stigma, which are 'consumption' characteristics, and energy, which we have assumed not to provide any direct utility, only indirectly in the production of income (leisure and consumption of non-calories). The non-calorie properties of food are assumed to be part of the other, composite, good. Thus, we here assume that the different 'characteristics' of food can be obtained as separate units. This is perhaps not a realistic assumption for localities where the variety in the available food is small, but in most places it seems to be a reasonable approximation.

10. The physical exercise required for the maintenance of cardiovascular and muscular fitness lays a further restriction on the minimum external activity that the individual can pursue. However, people who undertake even light physical work for a few hours per day will automatically get the required exercise.

11. This weight has been estimated to correspond to a BMI of around 12 (James *et al.* 1988). The weight below which risk of ill health sets in is estimated to correspond to a BMI of 18.5.

12. Over the convex part of the energy expenditure function, all linear combinations lie above the function (by definition). On the empirical side, a study of the energy cost of different household and agricultural tasks actually performed by

Gambian women indicates that the great majority of the tasks are much lighter
than estimated in laboratory experiments. The authors (Lawrence *et al.* 1985:
p. 759) further note: 'most activities were performed by our African subjects with
considerable economy of effort (i.e. there were few superfluous movements)' and
they were struck by 'the smooth performance of the tasks'.

13. The notion that 'smaller is better' in nutritionally constrained populations has
    been suggested earlier in an informal way (e.g. Seckler 1982, 1984).

14. Sahn and Alderman (1995) examined the effect of receiving a rice ration on the
    rural labour supply in Sri Lanka. They found that labour supply decreased by
    10–15 per cent after other influences had been controlled for.

15. The fact that a daily calorie intake of 2,700 is sufficient for the present author to
    stay in nutritional balance and perform his job, while a smallholder male farmer
    of the same age (and smaller body) in Mali expends above 4,000 calories on the
    average day (von Braun 1988) has, of course, nothing to do with income elasti-
    cities for calories. This author has an income which is perhaps 100 times the in-
    come of the smallholder in Mali (at official exchange rates); still, he eats less. The
    self-evident explanation is that the farmer's work is more energy-demanding.

4

Related Empirical Evidence

4.1. INTRODUCTION

Nutritionists and economists have focused on different parts in the nexus of linkages between the individual's work load, body size, energy expenditure, and income. Nutritionists have predominantly been engaged in modelling energy (calorie) expenditure/intake as a biological function of body size and physical activity (manual work intensity), while the relation to income and other economic variables has largely been unexplained. Economists, on the other hand, have mainly been preoccupied with estimating income elasticities for calories, i.e. the demand for calories as a function of income and prices, with insufficient regard for biological energy determinants. In other economic studies, the objective has been to investigate the reverse relationship, i.e. whether 'nutritional status' has an effect on labour productivity and, thus, income. In this chapter we shall examine the various theories and empirical tests of the nutrition–income linkages and also see how they relate to the model set up in Chapter 3 above.

4.2. NUTRITIONISTS' ESTIMATION OF CALORIE EXPENDITURE REQUIREMENTS

In the nutritionists' model of individuals' energy (calorie) expenditures (E_i), the two determinants are the Basal Metabolic Rate (BMR_i) and the physical activity level (PAL_i) (expressed as a multiple; cf. Chapter 2). The BMR_i for an individual is further modelled as a function of his or her body weight (W_i) and a vector of time-invariant personal characteristics, Z_i (mainly age and sex). The calorie expenditure function can thus be expressed formally as:

$$E_{it} = PAL_{it} \, BMR_{it} \, (W_{it}, Z_i). \tag{4.1}$$

When the individual is in energy balance during period t, his or her calorie intake (C_{it}) must equal expenditures (E_{it}).

Equation 4.1 thus allows us to estimate the energy expenditure requirement for a given body size and physical activity level (and given Z). (How this is done in more detail is discussed in Chapter 8.) When holding body weight (and BMR) constant, equation 4.1 corresponds to what is depicted as the short-term energy requirement function in the model developed in the previous chapter (Fig. 3.1), although its convex section is not allowed for in the above equation.[1] When both body weight and activity level are allowed to change simultaneously, the equation can be seen as a linear approximation of the long-run calorie expenditure function in that model.

A main concern for nutritionists has been to find the critical lowest body weight and *PAL*—and thus the lowest calorie expenditure/intake—that are consistent with health and physical functioning. They have not been seriously interested in the question how the individual's choice of actual physical activity level (PAL), i.e. work intensity, and of body weight (*W*), is related to economic variables such as relative prices and income earnings potential. The minimum body weight (for height) is estimated from correlations be-tween mortality risk and weight (in Western populations). The minimum en-ergy expenditures (by the FAO/WHO/UNU definition) are estimated on the assumption of a physical activity level that allows for a workload that is stated to be 'economically necessary'. (The difficulties involved in defining what is 'economically necessary' in operational terms are discussed in Chapter 8 below.)

4.3. CALORIE–INCOME ELASTICITY ESTIMATES

4.3.1. *Theory*

Empirical economists have for a long time been engaged in estimating in-come (or expenditure) elasticities for calories. The estimates that came forth before the mid 1980s were derived on the basis of the standard consumer de-mand model. In this model, calories enter as an argument in the individual's utility function, just as any other good, and the demand for calories is ob-tained by maximizing the utility function subject to his (or the household's) budget constraint. The standard (log) demand function for calories (*C*) de-rived from this model takes the form:

$$\ln C = a_0 + a_1 \ln Y + a_2 \ln P + e, \qquad (4.2)$$

where *Y* is the individual's income and *P* is the relative price vector of calo-ries obtained from different food items. The a_1 is the income elasticity for cal-ories, and the a_2 vector the price elasticities, to be estimated.

There are two main theoretical problems with using a standard consump-tion model to estimate the demand for calories in the poor country context (or anywhere). The first problem is that income is assumed to be exogenous, i.e. the possibility that calorie intake may have an effect on income, or that both calorie demand and income are endogenous variables, thereby inducing a simultaneity bias in the estimates, is not controlled for. The second is that demand for energy is assumed to enter the individual's utility function only.

The fact that demand for calories is (also) indirect, i.e. energy is an input (or intermediate factor) in the individual's labour production function, determined by his specific body constitution and the intensity of the work activity he performs (the two variables that nutritionists emphasize), is ignored.

Bouis and Haddad (1992) and others (e.g. Behrman and Deolalikar 1987, Pitt *et al.* 1990, Ravallion 1990; Bhargava 1991, and Subramanian and Deaton 1996) have more recently attempted to overcome some of the shortcomings of the 'old' estimation models. Their tests are based on equations similar to:

$$C = a_0 + a_1 A(W) + a_2 Y(A, \boldsymbol{P}, \boldsymbol{K}, \boldsymbol{X}) + \boldsymbol{Z}' a_3 + u \qquad (4.3)$$

where C is realized demand for calories, W is body weight, A is physical activity level, and Y is income. The three latter variables are in principle treated as endogenous by most of the authors (although not always in practice, see below). The exogenous variables are $\boldsymbol{P}$, which is a vector of prices for the commodities produced, $\boldsymbol{K}$, a vector of factors of production other than raw labour (such as land, fertilizers, capital goods, etc.), and $\boldsymbol{X}$, a vector of unobserved characteristics of the production process. Finally, when estimated on data for households rather than for individuals, a vector $\boldsymbol{Z}'$ is added which contains elements of household demographic characteristics (such as number of adults, children, sex, and age distribution, etc.). The a_i's are the coefficients (elasticities when in ln-form) to be estimated.

4.3.2. Estimation Technique, Measurements, and Data

In order to control for the possibility that income is an endogenous variable, most of the studies have used instrument variables and the two-stage least square (2SLS) estimation technique. Two of the studies are based on the simpler ordinary least squares (OLS) technique (Ravallion 1990, Subramanian and Deaton 1996). The calorie-intake variable is typically estimated by one or more 24-hour recalls, although some of the authors have somewhat longer recall periods. Household earnings are either estimated by reported income or expenditures. All the studies use cross-sectional data (in some cases a short panel).

4.3.3. Empirical Findings

The estimated income elasticities for calories derived in the early studies, based on some version of equation 4.2 and estimated by OLS, were usually quite high, in the 0.5–1.18 range (see Bouis and Haddad (1992: table 1) for a summary of results and a discussion of these).

The authors of the more recent studies have also ascribed to calories normal consumption goods properties, implying that they expect a positive relationship to endogenous income (or expenditures). The estimated size of the income elasticity, however, varies substantially. In one of the studies, the elasticity is very low and not statistically significant (Behrman and Deolalikar 1987); in three others it is relatively low (0.05–0.15), but significant (Pitt *et al.* 1990, Ravallion 1990, Bhargava 1991). In the remaining study (Subramanian and Deaton 1996), the elasticity is found to be comparatively high, i.e. above 0.40. The range is thus quite wide, although less so than in the early studies. The two studies reporting relatively high elasticities at the sample mean find it to decline with higher income. (See also Strauss and Thomas 1995: pp. 1902–4.)

In two of the studies, a relatively large share of the variance in household demand for calories is explained by the data (Ravallion 1990, Subramanian and Deaton 1996). In the study by Bouis and Haddad (1992: table A.3), the adjusted R^2s for the estimations, based on their preferred techniques and measurements, are below 0.10. Also, the models tested by Behrman and Deolalikar have low explanatory power (in addition to insignificant income coefficients). In the two remaining studies, no R^2s are reported.

4.4.   NUTRITION AND LABOUR PRODUCTIVITY

4.4.1. Theory

Nutrition is one of several factors economists have taken into consideration when estimating determinants of labour productivity in poor populations. The early contributions to this literature suffered from the same problems that beset the first attempts to estimate calorie-expenditure elasticities; most importantly, they did not control for simultaneity. In more recent years, a few studies have come fourth that have tried to control for this particular bias. The most well-known ones are Strauss (1986), Sahn and Alderman (1988), Deolalikar (1988), and Haddad and Bouis (1991).

Neither of these studies provide an explicit theoretical model explaining how 'nutrition' enhances productivity. They suggest, however, some hypothesis about the mechanisms through which 'nutritional status' may affect agricultural wages (and farm productivity). Haddad and Bouis (1991: p. 50) list the following: '(1) an enhanced ability to undertake piece-rate work, (2) payment based on worker's past performance, (3) payment based on worker's perceived work potential, and (4) positive correlation between nutritional status and unobserved characteristics such as individual initiative (mediated through, say, a preference for education)'. Sahn and Alderman (1988: p. 160) briefly refer to the 'nutrition wage efficiency hypothesis which requires a positive relationship between individual calorie intakes and higher wages, and presumably productivity.' Strauss (1986: p. 303) and Deolalikar (1988: p. 407) also refer to the 'nutrition-productivity hypothesis'.

The most elaborate econometric model used to test the impact of nutrition on farm productivity is one of Deolalikar's (who also provides an equation for wage determination); it takes the form (notations are slightly altered):

$$\ln Q = a_0 \ln E + a_1 \ln W + a_2 \ln L + a_3 \ln X + a_4 \ln K + u + v \quad (4.4)$$

where Q is farm output, E is the daily calorie intake (expenditure) of the individual during the period (individual and time subscripts are left out), W is body weight, L is actual family labour input, K is farm size, and X is a vector of variable inputs; u is an unobserved household-specific endowment and v is an error term. The wage equations tested by Deolalikar and by Haddad and Bouis are quite similar to 4.4, while the models tested in the other two studies (by Strauss and by Sahn and Alderman) are a bit different (see below).[2]

4.4.2. Estimation Technique, Measurements, and Data

In the small set of recent studies on the effects of nutritional status on labour productivity, these two entities are defined and measured differently. In Strauss and in Sahn and Alderman, nutritional status is measured by household calorie availability and intake, respectively. In the other two studies, both individual calorie intake and various anthropometric measures are used as alternative indicators of nutritional status. In two of the studies, productivity is measured by farm output in smallholder populations (Strauss and Deolalikar) while in the other two, agricultural labour wage is the productivity proxy (Deolalikar tests both a wage and a farm-output equation). The calorie intake variable is estimated by 24-hour recalls in three of the studies, and by food availability in the fourth (Strauss 1986).

In all the studies, the *2SLS* estimation technique is used to control for simultaneity; in Deolalikar (1988) random and fixed techniques are also used. In Haddad and Bouis (1991) these three techniques, as well as *OLS*, are used alternately.

4.4.3. Empirical Findings

The four studies have reached diverse results. On the one hand, Strauss (1986: p. 297) finds a 'highly significant effect of calorie intake on labour productivity, providing solid support for the nutrition-productivity hypothesis' for a sample of small farmers in Sierra Leone. His estimated output elasticity is 0.34 at the sample mean. Sahn and Alderman (1988: table 4) find a significant, but smaller effect of per-capita household calorie intake on wages for men (an elaststicity of 0.21), but not for women in a South-Indian sample. Haddad and Bouis (1991) conclude that by their preferred estimates, 'increased calorie intakes have little impact on productivity' (as proxied by wages). Deolalikar (1988) finds no statistically significant effects of 'calories' on either wages or farm output.

In the two studies which use anthropometric indicators of nutritional status, different results are also obtained. Deolalikar (1988: p. 411) finds that 'weight-for height has a significant effect of a fairly large magnitude, on both wages and output'. Haddad and Bouis (1991: pp. 59–61 and table 6) were not able to reproduce this result for weight-for-height, but found adult height to have a significant effect on wages. Strauss (1986: p. 297) reports not only the highest elasticities, but also the best 'fits'—in some of the tests the adjusted R^2s are in the 0.50–0.65 range. In Sahn and Alderman (1988), the R^2 is only 0.09. Haddad and Bouis (1991) do not report R^2s.

4.5. DISCUSSION

The highly diverse results in the recent studies, which aim at estimating demand elasticities for calories and also the reverse impact of 'nutrition' on productivity, are no doubt in part due to different estimation techniques, shortcomings in the data and the measurements, and other technicalities (discussed in further detail in Strauss and Thomas 1995). However, there is also the possibility that the diversity reflects the actual situation, i.e. there is no general systematic relationship between calorie intake (or body size) and income across households in either direction. In this section we shall explore this hypothesis a bit further.

4.5.1. Theories

The calorie consumption model predicts that by raising income, a household will consume more calories, just as it will all normal goods. The basic problem with this model is that it disregards physiological fundamentals. Energy (calories) is not a good that can be 'consumed' in the normal sense; whatever energy that goes into the human body through the food intake must come out in the form of energy expenditures, i.e. for the maintenance of BMR and for physical activity (see Chapter 2). A more plausible theory predicting a positive effect of income on calorie intake must be based on the assumptions that with higher incomes, people will choose to have (i) a larger body weight and/or (ii) a higher level of physical activity (i.e. work intensity).

In the theoretical model developed in the previous chapter, the individual chooses simultaneously the body weight and work intensity that maximize his income (net of calorie purchases). With an exogenous improvement in productivity, e.g. through a higher price of the good or service that he produces, the individual's optimal strategy is to increase his body weight as well as his work intensity (and therefore calorie expenditure/intake). From this model, one thus expects a positive association between the three endogenous variables income, calorie intake, and body weight in longitudinal data at the level of individuals. The 'sign' prediction is thus the same as in the standard consumption model, although the transmission mechanisms are different. However, this does not necessarily imply that higher income (or households) should be associated with higher calorie intakes *across* individuals (see section 4.5.6. below).

In the other set of studies, concerned with nutrition and labour productivity, the basic assumption is that if poor people eat more—i.e. have a higher calorie intake and/or a higher body weight (muscle mass)—they become more productive and earn higher incomes. The main difficulty with this hypothesis is in specifying how the line of causality runs more exactly. For once, a person's productivity can increase through a change in one of the exogenous parameters he faces (e.g. the market price of the product/service he produces goes up). He may then respond by working harder and eating more (to sustain the extra work effort) and he may put on weight, while at the same time his income increases. (This is, again, what the model in Chapter 3 predicts.)

This is different from arguing that a person can increase his productivity and income by simply eating more and put on weight, *given unaltered values of the exogenous parameters that he faces*. If poor people could increase their productivity and income just by indulging more calories—and spending less on other consumption—they would have incentives to do so. The rational individual would eat and work more up to the point where the marginal gain in productivity (income) is equal to the marginal cost of the additional calories needed to support the extra work effort and maintain a higher *BMR* (as predicted by the model in Chapter 3 above).

There is one important caveat, though. In a situation where the individual is in disequilibrium, in the sense that he has yet to find his optimum body weight, given his present constraints, improved nutritional status through 'over-eating', which builds up body strength (muscle mass), is rational behaviour.[3] In such disequilibrium situations, there may be a direct causal link from better 'nutritional status' to higher income.

4.5.2. Measurements and Data

In the literature under discussion it has proved difficult to find relevant and accurate proxies for many of the variables included in the tests. The proxy variables used for nutritional status, calorie intake, and body weight, are perhaps the most questionable. When it comes to calorie intake, this fact is admitted by most of the authors who still use it for want of more relevant measures. The question is whether 'calorie intake' reflects nutritional status in any meaningful way at all. This is the case only if a higher calorie intake is generally better than a low one from a nutritional point of view over the entire range observed. (Estimated calorie intakes range from 1,500 to 6,000 per day and per capita in some of the studies.)

In order to be undernourished, an individual must have an habitual intake below what is required to support a body weight and a work effort consistent with health and functional fitness. How many calories this requires varies from individual to individual depending on his height, age, sex, and what kind of work he or she is engaged in. Without taking all these variables into consideration (which no study has done), 'calorie intake' alone can say practically nothing about the nutritional status of an individual. Short adults with a sedentary job may be perfectly well nourished with a daily calorie intake of 2,000, while others, being tall and pursuing strenuous manual work, may require 4,000 calories in order to stay in energy balance at a health-consonant body weight.

Similarly, a low body weight by standards from the Western countries (where up to one-third of the population is obese), does not imply under-nutrition; it is only in the very low range of observed body weights that health is impaired (see Chapter 8).

The relevance of calorie intake as a proxy variable for nutritional status is one problem; to obtain unbiased and reasonably error-free measurements is yet another. The process of estimating the calorie intake of individuals and households (as well as of income, expenditures, etc.) has proved very difficult in the developing country context (see Chapters 6 and 7 for further details; see also Behrman 1992, Bouis and Haddad 1992, Strauss and Thomas 1995). Large random errors are likely to have inflicted substantial white noise on the estimates (Bhargava 1991). There is also the risk that some estimates are biased owing to systematic errors in the data. Of particular concern is the use in most of the studies of 24-hour recalls to estimate 'calorie intake'. Estimates for such short periods have proven to be utterly unreliable proxies for either 'habitual calorie intake' or 'nutritional status' (discussed further in Chapter 7). This shortcoming alone is sufficient to cast serious doubt on whatever result emerges in studies using such data.

4.5.3. Omitted Variables

The two variables that nutritionists have proven—without doubt—to be the main biological determinants of peoples' energy expenditures, body size and energy intensity of physical (work) activity, are not included simultaneously in any of the estimated equations. This is so in the calorie–income elasticity studies, as well as those aimed at estimating the effect of nutrition on labour productivity. In two of the former studies (Pitt *et al.* 1990, Bhargava 1991), variables that pick up the differences in calorie demand that stem from differences in individuals' BMR are included (weight and height), while this is not the case in the other studies. In none of the studies is there a variable that captures the influence on the calorie requirement which stems from differences in the energy intensity of the work activities of different households. Ravallion (1990: p. 492) is most explicit in saying that this may have induced a bias in his results, but also some of the other authors recognize this omission.[4]

4.5.4. Sensitivity to Estimation Techniques and Measurements

Most of the recent studies aimed at estimating calorie-expenditure elasticities have used instrument variables and 2SLS estimations in order to control for simultaneity. Two studies have used the simpler OLS technique; these are the ones that report the highest elasticities (Ravallion 1990, Subramanian and Deaton 1996). Bouis and Haddad (1992: table 4) provide a comprehensive test of the sensitivity of results to the choice of estimation technique and measurements. They apply four different techniques: OLS, 2SLS, 'Within' and Hausman-Taylor, to the same data set(s). Further, they use two different calorie estimates (availability and intake) and two different earnings variables (income and expenditures). After having controlled for the influence of other independent variables, they obtain elasticities that range from 0.03 to 0.59. The sensitivity to choice of estimation technique and variable definition and measurement is thus very high. Moreover, they do not find that the OLS method systematically yields higher estimates than 2SLS, which one would expect if there were a strong reinforcing effect from nutrition to income.

Three of the four studies aimed at investigating the effect of 'better nutrition' on labour productivity have used the 2SLS technique to control for simultaneity. Deolalikar used random and fixed techniques, and found that 'the Hausman specification test leads to a clear rejection of the random effects model' (Deolalikar 1988: p. 411). Haddad and Bouis (1991) examined the sensitivity to the estimated effect on wages of four different estimation techniques (OLS, 2SLS, Within and Hausman-Taylor) and three measurements of nutritional status (calorie intake, weight for height, and height). They found calorie intake and weight for height to be statistically insignificant with all four techniques and height to be significant with OLS and Hausman-Taylor (while the 2SLS tests were too unstable). The robustness to estimation model specification and to choice of nutritional-status proxy is thus low.

4.5.5. Simultaneity and Choice of Instrument Variables

None of the empirical studies under investigation treat all the three entities—calorie intake, body weight, and income—as endogenous variables: i.e. as determined simultaneously by roughly the same set of exogenous parameters (such as relative prices and household-factor endowments). In most of the studies, it is postulated, as discussed above, that there are causal effects in both directions between income and calorie intake—which the authors have attempted to control for by instrument variables and 2SLS.

To endogenize the variables on the right-hand side (RHS) that on theoretical grounds are likely to be endogenous is not sufficient for obtaining unbiased results. The instruments used must also be appropriate. This is discussed by Deolalikar (1988: p. 407) in his comment on the results by Strauss

(1986), obtained on cross-sectional data with 2SLS. He argues that 'such procedures implicitly treat individual/household effects as random variables, and this leads to inconsistent parameter estimates if the type of unobserved effects that influence labour productivity also affect nutritional requirements and intake'.

Since Strauss did not have access to body weight data, or the energy intensity of the various agricultural work tasks which his sample households performed, his instrumented estimates must be biased due to omitted variables. This means that it is 'technically' possible that Strauss's results reflect a causal link from hard work to higher calorie intake (which is a physiological necessity), rather than the other way around, which is his interpretation.[5] In Pitt *et al.* (1990), the chief objective was to explain intra-household differences in calorie distribution. In several of their tests aimed at that objective, a coded variable reflecting the energy intensity of the observed households' different work activity is included on the RHS. However, in the one equation used to estimate a calorie–income elasticity (their table 4), this variable is not included.[5] Similar omitted variable problems also beset most of the other studies using 2SLS to control for simultaneity, as no measure of the energy intensity of different work activities is included in the tests.

4.5.6. *Time-series Predictions versus Cross-sectional Observations*

The model presented in Chapter 3 above predicts that individual calorie expenditure (intake), body weight, and work activity (income) move in tandem in response to exogenous shocks. This prediction of the model, however, is confined to what happens in the case of a welfare-maximizing individual when he or she experiences changes in the exogenous variables over time. All the studies discussed above use cross-sectional observations of households/ individuals (or in two instances, a short panel). Results which follow from theoretical analysis of individual behaviour over time do not necessarily carry over to cross-section.

Whether or not calorie intake, body weight, and income should be expected to be positively associated across individuals (and households) depends on the respects in which the individuals included in the sample differ the most. If the sample comprises individuals who are engaged in one and the same job activity (e.g. subsistence farming), higher productivity (income) is likely to be associated with higher work intensity (and, consequently, higher calorie expenditure) and, possibly, a higher body weight.

On the other hand, if the main differences in incomes across households or individuals are due to the fact that they are engaged in different types of job activities, one could equally well expect a negative association. For instance, manual labour is generally highly energy demanding, and labourers often earn considerably less than people engaged in more intellectual activities, which require little energy for strenuous body movements.

The recent studies under discussion do not say much about the composition of the households in their samples as regards occupation, and discuss even less the energy intensities of different work activities. In most of the studies, the sample comprises households said to be engaged in agricultural work ('farmers'), without much further detail. The households within the forming sector may differ, however, in that some are owners of land, others are labourers, while still others are tenants. It may well be that hired labour has to work in the most strenuous, calorie-demanding tasks, while still earning the lowest incomes. Such a negative association may well neutralize other 'positive' links (associations) between income and calorie intake and, thus, explain the lack of strong correlations in most of the studies.

4.6.   SUMMARY AND CONCLUSIONS

In this chapter we have scrutinized various hypotheses and tests of interlinkages in the nutrition-cum-economics literature. A main finding is the lack of strong and robust associations between calorie intake, body weight, and income. Possible explanations are poor data quality, the use of inappropriate proxy variables, sensitivity to choice of econometric estimation specification, and several other 'technical' problems. An alternative, or rather supplementary, explanation is that the absence of strong associations reflects real phenomena. All the studies are based on cross-sectional observations (or short panels) of households or adult individuals. If these households/individuals are heterogeneous in terms of height, job activities, access to factors of production besides raw labour, etc., there is simply no theoretical reason to expect an unambiguous positive association between income, calorie intake (expenditure), and body weight. Or, at least, no such theory has been advanced so far.

The argument here that calorie intake, body size, and income should all be considered endogenous variables is not to say that poor nutrition and poverty (low income) are unrelated; they are intimately related in the sense that both variables are determined in general equilibrium by the same set of exogenous factors, e.g. factor endowments and prices. Some people are both inadequately nourished and poor because they have no or few factors of production besides their unskilled labour, and the product or service which they produce commands a low price in the market. The distinction between this explanation for individuals both having a low income and being undernourished and the conventional ones, which infer causality between income and nutrition one way or the other, may seem subtle, but different policy implications do follow.[6]

If both nutritional status (body weight) and income are endogenous variables, only changes in the true exogenous variables can induce (simultaneous) change in body weight and income—which will be in the same direction in some cases, in others not. In such a perspective, the adequate policy recommendation is that governments should concentrate their efforts on improving the very factors that determine the low productivity of the poorest population segments. This notion does not rule out that there may be situations where a case can be made for public intervention aimed directly at poor people's food consumption (e.g. in famines) or for nutritional education (see Behrman 1993, for a discussion). It is difficult to believe, however, that 'nutritional interventions' can be an efficient instrument for alleviating the long-term poverty and undernutrition problems (a question to which we return in Chapters 14–17).

NOTES

1. That the *PAL* multiple is not a constant, as in the (above) equation which is actually used by the FAO/WHO/UNU to estimate energy expenditures in people, but increases at high levels of physical activity is also acknowledged in the FAO/WHO/UNU (1985: annex table 6).

2. Disregarding the causality issue, equation 4.4 is approximately consistent with the theoretical model in the previous chapter if one makes a slight reinterpretation of some of the explanatory variable definitions. That is, the calorie expenditure (E), which has no direct influence on productivity in that model, can be seen as a proxy for work intensity, L the number of hours worked, and W a proxy for *BMR*.

3. This way of reconciling the model in Chapter 3 with the 'better-nutrition-can-raise-productivity' notion was suggested by Peter Timmer. Disequilibrium situations may be typical for many people in the developing countries at certain points in time (e.g. during the pre-harvest season). One may then conjecture whether poor people in such situations are likely to be caught in 'below-equilibrium traps' because they lack sufficient income (or the credit needed) to buy the extra calories required to work more and/or build up weight (muscle mass). Dasgupta (1993) did a calculation of the cost for an Indian labourer to increase his daily calorie intake by 600 calories per day. (Enough to maintain 10 kg of additional body weight.) He found that the cost of these calories correspond to about 4 per cent of a daily wage for such labour. This suggests that the investment cost for obtaining 'better nutrition' status in a disequilibrium situation is marginal.

4. In Pitt *et al.* (1990), the chief objective was to explain intra-household differences in calorie distribution. In several of their tests aimed at that objective, a coded variable reflecting the energy intensity of the observed households' different work activity is included on the *RHS*. However, in the one equation used to estimate a calorie–income elasticity (their table 4), this variable was not included.

5. It is notable that the other two studies using calorie intake as a proxy for nutritional status got insignificant results, while obtaining significant results for weight or height.

6. A notable but deliberate omission in this chapter and the literature referred to is that the nutritional situation of small children and, related, the intra-household allocation of resources, is disregarded. The determinants and consequences of child undernutrition/health-impairment will be the focal points in subsequent chapters (mainly 14–16).

PART III

5

Undernutrition: The FAO Estimates

5.1. INTRODUCTION

There are two sets of estimates of the prevalence of undernutrition in the world that are claimed to be comparable across regions/countries and over time. The first is of the aggregate estimates of the share of the households that are undernourished in the world's main geographical regions, provided mainly by the FAO (1992), FAO*a* (1996) and previously, at one point, by the IBRD (1986). The second set comprises estimates based on sample evidence on the anthropometric status of pre-school-age children at the level of countries, obtained by WHO (1995) and also used by UNICEF (Carlson and Wardlaw 1990, UNICEF 1993*b*). The two sets of estimates, derived with completely different methods, purport that 43 and 30 per cent of the population (children only in the latter case), respectively, in SSA have been chronically undernourished in recent years.[1]

As noted in the introductory chapter, the estimates diverge substantially more, however, when it comes to comparing the present situation in SSA with that in South Asia, the two regions with the most severe nutritional problems according to all sources. The FAO estimates suggest that the POU at the level of households is close to twice as high in SSA as it is in South Asia. The WHO/UNICEF estimates suggest completely the opposite situation; that the incidence of undernutrition in children is almost twice as high in South Asia as in SSA.

The question is whether the evidence is conflicting to this enormous extent because of (i) biases in one of the estimation methods (or both), (ii) because they are based on different definitions and measurements of undernutrition, or (iii) because small children in South Asia fare worse than those in Africa relative to adults. In this and the following chapters we shall try to resolve these questions and some related puzzling information on the nutrition situation in Africa in international comparison.

In the present chapter, the basic model used by the FAO to estimate the overall prevalence of undernutrition in various part of the world is presented in section 5.2. The different estimates of the POU that the FAO (and also the IBRD, using a similar method) have produced over the years are summarized in section 5.3. In section 5.4, a simple simulation exercise is conducted in order to examine the sensitivity of the results to alternative values of the exogenous parameters in the estimation model. Some concluding observations are presented in section 5.5.

5.2.   THE FAO MODEL

The FAO and IBRD have used similar models to estimate the overall prevalence of undernutrition in the major regions of the world, although they have attached different numerical values to the parameters that comprise the model. In this section we will focus mainly on the FAO's most recent version of the model (FAO*a* 1996); some differences with the earlier FAO versions and, occasionally, with the IBRD (1986) model will be pointed out *en route*.

5.2.1. *The Estimation Method*

The main features of the FAO model can most easily be described with the help of a simple graph (Fig. 5.1A). There is a population with a finite number of households and there is a given 'pool' of calories available for human consumption. The households have varying access to the available calories and are ranked according to their household per-capita calorie availability (HPCCA) along the horizontal axis in Fig. 5.1A. The distribution of the calories among the households is assumed to be log-normal and measured by the coefficient of variation (CV[1]). The national per-capita calorie availability in the population is abbreviated NPCCA. Out of all the households, those who have a household per-capita availability which fails to meet the per-capita minimum energy requirement, denoted the calorie cut-off point, CCOP[1], in Fig. 5.1A, are classified as undernourished. These are the households found in the cross-hatched area.

Alternatively, the POU estimates can be derived from the (seemingly) simple formula:

$$POU = \int_{c<r} f(c)\,dc \qquad\qquad (5.1)$$

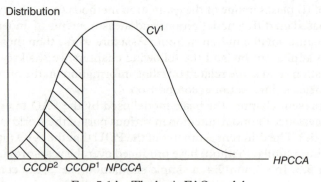

FIG. 5.1A. The basic FAO model

which contains three parameters only: c is the calorie intake proxy, r is the calorie requirement norm, and $f(c)$ is the density function of the distribution of the calorie intake proxy (for a more detailed algebraic exposition, see FAO*a* 1996: pp. 120–7).

5.2.2. Parameter Estimation Methods

The FAO method of estimating POU thus comprises three steps. The first is to estimate the per-capita calorie intake of the population at the national (country) level. The second step is to estimate the inter-household variance in the distribution of the calorie intakes. The third is to determine a calorie cut-off point below which households are classified as undernourished (the CCOP).

Quite obviously, the percentage of the population that falls out as 'undernourished' depends on where the CCOP is set. A lower cut-off point (e.g. at $CCOP^2$ in Fig. 5.1A) gives a lower prevalence of undernutrition for a given NPCCA and calorie distribution. It is notable that given the estimated distribution, an increase of the CCOP by a given percentage may give raise to a proportionally larger increase in the percentage of the population that is estimated to be undernourished. Exactly how sensitive the estimated prevalence of undernutrition is to the choice of CCOP is dependent on the distribution of calories. If the cut-off point is set in a part of the distribution where a large percentage of the population dwells, small changes in the CCOP may produce large changes in the estimated incidence of undernutrition (Ravallion 1990).

Secondly, it is also obvious that a smaller national per-capita availability of calories (a shift of the entire distribution to the left in Fig. 5.1A) would imply a higher percentage being undernourished for a given distribution and cut-off point. Again, a 1 per cent change in the NPCCA may induce a percentage-wise larger change in the estimated POU.

Thirdly, different distributions of calories across households produce different POU estimates (*cet par*) in a manner that is less obvious. In Fig. 5.1B, the same calorie distribution function (CV^1) as in the previous figure is depicted, but an additional curve which reflects a more uneven distribution—a higher coefficient of variation—has also been inserted (CV^2). One can think of the two distribution curves as representing two countries, where calories are distributed differently, but where the NPCCA is the same.

If we compare the areas representing the percentage of the population that falls out as undernourished in the two countries by applying the same CCOP, Fig. 5.1B reveals the result perhaps not immediately obvious. That is, we cannot say *a priori* that the country with the more uneven distribution (the CV^2 curve) will have a higher estimated incidence of undernutrition, or *vice versa*; this depends on the level at which the CCOP is set. If the cut-off point is set relatively high, we see that the households in areas a and c fall out as

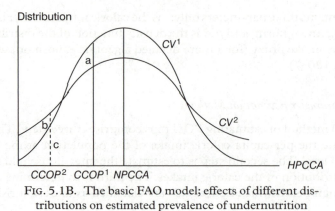

FIG. 5.1B. The basic FAO model; effects of different distributions on estimated prevalence of undernutrition

undernourished in the country with the relatively even distribution (CV¹). In
the country with the more uneven distribution (CV²), the households in
areas b and c come out as undernourished. Whether area a is larger or smaller
than area b depends on where the CCOP is set. However, if the cut-off point
is set to the left of the intersection of the two distribution curves, say at
CCOP² in Fig. 5.1B, the estimated incidence of undernutrition in the country with the more uneven distribution will be unambiguously larger than that
in the country with the more even distribution (*cet par*).

5.2.3. The Limited Aims with the FAO Estimates

In its previous *World Food Surveys*, the FAO claimed relatively modest ambi-
tions for its estimation method. The aim was to provide a panoramic picture
of the overall magnitude of prevalence of undernutrition in the world; a picture, however, that is detailed enough to allow comparison between large regions (such as Sub-Saharan Africa and South Asia) and changes over time.
The method was not (and still is not) aimed at identifying individual people/
households that are undernourished. Inherent in the method is that some
households will be erroneously classified as undernourished while they are
not; other households which are undernourished will be wrongly classified as
well-nourished (explained further in Chapter 9). The method is 'only' aimed
at providing unbiased estimates of the *share* of the population that fails to
meet the energy requirement norm. Finally, maldistribution of food within
households is not the concern: if a household is undernourished, all members are undernourished and *vice versa*.

However, with the *6th World Food Survey*, the FAO*a* (1996) has raised its
level of ambition. First, it has estimated the amount by which the most destitute are deficient, not just the share of the population that falls below the
calorie cut-off point. Secondly, the FAO*a* (1997) has published the POU
estimates for the 98 individual countries, on the basis of which its aggregate,
regional POU estimates reported in the *6th World Food Survey* were derived.

5.3. DATA AND ESTIMATES

5.3.1. Parameter Estimates

Per-Capita Calorie Intakes   The FAO uses the data on per-capita calorie availability at the level of countries, produced by the FAO, as proxies for 'average per-capita intake'. The availability data are obtained through a long series of conversions, from food-production and net-trade estimates, to the calorie content of the food supplies available for human consumption. The conversions allow for waste, seed, food used for industrial purposes, etc., as estimated in the so-called *Food Balance Sheets* by the FAOe (1986, 1996). (A more thorough description and critical assessment of these estimates is presented in the next chapter.)

Distribution of Calories   When it comes to the calorie distribution within the population of respective countries, the FAO uses households income/expenditure surveys to estimate a coefficient of variation. This procedure, however, is only used for the more-developed countries, for which surveys of 'acceptable' quality are available. For most other countries, the FAO estimates the inter-income-group distribution of calories on the basis of (i) calorie–income elasticities of the type analysed in Chapter 4 and (ii) estimates of the distribution of incomes. In still other (mostly African) countries, for which neither household survey data nor income distribution data are available, the FAO assumes that the calorie distribution is the same as in neighbouring countries. (These procedures will be assessed in Chapter 7.)

Calorie Requirement Norms   In establishing their calorie requirement norms, the FAO starts out from an equation similar to 2.2 in Chapter 2, where body weight, the basal metabolic rate, and the physical activity level are the three crucial parameters determining the energy requirement of the individual. The FAO uses a probabilistic approach to estimate the 'minimal critical' values of body weight and physical activity level that are consistent with health and functions. Moreover, the FAO method explicitly acknowledges that there are differences across households in minimum per-capita calorie requirement. It also assumes that there is a positive (but not perfect) correlation between actual intakes and minimum requirements. The CCOP is consequently set lower than average requirements (the so-called Recommended Daily Intake (RDI) as derived by the FAO in other contexts).[2] The CCOP is set at a level below which the FAO considers very few households could have an adequate calorie expenditure/intake, i.e. a satisfactory body weight and activity level. The FAO has taken different positions over the years on what these 'satisfactory' body weights and activity levels are (Table 5.1). The FAO approach is nevertheless more consonant with the notion of undernutrition as a health problem than that adopted by the World Bank in a similar study

(IBRD 1986). Here the Bank attached values to the body-weight and activity parameters from a notion of what it found to be a 'desirable' calorie intake. The IBRDs CCOPs are consequently higher than the FAO ones (Table 5.1).

5.3.2. The Estimated Prevalence of Undernutrition

The latest FAO estimates of the prevalence of undernutrition in the world are contained in Fig. 5.2. According to these estimates, the POU in 1990/2 was higher in SSA than anywhere else in the world. In fact, it was almost twice as high as in South Asia, the region with the second highest incidence (43 compared with 22 per cent). Moreover, SSA is the only region where the estimated POU has increased since the early 1970s. The estimated decline in East and South-East Asia is the most substantial, down from 41 to 16 per cent. Comparing the recent figures with those for 1979/81 suggests a slight increase in POU in Latin America, although from a level that is comparatively low.

In absolute numbers, the increase in undernutrition has more than doubled in SSA since the early 1970s, according to the FAO figures. In South Asia and in Latin America there has also been an increase in the number of undernourished during this period, although of a much smaller magnitude.

The overall message brought out by Fig. 5.2 is clear: according to the FAO, the food problems in the world are now heavily concentrated in SSA. Twice

TABLE 5.1. Different calorie-cut-off points used by the IBRD and FAO to estimate prevalence of undernutrition in SSA

Organization	Study (year)	Minimum BMI	BMR	Minimum PAL	Per-capita calorie cut-off point
			(adults)[a]		
IBRD	1986	22.0	AC[b]	1.70[d]	2,060
	1986	22.0	AC	1.60[d]	1,840
FAO	1985	20.0	AC	1.40[d]	1,648
	1985	20.0	LC[c]	1.40[d]	1,460
FAO	1992	18.5	AC	1.54[d]	1,788
FAO	1996	18.5	AC	1.55[d]	1,800

[a] The estimated calorie requirements for children below the age of 10 have been estimated from actual observed intakes from the average of 'sound and healthy' Western populations in all the studies.

[b] AC stands for the average estimated BMR for Caucasian populations.

[c] LC stands for the lower end of the intra-individual distribution of BMR, as suggested by Sukhatme.

[d] The 1.70 PAL allows for a full day's work in moderately heavy manual activities, but no strenuous social activities; 1.60 and 1.54 allow for the same working time, but in lighter physical activities; 1.40 allows only for 'base-line' physical activities and no physical work.

Sources: FAO 1992: table on p. 13; FAOa 1996 and unpublished FAO material.

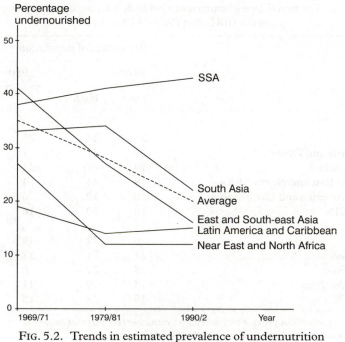

FIG. 5.2. Trends in estimated prevalence of undernutrition
1969/71 to 1990/2, by major geographical regions
Source: FAO*a* 1996: table 14.

as large a percentage of the population here is undernourished as in South Asia. The prevalence of undernutrition in SSA is also increasing, and so is the 'gap' with all other regions. It is further notable that there has been a 'convergence' across other regions, especially during the 1980s and early 1990s towards an estimated POU in the 12–20 per cent range. SSA does not comply to this general pattern; here the curve goes in the other direction, upwards.

5.4.   SENSITIVITY OF ESTIMATES

5.4.1. *Combining Different FAO and IBRD Parameter Values*

In order to get a feeling for the robustness of the estimation method, the FAO and the IBRD estimates of POU for 1970 and 1980 are reproduced in Table 5.2. Here we see that both organizations have produced two alternative sets of estimates for each year. They differ quite substantially, due to different choices of CCOPs and different estimations of calorie distributions.

In an important article, Beaton (1983*b*) attempted to quantify with greater exactitude which of the different parameter values explained most of the

TABLE 5.2. The prevalence of undernutrition in developing countries, as estimated by the IBRD and FAO, 1970 and 1980

Region	Percentage of population			
	1970		1980	
	Low	High	Low	High
IBRD[a]				
SSA	21	43	25	44
East Asia and Pacific	21	41	7	14
South Asia	19	47	21	50
Middle East and North Africa	18	35	4	10
Latin America and Caribbean	10	20	6	13
All LCDs	18	40	16	34
FAO[a]				
SSA[b]	20	29	19	26
Far East	21	31	17	25
Near East	15	22	8	12
Latin America	13	19	11	16
All LDCs	19	28	15	23

[a] Both organizations provide two alternative estimates (see text) for each year.
[b] Africa, excluding Egypt, Libya, Sudan, and SAU.

Sources: IBRD 1986: tables 2–3 and 2–4; FAO*a* 1985: table 3.4.

differences in the POU estimates produced by the FAO and IBRD. By combining three calorie cut-off points with three different estimates of how the 'available' calories are distributed in the population, all of which have actually been used by either the FAO or the Bank to obtain the estimates reproduced in Table 5.2, he derived a total of nine POU estimates for Tanzania (and for three non-African countries).

Beaton found the estimated POU in Tanzania to vary between 17 and 80 per cent (Table 5.3) depending on the combination of the parameter values used. Comparing numbers between rows a, b, and c (for a given column) reveals that rather little is explained by the differences in the estimated distributions of the calories. As can be seen by comparing numbers along rows, Beaton found that the bulk of the variance was explained by the different CCOPs. The highest estimates derived by Beaton were based on the CCOPs used by the IBRD, which are about 40 per cent higher than the lowest FAO ones (cf. Table 5.1). (See also Neiken 1988 and Waterlow 1989*b*.)

5.4.2. *Sensitivity of FAO Estimates of POU in Africa in 1990/2*

In this subsection we shall examine the sensitivity of the POU estimates from the FAO for the SSA countries for the years 1990/2 in a slightly different way. The CCOP is allowed to vary by plus or minus 10 per cent of the value

TABLE 5.3. Estimated share of the population with an energy-deficient diet in Tanzania (per cent)

Assumed calorie distribution	Assumed per-capita calorie requirement		
	FAO 1 1.20 BMR (0.65 RDI)	IBRD 1 1.50 BMR (0.80 RDI)	IBRD 2 1.67 BMR (0.90 RDI)
FAO calorie distribution 1	17	45	76
FAO calorie distribution 2	31	50	70
IBRD calorie distribution	23	52	80

Source: Beaton 1983b.

attached to this parameter by the FAO (which is considerably less variation than in Beaton's example). We shall further let the coefficient of variation in the distribution of calories across households vary by plus or minus 5 percentage points around the value estimated by the FAO. Finally, we go one step further than Beaton and also let the NPCCA vary by plus or minus 10 per cent of the FAO estimate. (Both the FAO and the IBRD estimates of POU for 1970 and 1980 were based on the FAO estimates of national per capita calorie availabilities, which Beaton (1983b) accepted at face value.)

One then obtains altogether 27 (3 × 3 × 3) combinations of parameter values, from three calorie cut-off points, three distribution functions, and three NPCCA estimates. These 27 combinations of parameters provide POU estimates that range from 21 to 61 per cent of the population in SSA (Table 5.4). By comparing numbers along rows (within respective panels), we see that by varying the CCOP from minus to plus 10 per cent of the FAO value (holding requirements and distribution constant), the estimated POU increases from 34 to 51 per cent (in panel b). Comparing rows for given columns within respective panels we see that the estimated POU varies by a factor of almost two when the NPCCA parameter is altered. Finally, comparing numbers for given rows and columns across panels, we see that the POU estimates are not very sensitive to alterations in the distribution parameter (in this interval), the same result that Beaton derived.

The FAO itself has provided a simple sensitivity test of its POU estimates (FAOa 1996: table 13). What the FAO does is to derive the impact on the POU estimates of varying the distribution parameter, i.e. the CV, for hypothetical countries with different levels of per-capita calorie availabilities. When the CCOP is held constant at 1,800 calories, FAO finds that varying the CV between 0.20 and 0.35 has practically no impact on the estimated POU (Table 5.5). For the hypothetical countries with higher levels of calorie availabilities, the POU estimates are considerably more sensitive to the alteration of the CV parameter. For instance, for a country with an NPCCA of 2,040, the POU moves from 30 to 42 per cent as the CV is increased from

TABLE 5.4. Sensitivity of FAO estimates of prevalence of undernutrition in SSA to alternative parameter values. Estimated percentage of population undernourished, 1990/2

Distribution	NPCCA[a]	Calorie cut-off point		
		1,620 (90% FAO)	1,800 (100% FAO)	1,980 (110% FAO)
a) More even	1,836 (90% FAO)	40	51	61
distribution	2,040 (FAO)	30	40	50
(CV = 0.25)	2,244 (110% FAO)	21	31	40
b) FAO estimated	1,836 (90% FAO)	43	52	60
distribution	2,040 (100% FAO)	34	43	51
(CV = 0.30)	2,244 (110% FAO)	26	35	43
c) More uneven	1,836 (99% FAO)	45	53	60
distribution	2,040 (100% FAO)	37	45	52
(CV = 0.35)	2,244 (110% FAO)	30	38	45

[a] National per-capita calorie availability.

Source: Author's calculations, based on the FAO model.

TABLE 5.5. Sensitivity of POU estimates to varying the distribution parameter

National per-capita calorie availability	Coefficient of variation (CV)			
	0.20	0.24	0.29	0.35
	Percentage undernourished			
1,700	65	64	63	63
2,040	30	34	38	42
2,450	7	12	17	23
2,940	1	2	6	10

Source: FAOa 1996: table 13.

0.20 to 0.35. The FAO concludes 'that the expected greater error in the CV compared with the per caput DES [Daily Energy Supply, NPCCA in the terminology used here] is not of great concern' (FAOa 1996: p. 43). This conclusion is consistent with the one reached above on the basis of the test which underlies the results reported in Table 5.4.

While the test carried out by the FAO itself is intended to provide a check of the sensitivity of errors in the estimated CV parameter only, the exercise can be interpreted in yet another way. That is, one can see the variation of the DES (our NPCCA) as a sensitivity test of errors also in the food availability estimates for a given country. Let us take the 2,040 DES case as the benchmark, which is in fact the actual calorie availability for the SSA countries for the years 1990/2 as estimated by the FAO. The estimated POU at the 1,700 and 2,450 DES levels can then be seen as indications of the sensitivity to errors of about plus or minus 20 per cent in the calorie availability figures. We then see that the FAO exercise (indirectly) confirms what we found earlier (Table 5.4), *viz.* that the POU estimates are highly sensitive to errors in the NPCCA data. The main difference is that the FAO does not discuss (in FAO*a* 1996) such possible errors and biases (which is what we shall do in the next chapter).

5.4.3. Correlation between POU and NPCCA

In order to provide an additional test of where more exactly the sensitivity of the POU estimates originates, Fig. 5.3 was constructed. In the figure, the POU and NPCCA estimates produced by the FAO (1992) were plotted for seven regions at five points in time. The graph reveals a very strong association between the two variables; in fact, NPCCA 'explains' 88 per cent of the variability in the estimated POU (as measured by R^2 adjusted). Or put the other way round, differences in CCOPs between the regions and in the estimated distribution of the calories only account for 12 per cent of the total variance.

That the observations for some regions lie above the regression line is due to either (i) a more uneven calorie distribution relative to other regions and/or (ii) a lower CCOP, and *vice versa* for observations found below the

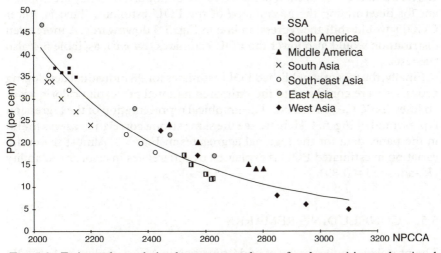

FIG. 5.3. Estimated correlation between prevalence of undernutrition and national per-capita calorie availability, by major geographical regions, 1970, 1975, 1980, 1985, and 1990

Source: ACC/SCN 1992.

line. That the CCOP is lower for some regions than others is explained either by the fact that some populations have a smaller average body mass and/or by the fact that that the ratio of adults to children is lower. East Asia (China), for instance, is consistently found to be above the regression line. People in China are not exceptionally large (see Table 11.6), but the ratio of adults to small children is much higher than, say, in South Asia or Africa, which implies higher per-capita calorie requirements.[3]

The strong association between prevalence of undernutrition and calorie availability means that differences in (estimated) calorie distribution and in cut-off points explain only a marginal share of the *inter-regional variation* in POU and its *development over time*. The strong association further reveals that a potential bias in the estimated NPCCA for the African countries (discussed in Chapter 6) would imply a large error in the estimated POU for this region. Fig. 5.3 suggests that if the estimated NPCCA for Africa is raised by 10 per cent, this would cause a drop in the 1990 POU estimates, from 43 to about 35 per cent (*cet par*). On the other hand, if the NPCCA is lowered by 10 per cent, the implication is that almost two-thirds of the population in SSA fall out as undernourished. (Note that all the observations for SSA lie close to the regression line.) This further corroborates the point made earlier: the accuracy of the NPCCA data for Africa is highly important for evaluating the reliability of the FAO's assessment of the POU in the region and for the question of where the world's food problems are now concentrated.

That the NPCCA variable explains such a large share of the *inter-regional* and *inter-temporal* differences in estimated POU does not imply that the CCOPs and the distribution parameters are unimportant. They are important for determining the *general level* of the POU estimates. That is, lower CCOPs would shift the regression line in Fig. 5.3 downwards. A more even distribution would also lower the POU estimates (*cet par*), as Table 5.4 also suggests.

Finally, the recently published POU estimates for 98 individual developing countries were correlated to the estimated national per-capita calorie availabilities (NPCCA) in 1990/2. The graphical representation of the regression is presented in Fig. 5.4. Here we see the same strong correlation as was found in the panel data for the regional aggregates in Fig. 5.3. Almost the entire variation in estimated POU is explained by differences in calorie availability (R^2-adjusted = 0.89).

5.5.   CONCLUDING REMARKS

The prevalence and severity of undernutrition in Africa implied by the POU estimates from the FAO are simply immense. What is claimed by the FAO is *not* that almost every second household (individual) here is inadequately nourished in the meaning that their calorie intake falls below a norm that

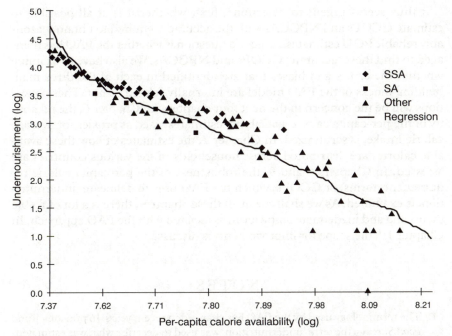

FIG. 5.4. Estimated correlation between prevalence of undernutrition and national per-capita calorie availability across 96 developing countries, 1990/2

allows for an active life and maintenance of a body size comparable to what is normal in Western populations. What the FAO estimates tell us is that almost one out of two households in Africa do not have enough to eat on a permanent basis to satisfy their biological internal body needs for energy at a weight that is consistent with health and/or to undertake relatively light physical work activities for normal hours.

In this chapter we have demonstrated that the POU estimates produced by the FAO are highly sensitive to rather slight, plus or minus 10 per cent, variations in the assigned values of two of the three parameters that comprise the estimation model: (i) the per-capita calorie availability and (ii) the CCOP, while being considerably less so to (iii) the estimated distribution of the calories across households (within the range considered). This sensitivity test thus suggests that only if the parameter values can be estimated with high accuracy, is the FAO method reliable enough to provide POU estimates that have some policy relevance.

The policy implications differ tremendously between when 20 or 60 per cent of a population is undernourished. If only 20 per cent are undernourished, there may be scope for targeted intervention so as to help them out. If more than half the population is undernourished, the only remedy would be general policies at the national level.

It thus seems urgent to determine, first, whether it is at all possible to estimate CCOPs and NPCCAs with the accuracy required to obtain reasonably reliable POU estimates. A second question is whether the FAO has managed to find these 'accurate' CCOPs and NPCCAs. We also have to examine whether the errors and biases that are identified in each of the three main building blocks of the FAO model are internally related or not. These questions will be the concern in the next four chapters. In Chapter 6, the reliability of the per-capita calorie availability estimates, used as proxies for average calorie intake, is scrutinized. In Chapter 7, the estimates of how these available calories are distributed across households in the various countries are assessed. In Chapters 8 and 9, the robustness of the per-capita calorie requirement norms, or CCOPs, which the FAO uses to delineate undernutrition, is examined. As we shall see in all these chapters, there is a lot of feeble theorizing and inadequate empiricism associated with the FAO approach. In Chapter 10, the scope for improvements is discussed.

NOTES

1. The terminology used by the FAO has changed in recent years. In previous *World Food Surveys*, the term 'undernutrition' was used to describe what was estimated. In the *Sixth World Food Survey* (FAO*a* 1996), the terminology is more ambivalent. Here the expressions 'inadequate food intake' and 'inadequate access to food' are introduced. On p. 44 it is stated that these terms 'cannot be equated with undernutrition as tends to be done in popular discussions'. However, already on the next page, the term undernutrition figures at the top of table 14. In figs 4 and 5 on subsequent pages, the headlines are 'trends in number and proportion of undernourished' and 'distribution of undernourished'. It thus seems as if the FAO has yet to make up its mind on what it really aims to estimate, and to clarify the distinction between 'inadequate food intake' and 'undernutrition' in more detail.

2. For the SSA countries, for instance, the *CCOP*, or 'minimum per-capita energy requirement', is set at 1,800, about 14 per cent below the estimated 'average per-capita energy requirement' of 2,100 (FAO*a* 1996: table 16).

3. The exact reason why the *POU* estimates for China are relatively high in comparison with the average cannot be identified, as the FAO does not publish details about how the organization has derived the estimates.

6

Calorie Availability in Sub-Saharan Africa

6.1. INTRODUCTION

Since the early 1960s, the FAO has published annual data on the 'calories available for human consumption' on a per-capita basis for almost 150 countries, including most of those in SSA. The FAO is, in fact, the only provider of estimates of the food (calories) 'available for human consumption' in the various countries of the world that are supposedly comparable over time and countries. The estimates are used by governments, other international organizations and, not least, by researchers in various contexts. Moreover, the FAO calorie 'availability' data are used as inputs in the estimates of the prevalence of undernutrition produced by the FAO*a* (1996), presented in Chapter 5 above. These estimates suggest that the proportion of the population in SSA that suffers from undernutrition is now almost twice as high as that in South Asia and that the chief reason is low availability of food. It is therefore important to assess the accuracy of the FAO calorie-availability estimates for the African countries, which is the objective of this chapter.

Following this introduction, section 6.2 describes in general terms the method by which the calorie-availability estimates in SSA are derived by the FAO, and the estimates for the period 1970–92 are presented. In section 6.3, the reasons why it is especially problematic to estimate calorie 'availability' in Africa are discussed. In sections 6.4–6.6, possible biases in the FAO estimates are scrutinized in greater detail. The chapter closes with a summary of the main findings and conclusions.

6.2. CALORIE AVAILABILITY IN SUB-SAHARAN AFRICA

6.2.1. *The FAO Estimation Method*

The FAO describes its estimation method as follows:

The total quantity of foodstuffs produced in a country added to the total quantity imported and adjusted for any change in stocks that may have occurred since the beginning of the reference period gives the supply available during that period. On the *utilisation* side, a distinction is made between the quantities exported, fed to livestock, used for seed, put to industrial and other non-food uses, or lost during storage and transportation, and food supplies available for human consumption at the retail level, i.e. in the form food leaves the retail shop or otherwise enters the household. The per-caput supply of each food item available for human consumption is then obtained by dividing the food supplies available for human consumption by the related data on the population actually taking part of it. Data on per-caput food supplies are expressed in terms of quantity and also, by applying appropriate food consumption factors, in terms of nutrient elements (calories, protein, . . .)' (FAO*e* 1993: p. 9).

The estimates of the number of calories 'available for human consumption' on a per-capita and per-day basis are reported in the so-called *Food Balance Sheets* (*FBS*), which are published regularly and revised and updated concurrently (FAO*e* 1980, 1984, 1991, 1994, 1996). The food production data that underlie the FAO calorie-availability estimates have been supplied by national governments in 'the form of replies to annual FAO questionnaires'. Wherever no official or semi-official figures are available from the countries themselves, the FAO obtains its own estimates. The calorie content of the various 'available' food items is derived from standardized conversion tables that the organization has produced.

6.2.2. The FAO Calorie Availability Estimates

Regional Availability 1970–92   For the SSA region as a whole, the FAO food-availability estimates suggest that the national per-capita calorie availability (NPCCA) has dropped slightly, but consistently, since the early 1970s (Fig. 6.1). The most alarming message brought out by Fig. 6.1 is not the slight fall

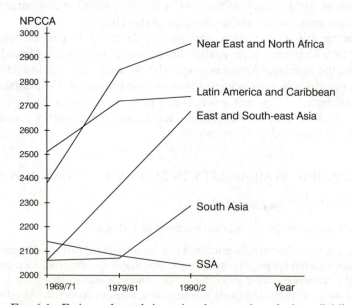

FIG. 6.1. Estimated trends in national per-capita calorie availability (NPCCA) 1969/71–1990/2, by major geographical regions
Source: FAOa 1996: table 1.

of the NPCCA in Africa over the years, but the sharp contrast to other developing regions. In 1969/71, the SSA countries had NPCCAs equal to the developing countries average. In all regions except SSA, the estimated NPCCA has increased, by between 9 and 30 per cent since the early 1970s. Even during the economically problematic 1980s, the NPCCA increased in all other regions, although only very slightly in Latin America (where it was initially at a higher level than in the other regions). If one assesses the food situation in the world in broad terms from the supply side, the FAO estimates suggest that the problems are now heavily concentrated in SSA.

Availability by Country   The latest data on NPCCA are for three years, 1990/2 (a three-year average), and they suggest a rather varied situation in the African countries (Table 6.1). In a dozen SSA countries, the per-capita

TABLE 6.1. Estimated national per-capita calorie availability in SSA countries as compared with India and Bangladesh and changes between 1979/81 and 1990/2

Country group	Estimated change in national per-capita calorie availability		
	Decline (1)	No change[a] (2)	Increase (3)
(a) Countries with a lower NPCCA than that of Bangladesh (<1,990) in 1990/2	Mozambique (−10) C. Af. Republic (−24) Sierra Leone (−14) Rwanda (−11) Chad (−8) Somalia (−15) Ethiopia (−10) Kenya (−8) Liberia (−26) Malawi (−16) Angola (−15)	Burundi	
(b) Countries with a NPCCA higher than that of Bangladesh but lower than India (<2,330) in 1990/2	Cameroon (−13) Malagasy (−11) Senegal (−6) Tanzania (−7) Zambia (−7) Zimbabwe (−7)	Congo Gabon Lesotho Namibia Niger Sudan Togo Uganda Zaïre	Botswana (+7) Burkina Faso (+27) Gambia (+14) Ghana (+9) Mali (+24) Nigeria (+7)
(c) Countries with a higher NPCCA than that of India (>2,230) in 1990/2	Cote d'Ivoire (−13)	Mauritius	Benin (+15) Guinea (+6) Mauritania (+24) Swaziland (+8)

[a] Less than a 5 per cent change.

Source: Base data from FAO*a* 1996: table 1 in appendix 2.

calorie availability in 1990/2 was lower than in Bangladesh. (In the rest of the developing world, only Afghanistan, Haiti, and Peru have a lower NPCCA than Bangladesh, according to the FAO*a* (1996: appendix 2, table 1).) In another 21 SSA countries, the situation is somewhat better, but still worse than in India. Only six SSA countries have an estimated NPCCA above that of India, according to the FAO.

A notable development over the 1980s is that the estimated NPCCA has declined in eleven of the twelve SSA countries that had the lowest food supplies in 1969/71. The countries that have experienced the largest decline (by more than 15 per cent) since the early 1980s are Angola, the Central African Republic, Ethiopia, Liberia, Malawi, and Somalia. Overall, there is a tendency that the SSA countries with the highest initial NPCCA had a better performance during the 1980s than the countries with low calorie supplies. Out of the 10 countries that have had an estimated increase in the calorie availability, only Nigeria is large. The other countries in this group are all relatively small, together accounting for less than 10 per cent of the population in the region.

6.2.3. Composition of Calorie Sources

The FAO *Food Balance Sheets* suggest that 93 per cent of the calories available for human consumption in SSA as a whole come from domesticated vegetable plants. In almost all the countries, the main sources of calories are staple cereals (mainly maize, sorghum, and millet) and roots and tubers (mainly cassava). These are what are usually labelled 'main vegetable food'. Roots and tubers form the main source of calories in about a dozen of the 34 SSA countries for which *FBS*s have been estimated (FAO*a* 1996: appendix 2, table 3). Most of these countries are found in Western and Central Africa. In almost all the countries, only a small part of the calorie supply comes from a range of 'minor' vegetable products (sugar, pulses, vegetables, fruit, etc.). According to the FAO, Africans are largely vegetarians. The share of total calories that comes from animal products, i.e. meat and offal, fish, animal oil and fat, eggs, milk, and milk products, is on the average 7 per cent. The main exceptions are some countries where milk is a major source of energy (e.g. Mauritania and Somalia). Since 1969/71, no major change has taken place in the relative share of different food items; this is the case also in South Asia, according to the FAO.

6.3.   SOURCES OF ESTIMATION ERRORS

To estimate the food available for human consumption from the supply side, using the *FBS* approach, is a complicated procedure. In the following we will focus mainly on the first links in the long chain of calculations that the FAO undertakes in order to produce data on NPCCA; i.e. the food production and net trade data. The subsequent calculations by the FAO of what happens on the long route from food production to calories available for human consumption are built on a host of assumptions and 'expert opinion'. This includes calculating post-harvest losses, storage losses, seed, food lost in the processing chain, industrial use of food material, food fed to animals, and food wasted at the household level. There is no possibility of assessing these steps in the FAO estimation procedure thoroughly, since the details are not published.

6.3.1. The FAO Food Production Estimates

For a variety of reasons, the difficulties encountered in estimating food production are especially severe in the African countries. Most African countries are large, sparsely populated,[1] and span a multitude of climatological zones and cropping systems. On average, some 70 per cent of the population makes a living by agricultural activities, and much of the food is produced for subsistence. Many peasants pursue mixed farming, i.e. both crop production and livestock holding. The number of minor crops is usually great (Eicher and Baker 1982). Furthermore, slash-and-burn shifting cultivation is still an important mode of production in many parts of Africa. The harvested area is then difficult to define, even with the best measurement technology. Moreover, nearly all food cultivation in Africa is mixed in various forms. The most common practice is that two or more crops are planted on the same soil. Things are also complicated by the fact that there is continuous cropping (a particular crop is not harvested at any particular time of the year) and 'relay' cropping (one crop is sown before another is harvested).

According to the FAO, what is called 'main vegetable food produced domestically' accounts for two-thirds of the total calorie intake in the average African country and is thus by far the most important item to be examined. Relatively accurate estimates of the production of this type of food can be derived with modern, scientific objective methods, based on detailed acreage enumeration and frequent random-yield sampling. In many of the (most developed) countries for which the FAO provide national *FBS*s, such scientific methods have been used. The FAO estimates of food production in the SSA countries are based on much simpler and less reliable methods.

Blades (1980), an OECD national account specialist, made a detailed examination of five SSA countries and concluded that the margin of error in agriculture production statistics was in the 25–46 per cent range (Table 6.2). Lipton (1986: pp. 3–4) goes as far as to say that, regarding the main staples in the four largest countries (Nigeria, Zaïre, Ethiopia, and Sudan), 'we have no idea of the levels or trends in output or consumption . . . over the past 5–20 years.' According to Lipton's assessments, the available estimates of small farmers' output of main staple crops are subject to unknown errors of at least plus or minus 20–40 per cent.

TABLE 6.2. The agricultural sector, estimated share of
GDP and error range in five SSA countries, 1970s

Country	Share of GDP (per cent)	Error range (per cent) (+/−)
Botswana	30	36
Kenya	32	25
Malawi	51	33
Nigeria	42	46
Tanzania	40	24

Source: Blades 1980: table 3.2.

A further indication that Blades and Lipton are correct is that when two or more independent food production series exist (e.g. FAO, USDA, and different national ones) for one and the same crop in a particular country, they usually differ considerably (Candler and Lele 1981, Paulino and Young 1981, Paulino and Sarma 1986, Sarma 1986, Adamu 1989). In some instances, the *level* differs by a factor of three; in others, the estimated *time trends* have different signs; in many instances drastic *annual changes* conflict. The FAO estimates are much higher than those of the USDA in some instances, while substantially lower in others (Table 6.3).

A World Bank report concludes that 'most analysts and decision makers believe that available estimates of agricultural output are unreliable and grossly inadequate' (IBRD 1989: p. 209, see also Chander 1990). Also, the FAO admits in special reports that their data for Africa, especially, are unreliable (e.g. FAO 1975, 1987*a*). In the foreword to a consultant report (Lipton 1985*a*), Leroy Quance, a former director of the Statistics Division of the FAO, writes that the databases for smallholder food production in Africa 'are dangerously weak'. In the FAO *FBS*s, where the estimated calorie content of the food is reported, there are three short paragraphs on 'accuracy' (cf. FAO*e* 1996: p. vii); in the annual *Production* and *Trade Yearbooks* even less is said on 'accuracy'.

6.3.2. The Food Trade Estimates

Trade statistics are sometimes thought to be less unreliable than most other statistics from the African countries. One could thus expect that the least problematic task facing the FAO would be that of estimating the calorie content in the (net) imported food (FAO*c*). This is not so for two main reasons.

First, as demonstrated in a study by Yeats (1990), employing the 'partner-match' method to check officially recorded African trade-flows, there is virtually no correspondence in many instances between the amount of exports reported by one country and that reported by the importing country (see also

TABLE 6.3. Ratio of FAO and USDA estimated production of selected cereals in SSA countries

Country	Maize		Rice		Wheat	
	1976–7	1985–6	1976–7	1985–6	1976–7	1985–6
Angola	1.13	0.95	1.00	1.00	1.30	1.43
Benin	1.30	0.98	—	1.00	—	—
Botswana	—	0.20	—	—	—	—
Burkina	—	0.99	—	—	—	—
Burundi	0.80	1.00	—	—	—	—
Cameroon	1.02	0.75	—	0.92	—	—
Chad	—	1.31	1.00	1.85	—	—
Ethiopia	—	1.08	1.02	—	—	—
Gambia	—	—	0.40	1.07	—	—
Ghana	0.88	0.97	1.24	1.27	—	—
Guinea	—	—	0.87	1.01	—	—
G. Bissau	—	—	1.77	0.99	—	—
Ivory Coast	0.49	1.14	1.05	0.91	—	—
Kenya	0.93	0.93	—	1.43	1.13	1.13
Lesotho	—	1.00	—	—	—	0.83
Liberia	—	—	0.97	1.02	—	—
Madagascar	1.13	1.00	1.24	0.98	—	—
Mali	1.22	1.25	1.37	0.88	—	—
Malawi	1.02	1.03	—	1.03	—	—
Mauritania	—	—	—	0.94	—	—
Mozambique	0.79	1.34	0.58	0.95	1.00	1.67
Niger	—	—	—	0.50	—	—
Nigeria	0.92	0.75	0.89	1.45	2.63	1.36
Rwada	—	1.09	—	—	—	—
Senegal	1.12	1.09	0.74	0.97	—	—
S. Leone	—	—	1.05	0.96	—	—
Somalia	—	1.09	—	0.40	—	—
Sudan	—	—	—	0.80	0.97	0.79
Swaziland	—	0.99	—	0.60	—	—
Tanzania	1.04	1.00	0.44	1.00	1.51	0.96
Togo	—	—	—	0.83	—	—
Uganda	1.84	0.71	—	—	—	—
Zaïre	1.25	1.00	0.85	1.00	0.67	1.67
Zambia	1.49	0.94	—	0.86	1.00	0.83
Zimbawe	1.00	1.65	—	—	1.06	1.08

Sources: FAO*b*, various issues; USDA, various issues.

Paulino and Tseng 1980). The second (related) reason is that a large share of food trade in the SSA region is unrecorded and unofficial. In many of the SSA countries, with overvalued exchange rates and/or governmental regula-tion of food prices below-the-market price, the incentives for unrecorded trade (smuggling) have been great. By their very nature, the size of officially unrecorded trade-flows are not easily quantified. Nevertheless, a few estima-tions have been undertaken and they point to an unrecorded food trade of be-tween 40 and above 100 per cent of officially recorded trade (Burfisher and Missanen 1987, Berg *et al.* 1985: pp. 75–77, Barad 1988). The FAO under-takes its own estimates of food trade, but in the absence of reliable national (or any other) data base, the estimates still contain large margins of error.

It also seems that the quality of the trade statistics from the African coun-tries has deteriorated. In their assessment of trends in the reliability of inter-national trade statistics in general, Rozanski and Yeats (1994: p. 125) found that 'starting in the late 1970s a quality breakdown in Sub-Saharan African countries' statistics occurred that was of sufficient importance to influence our overall [global] results. In these cases, international agencies were forced to 'piece together African trade profiles using any available (partial) statistics and this greatly compromised data quality.'

6.3.3. Conversion from Production to Consumption

Vegetable Products   The chain of 'conversions' that the FAO has to undertake in order to derive the calorie content of the food available for human con-sumption from food production (and trade) estimates is long. When it comes to 'main domesticated vegetable' food items, the main problems are the pre-harvest losses, losses during harvest, and post-harvest (transportation and storage) losses.

In the derivation of the NPCCA estimates, the FAO attaches a specific number of 'losses' to each crop and country. The same applies to the other 'diversions' of vegetable food materials in the transition from production to human intake. All this gives an impression of exactness which is not substan-tiated. There are several independent estimates of the post-harvest losses in staple crops in the African countries (reviewed by Schulten 1982). These independent studies show that there are large discrepancies between estim-ates of the same crop across studies (depending on methods used, time of storage, etc.) In most of the independent investigations it is explicitly acknow-ledged that the uncertainty is very large. In half the studies, the estimated losses are presented as a range rather than as a definitive figure, and in many cases the range is quite wide, mainly depending on the time of storage. The FAO is of course well aware of the difficulties, and has tried to improve on methods. The remaining estimation problems are nevertheless of such a magnitude that all figures for waste/losses are 'subject to large margins of error' (FAOe 1991: p. vi).

Animal Products   To derive estimates of calories available from animal products also requires a long chain of conversions. First one needs data on livestock numbers, then on (i) slaughtering rates, (ii) the average weight of the slaughtered animals, and (iii) the calorie content of the edible meat on (a) an animal, (b) a country, and (c) a yearly basis. Practically no African country undertakes comprehensive, frequent, and reliable livestock censuses and practically no national data exist on variables (i)–(iii). The FAO thus has to rely on 'expert opinion' and other subjective methods in order to estimate the calories in animal products that are 'available' for human consumption.

6.3.4. Size of Population

A further problem is that the population and demographic data needed to derive per-capita estimates are as shaky as any other statistics on Africa. In most of the African countries, the size of the population is not known with any degree of accuracy. In one-third of the countries, no census has been carried out during the past 20 years, and estimated population growth rates are obtained by the UN with indirect, less-reliable methods (UN 1992, Chamie 1994, Deaton 1995). The result from the 1991 census in Nigeria provides an interesting example. The census arrived at a population of 96 million people in 1990. The UN estimate for that year, estimated through projection from an earlier census in the 1970s, was 108 million, or a 10 per cent overestimation. Similar differences between before- and after-census estimates for other African countries are reported by Blades (1980: p. 70). A 5 per cent margin of error is the least we can expect when it comes to population estimates in the African region in general.

6.4. BIASED ESTIMATES: *A PRIORI* REASONS

6.4.1. Acknowledged Biases

The many errors that beset the NPCCA estimates go in both directions, and that there is a net bias of a particular sign cannot be ascertained *a priori*. The FAO itself mentions two possible biases. First, the organization (FAO*e* 1984: pp. 9–10, 1991) stresses that 'it is important to note that the quantities of food available relate to the quantities reaching the consumer but not necessarily the amount of food actually consumed, which may be lower than the quantity shown, depending on the extent of losses of edible food and nutrients in the household, e.g. during storage, preparation and cooking, . . ., plate-waste or quantities of food fed to domestic animals and pets, or thrown away'. That is, on this count there is a possible bias towards overestimation. Assessments of the size of waste at the household level find it to be rather small in the developed countries—in the order of less than 5 per cent (Dowler and Seo 1985). In the poorest countries, where the economic incentive not to waste food is stronger, one would expect less waste. In a nationwide study from Brazil, household food waste was estimated at 3 per cent (FAO/ESN 1990).

Secondly, the FAO says that when it comes to some minor food items, the coverage is not complete. Minor food items comprise vegetables, fruit, nuts, oilseeds, and oils, but also meat, game, and fish (McGlothlen *et al.* 1986). Although it is very difficult to quantify this omission, one study found that it has caused underestimation of total calorie availability by at least 5–10 per cent (Svedberg 1991*a*: pp. 122–8). The two biases admitted by the FAO are thus in different directions.

However, there is a whole range of other possible biases in the NPCCA estimates, which are not explicitly acknowledged by the FAO. Given that so few alternative data are available, it is not possible to say anything definitive about the size of these biases, but there are some indications of the orders of magnitudes involved. Before we turn to these, some *a priori* reasons for expecting a downward bias in the production estimates for major cereal crops need to be discussed.

6.4.2. Incentives for Underreporting

The first reason to suspect that the estimates of staple food production in Africa are downward biased is that there are incentives for underreporting at most levels. The smallholder farmers may gain by giving the public authorities the information—through whatever channel—that their production is lower than it actually is. First, in many an African country, trade in main staples is more or less strictly monopolized by a government marketing board, or has been until recently, and the prices paid to the farmers have been below these in the parallel, unofficial market (Bates 1981, Eicher and Baker 1982, Ahrin 1985). Thus, the incentives to sell on the unofficial, non-registered, and sometimes illegal markets have been strong. Secondly, at the extent to which farmers and pastoralists pay taxes that are related to their production volume, a way of keeping the tax burden down is to underreport production, whether crops or livestock. It should be recalled that the first crop estimations that took place during the colonial days were undertaken just for the purpose of extracting tax revenue from the farmers (Evenson and Prey 1994). Thirdly, in order to qualify for government (input) subsidies, various extension services and food aid, it may be profitable to give downward-biased information on productivity.

The national government agencies that supply the FAO with base data also have an incentive to keep food production estimates down in order to attract more food and other aid. The FAO itself has no incentive to overestimate food supplies; the organization's existence has for a long time been largely based on the notion of severe food supply problems in the underdeveloped countries. One does not have to go so far as to say that there is systematic falsification of data at the national and FAO levels. In the case of the FAO that would be unthinkable. However, one only needs to think that underreporting on behalf of the bureaucracies 'reflects nothing more than the persistence of honourable men attempting to dramatise their case through exaggeration', as argued by Poleman (1977: p. 387). Considering the unreliability of the base data, there is always scope for choosing 'low' numbers within the confidence intervals without violating acceptable practices.

6.5.   BIASED ESTIMATES: METHODOLOGICAL REASONS

The food items produced domestically comprise the bulk of the estimated total food consumption in the SSA, according to the FAO. Out of these food items, 'major vegetable food', i.e. cereals and roots and tubers, dominate. Production estimates of such items are conventionally derived by enumerating the acreage under cultivation (or crops) and multiplying by yield estimates.

6.5.1.   Acreage Estimates

Acreage enumeration is conducted in different ways in the 145 countries for which the FAO provides food production estimates. In the developed countries, most land on which 'main' cereal crops are grown is registered and updated each year by special statistical units, usually in the National Statistical Office. Thus, in most developed countries, acreage enumeration is not a great problem; yield sampling (see below) can be.

In developing countries in general, and in the SSA countries in particular, acreage enumeration is considerably more difficult and the methods used are much less reliable. In fact, when it comes to 'national methods of collecting agricultural statistics', there was no national statistical information at all for about half of the SSA countries in the mid-1970s (FAO 1975).[2] The situation had not changed much by the mid 1980s (Lipton 1987) and there are no indications of improvements later on either (Murphy et al. 1991). Only in two SSA countries, Kenya and Botswana, is a good share of the cultivated land registered and privately titled. 'Ghana, Lesotho, Mali, Burundi and Mauritania have recently passed laws encouraging land titling or registration' (Atwood 1990: p. 460). In spite of this, hardly any cultivated land is yet statistically registered in these countries or elsewhere in SSA. The great bulk of the land is not privately owned, but subject to communal ownership and cultivated by individual households under a great variety of more or less stable land tenure arrangements. Under such circumstances, the acreage under cultivation has been estimated by various subjective methods, including (i) ocular observation matched with acreage measurements from maps, (ii) cadastral surveys combined with triangulation estimation, and (iii) aerial photography.

Ocular Observation   The technique still most commonly used to estimate land under cultivation is subjective eye observation by field officers of the agricultural and other ministries. Their duties sometimes include not only the collection of data, but also extension work (Paulino and Young 1981: pp. 41–2). That these estimates taken by eye are highly unreliable is widely witnessed (Casley and Lury 1987: p. 191; Lipton 1985a: p. 8). The officials tend to include what they can see and exclude what they cannot see, with the consequence that small fields in remote areas are incompletely covered.

Cadastral Surveys and Acreage Estimation   To the extent to which direct, on-the-ground acreage estimation is conducted in the African countries, some type of cadastral survey is used to define the sample frame. The first problem is to find representative units of observation (the selection problem). Sometimes the household frame can be obtained from population censuses (usually obsolete) or tax-payer lists (usually incomplete). That is, the sample frame usually covers only a fraction of the total population at any given time. This may lead to overestimation of the acreage per household, if the inclusion in most types of available lists of relatively large and stable farms (households) is higher than of relatively small ones. On the other hand, there will usually be a downward bias in the extrapolation to the total population, since not all farmers in an area are likely to be included in the lists that define the base population (the sample frame). This exclusion has been estimated to be 10–15 per cent on the average (see Lipton 1985a: p. 7).

Alternatively, in the absence of land registers, information about acreage has to be obtained from the selected farmers themselves or from their 'headmen' (e.g. village chiefs). To the extent to which farmers fear being more heavily taxed, they will be unwilling to reveal the entire scope of their farming activity. In Africa, farmers' opportunity for adjusting their estimated holdings of land under crops downward is enhanced by several 'structural' characteristics of agriculture. Many smallholders cultivate a variety of small plots spread over large areas, the most remote plots being the most likely to be 'forgotten' without detection by the enumerating officer. Moreover, the facts that private title to land seldom exists, and that no formal registration of changes in tenure arrangement is made, make it easy for the farmer to claim that plots that she (or he) actually cultivates 'belong' to someone else.

Aerial Photography   This method is used in parts of two countries only, Kenya and Zimbabwe, in combination with on-the-ground inspection. This method also tends to underestimate the true area under crop cultivation. First, ground inspection can reject what photographic inspection indicates to be cultivated land, but cannot be used to identify cultivated plots that are not shown on the photograph, creating a downward bias. (If ground visits are made only during the main agricultural season after the long rains, as in Kenya, and not in the short-rain season (minor crops), another downward bias is induced.) Secondly, not all crops can be identified by aerial photography. Roots and tubers are the main examples; cassava can remain in the ground without any above-ground visibility for years. Thirdly, there is always the problem 'of concealment of cultivated areas in forest or under shade' (Lipton 1985a: p. 7). Finally, small plots, especially when spread over a large area where most of the land, but not all, is impediment, will not be detected on aerial photographs (Casley and Lury 1987: p. 190).

6.5.2. Yield Estimates

Yields are more difficult to estimate in the non-commercial agricultural sector in Africa than in most other places. The climatological and soil conditions tend to vary sharply from region to region and the variety of cropping systems is enormous (see p. 83 above). Under such circumstances, very refined and costly measurement methods, based on frequent and extensive cut sampling, are needed if accurate yield estimates are to be obtained. In the SSA, this is not the case: instead, rather crude methods are used, based on interviews of farmers and ocular observation by officials.

Sample Crop Cuts   Only in a few SSA countries are yield estimates obtained through 'objective' methods, such as random crop cuts. These methods were initiated in the 1960s in Nigeria, Ghana, Kenya, Botswana, and Uganda (FAO 1975, Paulino and Young 1981: p. 41). The Nigerian attempt largely failed (Lipton 1985a, Murphy *et al.* 1991: p. 5) and Nigeria belongs to the four big SSA countries where, according to Lipton (1986), the margin of error in main staple food estimation is ±20–40 per cent. Economic and political chaos in Ghana and Uganda for prolonged periods aborted attempts to build up objective crop-yield estimation methods. Only Kenya (Blades 1980) and, possibly Zimbabwe, have reasonable systems.

Casley and Lury (1987), in their review of the literature on crop-yield methods and experiments, maintain that the crop-cutting method normally leads to an overestimation of yields by '14–20 per cent of the measured total harvest'. The main reason is that 'however well-trained, the enumerator has a subconscious reluctance to accept the dictates of random co-ordinates if the resulting area is clearly "untypical" ' (ibid: p. 197). Controlled experiments in five SSA countries have shown crop-cuts to overestimate true crops (harvesting of entire fields) by more than that (Murphy *et al.* 1991: table 2.1). However, considering that only a few crops in a small number of countries rely on crop-cutting methods, the overall bias in total food production is considerably less or even the reverse (see below).

Farmer Interviews and Assessment by Officials   Interviews of farmers in combination with assessment by officials is by far the most common way of estimating yields in Africa. Casley and Lury (1987: p. 198) claim that interviews of farmers (in Nigeria and Kenya, and also in Asia) have proved fairly accurate in controlled experiments (see also Murphy *et al.* 1991). However, when farmers have reason to expect that a fair assessment of the crop size may lead to increased taxation or other costs, they have incentives to understate true yields, and there is some evidence to corroborate this hypothesis (Murphy *et al.* 1991: pp. 49–50). The official is often also responsible for agricultural extension work (Paulino and Young 1981: pp. 41–2). In such cases, he has an incentive to exaggerate yield increases in fields that can be attributed to his own extension efforts and to underestimate yields in other fields (Murphy *et al.* 1991: p. 2). The net result will depend on the amount of land under his extension responsibility relative to other land.

In short, when it comes to estimating yields with the primitive methods used in the SSA, one cannot expect a systematic bias in a particular direction. In places where simple crop-cuts are used, yields may be overestimated. In the great majority of countries where the farmers' own estimates and/or ocular assessment by agricultural extension officers are relied upon, there are conflicting biases of unknown size.

6.6.   COMPARATIVE EVIDENCE FROM INDIA AND PAKISTAN

In the above two sections we have argued that the incentive structure is such that we should expect acreage enumeration (and food production) to be underestimated in the African countries; we have also discussed several rather well-known reasons why the rough estimation techniques in use are downward biased. It is also known from other sources that subsistence agricultural production, which is a large sector in Africa,[3] is systematically underestimated (Heston 1994: p. 39). However, until more sophisticated estimation methods are introduced in the African countries, one cannot quantify the size of the underestimation. Some insights can be gained, though, from experience in other parts of the world.

When (reasonably) complete land registers replaced the earlier primitive estimation methods in South Asia, upward revisions followed. Evenson and Prey (1994) found that: 'Evidence from crop-cutting surveys in India and the Punjab in Pakistan indicate that during the 1950s and the 1960s output of major foodgrains was underestimated by official statistics' (based on subjective methods) by about 25 per cent in both countries. They found that this was due to downward biases in the acreage enumeration, while there was no systematic bias in the yield estimates, which is what we expect from the discussion above. In the third country examined, Bangladesh, they found less systematic evidence of early underestimation. Here also acreage was underestimated by 'subjective' methods, but yields, on the other hand, were systematically overestimated (Evenson and Prey 1994: table 4).

Experimental tests of the reliability of different kinds of 'interview surveys' in India also show that quick and low-cost surveys produce severely downward-biased estimates of the size of agricultural operations (area in acres). A comparison of three survey techniques in increasing order of complexity, time-intensity, and economic funding showed that the cheapest method resulted in a 30 per cent underestimation as compared with the most sophisticated method. When the same investigation was carried out in six different regions of India, in each and every region, the most sophisticated method yielded significantly higher acreage estimates than the 'intermediate' method, and this one in its turn, resulted in higher estimates in all regions than the simplest method (Zarkovich 1975: pp. 17–18 and table 2). There is no *a priori* reason to believe that the primitive acreage-estimation methods in use throughout Africa should be less biased than they proved to be earlier in South Asia.

That the production data underlying the NPCCA estimates in the African countries are unreliable and incomplete is a fact of which the FAO is fully aware, and has been for a very long time. The FAO has sponsored several conferences where experts from various professions have suggested methods of improving these statistics (e.g. Lipton 1985*a*, *b*, 1986). The FAO has also made efforts to improve data collection and the primitive estimation methods through its own extension work in the African countries. Not much has come out of these efforts, however. It is even likely that the production of agricultural statistics has deteriorated further in many of the countries (as has happened with trade statistics (Rozanski and Yeats 1994)) in the wake of economic and political upheaval.

The amazing fact is that the FAO continues to publish detailed figures in its annual official statistical publications (FAO*b*, FAO*c*, FAO*e*) year after year without much mentioning the poor quality of the data base in the African countries. In fact, the FAO provides estimates of the per-capita availability of protein and fat in grammes down to one decimal point in its *FBS*! This gives an illusion of exactitude that is hilarious to anyone who has spent a few hours studying the estimation methods and the quality of data, or travelled rural Africa for a few days. Moreover, the FAO*b* (1994: table 106) has provided NPCCA data for several countries in years when civil war or other disturbances have made all field estimations impossible in large parts of the countries, e.g. Angola, Ethiopia, Liberia, Mozambique, Sierra Leone, Somalia, Sudan, and Zaïre (now Congo).

In order to grasp the quality aspects of the FAO data for Africa one has to study 'background' FAO documents (often not published) and various consultants' reports that are not easily available to the general user of official FAO data. The contrast with most official USDA publications is stark; in these, there is a much more open attitude to revealing the unreliable and incomplete (implying underestimation) base data.[4]

6.7. CONCLUDING REMARKS

That there are large margins of error in the food availability estimates for the African countries is one thing; this has been pointed out repeatedly by several authors (cited above). Systematic biases are another problem, which has received less attention. The FAO itself acknowledges two such biases (in opposite directions): waste at the household level and incomplete coverage of minor food items.

In this chapter we have analysed the main theoretical arguments for expecting downward estimation of acreage under cultivation and, thus, food production of major crops. First, there are incentives for underreporting production at all levels. Second, the primitive methods used to estimate acreage tend to lead to incomplete coverage.

Although there is no *direct* empirical evidence from Africa on the size of the underestimations, there are other more indirect pieces of information that corroborate the notion of underestimation. First, studies from India and Pakistan show an underestimation of acreage and production by 25 per cent by the primitive methods used earlier (and still in vogue in Africa) when objective methods were introduced. Secondly, experimental studies, also from India, on the reliability of 'primitive' methods, when compared with more sophisticated methods, gave similar results. Thirdly, the estimates provided by the USDA of food production in the African countries, while giving widely differing estimates for individual crops at given times and in given countries, do not differ much in terms of broad averages from their FAO counterparts (Table 6.2 above). Since the USDA explicitly states that their estimates are incomplete on average, this is a further indication that the FAO production estimates are also downward biased.

All this is not to say that we can definitely conclude that, overall, the NPCCA estimates provided by the FAO for the SSA countries are substantially downward biased. There are many other errors in the hundreds of conversions needed to transform gross food production and net trade data to per-capita calorie-availability estimates that may imply overestimation, e.g. inflated yield estimates and 'waste and losses' estimated to be too low. We have not been able to say much on these counts because no alternative data are available. There are, however, additional methods for estimating calorie 'availability' and, thus, also for checking the reliability of the FAO estimates. This evidence comes from surveys of food intakes and household expenditures, which we shall analyse in Chapter 7. There are also, as we shall see in Part IV below, plenty of anthropometric indicators that provide a further possibility for checking the reliability of the FAO estimates of undernutrition in SSA (and elsewhere).

NOTES

1. The number of inhabitants per km^2 in SSA at large was 23 in 1991; the equivalent figure for South and South-east Asia was 171.
2. The excluded countries were: Angola, Benin, Burkina Faso, Burundi, Cape Verde, Central African Republic, Comooros, Cote D'Ivoire, Djibouti, Equatorial

Guinea, Gambia, Guinea Bissau, Mali, Mauritania, Niger, Rwanda, Sao T. & Principe, Senegal, Seychelles, Sierra Leone, Somalia, Sudan, and Zimbabwe.

3. Blades (1980) provides estimates in the 20–40 per cent range for a dozen SSA countries.

4. In a critical assessment of the FAO production data, Lipton (1985a, b) makes the obvious suggestions that the FAO should not hesitate to leave a country/crop observation blank in its publications when the margin of error is high, that the means by which published estimates are derived ought to be stated explicitly, and that the reliability of the statistics should be indicated by an index (a scale of 1 to 5, for instance). This has not been done in the latest *FBS* (FAOe 1996); the only indication of an increased recognition of the unreliability of the data is that no estimates are provided for a few countries which were included in earlier *FBS*s (FAOe 1984). In the *Sixth World Food Survey*, the FAOa (1996: 42) admits that the 'risk of error is likely to be particularly high in a few countries (Ethiopia, PDR, Somalia, Rwanda and Afghanistan)'. The proper procedure would be not to provide any data at all for these countries and add almost all African countries to the 'at risk' list.

7

Calorie Intake and Distribution: Estimates from the Consumption Side

7.1. INTRODUCTION

The share of the population that was undernourished in the early 1990s was the highest in SSA according to FAO estimates—almost twice as high as in South Asia. The main reasons why SSA stands out in terms of high prevalence of undernutrition is not that the estimated distribution of calories is any different from, or that calorie requirements are higher than, that in other regions. By far the most important reason is that the estimated per-capita availability of calories is exceptionally low in SSA. In the previous chapter we argued that because of the primitive methods used by the FAO, these estimates for the African countries are most likely downward biased, both in absolute terms and in relation to estimates for India and the rest of South Asia.

In this chapter we shall study evidence on calorie consumption in Africa and elsewhere, derived from the demand side. This evidence comprises various types of household surveys of food consumption or food expenditures. The first objective is to assess the accuracy and representativity of this evidence (section 7.2). Secondly, by comparing the data on calorie consumption to those derived by the FAO from the *FBS* production/trade data, hopefully we shall be able to say more about average food (calorie) standards in the SSA in international comparison (section 7.3). A third objective is to use food expenditure studies to try to answer the question of how cost-effective the calorie consumption of the African populations is in international comparison (sections 7.4 and 7.5). A fourth objective is to scrutinize the estimates of inter-household calorie distribution from food expenditure surveys that the FAO uses to estimate the prevalence of undernutrition (section 7.6).

7.2. HOUSEHOLD CONSUMPTION SURVEYS AND CALORIE INTAKE

7.2.1. Measurement Methods

Four principal methods have been used to estimate per-capita calorie consumption of households, and more rarely, of individuals, in Africa and other food-deficient areas. The most common and inexpensive procedure is recalls: the investigator simply asks people how much of different kinds of food they have consumed during a specific time period. The second method is to measure changes in food stocks and convert them into 'consumption' flows. The third method is to weigh the equivalent of the food actually observed to have been consumed by the individual or the household. The fourth method is to derive quantity estimates indirectly, from food expenditure data supplied in household income/budget surveys and food price data. The energy content of the estimated food consumed, whatever method used, is derived from standardized conversion tables.

7.2.2. Estimates

Direct estimates of calorie intake for a total of 85 sample populations in Africa are summarized in Schofield (1979) and in Hulse and Pearson (1981). The bulk of the evidence is for 1960–79, and a majority of the African countries are covered. The estimated daily per-capita calorie intake lies in the range 1,800–2,200 range in most cases; the estimated (unweighted) average in the 85 samples is 1,950 (Table 7.1).

There are relatively few estimates of calorie intakes in the 1980s and the 1990s. In the FAO/ESN *Nutrition Country Profiles* (1987–97), which are now available for almost all countries in the world, there is a section reporting on 'food consumption'. In most of these profiles, various estimates of calorie intakes for specific age groups based on small and local samples are presented, but very seldom (national) per-capita estimates. There are also a few recent Household Expenditure Surveys conducted by IFPRI with the more specific intention of providing the FAO with base data for the estimation of calorie distribution across households. In most of the World Bank's *Living Standard Measurement Studies* there is no information on calorie consumption on a per-capita basis. The *Nutrition Situation Surveys* published regularly by the special UN agency ACC/SCN, while providing a wealth of anthropometric

TABLE 7.1. Estimated per-capita calorie intake in SSA countries

Country or site (year)	Sample unit	Sample method	Estimated average calorie intake per capita
West Africa (1970s)	51 villages	Recalls/ weighing	1,968
SSA (1970s)	36 villages	Recalls/ weighing	1,936
Average	85 villages[a]	Recalls/ weighing	1,950

[a] Two studies were covered in both surveys.

Sources: Hulse and Pearson 1981: table 5; Schofield 1979: table 5.5.

indicators for almost all countries, do not collect and publish per-capita calorie intake estimates. (The few available estimates are presented in summary
form in Table 7.2.)

As is well known, there are as many difficulties involved in estimating food
intakes from consumption studies as there are in estimating food availability
from the supply side. (These difficulties are probably the main reasons why
very few estimates of calorie intakes have been produced lately.) The main
problems with food consumption surveys (FCSs) and household expenditure surveys (HESs) have been analysed in detail elsewhere (Poleman 1975,
1977, Dowler and Seo 1985, Grootaert and Cheung 1985, Deaton and Case
1988, Bouis *et al.* 1992, several contributions to von Braun and Puetz 1993).
In the following we shall thus focus only on some errors and biases which are
of particular relevance for the studies of those African countries which were
referred to earlier.

7.2.3. Selection Biases

Most of the FCSs conducted in Africa before 1980 underlying the estimates
summarized in Table 7.1 are not representative of the 'habitual' food standards of the national populations. There are three main selection biases in this
set of studies.

(1) Unrepresentative samples   In a majority of the surveys in African countries in the 1960s and 1970s, the focus was on rural groups that were found
to have nutritional problems prior to the examination, this being the very
reason why the investigations were carried out. The sample population was
intended to be representative for the national population only in four out of
the 51 studies covered in Dillon and Lajoie (1981: table 2, footnote a).
Schofield (1979: p. 11) does not discuss the representativity of the African 36
samples in her survey in any detail, but notes that 'in general . . . investigations are restricted to small, unrepresentative samples'. All this means is that
the estimates derived for these unrepresentative groups must be lower than
the national average of the country in question. How much lower cannot be
ascertained, but if a particular population group is at a nutritional disadvantage, one would presume that for this to be detected in the first instance, the
calorie 'disadvantage' must correspond to more than a few per cent.

(2) Seasonality   There is plenty of evidence showing large intra-year variations in per-capita calorie intake in countries with marked seasonality in
agriculture, which characterizes the majority of the countries in Africa. The
results from the studies replicated in Table 7.2 suggest that data obtained in
the lean season underestimate annual average calorie intake by about 10 per
cent on the average. (Also see Chambers *et al.* 1981: pp. 45–50; Rosetta 1986;
Tomkins *et al.* 1986; von Braun 1988; Sahn 1989.)

TABLE 7.2. Seasonal variations in estimated calorie intake in selected SSA countries

Region/country (years)	Estimated per-capita calorie intake				
	(1) Wet season	(2) Dry season	(3) Yearly average	(1)/ (2)	(1)/ (3)
(1) Average for 15 villages in West Africa (1970s)	2,191	2,458	—	0.89	—
(2) Average for 25 villages in West Africa (1970s)	1,885	2,102	—	0.90	—
(3) Senegal (1965)	1,527	2,197	1,867	0.70	0.82
(4) Chad (1965)	2,196	2,841	—	0.77	—
(5) Madagascar (1962)	2,074	2,440	2,223	0.85	0.93
(6) Gambia (1985/6)	2,159	2,269	—	0.95	—
(7) Nigeria (1971)	1,666	2,048	—	0.81	—

Sources: (1)–(2): Schofield 1979: pp. 53–4; (3)–(4): Hulse and Pearson 1981: tables 6 and 7; the remaining data are from FAO/ESN, various years.

In 18 out of the 51 FCSs from the Sahel countries covered in Dillon and Lajoie (1981: table 1), information is given on what time of the year the investigation was carried out. In 16 of these 18 FCSs, the study was conducted in the preharvest season, and in the remaining two, shortly before. Moreover, it seems that many of the studies have been carried out in a below-average year. Three of the four studies based on representative samples listed in Dillon and Lajoie (1981) were conducted in the Sahel during the famine years 1972–4, clearly an unrepresentative period.

(3) Urban versus Rural Samples   Almost all the FCSs discussed above have been carried out in rural areas. *A priori*, there is no particular reason to expect an unambiguous urban/rural difference. Urban people may indulge in fewer calories because they are engaged in less strenuous work activities than rural people. On the other hand, average household income is almost invariably higher in urban than in rural areas, which may mean higher food (calorie) consumption.[1] The six African studies replicated in Table 7.3 suggest lower consumption in rural areas in four samples and higher consumption in the remaining two; the evidence from non-African countries is also conflicting. We thus cannot say in which direction the rural focus in most African surveys has tilted the estimates—if at all.

7.2.4. Observation and Measurement Biases

The various methods used to estimate habitual calorie intake in sample populations (even if representative) entail several measurement errors and

TABLE 7.3. Estimated per-capita calorie consumption in rural/urban locations in selected countries

Country (year)	Total sample size	Per-capita calorie intake		
		Rural	Urban	Rural/urban
Côte d'Ivoire (1979)	1,930	2,139	2,043	1.05
Congo (1981)	—	2,200	2,550	0.86
Mali (1972)	1,838	1,825	1,950	0.94
(1978)	2,131	1,901	1,950	0.97
Zambia (1974)	—	1,907	2,047	0.93
Mauritius (1983)	1,215	3,366	2,657	1.27
Rwanda (1984)	5,100	1,956	2,296	0.86
Egypt (1981/2)	—	2,980	2,742	1.09
Pakistan (1985/7)	8,864	2,379	2,259	1.05
Vietnam (1966)	—	1,986	2,108	0.94
Panama (1971)	600	2,089	2,101	0.99
Colombia (1981)	3,330	2,295	2,184	1.05
Costa Rica (1982)	958	1,922	1,987	0.97
Haiti (1988)	—	1,741	1,930	0.90

Sources: FAO/ESN, various years.

biases, as many users of such methods have pointed out. Two main problems beset the recall method. One is that when interviewed, people tend to forget minor items consumed and/or snacks in between meals. Another is that when people are asked about their food-consumption habits, they are inclined to provide information which they think the investigators would like them to give, or what they think would benefit themselves (e.g. obtaining food supplements). It may also be that the poor tend to 'talk a good diet', i.e. to exaggerate their food intake, being ashamed of their deprivation. There are thus conflicting biases in the recall method, and to resolve the net outcome is an empirical matter.

The main disadvantage with the stocktaking method is that it usually covers storable food items consumed at home only; non-storable food items, as well as drinks, snacks, and meals eaten outside the home are normally excluded. The weight-of-the-food-consumed method also produces biased results, mainly for the same reason as the stocktaking method. It is also well known that (poor) people who are observed are likely to change their dietary behaviour, but there is no *a priori* possibility of saying how they change.

The studies providing calorie intake estimates *indirectly* from food expenditure surveys are beset by roughly the same selection and measurement problems as other types of calorie-consumption surveys. As there are very few such surveys available for African countries (discussed in section 7.5 below) we leave these aside for the moment.

7.2.5. The Ideal Estimates: The Doubly Labelled Water Method

While the type of surveys discussed so far are aimed at estimating peoples' calorie *intakes*, there is also one method for estimating calorie *expenditures* at the level of the individual. This is the so-called Doubly Labelled Water (DLW) method, which uses chemical substances to measure the carbon dioxide flux in the body between two or more points in time. Since the carbon dioxide flux is strictly proportional to the energy metabolized in the body, standard indirect caliometry can be used to estimate the energy expenditure. Through the energy balance identity, which states that energy expenditures must equal energy intakes plus changes in the energy stores (weight) in the body, the intake can be estimated indirectly (for more details, see Schoeller *et al.* 1990).

The DLW method provides very accurate estimates of energy expenditures under laboratory conditions, the margin of error being almost nil. The method can be used on 'free-living' populations, i.e. applied to people who carry out their normal day-to-day activities, but with slightly less accuracy, due, for example, to variations in the water content in the body that induce fluctuations in body weight unrelated to changes in solid tissue. Another problem is that when observed and measured, people may alter their habitual physical activity level; one also has to obtain estimates at several points in time in order to ensure representativeness. Presumably, it is mainly economic-cost considerations that have prevented this method, which has been available since the mid 1950s, to be used more frequently in the developing country context (it appears that only a handful of studies are available; see below).

7.3. COMPARING ESTIMATES OF DIFFERENT TYPES

So far we have discussed typical errors and biases in three types of studies aimed at estimating per-capita calorie consumption in poor populations: the *FBS*, FCS, and DLW methods. The two former types of studies are known to contain large margins of error and also to produce biased estimates for a variety of reasons, which were discussed above. All comparisons of estimates derived with these various methods thus have to take these imperfections into consideration. In the following, we shall nevertheless discuss what can be learnt—if anything—from such comparisons.

7.3.1. Comparing FCSs using Different Methods

Cross-checking of results obtained by recalls with those obtained through weighing the observed food intake in various sample populations in India suggests that the weight-of-the-food method produces lower estimates, ranging from 10 to 40 per cent. Only in some more recent studies, has the discrepancy been less (see Harriss 1990: p. 375 and the review by McNeill 1986).

It is therefore notable that the 85 dietary studies from Africa referred to above are all of the not-so-recent type (pre-1979). If one takes the average of the Indian figures (25 per cent) and assumes that it carries over to the half of the pre-1980 African studies that are based on 'weighting' and 'stocktaking', one arrives at the conclusion that per-capita food intake in these surveys from Africa is underestimated by 10–15 per cent. This is, of course, provided that the recall method is not generally *upward* biased, which comparisons with the DLW method suggest is not the case (see below).

There is little recent comparative evidence from Africa. Bouis (1994: table 1) obtained both repeated 24-hour recall estimates of calorie intake and indirect calorie consumption estimates from household expenditure data for one and the same population in Kenya (and also one in the Philippines). In both cases, the recall estimates were a few per cent higher than the indirect estimates derived from the household expenditure surveys. Although contrary to our earlier findings, these observations are too few to permit generalizations.

7.3.2. Comparing FCS with FBS Estimates

Country Estimates   Comparisons of per-capita calorie consumption estimates derived from various FCSs with calorie supply estimates from *FBS*s for individual countries have found the latter estimates to be higher (FAO 1983; Dowler and Seo 1985). The bulk of the evidence is from developed countries; here, both cross-sectional and time-series data suggest that the negative discrepancy ranges from 10 to 40 per cent, and tends to grow with higher per-capita income.

Comparisons from nine developing countries (in the 1970s) show positive and negative differences in about equal proportion (FAO 1983: p. 8). Four other FCSs from Asian countries all show a negative discrepancy (Dowler and Seo 1985: table 1). The evidence reported in these two reports, which do not include any study from SSA, thus suggests that *FBS* estimates are somewhat higher than the estimates derived from FCSs in most, but far from all, cases. This conclusion is corroborated by the evidence from some additional country comparisons reported in Table 7.4.

The main hypothesis usually advanced to explain the difference has been that waste and leakage at various stages in the long chain of events from food production to actual household intake has been larger than typically allowed for in the *FBS* estimates. Dowler and Seo (1985) provide rather convincing evidence from developed countries that this is not the case at the level of households.[2] They speculate a little about other explanations, but offer no definitive conclusion. They nevertheless argue that 'Household Consumption Surveys, despite their inherent sources of error, are more likely to give an accurate picture of calorie intakes [than *FBS* data]' (ibid: p. 288).

TABLE 7.4. Comparison of food-consumption survey (FCS) and food-balance-sheet (*FBS*) estimates of per-capita calorie consumption in selected countries

Country (year)	Sample size	FCS	FBS	Difference
Senegal (1968)	—	1,944	2,451	−507
Congo (1981)	—	2,250	2,090	160
Benin (1987–8)	869	2,058	2,279	−221
Zambia (1987)	—	2,070	1,918	152
Côte d'Ivoire (1979)	1,930	2,104	2,663	−559
Mali (1981–3)	—	1,808	1,898	−90
Gambia (1985–6)	2,159	2,214	2,229	−15
Nigeria (1971)	—	1,952	2,002	−50
Uruguay (1962)	5,767	2,594	2,782	−188
Peru (1971–2)	8,000	1,997	2,289	−292
(1977–8)	10,000	1,941	2,179	−238
Colombia (1981)	3,333	2,223	2,505	−282
Costa Rica (1982)	958	1,953	2,621	−668
Dominica (1986)	1,404	2,394	2,615	−221
Haiti (1988)	2,079	1,788	2,005	−217
Pakistan (1985–7)	8,864	2,180	2,186	−6
Egypt (1981–2)	3,300	2,843	3,088	−245

Sources: The food consumption survey data are from FAO/ESN, various years; the FBS data are from the FAO*b*, various years.

Aggregate Estimates   For the 1960–79 period, the FAO (1987*b*) estimates the average per-capita daily availability of calories in SSA as a whole at 1,964, on the basis of *FBS* data. The average for the FCSs reported in Table 7.1 is 1,950. In other words, there is hardly any disagreement between the FAO estimate, based on supply-side, aggregate data and the average of the sample estimates derived from demand-side, disaggregate data.[3] The small actual difference between the FCS and the *FBS* estimates is slightly negative, which may be interpreted as minuscule 'waste' of the food available at the household level.

At first sight, one might be inclined to take the almost-perfect congruity between estimates obtained in completely different ways as proof of the robustness of the estimation methods. But this finding is also consistent with the hypothesis that both the demand-side FCS estimates and the supply-side *FBS* estimates are downward biased (in roughly the same proportions). Earlier, we found three main reasons to believe that, in general, there is a downward bias in the available FCS estimates in the SSA due to: (i) inaccurate estimation methods, (ii) non-representative samples, and these samples being (iii) obtained at a non-representative time of the year. We also found reasons to expect that the estimates based on *FBS* data are most probably downward biased, mainly because (i) the area under crop cultivations is underestimated and (ii) most minor food items are incompletely covered (cf. Chapter 6).

Although it is impossible to put exact numbers on the degree of underestimation in the demand- and supply-side estimates for the African countries in general, both are likely to be in the range 10–20 per cent. As we shall see later on, this conclusion is consistent with the observation that the anthropometric status of the population in SSA is much better than in South Asia.

7.3.3. Comparing with the Doubly Labelled Water Method

Schoeller (1990) reports results from nine studies from developed countries where the DLW method has been used to check the accuracy of intake estimates based on recalls. In three of the studies, the recall estimates were roughly on a par with the DLW results; in six studies the recalls were substantially lower. This seems to corroborate our earlier conclusion, that the recall method is generally downward biased. (Also see Heymsfield *et al.* 1995, Martin *et al.* 1996.)

There are only two studies, however, that use the DLW method to check dietary recall estimates in developing countries: one from Chile and one from The Gambia. The first study found an almost perfect match between the two methods, while the Gambian study reported exceptional underestimation by the recall method; only 40 per cent of the actual calorie expenditures were 'recalled' (Singh *et al.* 1989). The reason for this enormous bias was not clearly understood, but the sample was nevertheless far too small (12 nonpregnant women) for the results to have any meaning in a general context. However, the DLW method is the most reliable one available, and a large number of comparative DLW and recall studies will have to be carried out before we can say more about exactly how large the biases are in studies using recalls and other unreliable methods for estimating calorie intakes (also see Black *et al.* 1996).

7.4. FURTHER USE OF FOOD EXPENDITURE SURVEYS

Some of the evidence on per-capita calorie intake reported in the preceding sections was derived from *Household Expenditure Surveys* (HESs). Such surveys can shed light on two additional questions of interest in the present context. One is the allocation of household expenditures on high- versus low-cost calorie food items, which will be our concern in the next section. Moreover, while *FBS* data say nothing about the distribution of calories across households, expenditure studies can be used for estimating distribution (which the FAO has done in order to derive its prevalence-of-undernutrition estimates;

to be analysed in section 7.6). All this is possible in principle; in practice most available HESs are not conducted in ways that permit addressing these questions.

7.4.1. Household Expenditure Surveys in SSA: Methodological Shortcomings

Almost 50 household-expenditure studies from about half of the SSA countries are listed in the FAOd (1988, 1996) *Review of Food Consumption (Expenditure) Surveys*. Unfortunately, very few of these can be used for estimating either low- versus high-cost calorie consumption, or the distribution of the calories. Most of the studies use food-item classifications which have been aggregrated too far and/or income groups which are too broad. In fact, in more than half the studies, no estimates are reported by income class, only the average for the entire sample. Moreover, many of the studies consider cash expenditures only; the imputed incomes of subsistence farmers, the largest and often the poorest population group in most African countries, are left out. Some of the studies report on the extent of non-responses, which in many instances are very numerous and not corrected for; in other studies, the problem is not even mentioned. Yet another problem is that in many of the studies, the average total expenditure of the poorest population groups grossly exceeds their average income, and no explanation or correction is offered.

7.4.2. Representativeness of Surveys

Most of the food expenditure studies covered in the FAO *Reviews* are based on non-representative population groups. In the huge majority of the studies, only urban populations are examined. The sample is rather small in many of the studies, especially those covering rural populations (while being very large in some of the others). The representativeness of the households in the samples is also open to question in many cases. Some include only households that can be identified from official records, which tend to leave out many of the poorest and nutritionally most-vulnerable households (e.g. the landless in rural areas and newly arrived immigrants in the urban sector).

Furthermore, although food expenditure studies have been conducted in a large number of countries, no such studies are available for many of the poorest countries, e.g. Burkina Faso, the Central African Republic, Mauritania, Angola, and Mozambique. The studies from many other countries in which per-capita income and food production are thought to have declined considerably over the past 10–15 years are rather dated. Moreover, in the handful of countries (Ghana, Kenya, Malawi, Nigeria, Sudan, and Zambia) where food expenditure surveys have been undertaken at two or more points in time, the surveys have been conducted in different ways, which defy intertemporal comparison.

7.5. LOW- VERSUS HIGH-COST CALORIE EXPENDITURES

From the above section, one can only conclude that the great majority of the 50-odd food expenditure surveys from Africa are useless for the purpose of estimating the cost-efficiency of diets, mainly because of non-representative samples and weak estimation methodologies. In this section we shall nevertheless take a closer look at the few surveys from which some relevant information can be obtained.

7.5.1. Hypothesis

Poor and rich people alike demand food in order to satisfy several biological needs and preferences. The energy content of the food is only one of these 'characteristics'; others are taste, bulk, texture, variety, and the social stigma associated with different food items. The time and cost it takes to prepare the food also enter the consumers' preferences. Different kinds of food contains these various characteristics in different proportions. By varying the consumption mix over both time and space, the consumer can normally obtain the optimal combination of the various components in food with due regard to their (implicit) relative prices and the budget constraint. The extent to which the various qualities of food can be demanded as separate goods depends on the variety of food supplied locally. In places with strong monoculture and great obstacles to trade, the joint-product property of the main staple food may impose restrictions on the possibility of obtaining a nutritionally balanced diet while satisfying the demand for other characteristics of food simultaneously.

On economic as well as common-sense grounds, one would think that the energy–protein content of food is the most basic of all economically constrained needs people have. If more than 40 per cent of the African population does not have the income needed to buy enough food to satiate the energy requirements for basal biological body functions and sustain a minimal work effort, as claimed by the FAO, the implications are plain. In such severely undernourished populations, one would expect that (i) the share of income spent on food and (ii) the share spent on low-cost-per-calorie food in total food expenditure are close to unity. By low-cost-per-calorie food we mean cereals, roots, tubers, pulses, and sugar; we understand high-cost-per-calorie food to be meat, fish, milk, eggs, vegetables, and fruit; when reported, we also include expenditures on meals outside the home. The basis for this classification is reported in Table 7.5, which presents estimates of the price per calorie contained in 13 different food-item groups in five developing countries. The price pattern is reasonably consistent over the five countries, although there are some notable deviations, e.g. meat and fish are comparatively cheap in India, and rice is expensive in Kenya.

TABLE 7.5. The hierarchy of calorie costs for seven countries, 1975

Food category	USA	India	Kenya	Korea	Brazil	Mexico	Japan
(1) Roots and tubers	100	163	100	208	114	400	163
(2) Sugars and honey	114	170	286	213	100	100	100
(3) Rice	136	147	790	148	253	200	191
(4) Other cereals and pulses	186	100	190	100	210	200	303
(5) Pork	186	151	438	298	834	1,200	1,122
(6) Milk and milk products	236	626	1,029	556	639	700	1,084
(7) Egg and egg products	255	653	1,019	494	1,858	3,300	388
(8) Lamb and mutton	273	312	648	287	1,566	5,500	413
(9) Beef	314	163	605	1,735	1,502	3,200	3,209
(10) Poultry	464	1,328	3,000	640	2,902	4,500	1,428
(11) Fruit	545	595	2,905	1,015	380	900	1,434
(12) Vegetables	1,632	895	2,471	377	8,468	6,000	2,216
(13) Fish	1,705	100	4,794	525	2,249	2,600	1,741

Note: The cheapest commodity in each country is set as base = 100.

Source: Chaudhri and Timmer 1986.

7.5.2. Evidence

In the four samples from SSA in Table 7.6, the share of food purchases in total expenditure is inversely related to income (as expected). The lowest-income quartile devote between half and three-quarters of their total expenditure to food. The highest-income quartile (not reported in the table) spend less than 40 per cent of their total expenditure on food purchases. All this is not very different from what is typical in less-developed countries in most of Asia and Latin America. The shares, however, are somewhat lower in the African countries than in India and Bangladesh, the two non-African countries with the most severe food problems in *absolute* terms, according to all sources.

The information of prime interest contained in Table 7.6, however, is the share of total food expenditure that is used to buy high-cost-per-calorie food items by the lowest income quartile. The striking observation is that the share is comparatively high in the African countries, ranging from 54 per cent in Malawi to 82 per cent in Mauritius. These shares are significantly higher than in Bangladesh and India and on a par with what is found in South-East Asia and in Brazil. Moreover, in all of these four African countries, the share of total food expenditure devoted to high-cost-per-calorie items by the poorest households deviates only marginally from that of the households with the highest incomes (not shown in the table).

TABLE 7.6. Share of food in total household expenditures and share of high-cost-per-calorie food items in total food expenditures, by the lowest-income quartile in selected developing countries

Country	Year(s)	National/ rural/ urban	Share of food in total expenditure	Share of high-cost-per-calorie food in total food expenditure
Sub-Saharan Africa				
Malawi	1979/80	Average for four towns	50	54
Zambia	1977	Urban	74	76
Mauritius	1981	Nationwide	55	82
Sudan	1978/9	Urban	59	67
South Asia				
Bangladesh	1981/2	Nationwide	73	27
		Rural	72	26
		Urban	69	35
India	1977/8	Rural	78	27
		Urban	72	40
	1983	Rural	73	33
		Urban	70	43
Pakistan	1979	Nationwide	55	53
		Rural	56	52
		Urban	50	60
Other Asia				
Philippines	1985	Nationwide	60	50
		Rural	69	48
		Urban	65	58
Malaysia	1980	Nationwide	50	70
		Rural	52	63
		Urban	43	81
Korea	1986	Urban	42	69
Americas				
Brazil	1974	Nationwide	60	53
		Rural	65	50
		Metropolitan areas	42	65
Guatemala	1978/9	Nationwide	65	50

Sources: Base data are from the FAO*d* 1986, 1988.

The poorest households in the African samples thus have a considerably less cost-efficient diet than their counterparts in India and Bangladesh. This does not seem to be explained by differences in the relative cost per calorie in the various kinds of food. The price of a calorie contained in meat/fish/

vegetables/fruit in relation to the price when contained in cereals/roots/ tubers is considerably higher in the one African country for which there are data, Kenya, than in India (Table 7.5).[4]

Undernutrition in SSA, if as severe as suggested by the FAO (see Chapter 5), is not easily reconcilable with the low cost-efficiency of food expenditures by the lowest-income quartile revealed in Table 7.6.[5] That the poorest households in the African countries have a relatively less cost-efficient diet than their counterparts in India is a further, albeit tentative, indication that the FAO estimates of calorie availability in the African region are downward biased and, consequently, that the FAO estimate of the prevalence of undernutrition, is upward biased, not only absolutely, but also relatively to South Asia. And as we shall see subsequently, the latter conclusion is, again, consistent with the finding of a substantially lower incidence of anthropometric failure in Africa as compared with South Asia.

7.5.3. Caveats

The picture revealed by Table 7.6 has to be interpreted with caution, however. First, the various surveys that underlie the estimates reported in Table 7.6 most probably contain many of the errors and biases that beset most expenditure surveys in developing countries (as discussed above). It has not been feasible to scrutinize the surveys we have used here in any detail, in order to ensure strict comparability. Secondly, the various surveys use slightly different aggregates of food items, i.e. some of the studies report expenditures on meals outside the home separately (an item then included in the high-cost-per-calorie food category), while other do not (instead it is included in a residual as 'other' food items). Since the surveys of India and Bangladesh do not report 'meals outside the home' separately, the estimated share of expenditures going to high-cost food items may be downward biased. However, re-estimation, including the residual 'other food items' in the high-cost category, for India and Bangladesh, only altered the estimated shares by a few percentage points.

Also, the representativity of the samples reported in Table 7.6 is questionable. The four SSA countries may not be representative for most of Africa; Mauritius especially is a questionable case. They may also be too few to permit generalizations. Moreover, all but one sample from the African countries are from urban areas, and these estimates would best be compared with urban estimates elsewhere.

7.6. DISTRIBUTION OF CALORIE INTAKE

The FAO estimates of the distribution of calories used in the estimations of the prevalence of undernutrition in SSA and other regions are partly derived from HESs and partly from income distribution estimates.

7.6.1. Measurements

In earlier sections we have discussed errors and biases in different types of surveys (*FBS*s, FCSs and HESs) when it comes to estimating *average* calorie intake in a population. There are also several typical errors and biases in the estimated *distribution* of calories across households (which beset almost all HESs produced before the 1990s).

The first is that the poorest households, which are the most difficult to locate, are underrepresented and also figure highly among the non-responding. The second is that the food-item aggregates that are used are too broad. This typically leads to an underestimation of the calories consumed by the poorest and an overestimation for the relatively rich. The reason is that within each food category, there are different food items with different prices per calorie, and the poor tend to buy relatively more of the cheaper calorie items. A third is that in most HESs, no correction has been made for food received or given as gifts, or as compensation for work for households members. Some recent studies suggest that this omission has distorted the results in previous studies to a considerable extent (Bouis and Haddad 1992). The poor typically are net receivers of food gifts and the relatively rich households are net givers. It may also be that food wastage at the level of households is greater in relatively well-off households than in the poorest ones.

For these and other reasons, the FAO also finds most available *Household Expenditure Surveys* (FAO 1992: p. 17) much too unreliable and non-representative to be used for estimating calorie distribution. This is so not only for the African countries (for the more specific reasons spelt out in section 7.4 above), but also for developing countries in other parts of the world. The FAO has therefore recently commissioned HESs for three Asian and two African countries from IFPRI researchers.

The IFPRI surveys are probably more reliable and unbiased than most previous surveys. This is not only because they are based on state-of-the-art estimation methods in general,[6] but also because they have been designed especially with the aim of estimating distribution of calories (which has not been the prime objective in the great bulk of previous studies). The methods used in the IFPRI surveys further allow one to distinguish between inter-household variance in calorie intake and within-year variance. This is perhaps the most important innovation in these surveys compared with most earlier ones.

In addition to the IFPRI surveys, the FAO has based its estimates of the distribution of calories on earlier FCSs and HESs from Bangladesh, China, Colombia, Indonesia, Mexico, Pakistan, Peru, Philippines, and Venezuela (FAO 1992: p. 22). These surveys have been reprocessed in collaboration with national statistical organizations in the respective countries in order to fit the FAO needs. The fact that they were not originally intended for estimating inter-household distribution of calorie intake has probably meant that they are less accurate than the IFPRI surveys.

All in all, the FAO has estimates of calorie distribution from HESs for some 18 countries. Since these countries include China, they account for some 75 per cent of the population in the Third World. There are an additional 34 countries for which there are no acceptable HESs, but for which there are some data on income distribution. For these countries, the FAO estimates the distribution of calorie intake with the help of income–calorie elasticities (for details, see FAO 1992: pp. 22–3). For the remaining 47 countries, for which there are neither HESs nor income distribution data, the FAO estimates calorie distribution as the weighted average for the region to which the country belongs. The latter group includes almost all countries in SSA.[7]

7.6.2. Estimates

The IFPRI estimates for the five countries which are used by the FAO as 'benchmarks' for estimating distribution of calories are reproduced in Table 7.7. We see that factoring out the within-year variance reduces the total inter-household variance considerably. This indicates that estimates obtained at one point in time only (which most early estimates did) contain selection bias. We also see that the estimated inter-household distribution of calories varies notably between the different surveys.

The main problem with the benchmark studies from IFPRI is that of representativeness. The studies are from five counties only, which may not be representative for the other 100-odd countries underlying the FAO regional POU estimates. Moreover, the small samples from these five countries may

TABLE 7.7. Estimated decomposition of the coefficient of variation (CV) in five household food-consumption surveys conducted by IFPRI researchers

	Kenya	Zambia	Bangla-desh	Philip-pines	Pakistan
Sample size	276	116	301	406	925
Coverage	1 district	10 villages	8 villages	1 district	4 districts
No. of survey rounds	4	12	3	4	6
Reference period	1 day	1 week	1 day	1 day	1 week
Years of survey	1984/5	1985/6	1982/3	1984/5	1986/7
Estimated mean intake (household per-capita)	1,892	2,172	2,232	1,855	2,280
Estimated CV					
Between households	0.17	0.37	0.21	0.26	0.27
Between rounds	0.04	0.08	0.03	0.04	0.14
Residual	0.31	0.32	0.25	0.30	0.38
Total	0.35	0.50	0.33	0.40	0.49

Source: FAO 1992: tables 20 and 22.

not be representative even for these countries. Most notably, the highest disagreement is between the estimates for the two African countries. The between-household estimate for Zambia ($CV = 0.37$) is above the acceptable range set up by the FAO (see footnote 7) and the estimate for Kenya is below ($CV = 0.17$). How the regional estimate for SSA, at 0.30, is projected from these two highly different sample estimates is not made clear by the FAO.

However, after all the manipulation with the national distribution data, when the estimates for individual countries are aggregated to the regional level, only small inter-regional differences in the CVs remain; they are all in the narrow range between 0.28 and 0.32 (FAO 1992: p. 13). It is thus not very surprising that hardly anything of the inter-regional differences in the POU estimates is explained by differences in the estimated distribution of calories between the major regions (see Table 5.4). Almost all the differences in the POU estimates are explained by different estimated per-capita food availabilities. The levels of the POU estimates, on the other hand, are influenced more by the distribution estimates.

7.7. SUMMARY AND CONCLUSIONS

The main conclusion that emerges from the analysis in this chapter is that few definitive, firm conclusions can be drawn. Most of the scant data available on food consumption and food expenditures are simply too unreliable and biased, especially for the African countries. Probably, they are no less unreliable than the FAO *FBS* data. The comparison of these consumption-side and the supply-side data sets, conducted in order to find out more about the 'true' nutritional situation in Africa in international perspective, has thus not carried us very far. The highly tentative and uncertain findings can be summarized in four points.

- Most of the estimates of calorie intakes from FCSs in Africa are likely to be downward biased because the estimation methods tend to encourage underreporting of the food consumed.
- Most of these surveys are non-representative, i.e. conducted on sample populations with below-normal calorie intake at the time of estimation.
- There is a close resemblance between the calorie-consumption estimates from FCSs and *FBS*s, especially for the pre-1980 period. This can either be interpreted as proof of robustness of both estimation methods or, alternatively, that both methods are about equally downward biased, the tentative conclusion we draw here.
- The few *Household Expenditure Studies* available suggest that the poorest households in the African countries have a higher share of high-cost food items in their food expenditures than their counterparts in South Asia. This observation is difficult to reconcile with the significantly higher incidence of undernutrition in Africa than in South Asia, as purported by the FAO.

However, this evidence is too scant, unreliable and, possibly, too unrepresentative to allow more definitive conclusions.

When it comes to the second main objective of this chapter, *viz.* to assess how the estimates derived by the FAO on the distribution of calories across households in different countries have been obtained, at least one affirmative conclusion can be reached. As we have seen, there are only two studies providing estimates of the inter-household distribution of calorie intakes in SSA that are technically acceptable. The two studies are based on small local samples and are not representative of the national population in the countries where they were conducted (and even less so for the other 45 countries in the region). We can thus conclude that there is no empirical basis at all for the distribution data that the FAO uses in its estimation of the POU in Africa (and also some other parts of the world).

NOTES

1. The extensive anthropometric evidence presented in Chapter 11 shows the nutritional status to be significantly better in urban than in rural populations, which implies a larger calorie expenditure for the BMR.
2. Studies from the USA and UK suggest that waste at the household level is in the order of less than 5 per cent. The only study carried out in a developed country that I have come across is for Brazil, which puts waste at around 3 per cent (FAO/ESN 1990).
3. About half of the 68 dietary studies from Africa covered by Schofield (1979: table 4.1) are based on the food 'weightment method'. The remaining surveys rely mainly on stocktaking and recalls.
4. It is further notable that in the Kenyan diet the estimated share of meat is only marginally higher than that in the average African country (see FAO*a* 1996: appendix 2, Table 3).
5. There are also some sample observations suggesting that people with low calorie intakes have cost-inefficient diets; see Shah (1983) and Behrman and Deolalikar (1990).
6. The International Food Policy Research Institute (IFPRI) has emerged as a major research centre for household surveys in developing countries which have gained considerable insights into estimation problems and data requirements (for recent accounts, see von Braun and Puetz (1993) and Bouis and Haddad (1992)).
7. When the FAO obtains an estimate of the coefficient of variation (CV) in the calorie distribution outside the range 0.20–0.35, it adjusts these estimated CVs to 0.20 or 0.35 (the reason for this is explained in FAO 1992: footnote 3).

8

Minimum Calorie-Expenditure Requirements for Individuals

8.1. INTRODUCTION

The per-capita calorie cut-off points (CCOPs) used by the FAO and IBRD in their estimations of the prevalence of undernutrition among households in Africa over the past 20 years have varied from 1460 to 2060 (Table 5.1). Behind these absolute, precise numbers lie a host of different assumptions and estimates of the values of the parameters from which the CCOPs are derived. In essence, the construction of a CCOP entails two main steps. The first is the estimation of the minimum energy requirement that is consistent with health and functional fitness at the level of individuals and households. The problems involved at that stage will be the subject of this chapter. The second step is to aggregate individual energy requirements into the calorie cut-off point. This basically means that one has to estimate the distribution of household per-capita minimum requirements, and also how this distribution is related to the distribution of estimated intakes. The problems encountered at that stage are analysed in Chapter 9.

8.2. ESTIMATING INDIVIDUAL AND HOUSEHOLD MINIMUM ENERGY REQUIREMENTS

8.2.1. Individuals' Minimum Energy Requirements

People need energy (calories) for two main purposes. One is to maintain the internal functions of the body, i.e. heat generation, respiration, blood circulation etc., usually referred to as the basal metabolic rate (BMR). The other is to pursue external physical activity, such as work. The individual's total energy expenditure requirement is conventionally modelled as the product of his physical activity level (PAL) and his BMR. That is, the amount of energy he expends in accomplishing a given level of physical activity is assumed to be proportional to his BMR (as a multiplier). The BMR, in turn, is expressed as a function of his body weight.

The minimum energy expenditures ($E_{it}^{\star}$) at the level of individuals can thus be written as:

$$E_{it}^{\star} = PAL_{it}^{\star}[BMR_{it}(W_{it}^{\star})], \tag{8.1}$$

where subscript i stands for the individual and t for the specified time period. The '$\star$' marks the particular minimum value of the respective parameter that is considered compatible with health and 'economically necessary work'.

8.2.2. From Individuals to Households

The next step in the construction of CCOPs by the FAO and IBRD is to aggregate estimated individual minimum-energy-expenditure requirements to household per-capita minimum requirements ($EH^\star$). These estimates are derived from the following formula:

$$EH_{ht}^\star = \Sigma \varphi_{it} \, PAL_{it}^\star \, [BMR_{it} \, (W_{it}^\star)] \qquad (8.2)$$

where φ_{it} is the weight (share) of individual i during period t of the total energy requirements of household h.

In the construction of their per-capita calorie cut-off points for households, the FAO and IBRD do not provide separate estimates for all the different households (or groups of similar households) in the various populations. What they do is to derive the minimum requirement in a representative household that has a demographic composition equal to that of the total population as a whole in the respective country. That is, the weights (φ_{it}) are derived from the age and gender structure of the population in the respective country, also taking inter-country differences in one anthropometric characteristic into consideration (the average height of adults).

The establishment of minimum values for weight and physical activity is not without problems, as we shall see, but there is broad agreement on some of the issues involved. It is widely agreed that the main determinant of the energy requirement for BMR is body weight. It is also agreed that there are differences in BMR between the sexes and age groups. Women have a somewhat lower BMR than men per kilo of body weight, and it declines with age for both sexes. That energy expenditure for a given physical activity is approximately proportional to the BMR also seems to be non-controversial. In dispute are: (i) what constitutes the minimum acceptable body weight, (ii) the functional form of the relationship between BMR and body weight, and (iii) whether the BMR/kg is constant or can adjust to intake or body weight. These are the issues to be analysed in the next section (8.3). In the subsequent section (8.4) we shall discuss a further controversial issue: (iv) the problems involved in establishing the minimum physical activity level that is consistent with avoidance of undernutrition.

8.3. BODY WEIGHT AND BMR

8.3.1. Minimum Body Weight

Adult Weight   Since weight (W) is strongly correlated to height squared (H^2) in healthy populations, the critical low weight is conventionally derived from the Body Mass Index (BMI):

$$BMI = W(kg)/H^2(m). \tag{8.3}$$

The critical low weight $(W^\star)$ for an adult individual is thus determined by the 'acceptable' body mass index $(BMI^\star)$ and his *de facto* height (H):

$$W^\star = BMI^\star H^2 \tag{8.4}$$

The $BMI^\star$ that the international organizations have found appropriate has changed considerably over time. The calorie norms used by the IBRD (see Table 5.2) were constructed using a $BMI^\star$ of 22. In the *Fifth World Food Survey* (FAO*a* 1985), the $BMI^\star$ was 20. The most recent estimates put $BMI^\star$ at 18.5 (James and Schofield 1990, Waterlow 1992), and this figure is also underlying the construction of the CCOPs for the *Sixth World Food Survey* (FAO*a* 1996).

There are two fundamentally different principles behind the IBRD and the FAO approaches to the derivation of acceptable weight norms. Which approach is the more suitable depends on what question is posed. If the question is normative, i.e. how much food (calories) do people in a developing countries need to have a body weight (and work intensity; see below) that one may find desirable (e.g. the 'normal' weight in developed countries), the IBRD approach is justifiable. If the question is positive, i.e. what body weight (and PAL) is necessary in order to avoid health and functional impairment, the FAO approach is more appropriate. Since the interest in this study is undernutrition from a medical point of view, not 'desirable' food standards in a normative sense, we will focus solely on the FAO approach in the following.

The lowering of the $BMI^\star$ by the FAO, from 20.0 to 18.5, merits some comment. Only some ten year ago, the FAO and the international nutritionist research community were in broad agreement that the critical weight for height corresponded to a BMI of around 20. This notion was based on evidence from the developed countries, not least a very large investigation of the relationship between BMI and excess mortality in Norway (Waaler 1984). That study shows mortality to pick up notably already at BMI 21.0, both for men and women. However, there is at least one serious limitation with the Norwegian study (and also similar other ones): it does not control for influences other than BMI on excess death risk. It may well be that thin people with high mortality risk in developed countries (where primary undernutrition is not a problem) are overrepresented by individuals suffering from chronic disease, with abnormal smoking and drinking habits, etc., which give rise to wasting and excess mortality simultaneously (Thuluvath and Triger 1994).

The new evidence that the FAO refers to when lowering $BMI^\star$ from 20 to 18.5 comprises a handful of studies in which a significant share of 'apparently healthy and productive' individuals in developing country samples have been found to have a BMI around 18.5, and some even below that, in the 15–16 range. (See FAO*a* 1996: Appendix 4 for a brief but succinct summary of the new evidence.) A *BMI** equal to 18.5 may thus be consistent with health and functional fitness (for otherwise healthy people), but there is no firm evidence from developing countries to show that health risks are picking up considerably at this very weight for height; and no causal links have been proved. (It is notable that the lowest BMI compatible with life is 12, as suggested by clinical evidence (James *et al.* 1988).)

There is also the question of body weight as an 'insurance' mechanism. Many poor people in the developing countries face the risk of involuntary sudden decline in weight in the wake of illness or economic shocks—with subsequent increased overall health risks. One may thus argue that in developing countries, where morbidity is substantially higher than in developed countries, and where credit and insurance markets are non-existent or imperfect (Dasgupta 1993), poor people must have a buffer in the form of some 'excess' weight. There are also seasonal swings in work intensity that have to be countered by changes in body weight if people are poor and credit markets are imperfect. From this perspective, a *BMI** of 18.5 may seem unduly low. One cannot, however, raise the critical low body weight to take such risks into consideration without invoking normative value judgements of what degree of 'insurance' the weight norm should allow for and what alternative insurance mechanisms one should consider in different countries.

Nevertheless, the gradual lowering of the *BMI** by the FAO, from 22.0 to 18.5, has meant substantial downward revisions of the critical low weight for adult men and women. As can be seen from Table 8.1, this weight for average height (the 50 percentile) has been lowered from 62 to 52 kg for adult men in Africa. For women the corresponding reduction is from 54 to 46 kg. In relative terms, this means a 16 and 14 per cent decline, respectively.

The convention that energy expenditure for physical activity is estimated as a multiple of the BMR, and the latter as a monotonic positive function of body weight (see equation 8.1), make the choice of minimum body weight for adults essential. If this weight is set too high or too low, the bias thus induced in total energy requirement will be magnified by the convention of estimating energy expenditures for physical activity as multiples of weight.

TABLE 8.1. Estimated critical lower weight for adults (men and women) with different heights and lowest acceptable BMI

Height men/women (cm) in the SSA	Centile	Lowest acceptable weight					
		Men (BMI)			Women (BMI)		
		22.0	20.0	18.5	22.0	20.0	18.5
168/157	50	62	56	52	54	49	46
159/148	5	56	51	47	48	44	41

Source: Height data from Jürgens *et al.* 1990.

Height of Adults   In the *Fifth* and *Sixth World Food Surveys*, the FAO has used the average actual heights of adults in the various populations in the world as norms in the construction of the CCOPs. (Once grown up, a person's height cannot be altered by their eating more.) An alternative, which would be more consistent with the 'critical minimum' approach used by the FAO to define the critical minimum weight (for given height) would be to set the reference height at the low end of the distribution (at say the fifth centile (159 cm) rather than at the average (168 cm); see Table 8.1).

Children's Weight   In the *Fifth World Food Survey* (FAO*a* 1985), the reference weight for age for children was set at the '*lower limit* of the range of acceptable weight for height' for sound and healthy children in the Western countries (NCHS reference sample). In the *Sixth World Food Survey* (FAO*a* 1996: table 5, appendix 3), the reference child weight is set at a level corresponding to 'the *median* of acceptable weight for height' (italics added). This new practice is in violation of the basic 'critical minimum' approach that was followed earlier (and is still applied to adults), and also in contrast to the worldwide accepted method to assess children's nutritional status by anthropometric devices. The standard cut-off points used in anthropometric studies for children is 90 per cent of median height for age and 80 per cent of median weight for age of the reference population. (Or alternatively, at two SDs below the median NCHS reference norm, which corresponds to the third to fifth centiles of the reference population.)

   Why the FAO does not apply the same 'critical minimal' approach that it uses for adults in deriving calorie requirements for children is not made clear. The reason seems to be a notion that children are more vulnerable to nutritional stress than adolescents and adults. However, there is some evidence on nutritional (anthropometric) status of children and subsequent morbidity and mortality which can be used to find the 'critical minimal' weight and height for children that are safe (Pelletier 1994; this and related evidence is analysed more thoroughly in Chapter 14).

8.3.2. Body Weight and BMR

One model of the relationship between BMR and body weight takes the form of a linear equation with a positive intercept; this is the model underlying the FAO/WHO/UNUs (1985: table 42) estimates of BMR. This model implies that as body weight falls, the estimated total BMR declines less than proportionally and the BMR/kg goes up. With this model specification, the estimated BMR/kg for small people (in developing countries) is thus higher than for large people (in developed countries). The main theoretical support for this model (i.e. higher BMR/kg in small people) is that the energy expenditure for each and every specific basal body function (organ) is more or less fixed, but that the 'sum' alters with changes in body composition as weight changes. That is, as weight decreases (for a given height), the ratio of fat to lean body tissue normally goes down and the energy expenditure for the maintenance of fat stores is lower than for the sustenance of the functions of lean body tissue (see Soares and Shetty 1991).

Others have argued that a quadratic (concave) relationship between BMR and body weight has a stronger theoretical underpinning (cf. next subsection) and/or fits the empirical observations better. Still others have suggested that BMR should be estimated on the basis of a more extensive model, including variables such as height and body composition, e.g. fat/lean body tissues (Butte *et al.* 1995). The conventional wisdom of today, however, seems to be that the results are not significantly affected by the choice of functional form and/or the inclusion of variables in addition to weight, as suggested by a comprehensive review of the world literature (Schofield 1985).

8.3.3. Intra-individual Adaptation of Metabolism

Most nutritionists, whether they tend to lean towards the Adjustment and Adaptation or the Genetic Potential paradigms of undernutrition, would probably accept that there is a range over which the individual can adjust their body weight (and PAL) without harmful effects on health and functions. (The differences are in what exact low body weight and physical activity level should be acceptable.) A more controversial issue is whether the human body can adapt permanently to low energy intakes by lowering energy expenditures for the BMR. Several nutritionists claim that there is a mechanism that reduces metabolism when weight goes down, i.e. there is phenotypic adaptation to low intake over time. There are basically two possible ways in which this could happen.

One is that there is an increase in pure metabolic 'efficiency'. It is important to note that what is argued is that the adaptation takes place within a certain range without any 'costs' in terms of health impairment or reduced work capacity (Sukhatme and Margen 1982). The other mechanism is that when food intake declines, the body reduces the energy 'wasted' in thermogenesis (heat production). Sukhatme and Margen (1982) and Srinivasan (1983) argue that heat generation is a large and flexible part of total energy expenditure, not small and fixed as postulated, for instance, by the FAO/WHO (1973), FAO (1992) and FAOa (1996). In the case in which the energy dissipated as heat is substantial and will be regulated through homeostasis, 'energy requirements for BMR are not constants, but must be designed in a probabilistic sense' (Srinivasan 1983: p. 9).

In its study from 1986, the IBRD did not allow for intra-individual adaptation of metabolism in the construction of the CCOPs. The FAO has changed its position on this issue back and forth over the years. In the *Fourth World Food Survey* (FAOa 1975), the CCOPs were established with no allowance for intra-individual adaptation. In the *Fifth World Food Survey* (FAOa 1985) an ambivalent approach was adopted. One set of POU estimates were derived on the assumption of considerable intra-individual lowering of metabolism (per kg of body weight) when energy intake and body weight decline. Another set of POU estimates were derived on the assumption of no adaptation of metabolism. (The different assumptions concerning adaptation alone accounted for a huge difference in the estimated POU; see Chapter 5, Table 5.4.) In the *Sixth World Food Survey* (FAO*a* 1996), the organization is back at its position of 20 years earlier: intra-individual differences in metabolism are not thought to be large enough to warrant consideration.

It is very much debated, both at the theoretical and empirical levels, whether there can be intra-individual adaptation to low intake (Dasgupta and Ray 1990, Osmani 1990, 1992*b*). An increasing number of scholars seem to accept the possibility (e.g. Srinivasan 1981, 1992, Payne 1992), while many others do not (Beaton 1983*a*, Waterlow 1990*b*, Gopalan 1992). The empirical evidence on intra-individual adaptation available so far does not permit a definitive stand one way or the other.

There are experimental studies that show BMR/kg to *decline* with lower body weight (Serog *et al.* 1982, Bessard *et al.* 1983, Barrows and Snook 1987). However, when changes in body composition (lean to fat body tissue ratio) are controlled for, most studies find 'no evidence for adaptive thermogenesis' (Ravussin *et al.* 1985, Davies *et al.* 1989, Bianca *et al.* 1994). Still other studies find reductions in body-composition-corrected metabolism at rest at low weights (Bessard *et al.* 1983, Barrows and Snook 1987). The divergent results seem to be at least partly explained by the fact that in some studies the lower thermic effect of food digestion at small intake has been considered, in other studies not.

It thus appears that, so far, no conclusive evidence exists of intra-individual adaptation to habitually low food intake. In order to settle this question definitely, 'more prolonged monitoring would seem to be necessary to establish that very low calorie diets are responsible for a reduction in total dietary-induced thermogenesis' (Davies *et al.* 1989, also see Healy 1989, James 1989, Waterlow 1992). Before this is done it does not seem scientifically possible to take a definitive stand, as the FAO has done, one way or the other concerning intra-individual adaptation of metabolism.[1]

8.3.4. *Inter-individual Variance in Metabolism*

Many earlier studies found inter-individual differences in metabolism between people of the same weight/sex/age/race to be in the 7–9 per cent range. In most of these investigations, however, no controls of different ratios of fat/lean body mass and water content in the body were made. Later studies have found that when these factors are controlled for the coefficient of variation is around 2 per cent; the difference that can be attributed to genetic factors thus seems to be almost negligible (James *et al.* 1988: p. 971, Nelson

1989, Waterlow 1992). The FAO*a* (1996) has not explicitly considered inter-individual differences in metabolism in its CCOP estimates.

8.3.5. Inter-ethnic Variance in Metabolism

The evidence on metabolism in different populations summarized in the survey by Schofield (1985) is still the most extensive source of information on this subject. The studies surveyed are mainly from developed countries, although they include a small subsample of data from developing countries. The latter show the estimated BMR/kg to be on average 10 per cent lower (average for different age and gender groups) in Asian, African and Latin American populations than in Caucasian populations. More recent and extensive surveys of evidence on metabolism in Third World populations also found it to be lower than in Caucasians (Henry and Rees 1991, Bianca *et al.* 1994, Hayter and Henry 1994). The results are consistent across studies and methods.

In setting up their reference BMR, the FAO*a* (1996) uses the information on BMR from Schofield which is almost exclusively from developed countries and Italy in particular, where the BMR in the population, as estimated, is exceptionally high even by developed country standards (Hayter and Henry 1994). The FAO does not allude to, or allow for, inter-racial differences. Ignoring this factor implies that the CCOPs for the populations in the developing regions are set about 10 per cent higher (recalling that energy expenditures for physical activity are calculated as a multiple of BMR). However, so far it has not been possible to say whether the main explanation is geneotypic differences along ethnic lines, phenotypic adaptation to lower intakes (*à la* Sukhatme; cf. above), or different climatological environments (on the latter possibility, see Askew 1995). Studies of metabolism in people migrating between 'tropical' and 'temperate' regions is a promising way to find out, but the available evidence is so far too scant to permit any definitive answers (see Hayter and Henry 1993).

8.4.   MINIMUM PHYSICAL ACTIVITY

To estimate the minimum level of physical activity that a person must pursue in order to avoid undernutrition is by far the most difficult task in establishing minimum energy requirements for individuals. Physical activity has two main facets that both have to be considered. One is that a person has to undertake some physical activity in order to maintain cardiovascular, respiratory and muscular fitness. The other is that he or she normally must pursue some (physical) work activity to earn an income that permits him/her to eat.

8.4.1. *Biological Minimum Physical Activity Requirement for Adults*

There seems to be rather wide agreement among physiological nutritionists that the minimum level of physical activity that is consistent with health and physical fitness corresponds to about 1.40 times the BMR during non-sleeping hours (or 1.27 over the 24 hours). An energy expenditure of this size allows for sitting up or strolling around pursuing very light household chores, but not for any physical work beyond that (FAO/WHO/UNU 1985, James and Schofield 1990).

8.4.2. *Economical Minimum Physical Activity Requirement for Adults*

The second facet that has to be considered is that most people (especially in poor countries) have to be engaged in at least some manual physical work in order to earn an income that is sufficient to buy (or produce) the food required for BMR and the work activity itself (as the model in Chapter 3 shows more formally). This is where the most tricky part of establishing the critical low energy expenditure norm comes in, and where the lack of an established estimation methodology is the most glaring.

The FAO and IBRD have taken different approaches when it comes to determining energy requirements for external physical activity. The IBRD (1986) study sets the PAL at 1.67 (times BMR), derived as 90 per cent of the recommended daily intakes (RDI) as estimated by FAO/WHO (1973). A PAL of this size implies that the adult person in less-developed countries can engage in rather heavy manual labour for 7 hours per day. At the other extreme, the FAO*a* (1985), sets the PAL at 1.4 (times the *BMR*), which allows for very little physical work activity.[2] In the *Sixth World Food Survey* (FAO*a* 1996), the PAL multiple is set at 1.55 times the BMR for men and at 1.56 for women, which allows for light work activity for normal hours.

Even the most casual observation of any (poor) population reveals that the economic return of physical work effort differs substantially among individuals because of differences in their physical productive assets (land, capital, etc.), their human capital, and a host of other factors. (This was analysed more formally in Chapter 3.) The lowest PAL that permits the person to avoid undernutrition is thus highly individual-specific; it can easily vary from 500 to 2,000 calories expended per day for an adult man (see section 8.5 below).

In a 'critical minimal' perspective, it is difficult to imagine how a substantial part of the adult population in Africa, in which up to 70 per cent are engaged in non-mechanized agriculture and related activities, should be able to work much less than is implied by a PAL of 1.55 without affecting health. A 1.55 BMR is well below the 1.67 BMR used in the IBRD study and it is notably above the 1.40 times BMR that allows for very modest physical activity. A PAL of 1.55 may enable some individuals to earn a basic living, given the present limited knowledge about the distribution of the minimum workload necessary for economical survival in any one population. It has to be remembered, however, that this exact level of PAL is not derived from any theoretical model (or reasoning) and the FAO has not presented any empirical support whatsoever for this particular number.[3]

There is some empirical information on the actual physical activity level (PAL), as measured by the DLW method (the only reliable one) of 'free-living' adult individuals in developing countries, but it is extremely scant. In their assessment of 574 DLW measurements of PAL, Black et al. (1996) report only six from such countries; the rest are from 'affluent societies'. The average PAL observed in these six populations ranges from 1.61 for poor non-working Guatemalan mothers to 3.02 for Gambian male labourers (see Table 8.2). The averages, minus 2 SD, suggest PALs in the lower tail of the distributions below 1.27 in all of the three female samples, and around 1.60 in the male ones. These numbers suggest that the PALs in the lower tails for people of working age are in accordance with the FAO PAL for males (1.54), but not for women (1.55). The number of observations is far too scant, however, to permit any reliable conclusions regarding the validity of the FAO 'guesstimates'.[4]

8.4.3. Minimum Physical Activity for Children

The physical activity allowed for children in developing countries by the most recent FAOa (1996) norm is based on estimated actual calorie intake of 'sound and healthy' children in Western populations. (In FAOa 1985, an upward allowance by five per cent was made on the notion that nowadays Western children are not active enough, but this was abolished in 1996) It is notable that this estimation procedure is not in line with the 'critical minimum' approach that is followed by the FAO in most other instances, particularly for adults. There are studies indicating that children's mental and

TABLE 8.2. Estimated PAL in free-living subjects with the DLW method in developing countries

Subjects	Estimated Physical Activity Level (PAL)		
	Average	SD	Average −2 SD
(1) 15 poor Guatemalan mothers[a]	1.61	0.17	1.27
(2) 6 thin Chilean male labourers	1.78	0.13	1.52
(3) 10 Gambian women farmers	1.97	0.40	1.17
(4) 7 Gambian women farmers	1.74	0.32	1.10
(5) 16 Gambian male labourers	2.96	0.66	1.64
(6) 16 Gambian male labourers	3.02	0.70	1.62

[a] Not working.

Source: Black et al. 1996: appendix table.

psychomotoric development can be delayed and impaired in the absence of physical activity, but few (if any) such studies find the impairment to set in immediately below the physical activity level of the *average* 'sound and healthy child' in the West (see Chapter 14).

It is further noteworthy that there is a growing literature that indicates that energy expenditures in children in the developed countries, as measured by the DLW method, are significantly below previous estimates and current recommendations (Davies *et al.* 1995 and references therein). The authors argue, however, that 'the reasons for the differences should be thoroughly investigated before major changes are made to international [i.e. FAO/WHO/UNU] or domestic recommendations for energy requirements' (ibid: p. 364).

8.4.4. Sensitivity of Requirement Norms

In this subsection we shall demonstrate how wide the differences in estimated minimum 'energy requirement' will be depending on what values we attach to the 'critical minimum' height, body weight, BMR/kg and PAL. We shall derive the total minimum energy expenditures for adult men, using different values of these entities. The results are reported in Table 8.3. We have four men who differ in height and body weight. The man depicted in the first column is 168 cm tall, which is the average for African adult men, and weighs 56.6 kilos (implying a BMI of 20). Depending on how much he works (the PAL) and what his metabolic rate is (BMR/kg/day), he has a total daily energy expenditure of between 1,839 and 2,248 calories. The man in the second

TABLE 8.3. Estimated daily calorie-expenditure requirement for adult men in Sub-Saharan Africa for different height, weight, BMR, and PAL

	Height/weight combination			
Height (m)	1.68	1.68	1.59	1.59
Weight (kg)	56.6	52.2	50.6	46.8
BMI	20.0	18.5	20.0	18.5
	(1)	(2)	(3)	(4)
(a) PAL = 1.55				
BMR/kg/day				
25.8	2,248	2,074	2,010	1,859
23.2	2,022	1,865	1,809	1,672
(b) PAL = 1.40				
BMR/kg/day				
25.8	2,044	1,886	1,827	1,690
23.2	1,839	1,695	1,644	1,520

Sources: Heights: Jürgens *et al.* 1990 (see Table 8.1). Weights: derived from a BMI of 20.0 and 18.5, respectively. BMR/kg/day: FAO/WHO/UNU 1985: table 42 (25.8) and a 10 per cent lower figure (23.2), based either on intra-individual adaptation or lower metabolism in non-Caucasian populations (see text). PAL: FAO*a* 1996 (1.55) and FAO*a* 1985 (1.40).

column is different from the first in one respect: he has a lower weight (corresponding to a BMI of 18.5). The men in columns (3) and (4) are shorter; their stature is 159 cm only (corresponding to the 5th centile in the African population). The highest estimate (2,248 calories) in Table 8.3 is almost 50 per cent larger than the lowest (1,520). The estimated minimum energy requirement for individuals is thus highly sensitive to the values of height, BMI, BMR/kg, and PAL that one starts out with.

8.5. SUMMARY AND CONCLUSIONS

Estimation of the minimum energy expenditures that mark undernutrition in an individual entails several steps that are not easily resolved scientifically, and there is no consensus on most of the issues. On some of the issues involved, the FAO*a* (1996) has chosen values of the 'exogenous' parameters that are at the low end of what seems to be the range over which there is controversy. FAO has chosen a critical minimum body weight for adults using a BMI of 18.5, which seems low if one accepts the 'insurance' aspect of body weight. The FAO has also chosen a critical minimum physical work activity that adults must pursue in order to avoid undernutrition that may seem low in countries where most adults are engaged in non-mechanized agricultural activities. However, the main problem here is that there is no empirical foundation whatsoever.

In other instances, the FAO has used parameter values that are at the high end of the disputed range. First, the FAO has not made any allowance at all for intra-individual adaptation to low calorie intakes. This is an 'extreme' assumption considering that this controversial issue is far from resolved. Secondly, the FAO has not made an adjustment for the nowadays rather well-documented observation that BMR per kg of body weight in non-Caucasian populations is lower than in Caucasians. Thirdly, the FAO has assigned (high) values to the *minimum critical* energy expenditure requirement for children below the age of five that has little support in the mainstream scientific literature.

The simple exercise conducted in section 8.5 above illustrates the sensitivity of individual energy requirements to the assumptions made with respect to minimum body weight, the relation between BMR and body weight, intra- and inter-individual differences in BMR, and the minimum required physical work activity.

The main problem with the individual energy requirement norms produced by the FAO is not that they are based on 'wrong' assumptions and parameter values. The main problem is that today there are no scientific ways of finding out what the 'right' parameter values are in most instances (e.g. concerning intra-individual adaptation to low intakes and 'necessary' work activity). For as long as these and some related problems remain unresolved, the whole exercise of estimating calorie requirement norms for individuals will continue to be highly ambiguous and, perhaps, futile.

NOTES

1. In FAOa (1996: p. 37), it is claimed that 'recent research has led to a growing consensus that, for a person with a given body weight and level of activity, the range of any possible variation in the metabolic efficiency of energy utilised is very small.' The FAO refrains, however, from citing this 'new evidence'.
2. This is the approach suggested by Sukhatme (1978) and endorsed by Cutler and Payne (1984).
3. The difficulties encountered in trying to estimate an 'economically necessary' work activity level were the chief reason why no such activity was allowed for in the CCOPs established by the FAOa (1985) in its *Fifth World Food Survey*. In the *Sixth Survey* (FAOa 1996: p.37) it is claimed that 'Today, more detailed information is available' and a reference to James and Schofield (1990) is provided. This book contains very extensive and valuable information on calorie expenditure requirements for a large number of job activities that are common in developing countries, but the question of how to derive the energy expenditures that are 'economically necessary' is not dealt with.
4. The large number of studies carried out in the 'affluent societies' are with few exceptions confined to such small samples that the within-sample variance has little meaning. Moreover, estimation methods and the criteria for selecting the observed individuals (e.g. age, sex, lean/obese, etc.) vary a great deal across the studies. About 40 samples comprise 'free-living' individuals in 'non-special conditions' (such as athletes) for which BMR has been measured, not estimated. In these samples, a very high proportion of the average group estimates of PAL for males falls in the relatively narrow range 1.65–1.85 and in the range 1.54–1.67 for females (Black *et al.* 1996: appendix table).

9

From Individual Calorie Requirements to Per-capita Calorie Cut-off Points

9.1. INTRODUCTION

Different households in a population have different minimum per-capita energy requirements. One reason is that different individuals of the same sex and age, as discussed in Chapter 8 above, have different minimum energy requirements due to differences in stature and work activities. Different households also have different age and gender compositions, which influence their per-capita requirements. Consequently, in any one population, there will be a distribution of minimum household per-capita energy requirements. Moreover, actual calorie intakes are also distributed unevenly across households and this distribution and the distribution of requirements are interrelated. In order to obtain an unbiased estimate of the share of households that are undernourished in a population, i.e. have an actual per-capita intake that is below their particular household requirement, we need household-specific data on both the distributions of habitual intake and of requirement.

Unfortunately, there is not a single data set available in which these household-specific intakes and requirements have been estimated simultaneously in a Third-World population. Therefore, in order to provide estimates of the prevalence of undernutrition in a population, several assumptions have to be made regarding the joint distribution between intakes and requirements that have no empirical base. In this chapter we shall probe into the difficulties in obtaining reasonably unbiased household energy requirement norms and, thus, POU estimates, when the base data are largely lacking.

The plan of the chapter is as follows. In section 9.2, a hypothetical case for when perfect data are available will be analysed and contrasted with the *de facto* situation with less-than-perfect data. In section 9.3, the assumptions made by the FAO, in its attempt to estimate the CCOPs that are subsequently used to delineate the undernourished, are scrutinized. In section 9.4, we point to a flaw in the construction of CCOPs which has not been recognized previously and which is likely to have induced a relatively large bias in the POU estimates. A short summary and some concluding remarks are offered in section 9.5.

9.2.   CALORIE CUT-OFF POINTS AND REQUIREMENT/INTAKE DISTRIBUTION

9.2.1.   Estimating the Prevalence of Undernutrition in the Ideal Situation

As a benchmark case, let us start by analysing the 'ideal situation' when it comes to estimating POU at the household level in a large population. The ideal situation is when we have correct information on the actual distribution of calorie intakes across households and we also know their minimum energy requirements (both on a per-capita basis).

The ideal situation can be illustrated in Fig. 9.1A. Along the horizontal axis, the households with the lowest (x) to the highest per-capita requirements $(\bar{x})$ are ranked from the left to the right, with a mean at $X^\star$. The households with the lowest minimum household per-capita calorie requirements (HPCCR) are those with a high proportion of small children—who have low energy needs (small bodies)—and where the adults are engaged in light physical work activities which are relatively well-paid, signifying that they do not have to work very hard to satisfy the minimum food needs of the household. The households at the higher end of the distribution comprise mostly adults and adolescents and most members of the households are engaged in low-paid heavy manual work activities, which means that they have to work hard for long hours to earn the income that is required to 'survive economically'. The households near the mean of the distribution are likely to have a 'normal' demographic composition (i.e. similar to the average for the population) and to be engaged in medium strenuous physical work activities that earn average incomes.

The actual habitual per-capita intake of respective households is measured along the vertical axis. The range is from a low intake of y to a high intake of $\bar{y}$, with a mean at $Y^\star$. The ellipse encloses the distribution of household intake/requirements. That the distribution is depicted as an ellipse, stretching out in the south-west to north-east direction, reflects an assumption that there is a positive (but not perfect) correlation between household intake and requirement in the population. Furthermore, it is assumed—for the time being—that the households are evenly distributed within the ellipse.[1] The dot in the middle of the ellipse marks the intersection of average household intake and average requirement in the population. Average per-capita intake is assumed to be higher than the average per-capita minimum requirement $(Y^\star > X^\star)$, which is the actual situation in all major geographical regions of the world—except SSA—according to FAO estimates (although not all individual countries; see FAO 1997a). This means that the largest part of the area within the ellipse lies to the north of the 45° line.

The households above the 45° line have a higher habitual calorie intake than they require to avoid undernutrition. The households on the line have intakes that exactly match their minimum requirements. The households

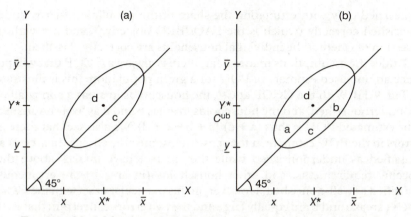

FIG. 9.1. Model for the estimation of prevalence of undernutrition when
household requirements are known and when they are not known

below the 45° line have intakes that fail to meet their specific requirements.
In the hypothetical case of perfect information about household-specific
requirements and actual intakes, an unbiased measure of the prevalence of
undernutrition in the population is area c as a ratio of the areas c + d in Figure
9.1A. That is, the households whose actual habitual intakes fall below their
household-specific minimum requirements as a share of the total number of
households in the population. It is notable that there is no need to construct
a CCOP in this case of perfect information; we simply count the number of
households with intakes that fall below their household-specific energy requirements (the 45° line). That number related to the total population gives
us an unbiased measure of the POU.

9.2.2. Estimating Undernutrition in the Actual Situation

The reality which we face is that there is not a single data set on household-
specific minimum energy requirements and actual intakes in a Third World
population. We only know *a priori* that the per-capita minimum requirement
must differ across households (for reasons discussed above). We have some
imperfect knowledge about the shape of the distribution of calorie intakes
across households (see Chapter 7) and the mean (see Chapter 6); but no information whatsoever about how the intake distribution relates to the requirement distribution (Kakwani 1992, Srinivasan 1992).

In order to illustrate how the POU is estimated in the actual situation, we
turn to Fig. 9.1B. Assume as before that the true per-capita requirement/
intake distribution is encompassed within an ellipse and that the observations are perfectly evenly spread within this area. (The latter assumption will
be relaxed later on.) The difference now is that we do not know the require-
ment/intake vector of the individual households. Suppose further that we are

concerned only with estimating the share of the population that is under-nourished correctly (which is the FAO/IBRD objective), and not with the question of whether the individual households are correctly classified.

Under the assumptions made so far, there is always a CCOP that will produce an unbiased estimate of POU for a given population; this is illustrated in Fig. 9.1B. With the CCOP at C^{ub}, the households in areas a and c fall out as 'undernourished' and the households in areas b and d as 'well-nourished'. The estimated POU is thus $(a + c)/(a + b + c + d)$. We also see that there are errors in the POU estimate in the sense that some households (in area a) are classified as undernourished while they in fact have intakes above their specific requirements, and other households (in area b) are erroneously classified as well-nourished. However, in this particular case, with the CCOP at C^{ub}, areas a and b are equally large and the two errors cancel out; that is, the type II error (area a) and type I error (area b) are of equal size, but with different signs, which leaves the POU estimate unbiased.

9.3.   THE FAO AND IBRD CALORIE CUT-OFF POINTS

In estimating the POU in the various regions of the world, the FAO and IBRD face a situation like the one depicted in Fig. 9.1B. They have data on the mean and variance of the household calorie-intake distribution, although these data are far from perfect (as we saw in Chapters 6 and 7). They do not have any empirically supported data on the distribution of per-capita household requirements and, consequently, none on how the intake and requirement distributions interrelate. They assume for good reasons that there is a positive correlation between household intake and requirement, but they do not know the correlation coefficient and the correlation slope. In the absence of these crucial data, the two organizations' objective, i.e. to find the CCOP that makes the two unavoidable errors cancel out (C^{ub} in Fig. 9.1B), is a mission impossible, as we shall see in this section.

9.3.1. Comparing FAO with IBRD

The effect on the estimated POU of the different CCOPs chosen by the IBRD and the FAO can be illustrated with the help of Fig. 9.2A and 9.2B. We retain the assumption that the 'true' distribution of intakes and requirements in the particular population under study is represented by the ellipse. In the case of the high IBRD cut-off point, at C^{IBRD} in Fig. 9.2A, which is close to the average requirement ($X^\star$), the households in areas a and c fall out as un-dernourished. The type I error is represented by area b and the type II error by area a. The bias in the POU estimate is thus $(a - b)/(a + b + c + d) > 0$, which means that the POU is overestimated.

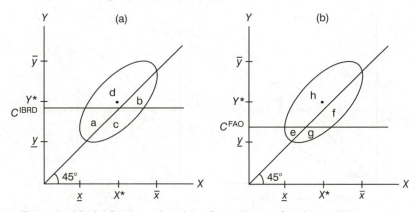

FIG. 9.2. Model for the estimation of prevalence of undernutrition; errors and biases related to choice of cut-off point

Other things being equal, a lower CCOP, used by the FAO and corresponding to C^{FAO} in Fig. 9.2B, means that (i) the estimated POU becomes smaller ($e + g < a + c$) and (ii) a downward bias is induced ($e - f < 0$). From this example one cannot conclude, however, that the FAO method to derive CCOPs always leads to lower POU estimates than does the Bank method; this depends on other factors as well (to be discussed in subsequent subsections).

In the construction of their respective CCOPs, the IBRD and the FAO have only been guided by what they find reflects the minimum per-capita requirement that is consistent with health and functional fitness for a household with the 'average' demographic composition. Given this approach, it is not surprising that the differences in CCOPs derived for different regions of the Third World varies so little, ranging from 1,790 in South Asia to 1,880 in East Asia (China) and South-East Asia: this is only a 5 per cent difference (FAO*a* 1996: table 16). These minor differences are explained only by differences in average adult height (smallest in Asia) and in the demographic composition of the average household (e.g. the largest proportion of small children is in Africa). No other concerns seems to have influenced the estimated differences in the regional CCOPs.

What is forgotten in this endeavour is that the objective with the CCOP is to produce unbiased POU estimates, nothing else. As we shall see in the following subsections, in order to obtain unbiased POU estimates, the construction of the CCOPs must take into consideration factors in addition to the minimum requirements for health and 'economic needs' for the household with the 'average' demographic composition and work intensity.

9.3.2. The Inter-linkage between the CCOP and the NPCCA

Consider now the two cases depicted in Fig. 9.3A and B. They can be taken to illustrate the situation in two countries (A and B) which differ in one

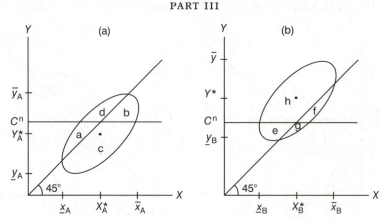

FIG. 9.3. Model for the estimation of prevalence of undernutrition;
errors and biases related to differences in NPCCA

respect only: they have different per-capita calorie availabilities and, thus, average intake (as measured along the vertical axes). They have the same requirement distribution (mean and variance) and the same distribution of the intake around different means (Y_A^* and Y_B^*, respectively). The distribution sets—the ellipses—are thus identical in shape, the only difference being this set lies further to the north in country B, with the higher per-capita calorie availability. If the same CCOP is applied to the two countries, say C^n, we see that in country A, with the low average calorie availability (Y_A^*), the bias induced is towards an underestimation of the POU (area $a - b < 0$). In country B, with a relatively higher average calorie intake (Y_B^*), the bias goes in the other direction, i.e. there is an overestimation of the POU (area $e - f > 0$).

In order to obtain an unbiased estimate of the POU in country A, the CCOP should be set somewhat higher than C^n (so that areas a and b become of equal size). For the estimated POU to be unbiased in country B, the CCOP should be set lower than C^n. *That is, even when two countries have the same calorie-requirement distribution (mean and variance), the CCOPs that produce unbiased POU estimates will be different.* This has not been allowed for in the POU estimates produced by the FAO. Since the estimated NPCCA varies from 1,590 in the most destitute SSA country to 3,510 in Turkey (FAO*a* 1996: appendix 2, table 1), the choice of (approximately) the same CCOP for all countries is bound to induce biases of different sizes in the POU estimates that distort the comparability across regions and countries.

In the cases depicted in Fig. 9.3, the application of one and the same CCOP leads to underestimation of the POU in the country (A) with low food availabilities and the high true incidence of undernutrition (area c + b) and overestimation of POU in the country (B) with more plentiful food supplies and a lower prevalence of true undernutrition (g + f). That is, the true difference in POU between the two countries is larger than the estimated difference. However, for CCOPs other than C^n, there may be biases in other directions, or the biases may be in the same direction, but of different sizes. The concluding point here is not that we can say that the application of (approximately) the same CCOP for all countries (regions) by the FAO has meant that there is a systematic tendency to underestimate POU in the countries with low food supplies and to overestimate POU in more food-abundant countries. The point is simply that, inevitably, there will be biases when one and the same CCOP is used irrespective of differences in food supplies.

9.3.3. *CCOPs with Different Requirement and Intake Distributions*

To complicate things further, the relative size of the type I and II errors also depend on the relative variance in the distribution of intakes and requirements, respectively. To illustrate this point, suppose that we have two countries, C and D, where average intake and average requirement are the same. In Fig. 9.4A, we have country C, where the range within which the actual intakes of households vary (between $\underline{y}_c$ and $\bar{y}_c$) is smaller than the range within which minimum requirements vary ($\underline{x}_c$ and $\bar{x}_c$). In country D (Fig. 9.4B), the opposite relation holds, i.e. the spread of actual intakes is larger than the spread of requirements. The correlation slope, however, is positive in both countries: it is smaller than unity in country C and larger than unity in country D.

Let us now compare the two situations. There will be an underestimation of the POU in country C (Fig. 9.4A), with a relatively low spread in intakes but a large spread in requirements (area a – b < 0). In country D (Fig. 9.4B), where the largest variance is in intakes, area e exceeds area f, and the POU estimate is upward biased. Again, the CCOP in country C must be raised somewhat above C^n if the POU estimate should be unbiased and *vice versa* in country D. One and the same CCOP cannot produce unbiased estimates in

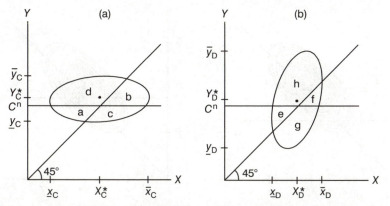

FIG. 9.4. Model for the estimation of prevalence of undernutrition; errors and biases related to differences in the distributions of intakes and requirements

two countries (populations) where the intake and requirement distributions are different. This is so even when the two countries have the same average intake and requirement. Since there are no data on either the variance in requirement or the correlation slope, there is no possibility that the FAO can have obtained 'correct' values of these parameters in the construction of the CCOPs (see Svedberg 1999*b* for more detail).

9.3.4. *Introducing Normal Distribution of Intake and Requirement*

In the analysis so far we have retained one simplifying assumption throughout: that the intake/requirement distribution is perfectly even within an 'ellipse'. This is, of course, not the case in any real population, but we know rather little about the actual distributions anywhere. A fair assumption is that the highest density is to be found around the mean of both the requirement and intake distributions and that it becomes increasingly less dense at the ends. That is, the two distributions are likely to have the approximate normal or log-normal properties, although with different means and variances.

In Fig. 9.5, iso-contours have been inserted within the ellipses, indicating higher densities around the mean of the intake and requirement distributions than towards the edges of the ellipse. (The situations in the two figures are otherwise the same as in Fig. 9.2A and B, where we have one country and we compare two situations with different CCOPs.) The choice of a low CCOP (C^l) in Fig. 9.5A means that it cuts the ellipse at a part where the density is relatively low, signifying that rather few households fall within in this area. The higher CCOP (C^h) in Fig. 9.5B will cut the distribution at a part where the density is relatively higher, i.e. a high proportion of the population are found. In this case the difference in the estimated prevalence of undernutrition between the low and high CCOPs will be larger than in the cases depicted in Fig. 9.2.

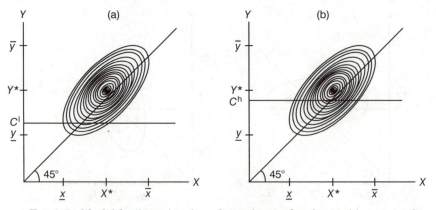

FIG. 9.5. Model for the estimation of prevalence of undernutrition; normal distributions of intakes and requirements

When the distributions are normal (or log-normal), one cannot, of course, estimate the size of biases just by comparing the size of the areas representing type I and type II errors. The various areas will now contain different densities and a small area near to the mean of the distributions may contain more households than a much larger area towards the edges of the distribution.[2] In order to produce unbiased POU estimates we thus have to know the distributions in detail. Empirically, the problem is that we have little information on the variance in either of the two distributions, and also the mean values are imperfectly known. The most serious problem, however, is that we have no empirically based information on how the distribution of calorie intakes (availabilities) relates to the distribution of requirements in any single population.[3]

9.4.   ONE-DIMENSIONAL CCOPS AND TWO-DIMENSIONAL UNDERNUTRITION

In this section we shall point out a further problem with the use of a single-dimension CCOP to estimate the POU that has not been considered by the FAO or other users of CCOPs.[4] The problem is that a single-dimension energy cut-off point is used to delineate undernutrition, which, by the FAO definition (and most others), is a two-dimensional phenomenon. That is, a person can be undernourished in either or both of two ways. One is that he or she has an habitual intake that is insufficient to support the energy expenditures required for basal metabolism at a body weight that is consistent with health in a probabilistic sense. The other dimension in which a person can be undernourished is that that he or she has a PAL that is insufficient for pursuing the minimum level of physical activity that is required for maintaining body fitness and health and/or to earn a minimum living through (manual) work. In the following sub-sections, it is shown that the use of a single-dimension CCOP will unambiguously lead to an underestimation of the POU (cet par).

9.4.1.   The Model

The minimum acceptable daily calorie requirement for the reference adult male (RA), upon which the CCOPs used by the FAOa (1996) are derived, is calculated roughly as follows (not all details are published):

$$RA = PAL^\star \times BMR/kg \times W^\star = 1.55 \times 25.8 \times 52.2 = 2,087 \qquad (9.1)$$

The number attached by the FAO to the PAL* for adult males is 1.55 in all countries (regions) of the world. Also the BMR/kg is taken to be the same world-wide (25.8 per day). The 'minimum acceptable' body weight (W*), derived from a BMI of 18.5, differs slightly across countries due to differences in the average stature of adult males (same for females). The number

52.2 in equation (9.1) is the weight derived from a stature of 168 cm, which is the average height of male adults in SSA. The number of calories required for BMR is thus set at 1,347 and the number of calories for minimum physical activity (PAL*) at 740 (2,087 – 1,347)

In Fig. 9.6, we have calories spent on physical activity along the vertical axis (PAL) and calories spent on basal metabolism along the horizontal axis (BMR). The RA at 2,087 is depicted as a negatively sloping 45° line. This line marks the various combinations of PAL and BMR that 2,087 calories can be spent on. Of course, not all combinations on the 45° line are observed in the population, as some are not consistent with survival. The ellipse demarcates the *de facto* distribution of the (PAL, BMR) combinations of different individuals in the population.

In Fig. 9.6, the ellipse has been drawn with the largest spread in the southwest to north-east direction. This reflects an assumption that people with relatively large bodies (weight) and BMR tend to spend more calories in absolute terms on physical activity than do small people. This seems to be a plausible assumption considering that the amount of energy (number of calories) that a big person has to exert to accomplish a given physical activity (e.g. walking a certain distance at a given speed) is larger than that for a small person.[5] The ellipse in Fig. 9.6 thus depicts a situation in which it is assumed that small and large people work equally as much on the average, but that there are variations (within the ellipse) across individuals for other reasons.

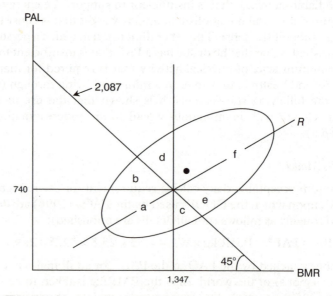

FIG. 9.6. Underestimation of the prevalence of undernutrition; one-dimensional cut-off point and two-dimensional undernutrition

The method used by the FAO to derive POU estimates boils down to calculating the share of individuals that have a calorie intake (approximated by 'availability') below 2,087 (RA). In Fig. 9.6, these are the observations found in the ellipse below the 45° line. The undernourished individuals comprise three different 'categories':

(1) those who are underactive and underweight (area a);
(2) those who are underweight but active enough (area b);
(3) those who are underactive but have sufficient weight (area c).

According to the FAO method, the remaining observations in the distribution are classified as well-nourished (areas d, e and f). However, as we can see from the graph, the individuals in area d are underweight while being active enough and the ones in area e are underactive but have acceptable weights. They are thus, just as the individuals in areas b and c, undernourished in one of the two dimensions underlying the definition of undernutrition used by the FAO, but sufficiently well off in the other. The method used by the FAO to estimate POU is thus biased as individuals in areas d and e are wrongly classified as well-nourished while in fact they are undernourished in one dimension (weight or activity).

9.4.2. The Simulated Size of the Bias

The size of the bias depends on several factors. It is nil only in the case when all individuals' households in the population spend their energy on PAL and BMR in the same proportion (roughly one-third for PAL and two-thirds for BMR). That is the case when the entire (PAL/BMR) distribution in the population lies along a positive line such as the one marked R in Fig. 9.6, and this line also has to go through the (740; 1,347) vector point. That is, the ellipse collapses into the R line, which is the implicit assumption underlying the construction of the CCOPs by the FAO. When different individuals and households have different PAL/BMR ratios, which must be the case in all real populations, there will be biases, and the larger the variance in this ratio, the larger the estimation biases.

In a paper in progress, Svedberg (1999c) simulated the size of the bias in the POU estimates for different values of the exogenous parameters (per-capita calorie availability, mean and variance of the PAL/BMR distribution, the shape of this distribution, the correlation between PAL and BMR, etc.) from an algebraic version of the above model. The simulated underestimation of POU due to misclassification of adults in areas d and e in Fig. 9.6 ranges from 10 to 13 per cent of the study population, depending on the numerical values attached to the exogenous parameters in the model.

Even the lowest simulation result suggests a substantial underestimation of POU, because the two-dimensionality of undernutrition is not taken into consideration. That the numbers are this high is mainly a consequence of the fact that the simulations were conducted on the basis of an NPCCA of 2,040, reflecting the FAO's actual estimate for the average SSA country. When we choose a higher NPCCA, of say 2,600, the underestimation of the POU becomes significantly smaller.

9.4.3. Further Considerations

There are a few qualifications and clarifications to the above analysis that merit further comment. First, it should be remembered that the health risks associated with low body weight are not compensated for by a high physical activity level, and *vice versa*, as far as we know. It may even be that a high activity level for an underweight person adds to the health risks he runs. It is also notable that the individuals in area b in Fig. 9.6, which are classified as undernourished by the FAO estimation method, like those in area d, are undernourished only in the weight dimension. For a given level of PAL, the individuals in area d are more underweight than those in area b, but this is irrelevant to the FAO estimation method, which is concerned only with de-lineating those above from those below the calorie cut-off point ('headcount-ing'), not with the severity of undernutrition in individuals in a relative sense. A parallel case applies to households in areas d and e.

Secondly, the individuals in areas d and e are relatively better off than those in areas a, b and c, as they have access to more calories (their combined PAL and BMR lie to the right of the 45° line in Fig. 9.6). It may appear that they do not have a problem with the total amount of calories, and that their prob-lem is that they have 'misallocated' the calories between PAL and BMR. The question is whether people in area d can escape undernutrition by expending fewer calories on PAL and more on BMR (having a higher body weight) along the negatively sloping 45° line corresponding to their total calorie avail-ability. In a parallel fashion, can people in area e reduce their body weight (BMR) and spend the calories on physical activity instead? That is, can people in both areas d and e move to area f, and thus escape undernutrition?

Introducing some economics into the analysis will lay restrictions on the possibility for people of shifting position, especially for those in area d. If people here expend most of their PAL energy in work activity, a reduction in PAL will lower income and, thus, lower their ability to buy food and maintain their total calorie intake. That is, they will no longer be on the same 45° trade-off line between PAL and BMR, but on a lower one. When it comes to house-holds in area e, the possibility of moving to area f is not constrained for the same economic reasons. In fact, they can reduce their body weight at least a little without running health risks, as there is a margin between their actual weight and the critical low one. If they do that and spend the calories thus freed in physical work activity they can both escape health risks associated with inactivity and earn a higher income that will shift them out to a higher total-calorie 45° line.

However, we are now entering problems that are not possible to tackle with the model used by the FAO to estimate POU. Within that model, it is not feasible to distinguish between people who are undernourished because they face a situation that they cannot change and people who are undernourished because they have made 'stupid' decisions. It is well documented that many households with a very low per-capita calorie intake, well below the CCOPs used by the FAO, have a relatively per-calorie cost-inefficient diet. That is, they spend their money on food items with a high cost-per-calorie content, presumably in order to satisfy other needs than to be well-nourished in the energy dimension, e.g. to get variety in the diet (see Pitt 1983, Shah 1983, Behrman and Deolalikar 1990). With the FAO aggregate method used to estimate POU, one cannot answer the question of why they are undernourished; that is a far more complicated question that requires other analytical tools.

9.5.   SUMMARY AND CONCLUSIONS

The whole idea of using a single CCOP to delineate the undernourished in a population where the joint intake/requirement distribution is unknown rests on the presumption that the type I and type II errors should cancel out. Otherwise, the POU estimates will be biased. Since the two errors induced by using a single CCOP go in different directions, there must be one CCOP that gives rise to two equally large errors (of opposing signs) and, thus, produces an unbiased POU estimate for a particular population. However, in order to find this unique CCOP, one needs information on the joint distribution of household per-capita intake and per-capita requirement in the population. Since these data are not available, the FAO estimates of the POU contain biases, the size and the sign of which is the focal point in ongoing research (Svedberg 1999b).

Moreover, the use of (approximatively) the same CCOP to estimate the POU in different populations (countries), where (i) the mean per-capita calorie availability, (ii) the variance in the distributions of intakes and requirements and (iii) the inter-linkage of the intake and requirement distribution do differ, means that the biases will vary in extent among different countries (regions). One would thus expect there to be not only biases in the *level* of the POUs produced by the international organizations—the *comparability* between estimates for the various geographical regions must also be tainted.

In section 9.4 it was further shown that there is yet another bias in the FAO CCOPs, a bias that induces an unambiguous underestimation (*cet par*) of the POU in all populations, although of different sizes. This is because a single-dimensional cut-off-point has been use to delineate undernutrition, which is a two-dimensional problem.

In this and the previous chapter we have highlighted the many steps that are required to establish a CCOP. Each step is beset by several methodological and empirical problems that induce ample possibilities for large margins of error in the POU estimates and, in most instances, also biases. In a previous chapter (5) it was shown that the estimated POU is highly sensitive to even rather small variations in all the parameters comprising the estimation model. Considering these two facts, one must ask the following questions: is it possible to refine the FAO estimation method so that reasonably reliable and unbiased POU estimates are provided? Or is the entire FAO approach to the estimation of undernutrition a futile exercise that will never provide meaningful results? Are there other, more accurate ways to estimate the prevalence of undernutrition? These are the questions addressed in the next and following chapters.

NOTES

1. The diagrammatic technique used in this section to analyse biases in the estimation of POU with single CCOPs was first applied by Anand and Harris (1992). As they show, if the correlation between intake and requirement were perfect, the ellipse would collapse into a straight line, a case which they analyse in more detail.
2. As we saw in Chapter 5, the FAO and the IBRD have assumed the intake distribution to be log-normal (based on some empirical evidence; see Chapter 7) in all countries, but what assumption they have made regarding the shape of the requirement distribution is unclear, since it has not been published.
3. In a forthcoming paper, Svedberg (1999b) simulated the type I and type II errors in the FAO estimates of POU for the five major geographical regions. The simulations were undertaken with various combinations of assumed values of (i) the coefficient of variation in the calorie requirement distributions and (ii) the correlation between intakes and requirements. The tentative results suggest that for all combinations of 'plausible' values of these two parameters, the FAO has seriously underestimated (cer par) the POU in all regions.
4. In a technical appendix to the Fifth World Food Survey, the problem to be discussed here is mentioned, but no analysis of how it affects the POU estimates and what implications it has for the derivation of CCOPs is provided.
5. In fact, estimates show it to be approximately proportional to BMR, and, thus, body weight (FAO/WHO/UNU 1985: annex 1). This is the very reason why energy expenditure for physical activity is conventionally expressed as a multiple of the BMR.

10

Aggregate Estimations of Prevalence of Undernutrition: Scope for Improvements?

10.1. INTRODUCTION

The model used by the FAO to estimate the overall prevalence of under-nutrition (POU) in the main regions of the world—and most recently, in indi-vidual countries—may look very simple as it comprises three parameters only: national per-capita calorie availability (NPCCA), the inter-household distribution of the calories available, as measured by the coefficient of vari-ation (CV), and a calorie cut-off point (CCOP). As we have seen in previous chapters, however, there is little we know for a fact regarding the 'true' values of any of these three parameters in any one population. The estimation of each parameter involves a long chain of calculations, most of which are based on imperfect data and more or less ambiguous assumptions.

The main objective of this chapter is to assess the possibilities for improv-ing the FAO method of estimating prevalence of undernutrition (in section 10.3). In section 10.4, as a bridge to Part IV of the study, we shall also point at alternative methods for answering the policy questions for which we need nutritional indicators. However, we shall start this chapter by providing a quick summary of what we have found in the previous five chapters (section 10.2).

10.2. SUMMARY OF MAIN FINDINGS

10.2.1. Sensitivity of the Undernutrition Estimates

In Chapter 5, a test of the robustness of the POU estimates produced by the FAO was conducted. The test required that we varied the CCOP and the NPCCA parameters by ±10 per cent, and the coefficient of variation (CV) in calorie intake across households by 5 percentage points, around the values attached to these parameters by the FAO for the Sub-Saharan African coun-tries (for which the base data are the least reliable, as the FAO also admits). We then obtained POU estimates ranging from 21 to 61 per cent of the popu-lation (Table 5.4). In subsequent chapters, the empirical foundations for the ±10 per cent ranges of uncertainty in the NPCCA, CV, and CCOP para-meter estimates were provided.

10.2.2. The National Per-capita Calorie Availability Estimates

Most independent observers of the FAO estimates of NPCCA for the African
countries find them unreliable. Blades (1980) and Lipton (1987), supported
by Heston (1994), conclude that the *margin of error* in the estimates for the
main staple foods in seven (including some of the largest) African countries
is at least ±20–40 per cent. Also, a leading proponent of the FAO has labelled
them 'dangerously weak' (in a non-published report).

In Chapter 6, we further found reasons to expect the NPCCA estimates to
be *downward biased* for the African countries in general. One reason is the incomplete coverage of minor food items. Another is that the primitive subjective methods used throughout the region to estimate acreage produce
numbers on the low side. There are several *a priori* reasons for expecting this.
The supporting empirical evidence is mainly from South Asia. Here the
estimated acreage increased by some 25 per cent when the earlier subjective
methods were replaced by objective methods. Also, controlled experiments
in India show the subjective methods to produce estimates that are some 25
per cent too low.

There is thus reason to believe that the primitive NPCCA estimates for the
African countries are not only too low in absolute terms, but also in relation
to estimates for South Asia and most other developing countries, where more
objective estimation methods are in use. This implies that the POU estimates
for SSA are upward biased in relation to the POU estimates for other regions,
inclusive of South Asia (*cet par*).

10.2.3. The Calorie Distribution Estimates

In the *Sixth World Food Survey* the FAO*a* (1996) bases the calorie distribution estimates for the SSA countries on two food expenditure surveys from
Kenya and Zambia, respectively, produced in collaboration with the IFPRI.
These surveys are based on samples comprising a few hundred households in
a dozen villages—they are not nationally representative.[1] For the other 48
SSA countries, for which no reliable household survey data exist, the FAO
estimates the distribution of calories indirectly, from estimated income distribution data, using assumed (not estimated) calorie–income elasticities. As
was argued in Chapter 4, the whole concept of calorie–income elasticities is
questionable, and the numbers produced by different empirical studies differ considerably. The fact is that the data used by the FAO on calorie distribution across households in the African countries have no empirical
foundation (Chapter 7).

10.2.4. Individual Calorie Requirement

The first step in the construction of the CCOPs used by the FAO to estimate POU is to find the minimum body sizes, basal metabolism, and

physical activity that are consistent with health and fitness at the level of individuals.

Body Weight   In constructing the latest CCOPs, the FAO lowered the critical minimum body weight for adults, from a BMI of 20 to one of 18.5, in response to new research findings, which may seem reasonable. The FAO minimum energy expenditure norm for children, however, is derived on the basis of a 20 per cent larger body weight than the anthropometric norms used worldwide to assess the nutritional status of children (see Chapter 11).

Basal Metabolism   The stands taken by the FAO when estimating BMR/kg of body weight in developing country populations are controversial in two main respects, as argued in Chapter 8. First, the FAO has chosen to ignore new information on inter-ethnic variance in basal metabolism. There are now several studies showing the estimated BMR/kg to be about 10 per cent lower on average in 'tropical' populations than among Caucasians,[2] the BMR norm for the latter being used by the FAO worldwide. The second concerns the possibility that the human body can adapt permanently to low-energy intakes by reducing energy expenditures for BMR. The FAO has taken sides in this unresolved controversy, not by providing convincing theory and empirical evidence, but simply by denying its existence.

Physical Activity   The FAO estimates of minimum energy requirements for the 'economically' necessary physical (work) activity level (PAL) for individuals or households are not empirically based. Even the most casual observation of any (poor) population reveals that the economic return for physical work effort differs substantially among individuals because of differences in their physical productive assets (e.g. land and physical capital), their human capital, and a host of other factors. The PAL that permits the person to avoid undernutrition is thus highly individual-specific and can easily vary between 500 and 2,000 calories per day for an adult man. In the *Fifth World Food Survey*, the FAO 'resolved' this problem by not allowing for any physical work activity at all for adults in its CCOPs. In the *Sixth World Food Survey*, the critical minimum work activity is set at 1.55 times the BMR on an *ad hoc* basis. There is as little empirical support for this number as there is for a 10 per cent higher or lower figure.

10.2.5. The Calorie Cut-off Points

There is not only uncertainty regarding the values of the minimum body weight, BMR, and PAL at the level of individuals. There are also problems with the *aggregation* of individual minimum energy requirements—whatever they are—to a calorie cut-off point. In fact, this is the most complicated step in the entire procedure that underlies the estimation of POU, as demonstrated in Chapter 9. Here we shall recall only two such problems. The first is how to estimate (i) the distribution—the coefficient of variation—of minimum per-capita calorie requirements across households, and (ii) the relation of this distribution to the distribution of intakes—the correlation coefficient —in a population. The second problem is that of integrating into the estimation procedure the fact that people can be undernourished in one of two dimensions, through being underweight or being underactive, even when having a calorie intake above the one-dimensional calorie norm used by the FAO.

In the absence of empirically based data on the parameters that are needed to incorporate these two 'complications' into the construction of the CCOPs, the FAO has simply ignored them. Simple simulations show that the CCOPs are highly sensitive to these 'omissions'. When different numbers within plausible ranges are attached to the missing parameters, the ensuing CCOPs tend to vary by more than ±10 per cent around the values the FAO has attached to them (Svedberg 1999b, c).

10.3.   THE SCOPE FOR IMPROVING THE FAO ESTIMATES

In order to be able to produce reasonably reliable and unbiased POU estimates with the FAO type of model, improved methodologies and data are required in a multitude of dimensions. In this section we shall start by identifying improvements that can be accomplished through application of already existing knowledge at little cost. Subsequently, we shall identify some improvements that seem feasible in the longer term, provided that enough financial funds are made available. Finally, we shall point to areas where there does not seem to be much scope for improvement, almost irrespective of the costs and time allowed.

10.3.1. Possible Improvements in the Short Term

Among the issues discussed above, there are two that seem to be resolvable without much additional effort. One improvement would be to base the CCOPs for the developing countries on a 10 per cent lower BMR/kg of body weight in accordance with new findings of lower metabolism in non-Caucasian people. The second would be to lower the critical body weight for children in order to assure consistency with anthropometric norms and also with the probabilistic approach followed by the FAO in assigning minimum weights for adults. Revisions on these two accounts would lower the CCOPs (cet par) by about 10 per cent and the estimated number of undernourished in the world would fall from 841 million to less than 650 million. But that would still be a highly uncertain number, as there are many remaining difficulties (see below).

10.3.2. Possible Improvements in the Long Term

There are some other stages in the long and complicated procedure of estimating POU with the FAO method that could be improved by applying already established methodology, but at a high economic cost.

The national per-capita calorie availability estimates, especially but not exclusively for the African countries, could be improved by introducing objective scientific methods for acreage enumeration and crop yield estimation. In the mid-1980s, Minhas (1986), a leading Indian expert on food production estimations, thought that it would take at least 10 years before reasonably reliable food supply estimates could be produced in the African countries, if stern action were to be taken immediately. No such action has been taken. On the contrary, the agricultural production statistics, like the trade statistics, have deteriorated in many of the African countries.[3]

The inter-household distribution of calories is another area where existing estimation technology permits more reliable estimates than presently obtained in the African (and many other) countries with primitive methods. By conducting large and nationally representative HESs in most of the countries, applying state-of-the-art estimation technology, the FAO could derive distribution estimates that would be far more accurate and less biased than the present ones.[4]

The catch is, of course, that carrying out reliable and nationally representative HESs and modern food production estimations in all the African countries would be an enormously costly and time-consuming operation that the FAO probably would have difficulties raising the funding for (we shall return to this question in the final chapter). To expect the national governments in Africa to be prepared to underwrite these costs is unrealistic. In the past they have paid little attention to such surveys, and in present-day economically constrained and politically chaotic Africa, the introduction of costly scientific acreage (and yield) estimation methods probably stand low on their priority lists.[5,6]

10.3.3. Remaining Unresolvable Problems

Even if the problems discussed in the above two subsections were to be resolved, the FAO would still face the almost impossible task of finding the CCOPs that produce unbiased POU estimates. One would then need data on how the two distributions, actual calorie intake, and minimum requirements of the households interrelate in each and every country. The minimum requirement for the individual household is dependent on what kind of work the members are engaged in and what the economic return for that work is, variables which are not easily observable. One would also need data on how households/individuals allocate their energy expenditures between BMR and PAL.

With data in all these dimensions, however (which would be difficult and costly to obtain for samples sufficiently large to ensure national representativeness), one would not need to construct CCOPs. With such data, one simply derives the POU by dividing the estimated number of households that have calorie intakes below their specific requirement by the total number of households (as was shown in Chapter 9).

10.4.   ARE ALTERNATIVE METHODS CALLED FOR?

Given the poor prospects for producing reliable and unbiased POU estimates in the forseeable future by the aggregate method used by the FAO, one must ask whether further work along that line is warranted. This question boils down to three subquestions. First, what important policy questions can POU estimates of the FAO type—even if reasonably accurate in the distant future —provide answers to? Secondly, are there other methods to answer these questions that are less costly and/or more accurate? Thirdly, are there important questions that the FAO method can answer while alternative methods cannot? Nutritional indicators are used chiefly to (i) estimate levels of POU, (ii) monitor its change over time, and (iii) to identify undernourished households or individuals for targeted intervention.

10.4.1. Estimating Undernutrition by Country

In the background preparations for the *Sixth World Food Survey*, POU estimates were derived for individual countries by the FAO. In the published official document, however, the FAO*a* (1996) only reported the aggregated POU estimates for the five major geographical regions that were reproduced in Fig. 5.2. The reason for not publishing the estimates for the individual countries was, the FAO then maintained, that they were too unreliable. The regional estimates, it was argued, are more reliable as *random* errors in the individual country, estimates tend to cancel out when aggregated to the regional level. The FAO subsequently changed its mind, however, and published estimates for 98 countries for the years 1969/71 and 1990/2[7]; the very same estimates that were not reliable enough to merit publication a few months earlier.[8]

Even if one is inclined to believe that random errors in country estimates tend to be largely offsetting when aggregated to the regional level, and that the biases pointed to in Chapters 8 and 9 are 'small', what policy-relevant question can *regional* POU estimates for a particular year be of help in answering? Only one question comes to mind: is the POU in, say, Sub-Saharan Africa larger or smaller than in South Asia? As we have already seen in Fig. 1.1, anthropometrics is an alternative method that is capable of providing estimates of POU also at this broad level. Moreover, while the FAO estimates suggest that undernutrition is far more prevalent in Sub-Saharan Africa than in South Asia, anthropometrics indicate that it is the other way around. We shall come back to this puzzle in Chapter 18, but the explanation probably lies in the systematic underestimation by the FAO of food supplies in Sub-Saharan Africa and, consequently, overestimation of POU (*cet par*).

However, if the 'international community' wishes to pursue a policy of direct intervention, reliable and unbiased estimates of POU at the country level must be available. If such estimates are to be produced with the FAO approach, the minimum requirements are that objective acreage estimation methods are introduced, and that nationally representative and detailed HES are carried out in each and every country. Such methods and surveys are costly and, again, nationally representative anthropometric surveys may be a more inexpensive and reliable way of obtaining estimates of the nutritional status of national populations.

10.4.2. Monitoring Changes in Undernutrition over Time

The changes in the estimated POU in respective regions (Fig. 5.3), and in the individual countries, over the 1969/71–1990/2 period (FAO 1997*a*) are almost exclusively explained by changes in the estimated availability of calories. This is because the POU estimates for different years are derived on the assumption that the calorie distribution within each country has been unaltered over time (since no data on changes in distribution are available) and that almost identical CCOPs are used (FAO*a* 1996: table 16).[9]

In order for the international community to be able to monitor progress towards the 2015 goal, the objective acreage surveys and representative HES called for in the previous subsection must be repeated regularly; otherwise, the monitoring of POU will be meaningless. This is a tall order and, again, anthropometrics offer an alternative way of estimating trends in the incidence of undernutrition.

10.4.3. Identifying Undernourished Individuals and Households

Even in a utopian scenario, where the proportion of undernourished can be estimated without bias with the FAO method, it will continue to be non-applicable for many other purposes for which we need nutritional indicators. This is because the FAO method, irrespective of how refined it may become in the future, cannot be used for assessing the nutritional status of individuals and specific households.

The FAO itself claims to be capable 'only' of estimating the *proportion* of a population that is undernourished, not that it is able to *identify* the undernourished households (FAO 1996*a*: pp. 120–7). The FAO's POU estimates will always contain type I and type II errors; this is a built-in feature of the basic approach of using CCOPs (see Chapter 9). The FAO claims implicitly that the false positives and negatives are of equal size, leaving the estimated proportion of undernourished unbiased. Irrespective of the substance of this claim, in order to be able to assess the nutritional status of particular households, the FAO would not only have to know their calorie intakes, but also their household-specific requirements; and that is something the FAO knows nothing about.

The fact that the nutritional status of households and individuals cannot be estimated with the FAO approach (even if improved as discussed above) means that it fails to answer several questions of policy relevance (Svedberg 1999a). First, the method cannot shed light on the intra-household allocation of nutrients and, thus, address the question whether women and young children are the prime victims of undernutrition; a main concern for many people. Secondly, since undernourished individuals cannot be identified by the FAO method, it cannot be used for targeting interventions. Thirdly, the method cannot be used for assessing the nutritional consequences of changes in economic policy, for example the structural-adjustment programmes that some 50 developing countries have agreed to undertake in collaboration with the World Bank and the IMF.

Perhaps the most attractive feature of the anthropometric approach to the estimation of undernutrition is the fact that the unit of observation is the individual. Anthropometric assessments can hence be used for all the policy-relevant purposes listed above, which the FAO method is incapable of.

10.5. CONCLUDING REMARKS

It is important to emphasize that what has been claimed here is not that the FAO's position on the issues discussed is all 'wrong'. What we have claimed is that many of the FAO stands are *ad hoc* and that alternative values of the three parameters that comprise the model used to estimate POU are as plausible and as well (or as poorly) supported by the scant empirical evidence available. The FAO model is simply too sensitive to relatively small alterations in the values of the 'exogenous' parameters, values that can only be estimated within broad confidence intervals. No policy-relevant information emerges from a method that is incapable of saying more than that the prevalence of undernutrition in, say Sub-Saharan Africa, is between 21 and 61 per cent.

To claim that the FAO type of model is impossible to improve, and that the information concerning the appropriate values of the three parameters that comprise the model will never materialize, may be going too far. But there is certainly a long way to go, considering that one has to start almost from scratch on many of the issues involved. The main problem is that of constructing CCOPs that produce unbiased POU estimates with the FAO method. This is such a complicated endeavour that there is serious doubt as to whether it can ever be accomplished. The data needs are simply too great, and the economic cost for obtaining these data would be enormous.

Finally, it should be recalled that even in the unlikely event that the data problems could be resolved in the distant future, we would still be left with a tool that was capable only of saying what proportion of a population was undernourished and how this proportion might change over time. The FAO model would still be much too blunt to answer the crucial questions of *Who* the undernourished are, *Where* they are, and *When* and *Why* they are undernourished. If the anthropometric method can produce reasonably reliable answers to these questions, as well as providing unbiased estimates of the prevalence of undernutrition and its change over time, there would be little need for the FAO method, even if it was improved. The possibilities offered by the anthropmetric method are assessed in Part IV below.

NOTES

1. The inter-household variation in calorie intake differs considerably between the two samples: the estimated CV is 0.17 in the Kenyan sample and 0.37 in the Zambian one (FAO*a*: p. 141). This is an indication that there may be large differences across the African countries that have not been accounted for.
2. So far it has not been possible to say whether the explanation is geneotypic differences along ethnic lines or phenotypic adaptation to lower intakes (*à la* Sukhatme).
3. This definitely happened in Burundi, Angola, Ethiopia, Liberia, Mozambique, Rwanda, Sierra Leone, Somalia, Sudan, Uganda, and Zaïre during long periods of civil war and other disturbances that made large parts of these countries inaccessible for enumerators and other officials. Despite this, the FAO continued and continues to publish detailed estimates on per-capita calorie availability for these countries. (See FAO*b* 1994: table 106.)
4. The two surveys from Zambia and Kenya produced in collaboration with the IFPRI are a step in that direction, but these are not nationally representative and are from two of the about 50 SSA countries only.
5. Moreover, there are an additional 90 countries (many only recently national states) for which no FBS data are available at all.
6. It is also possible, but not certain, that if enough research funds were devoted to it, the question of intra-individual adaptation of BMR to low-energy intakes could be resolved. No presently known technology exists for answering this question.
7. At the *World Food Summit* many delegations rightfully and forcefully argued that in order to direct policy, much more detailed 'hunger maps' than offered in the main document presented by the FAO*a* (1996) on this occasion, were required. Quickly, the FAO (1997*a*) published the individual country estimates. One cannot but suspect that the FAO feared that its *Food-Balance-Sheet* approach would otherwise be replaced by other methods for estimating undernutrition (anthropometrics or multi-purpose household surveys) that other international agencies (mainly the WHO and the World Bank) have more competence in conducting, and also the mandate to undertake.

8. As a response to a resolution adapted at the *World Food Summit* in late 1996 to extend the 'mapping of hunger' to the subnational level, the FAO (1997c) has expressed its willingness to provide such estimates, based on the model which has been critically assessed in the five previous chapters. Such subnational estimates would be as unreliable as national, or the supernational, estimates discussed previously, for very much the same reasons. In addition, however, subnational POU estimates would have to be based on very detailed estimation of food production at the district level. This would require each and every country to undertake modern objective acreage enumeration and yield sampling in the entire country, something no single SSA country does today. Moreover, subnational POU estimates obtained by the FAO method would require detailed statistical coverage of *intra-country* trade in food products, which are not available for any SSA country, or, for that matter, for any other developing country. Subnational POU estimates obtained by the FAO method are therefore impossible to derive in the short as well as the rather long term—if ever.

9. The CCOPs underlying the regional POU estimates at different times have taken into account changes in demographic composition (age structure), but these changes are minuscule over such short periods.

PART IV

PART IV

11

Anthropometric Indicators of Undernutrition: Measurements and Evidence

11.1. INTRODUCTION

There are two main sets of estimates of the prevalence of undernutrition in the world that are claimed to allow comparison over time and space. One set of such estimates are provided by the FAO on the basis of the aggregate method that was scrutinized in the previous six chapters. The other set of estimates are based on anthropometric measures. Until quite recently, this type of estimate was derived using a large variety of methods and measurements, and therefore they were not generally comparable across countries and over time. Since the early 1990s, however, estimates for almost 90 developing countries have come forth, based on more uniform measures and methods. This has improved the possibility of making international comparisons and, less frequently, of monitoring changes over time. Most of the new data sets have been compiled by the WHO and are used extensively by UNICEF, the ACC/SCN, and the FAO/ESN.[1]

The anthropometric indicators allow us to derive POU estimates in an alternative way, which makes possible comparisons with the estimates obtained by the FAO with its aggregate method. The anthropometric method also permits estimates of differences in nutritional status between rural and urban areas, for children of different age and sex and between children and adults. In combination with 'social' and economic observations, anthropometric indicators can also be helpful in identifying reasons for nutritional inadequacy. The anthropometric measures thus have a broader application potential than the aggregate POU estimates which we scrutinized earlier.

The overall aim of this and the subsequent two chapters is to assess the anthropometric measures as indicators of undernutrition. In this chapter we present the anthropometric measurements in use and a brief overview of the available empirical estimates. In Chapter 12, measurement and selection errors and biases in the estimates are identified. Chapter 13 addresses the more conceptual question of to what extent the conventional anthropometric indicators capture different aspects of what are considered symptoms of undernutrition.

The rest of the present chapter is organized as follows. In section 11.2, the anthropometric measures most commonly used are presented. Section 11.3 contains a summary review of the evidence on the anthropometric status of children in the SSA countries. In section 11.4, these estimates are subjected to international comparison. In section 11.5, the meagre evidence on the anthropometric status of adults is presented. The anthropometric status of adults and children are compared in section 11.6. Finally, a short summary of the main findings is offered in section 11.7.

11.2. MEASUREMENTS, DATA, AND NORMS

The anthropometric approach rests on the presumption that people's physical appearance reflects their nutrition (and health) status, i.e. if energy intake and expenditure balance at a level that is too low, this will show up in body constitution. This means that neither the energy intake nor the energy expenditure has to be measured. The anthropometric approach is therefore more simple and—above all—less reliant on the collection of inherently difficult-to-estimate data than the aggregate calorie-intake/requirement approach. (As we shall see in the two subsequent chapters, this is not to say that the anthropometric method is devoid of problems.)

11.2.1. Child Measurements

In setting up an anthropometric norm for children, the first question is what 'outcomes', or body-composition abnormalities, are the most reliable indicators of nutritional inadequacy. Many measures have been used in the literature. Since the early 1980s, it seems that nutritionists have found height and weight to be the most relevant ones (Waterlow 1984, Payne 1992). The bulk of the recent anthropometric evidence from Africa (and elsewhere) is thus based on height and weight measures. In earlier times, head and arm circumference, triceps skinfold, and a few other measures were frequently used. Following the Waterlow (1972, 1976) classification scheme, the more specific indicators used to assess children are: height for age (stunting), weight for height (wasting), and weight for age (underweight). The three different indicators are intended to capture different aspects of child undernutrition that have partly different aetiologies and time dimensions (to be further elaborated in Chapter 13).

The height-for-age indicator is mainly used for monitoring permanent, or chronic, undernutrition in children. The underlying theory is that chronic undernutrition in childhood retards growth in stature, although there is no concensus on the relative importance of nutrition, on the one hand, and disease and unfavourable socio-economic environment, on the other (Eveleth and Tanner 1990, Waterlow 1992), discussed in more detail in Chapter 14.

The weight-for-height indicator is used to monitor wasting, which is taken to reflect short-term, or temporary, undernutrition. The weight-for-age indicator is intended to capture both long-term (stunting) and short-term (wasting) undernutrition. It has been the indicator used most frequently by WHO, UNICEF, and other international organizations concerned with the health status of children, and most of the available empirical evidence is in this dimension.

11.2.2. The Height and Weight Norms

The second step in setting up an anthropometric norm is to decide what are the 'normal' height and weight in a population. The norms in use are almost without exception obtained from a Western population. The average child's height in such a population is taken to represent the genetic growth-potential for the average child worldwide. The average weight of the children in the reference population is not necessarily assumed to represent a genetic potential for weight, but a weight which imposes no hazards for health or mental and physical capabilities. The most commonly applied norm nowadays is from the US National Center for Health Statistics (NCHS), which UNICEF, WHO, and the FAO agreed to use in 1981; before that, the proliferation of norms was bewildering (WHO 1986).

The use of the same height-for-age norm (from the US) as the benchmark for what is normal (nutritionally unconstrained) stature in children in all parts of the world implies an assumption that all races and ethnic groups in the world have the same genetic potential for growth in the early age. (The empirical support for this assumption is discussed in Chapter 12.)

11.2.3. Acceptable Deviation from the Norms (the Cut-off Points)

The third step in deriving estimates of undernutrition with the anthropometric method is to find the unacceptable downward deviations from the height and weight norms (the cut-off points). In principle, there are two ways of establishing cut-off points.

One takes its starting point in what is statistically abnormal in the reference (Western) population. In populations in which nutritional inadequacy is absent (or very small), there is a distribution of heights and weights (for age): some children are short and/or light-weighted for genetic reasons, others are tall and/or heavy. The cut-off points used to delineate undernourished children in Third World populations are derived from the lower ends of the height and weight distributions in the reference population. This method is used by WHO, UNICEF, other international organizations engaged in monitoring the status of children in the world, and also by most independent researchers collecting and using anthropometric indicators.

In earlier times, there was no consensus on what precise 'statistical deviation' should be used to delineate the undernourished. Regarding height for age, for instance, some authors set the cut-off at 10 per cent below the median reference height; others at 2 standard deviations (SD) below; still others below the third (or fifth) decile in the reference population. (As demonstrated by Mora (1984), the estimated POU can be highly sensitive to which particular measure of deviation is used.)[2] However, since the early 1980s, the international organizations have agreed to use the 2 SD measure to delineate undernutrition in all child populations in order to accomplish comparability across countries and over time. This measure has also been accepted by most independent collectors and users of anthropometric indicators.

The second method for establishing cut-off points is to estimate at what downward deviations from 'normal' height and weight there are measurable statistically significant increased risks of health impairments and other dysfunctions in children. This method has a better theoretical foundation in the Adjustment and Adaptation paradigm of undernutrition (cf. Chapter 2). In practice, however, this method is seldom used for assessing children, while it is for adults (for reasons to be elaborated in Chapter 14 below).

11.3.   THE ANTHROPOMETRIC STATUS OF CHILDREN IN SSA

This section presents evidence on the anthropometric status of children under the age of five in the SSA countries. Most of the original data are from WHO and used by UNICEF, the ACC/SCN, and the FAO/ESN. The data allow for comparisons across African countries, developments over time, and comparisons with other parts of the so-called Third World. This data base also allows us to estimate differences by age, sex, and rural/urban location.

11.3.1.   Height and Weight Failure of Children in SSA

Estimates of the incidence of undernourished children in 33 SSA countries (for one particular year in the 1985–94 period) are summarized in Table 11.1.[3] The table suggests the highest incidence of undernutrition with the height-for-age indicator; almost 40 per cent of the children in SSA are stunted. A somewhat smaller share, about 30 per cent, are underweight, i.e. have a weight-for-age below the cut-off point. About 8 per cent of the children have a weight-for-height below the norm.

There are wide differences across the African countries. The estimated prevalence of underweight children ranges from below 6 per cent to almost half the child population. Ethiopia, Mauritania, and Madagascar are at the top the list, but the estimated incidence of the underweight is considerably above the average also in Burundi, Niger, Tanzania, and Nigeria. The lowest figures are reported for the Seychelles and Swaziland. In almost all the SSA countries, stunting is somewhat more prevalent than being underweight.

TABLE 11.1. Prevalence estimates for three anthropometric indicators, latest year (percentage below −2 SD of NCHS reference median for 0–59 month-olds)

Country by region	Year(s)	Underweight (weight for age)	Stunting (height for age)	Wasting (weight for height)
Eastern and Southern Africa				
Botswana	1987	15	44	—
Burundi	1987	38	48	6
Ethiopia	1992	48	64	8
Kenya	1993	22	33	6
Lesotho	1992	15	33	2
Madagascar	1992	39	51	5
Malawi	1981	27	49	5
Mauritius	1985	24	22	16
Namibia	1992	26	28	4
Rwanda	1992	29	48	3
Seychelles	1988	6	5	2
Swaziland	1983–4	10	30	1
Tanzania	1992	29	43	6
Uganda	1988	23	45	2
Zambia	1992	25	40	5
Zimbabwe	1988	12	29	1
West and Central Africa				
Burkina Faso	1993	30	29	13
Cameroon	1991	13	24	3
Cape Verde	1985	19	26	3
Congo	1987	24	27	5
Côte d'Ivoire	1986	12	17	9
Ghana	1994	27	26	11
Guinea–Bissau	1978–80	23	—	—
Liberia	1976	20	37	3
Mali	1987	31	24	11
Mauretania	1991	48	56	16
Niger	1992	36	32	16
Nigeria	1990	36	43	9
Sao Tomé & Principe	1986	17	26	5
Senegal	1993	20	22	9
Sierra Leone	1990	29	35	9
Togo	1988	24	30	5
Zaïre	1975	28	43	5
SSA (*average*)		31	39	8
India	1992	61	62	19
Bangladesh	1990	66	65	16

Sources: UNICEF 1993*b* and WHO Global Database, cited in FAO*a* 1996: appendix 2, table 8.

It is notable that undernutritition as indicated by wasting (weight-for-height) is considerably lower than for the other two indicators, 'only' 8 per cent in SSA as a whole. The only SSA countries in which estimated wasting is considerably higher are Niger, Mauritania, and, perhaps surprisingly, high-income Mauritius. In about half the countries, the prevalence of wasted children is in the 1–5 per cent range, which is about the same as in the reference populations. In Africa as a whole, more than 90 per cent of the children thus have an 'acceptable' weight for their height, while only 60 per cent have an 'acceptable' height for their age. This means that it is extremely important to make clear what is the most serious threat to child health and well-being: height or weight failure. If modest height failure poses no serious problem, while being underweight does, undernutrition among children in Africa is rather modest. If, however, height failure is the main problem, the situation is considerably worse. (This question is assessed in Chapter 14.)

11.3.2. Change over Time

Measures of anthropometric performance of children below the age of five, conducted with methods that permit inter-temporal comparison according to the ACC/SCN, are available for 11 SSA countries (Fig. 11.1). In three of these, Kenya, Tanzania, and Zimbabwe, the estimated trend in the incidence of underweight children (the only indicator for which changes over time are reported) is downwards; in the other eight countries, it is upwards. According to the Statistics and Monitoring Section of UNICEF (1993a: fig. 7), inter-temporally comparable data (on the incidence of underweight children) are

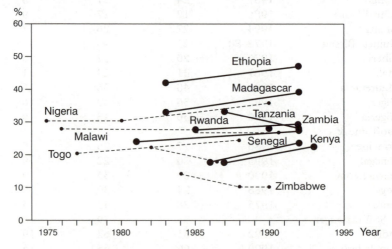

FIG. 11.1. Estimated trends in the percentage of children who are underweight in selected SSA countries

Source: ACC/SCN 1994: p. 2.

available for three SSA (partly different) countries only. In two of these, Togo and Cape Verde, the trend is downwards; in Zambia it is upwards. At the continental level, the ACC/SCN finds that the estimated incidence of underweight children in the SSA has remained more or less unaltered between 1975 and 1995 (Fig. 11.2).

11.3.3.   Anthropometric Status by Rural/Urban Area and Regions

Within each and every country in SSA, the incidence of undernutrition is higher in rural than in urban areas and most of the differences are statistically significant (Table 11.2). In half the countries, rural undernutrition is nearly twice that in urban areas. This is by the weight-for-age indicator; similar evidence is not available for other indicators.[4]

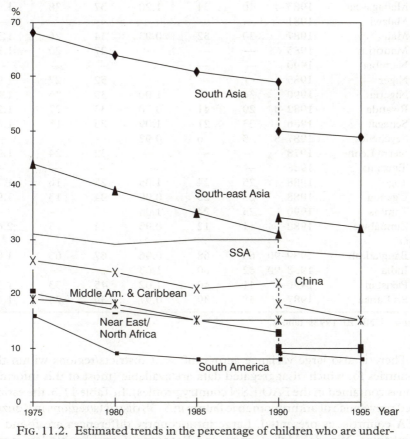

FIG. 11.2. Estimated trends in the percentage of children who are underweight, by major geographical regions, 1975–95

Sources: ACC/SCN 1992: table 1.2 (1975–90); ACC/SCN 1997*a*: table on p. 9 (1990–95).

TABLE 11.2. Prevalence of underweight children, by gender and rural/urban location, in selected countries, 1980s

Country	Year	Gender			Location		
		Male	Female	M/F ratio	Rural	Urban	R/U ratio
Africa							
Burundi	1987	38	39	0.96	39	20	1.93
Cape Verde	1985	20	18	1.09	—	—	—
Congo	1987	25	23	1.08	—	—	—
Côte d'Ivoire	1986	14	11	1.21	14	10	1.33
Djibouti	1990	—	—	—	30	20	1.50
Ghana	1987–8	27	27	0.98	31	23	1.38
Lesotho	1981	16	15	1.04	—	—	—
Madagascar	1983–4	40	34	1.20	37	28	1.30
Malawi	1981	—	—	—	—	—	—
Mali	1987	30	32	0.93	34	26	1.32
Mauritius	1985	—	—	—	27	20	1.32
Namibia	1990	—	—	—	—	—	—
Niger	1985	—	—	—	52	27	1.90
Nigeria	1990	36	36	1.00	39	36	1.46
Rwanda	1982–3	29	41	0.70	33	27	1.26
Senegal	1986	23	21	1.09	25	15	1.66
Seychelles	1987–8	5	6	0.92	—	—	—
Sierra Leone	1978	—	—	—	32	24	1.33
Tanzania	1988	—	—	—	—	—	—
Togo	1988	25	24	1.05	28	16	1.75
Uganda	1988	23	23	0.99	24	13	1.90
Zambia	1990	25	24	1.04	—	—	—
Zimbabwe	1988	11	12	0.95	14	5	2.62
Asia							
Bangladesh	1989–90	65	68	0.96	67	63	1.06
India	1988–90	62	60	1.03	—	—	—
Pakistan	1990–1	41	40	1.02	45	33	1.37
Sri Lanka	1987	38	39	0.97	39	28	1.40

Source: UNICEF 1993*b*: table 2.

There is also large variance across different districts/regions within the countries for which disaggregated data are available (most of this information is contained in the FAO/ESN country profiles). In Table 11.3, the estimated prevalence of anthropometric failure in 5–38 districts/regions in a dozen SSA countries is presented. Large intra-country differences are found in Zimbabwe, Nigeria, Mali, Congo, and Botswana. Considerably less intra-country differences are observed in Benin, Cameroon, Malawi, and Kenya. Nevertheless, in most of the countries, the intra-country differences are as

TABLE 11.3. Incidence of anthropometric failure of children, by district in selected countries

Country (year) (age group)	Anthropometric indicator	Number of districts	Prevalence of anthropometric failure	
			lowest	highest
Zimbabwe (1988)	Wt/Age	10	3	16
(3–60 months)	Ht/Age	10	11	37
	Wt/Ht	10	0	2
Nigeria (1983–4)	Wt/Ht	38	3	36
(0–60 months)				
Nigeria (1987)	Wt/Age	5	25	40
(0–60 months)	Ht/Age	5	24	37
	Wt/Ht	5	0	21
Sudan (1986–7)	Wt/Ht	12	9	36
(0–60 months)				
Benin (1987–8)	Wt/Ht	6	13	17
(0–60 months)	Wt/Age	7	29	39
Congo (1987)	Wt/Age	9	17	42
(0–60 months)	Ht/Age	9	19	58
	Wt/Ht	9	2	9
Burkina Faso (1987)	Wt/Ht	8	11	26
(12–48 months)				
Niger (1985)	Wt/Age	7	44	59
(0–60 months)	Ht/Wt	7	7	16
Botswana (1990)	Wt/Age	17	7	26
(0–60 months)				
Zambia (1987)	Wt/Age	9	12	35
(0–59 months)				
Mali (1975)	Wt/Age	7	3	27
(0–59 months)				
Malawi (1982)	Wt/Age	8	32	37
(0–60 months)	Ht/Age	8	47	65
	Wt/Ht	8	0	3
Kenya (1982)	Ht/Age	6	22	39
(1–4 years)				
Cameroon (1978)	Wt/Age	8	13	27
(3–59 months)	Ht/Age	8	14	31
	Ht/Wt	8	1	1
Pakistan (1987)	Ht/Age	5	34	57
(0–60 months)	Wt/Ht	5	9	12
Peru (1984)	Wt/Age	7	3	25
(0–60 months)	Ht/Age	7	16	63
	Wt/Ht	7	0	1
Brazil (1989)	Wt/Age	9	17	40
(0–59 months)				

Source: FAO/ESN Nutrition Country Profiles, various issues.

large as the inter-country differences in Africa. This is an indication that nutritional inadequacy to a large extent is a problem of uneven access to food, health facilities, and other resources which affect child anthropometric performance within the SSA countries.

11.3.4. Anthropometric Status by Age

The estimated incidence of children with low birth weight (LBW), i.e. less than 2.5 kg, is about 13 per cent on average (unweighted) in the 17 SSA countries for which the IBRD judges the statistical base to be reasonably reliable. The range is from a low of about 5 per cent in Ghana and Zimbabwe, to a high of 32 per cent in Togo (IBRD*a* 1995: table 27). According to UNICEF, the average incidence of LBW in SSA was about 16 per cent in the early 1990s (Fig. 11.3).

The estimated prevalence of the underweight by age cohorts (1–5 year-olds) are available for 23 SSA countries. The average for these countries is shown in Fig. 11.4. During the first year, there is a sharp increase in the incidence of those who are underweight, from about 13–16 per cent LBW to almost 30 per cent underweight between the ages of 1 and 2. After that, it tapers off slightly to reach a little above 20 per cent by the age of between 4 and 5. Although the levels differ considerably across the SSA countries, this sharp increase in the early years, and the subsequent slight drop, is found in almost all the countries for which age-specific estimates of underweight are available (UNICEF 1993*a*: table 3).[5]

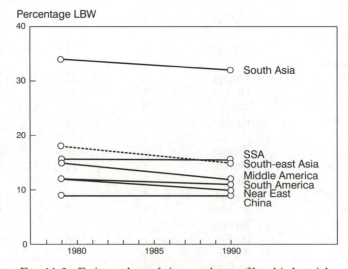

FIG. 11.3. Estimated trends in prevalence of low birth weight
(<2.5 kg) 1980–90, by major geographical regions
Source: ACC/SCN 1992: p. 55.

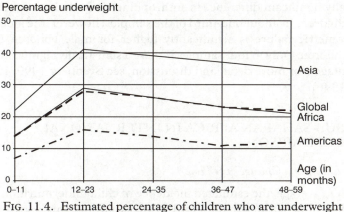

Percentage underweight

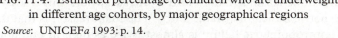

FIG. 11.4. Estimated percentage of children who are underweight
     in different age cohorts, by major geographical regions

Source: UNICEF*a* 1993: p. 14.

11.3.5. Anthropometric Status by Gender

In Table 11.2, estimates of anthropometric failure in the underweight dimension are presented for two dozen SSA countries. In most of the countries
there is no (statistically significant) difference between male and female children. There is, however, much more extensive evidence on differences in anthropometric status along gender lines in Africa.

In Table 11.4, summary statistics are reported from four surveys of evidence on the anthropometric status of children by sex in the SSA countries.
Altogether 160, what is claimed to be nationally representative, sets of anthropometric data from almost every country in the region have been examined in the four surveys, not only in the underweight dimension, but
also for stunting and wasting. In about two-thirds of the samples there is no

TABLE 11.4. Summary of evidence on gender differentials in anthropometric status
     of children aged 0–59 months in SSA countries

Study	Number of samples showing			Total
	Anti-male bias[a]	Anti-female bias[a]	No bias	
Svedberg (1990)	5	0	4	9
Klasen (1996)	21	3	45	69
Carlsson and Wardlaw (1990)	11	1	11	23
Svedberg (1996)	16	0	43	59
Total	53	4	103	160

[a] Statistically significant (χ^2-test).

Sources: Svedberg (1990), Carlsson and Wardlaw (1990), Klasen (1996), Svedberg (1996).

statistically significant difference in anthropometric status between male and female children. In about one-third of the samples, however, the incidence of anthropometric failure is significantly higher for male children than for female children. Only in four samples is there a statistically significant female disadvantage (for more detail and discussion, see Svedberg 1990, 1996 and Klasen 1996).

11.4.   SUB-SAHARAN AFRICA IN INTERNATIONAL COMPARISON

11.4.1.   Levels and Change over Time

Levels   On average, the estimated incidence of child undernutrition is lower in the SSA countries than in the Third World as a whole; this is so by all three anthropometric indicators (Table 11.5). The main reason is that the prevalence of anthropometric failure is almost twice as high in populous South Asia as compared to SSA by all three indicators. However, also in East Asia and the Pacific, the incidence of undernutrition by the weight-for-age and the weight-for-height indicators is higher than in SSA. It is also notable that no African country has a higher estimated share of undernourished children than found in India and Bangladesh by any of the indicators. In the Americas, the prevalence of undernutrition by the height-for-age indicator in Bolivia, Haiti, Honduras, Peru, and Guatemala is on a par with, or above, the average for the SSA countries. In the first two countries, the weight-for-age indicator also suggests a higher incidence of undernutrition than in Africa.

Changes Over Time   Fig. 11.2 suggests that no long-term improvement in the anthropometric status of children (with the underweight indicator) has taken place in SSA between 1975 and 1990. On comparing SSA with other major geographical regions in the World, we see that in South and South-East

TABLE 11.5. Prevalence of anthropometrically failed children under 5 years of age, by major geographical regions (per cent)

Region	Underweight (weight-for-age)	Stunting (height-for-age)	Wasting (weight-for-height)
SSA	31	39	8
Middle East and North Africa	23	33	7
South Asia	60	63	12
East Asia and Pacific	37	38	8
China	21	32	4
Americas	11	21	3
Total (developing countries)	36	42	8

Source: UNICEF 1993*b*.

Asia there has been a significant decline over the entire 1975–90 period. In the other regions, there was a decline during 1975–85, but in China and Middle America/the Caribbean, there was a slight increase between 1985 and 1990. Revised estimates for the 1985–95 period appear in Fig. 11.2.[6] According to these (highly preliminary) estimates, the prevalence of underweight children in SSA dropped by one percentage point between 1990 and 1995. The most notable message brought out by the recent estimates, however, is that the previous rather marked decline in most other regions seems to have slowed down considerably in the 1990s. (Whether this is a statistical artefact rather than a real phenomenon is discussed in the next chapter.)

11.4.2. Rural/Urban Differences

In Table 11.2 above, estimates of the prevalence of the underweight among small children are presented, showing the situation to be considerably worse in rural than in urban areas in the African countries. Although data are only reported for a few non-African (Asian) countries in that table, the rural disadvantage in this respect is a global phenomenon, although the rural 'bias' seems to be more pronounced in Africa than elsewhere (UNICEF 1993a: table 2). Also, the large intra-country differences reported in Table 11.3 are not unique for the SSA countries. Millman (1992) reports the estimated prevalence of the underweight in 10 Indian states, which ranged from 27 to 48 per cent. (The average for India in that sample is considerably lower than in the UNICEF estimates, mainly because another (lower) weight-for-age norm is used in the former.)

11.4.3. Differences by Age and Gender

According to the IBRDa (1995: table 27), except for Togo, there is no country in Africa which has an incidence of LBW as high as that in Bangladesh, Pakistan, or Sri Lanka (no data for India are presented). Notable is that Sri Lanka has an estimated incidence of LBW (22 per cent) that is almost twice as high as the African average (13 per cent).

The WHO/UNICEF (ACC/SCN 1992) have provided (admittedly rough) estimates of the prevalence of LBW on a regional basis for the 1980s (Fig. 11.3).[7] These estimates reveal the same picture as the more selective IBRD data. The LBW share is by far the highest in South Asia (above 30 per cent). It is the second highest in SSA, but the difference between SSA and the other five regions is not that dramatic. (It is notable that the prevalence of LBW is as high as 6–7 per cent in the developed countries, the same as in Ghana and Zimbabwe.) The main difference between SSA and the rest of the world is that the estimated LBW share has not declined here during the 1980s.

When it comes to gender differentials in anthropometric status in young children, the SSA countries seem to be different than most other places. In the SSA countries, it is quite common that boys have a statistically significant inferior anthropometric status *vis-à-vis* girls, but almost never the other way around (Table 11.4). In the rest of the developing world, the pattern is more varied. In some Asian and American countries, female children are at a disadvantage in terms of anthropometric status, in others vice versa. The notion that female children worldwide are at a nutritional disadvantage *vis-à-vis* male children has no support in the anthropometric evidence now available.

11.5.   ANTHROPOMETRIC STATUS OF ADULTS

The use of anthropometric measurements to assess the nutritional (and health) status of adults (as well as children above the age of five) is a rather recent phenomenon. There are few well-established anthropometric measures for adults, and the available empirical evidence is scant when compared to that concerning children. Moreover, since adults and small children are assessed with different anthropometric methods, and because cut-off points are derived from different principles, there are only limited possibilities for assessing their relative status in a given country (see next section).

11.5.1.   Measurements and Norms

There are two main types of anthropometric indicators for adults that seem to have gained reasonably wide recognition. The first is similar to those used to assess small children. This is the estimated share of the adults in a population who fall below some height or weight norm. Only for weight is there a relatively well-established norm: weights below those corresponding to a BMI of 18.5. (This number also underlies the CCOPs estimated by the FAO; cf. Chapter 9 above.) The ACC/SCN (1992: Chapter 4) has also used the share of women with a weight below 45 kg on the indication of increased obstetric risks. The same organization also estimates the share of women with a height below 145 cm, again on the basis of perceived increased health risks. Finally, the share of adult women with an arm circumference below 22.5 cm is estimated.

The second type of anthropometric measure in use is the *average* height of adults in the Third-World populations related to average height in a reference population. The reference population is usually one in which there is no reason to expect nutritional (i.e. energy) inadequacy to have prevailed for a few generations. The Northern European populations have the *de facto* highest stature in the world and are used below as a reference norm. Notable is that the stature of an adult tells us nothing about his or her *current* nutritional situation; it is only used as an indicator of the 'historical' nutritional (and health) record during childhood and adolescence. Moreover, the average height of people in a population tells us nothing about the *incidence* of stunting; it can be used only to compare averages for different populations. This is usually done on the presumption that all races and ethnic groups (with some reservations) have the same average genetic potential for *final* growth in stature (to be discussed in Chapter 12).

11.5.2. Evidence on Adult Anthropometric Failure

Incidence of Stunting and Wasting   The main evidence available is for women of reproductive age (15–49 years) collected by the ACC/SCN (1992). The base data were compiled from 340 studies from all around the world, carried out since the late 1970s. The data for women are acknowledged to be less 'secure' than the corresponding data for children, but claimed to 'give a reasonable estimate of the extent of the problem' (ACC/SCN 1992: pp.53, 73–4). The lack of similar data for males defies direct gender comparisons, but in combination with data on average height, something can still be said on gender differentials for adults (see below).

The principal findings are contained in Fig. 11.5. By most of the four indicators, women in SSA come out relatively favourably in international comparison. The share of stunted women is found to be very small in comparison with all other regions except China. In fact, by the height indicator, the incidence of failure in South Asia and South-East Asia is about five times higher than in SSA. Also, the two weight indicators, as well as the arm circumference measure, suggest that women in SSA have a considerably better anthropometric status than women in Asia, and are roughly on a par with women in Latin America.

Adult Average Height   In Table 11.6, estimates of the average height of male and female adults in ten different geographical Third-World regions are presented, as well as the height of the fifth centile (the five per cent shortest). Estimates for Northern Europe have been included in the table to facilitate comparisons of relative anthropometric failure across regions. SSA, together with East Asia (China) and South-East Asia, is found somewhere in the middle; the average height of both males and females is the smallest in Southern India and in Latin American Indian populations. It is the highest in the North African, Near Eastern and Latin American populations of European and African origin.

Males are on the average 5 to 10 per cent taller than females in the various regions, according to Table 11.6. The smallest difference is found in North Africa, the Near East and North Asia, and the largest in West Africa, South China, and the Indian populations in Latin America. West and South/East Africa have figures close to those in Northern Europe, which is also the case with populations in Northern India and Latin America of European and African decent.

It is of further note that the male:female ratio of the fifth centile is not very different from the 50th centile in most of the regions. This is an indication

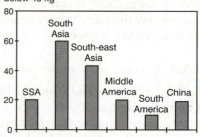

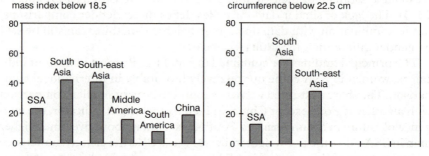

FIG. 11.5. Estimated anthropometric failure in women aged 15–49 years, by major geographical regions, 1980s

Source: ACC/SCN 1992: p. 53.

that in the most deprived segment of the population, female nutritional status relative to that of males is roughly on a par with that in the population at large; the main exception is South China. (The reliability and representativeness of these data are discussed in the next chapter.)

11.6. COMPARING CHILDREN WITH ADULTS

The weight norms (cut-off points) for adults have been derived from body weights that have been estimated to correlate with increases in health risks. The weight norms for small children have been derived from what is 'statistically abnormal' in Western populations. This means that we cannot compare the prevalence of the underweight among children and adults, respectively, *within* a country or region in a meaningful way.

However, the available estimates of incidence of anthropometric failure in children and adult women allow some interesting comparisons along age lines of relative anthropometric status *across* main geographical regions. In Fig. 11.6, the estimated prevalence of stunting and the underweight in

TABLE 11.6. Average height of adults, by major geographical regions, 1980s

	Height in cm				Male/female ratio		Height in per cent of North European			
	Males		Females				Males		Females	
Centile	5	50	5	50	5	50	5	50	5	50
West Africa	156	167	144	153	1.08	1.09	91	92	91	91
S.E. Africa	159	168	148	157	1.07	1.07	93	93	94	93
North Africa	158	169	150	161	1.05	1.05	92	93	95	95
Near East	162	171	154	161	1.05	1.06	95	95	97	95
North India	158	167	145	154	1.09	1.08	92	92	92	91
South India	153	162	139	150	1.10	1.08	89	90	88	89
North Asia	156	169	150	159	1.04	1.06	91	93	95	94
South China	161	166	143	152	1.13	1.09	94	92	91	90
S.E. Asia	153	163	144	153	1.06	1.07	89	90	91	91
Latin America										
Indian pop.	152	162	139	148	1.09	1.10	89	90	88	88
Other pop.	165	175	152	162	1.09	1.08	97	97	96	96
North Europe	171	181	158	169	1.08	1.07	100	100	100	100

Source: Base data from Jürgens *et al.* 1990: section 6.

children (aged 0–5) and adult women (aged 15–49) are plotted for six main geographical regions (no data for women are available for North Africa and Near East). When it comes to the prevalence of underweight people, there is a high correlation between children and women across regions. The prevalence of the underweight among both children and women is by far the highest in South Asia (about 60 per cent for both groups) and the lowest in South America (about 10 per cent). The two 'outliers' are South-East Asia and SSA. In both regions, about 30 per cent of the children are stunted, but the estimated incidence of stunting among women is more than twice as high in South-East Asia as it is in SSA (43 and 20 per cent, respectively).

The picture is slightly different when it comes to the relative prevalence of stunting. There is a weaker 'correlation' between the observations, reflecting that the incidence of stunting in women relative to that in children (according to the measures used) is more varied across the regions. Also in this dimension, the overall situation is worst in South Asia. And as in the case of prevalence of the underweight, South-East Asia and SSA are the main 'outliers', falling above and below the 'implicit' regression line, respectively.

The main observation emerging from Fig. 11.6 is that children are relatively far worse off in relation to adult women in SSA compared with all the other regions, and that the opposite holds in South-East Asia. There are three main possible lines of explanations for these observations. One is that there are biases of different kinds in the measurements. The second is that the norms used are different and not comparable. The third is that there are

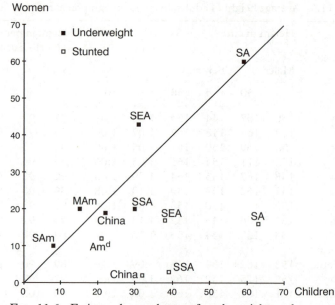

FIG. 11.6. Estimated prevalence of underweight and stunted women[a] (15–49 years) and young children[b] (0–5 years), by major geographical regions,[c] 1980s

Sources: ACC/SCN 1992; UNICEF*a* 1993.

[a] Percentage of women with weight below 45 kg; height below 145 cm
[b] Percentage of children with weight below –2 SD of the NCHS median norm
[c] SA = South Asia; SEA = South-East Asia; SSA = Sub-Saharan Africa; SAm = South America; MAm = Middle America and the Caribbean
[d] Am = Americas (no separate data for South and Middle America are available).

'factual reasons'. It could be, for instance, that children in SSA are more discriminated against in the intra-household distribution of food and health facilities than in other regions. But it could also be that children are more frequently ill in Africa for other reasons and that this explains the relatively high incidence of anthropometric failure and high mortality (the latter is well above that in South Asia). (This hypothesis will be tested in Chapter 12.)

11.7.   SUMMARY AND CONCLUSIONS

The bulk of the evidence on anthropometric failure in the world is focused on children below the age of five and refers to height and weight. With the standard cut-off points, almost 40 per cent of the children in the SSA countries are stunted (low height for age), about 30 per cent are underweight (low weight for age), and less than 8 per cent are wasted (low weight for height).

The incidence of anthropometric failure by all three indicators is almost twice as high in India and Bangladesh, and no single SSA country is comparable with the South Asian countries.

There are large variations across the African countries and also within them. The incidence of anthropometric failure in rural areas is almost twice that in urban areas, and there are large differences across districts. Comparing different age groups, one finds a drastic increase in the incidence of anthropometric failure from birth up to the age between 1 and 2 years, and, subsequently, a slight decline. A comparision of children of the two sexes, reveals that male children are found to be at a disadvantage much more frequently than female children in the SSA countries, while the opposite is common in Asia and America.

When it comes to the anthropometric status of adults, there are few commonly accepted norms and the available empirical evidence is relatively scant. It suggests that, with the exception of China, the incidence of stunting among women in SSA is much lower than anywhere else in the Third World. The incidence of underweight people (by two indicators) is also lower in SSA than in South Asia and South-East Asia, and comparable to that in Latin America. The average adult in SSA is taller than in South India, South-East Asia, and Indian populations in Latin America, but smaller than in North Africa, the Near East, and Latin America.

The average heights of adult males and females in the SSA countries in relation to the average heights of males and females in Northern Europe are about the same, indicating that there is no large gender differential. This is the case also in most other regions; the main exception is in the Indian population in Latin America, where males have a relatively better anthropometric status in the final height dimension.

In this chapter, the most widely used anthropometric indicators of nutritional status, along with a brief summary of the available evidence for Africa in international comparison, have been presented without much comment. In subsequent chapters, a critical assessment of this evidence will be undertaken. In Chapter 12, errors and measurement biases in the data are identified and analysed. In Chapter 13, the more conceptual question of how well anthropometric measurements indicate nutritional status is addressed.

NOTES

1. The ACC/SCN, the Administrative Committee on Co-ordination/Subcommittee on Nutrition, is a UN agency coordinating work on nutrition by WHO, UNICEF and the FAO. The ESN is a division of the FAO which has responsibility for the Nutrition Planning, Assessment and Evaluation Service. Its main publications are the *Nutrition Country Profiles*, which contain data not only on the anthropometric status of children, but also a large number of other indicators of the food and nutrition situation in individual countries.

2. Mora (1984) estimated the prevalence of undernutrition in a given child population with three different statistical cut-off points. The difference between the
highest and lowest estimates was more than 10 percentage points in some instances.

3. There are more anthropometric observations of pre-school children in SSA from
the 1960s and the 1970s. (For collections of such data, see Eveleth and Tanner
1976, 1990; Schofield 1979, Benefice *et al.* 1981, Dillon and Lajoie 1981, Keller
and Fillmore 1983, Haaga *et al.* 1985, ACC/SCN 1987, 1988, 1989, Kumar 1987,
Svedberg 1991*a*, Test *et al.* 1987, UNICEF 1985*b*, Gorstein and Akre 1988). The
samples covered in these studies were, however, based on such a variety of
methods, norms and cut-off points that no meaningful comparisons across countries or over time could be undertaken.

4. It is of some interest to note that this result is contrary to what has been found in
historical data from the now developed countries. In eighteenth-and nineteenth-
century Britain, 'military records show clearly that birth and residence in the
urban areas, in particular London, was associated with shorter height' (Floud
1992: p. 237). Additional evidence in the same vain and discussions are presented
by Komlos (1990) and Steckel (1995: pp. 1921–2).

5. The only exceptions are The Seychelles and Mauritania, where it increases monotonically with age.

6. The estimates for the period 1975–90 are not strictly comparable with the estimates for the period 1985–95. The largest discrepancy is for the South Asian countries, due to the introduction of a revised estimation method in India. The revised
estimate for India in 1990 is 53 per cent underweight, whereas with the previous
method, it was 61 per cent (ACC/SCN 1997*a*).

7. These data are from WHO and UNICEF; the Bank claims that 'UNICEF sources
are not strictly comparable across countries because they are compiled from a
combination of surveys and administrative records that may not have national
coverage' (IBRD*a* 1995: p. 240).

12

Anthropometric Indicators:
Measurement and Selection Biases?

12.1. INTRODUCTION

The measurement of heights and weights of individual children and adults poses no serious problems; with modern equipment these measures are relatively easy and inexpensive to obtain, even under primitive field conditions (Eveleth and Tanner 1990: chapter 2). Moreover, small measurement errors in height and weight tend to leave the estimated averages unbiased (Bairagi 1986). There are, however, at least three other potential sources of measurement biases in the anthropometric indicators presented in the previous chapter. The first is that the height norm used as a proxy for 'normal' average height in all populations may not be appropriate (section 12.2). The second is that the weight norms may be inadequate; the third is that the reported age of children contains a bias (section 12.3). There is also some doubt regarding the representativeness of part of the available anthropometric evidence (selection bias) discussed in section 12.4. The problems encountered when estimating time trends in the prevalence of anthropometric failure are scrutinized in section 12.5. Some concluding remarks are offered in section 12.6.

12.2. GENOTYPIC VERSUS PHENOTYPIC HEIGHT DIFFERENTIALS

12.2.1. Theory and Test Methods

The height norms used to estimate the proportions of children and adults that are undernourished in various populations, as reported in the previous chapter, are based on the assumption that the genetic potential for growth in stature does not differ among human races and ethnic groups. This notion is shared by many human biologists and geneticists, but there is no consensus. According to Tanner (1976), for instance, Asians (that is Chinese, Japanese, and Indo-Malays) have a somewhat smaller potential for growth than Caucasians. Roberts (1985) claims that some 'tribal' ethnic groups in the Far East are shorter for genetic reasons. 'Africans', for their part, are usually lumped together, and it seems to be widely believed that they have approximately the same potential for growth in stature as Caucasians (Eveleth and Tanner 1976, Tanner 1976, Payne 1992).

Eveleth and Tanner (1990: p.15) is the most extensive source of information available so far on the issue; they argue that 'both the size and tempo are different' [in child growth up to age five] . . .' It simply will not do to use an American or British standard to judge the growth of Japanese or Hong Kong infants or children'. They also cite a study (van Loon *et al.* 1986) in which 'the use of such [uniform] standards in Africa has been severely criticized'. If so, this is to say that we do not know to what extent the observed differences in height in the world are genotypical or phenotypical. That is, we do not know whether the enormous variation in the prevalence of height-for-age failure across countries has to do mainly with genes, or whether small (or large) stature is predominantly the outcome of external factors.[1]

12.2.2. Theory: Adaptation

From a purely theoretical point of view, the natural selection mechanism suggests that there should be adaptation of the genetic potential for growth in populations that have been confined to a specific environment for a long time. To take a few examples from Africa: the Bushmen and Pygmies have lived in rather special places (deserts and rainforests, respectively) for thousands of years in relative isolation. A small body could constitute a survival advantage in such places, which may explain their extremely short adult stature. The Nilotic people, on the other hand, have for several generations made their living mainly as nomadic cattle herders. Being able to walk long distances and spot *predatory* animals may constitute a survival advantage in this environment; and explain their exceptionally tall stature (not only in comparison with other African peoples, but also worldwide; see next section). However, few populations have lived for many generations in highly specialized and isolated locations. Most populations have been in contact with other populations, signifying intermarriage and renewal of the gene pool and, consequently, there has been no or little adaptation of adult stature to a specific, special environment.

12.2.3. Evidence on Child Growth-rate Potential

Perhaps the most notable result reported in the previous chapter was the exceptionally high incidence of stunting (and of underweight) among children in South Asia, some Central American countries with large Indian populations, and, although to a lesser extent, in South-East Asia. The data actually suggest that the incidence of stunting in South Asia is almost twice as high as in other parts of the world, including SSA (Table 11.4). All of these estimates are derived on the assumption that the genetic potential for growth during early childhood is the same in all populations. What, then, is the empirical evidence on the genetic potential for child growth in different populations?

In assessing growth potentials, a distinction between two issues has to be made. The first is whether the genetic potential for growth during childhood is the same in all populations, or whether the growth path (growth at different ages), or what Eveleth and Tanner (1990) call 'tempo', differs. The second question, which may be unrelated to the first, is whether all races and ethnic groups have the same genetic potential for final adult stature.

When growth retardation in a population is phenotypical, normal growth in stature can be achieved within one or two generations if the external constraints on growth are removed. This means that there are methods of differentiating between phenotypic and genotypic short stature in a deprived population (but not in an individual). One is to study subsamples of individuals for which adequate nutrition and health care is not a serious problem (usually the most well-to-do classes). The second is to examine differences in growth between individuals with the same ethnic origin, but who live in separate environments with different constraints on growth (e.g. blacks living in Africa and the US, respectively). A third is to measure height differences between ethnic groups which share the same environment and face similar economic constraints.

Africa   There are more than a dozen studies suggesting that children of mixed Sudanese and Bantu ethnic origin (the majority of the population in Western, Eastern and Southern Africa) living in the US and UK have the same (or even slightly higher) height for age as Caucasian children. Also, examinations of privileged children in Ethiopia, Kenya, Malawi, Nigeria, and Uganda, have found them to have an average height similar to that of children in the West.[2] Some of this evidence is reproduced in Table 12.1 (i.e. the results from studies that have presented their findings in a way compatible with the presentation of this table).

India   An anthropometric survey based on 32,000 individuals (both children and adults) in 15 major cities all over India, conducted by the Indian National Nutrition Monitoring Bureau, provides the most extensive anthropometric database available for this country (not considered by Eveleth and Tanner 1990). The results were reported by five income groups (Gopalan 1992: pp.43–4). The average heights for males and females of different ages in the most well-to-do group are reproduced in Table 12.1. The table suggests that at 5 years of age, the Indian well-to-do children and their Caucasian cousins in the US and Europe have almost identical heights. This applies to both females and males.

Gopalan (1992) reports additional results from another Indian survey, showing differences in height between children (sexes combined) from poor agricultural day-labour families and from 'highly affluent' families, respectively.

TABLE 12.1. Average height of well-to-do children and adolescents in different countries, by age and sex

	Males (cm)				Females (cm)			
	Age (years)[a]				Age (years)[a]			
	3	5	12	16	3	5	12	16
Africa (well-to-do)								
Kenya (Nairobi)[c]	96	110	147	—	95	109	150	—
Nigeria (Ibadan)	97	111	—	—	96	109	—	—
African ancestery[c]								
US	95	112	148	171	94	109	154	165
UK[d]	—	—	—	—	—	—	—	—
Asia								
India (urban well-to do)	—	110	144	165	—	108	140	156
China (urban)[b]	95	109	144	165	94	108	147	159
Indonesia (Jakarta)[b]	97	108	—	—	97	107	—	—
Japan (national)[b]	92	106	147	169	92	105	149	157
Asian ancestry (UK)								
Sikhs[b]	—	111	—	—	—	109	—	—
Pakistani Muslims[b]	—	110	—	—	—	108	—	—
Indian Hindus[b]	—	116[e]	—	—	—	108	—	—
Americas								
Mexican-Americans[b]	95	108	149	169	93	107	150	159
Europe								
Denmark	97	111	149	174	96	111	150	165
Sweden	96	110	149	175	95	109	151	162
United States								
NCHS	95	110	150	173	95	109	152	164

[a] The choice of ages reported here is based on consideration of growth spurts.
[b] Not well-to-do, but average.
[c] Two different sources for different age groups.
[d] No data for the age categories were used here, but heights were on a par with the NCHS norms for other age groups.
[e] Probably a misprint.

Sources: Gopalan 1992 (India); Stephenson *et al.* 1983 (NCHS); Eveleth and Tanner 1990 (rest).

At the age of 5, the average height of children already differs by almost 20 cm (89 versus 108) between the two groups. In the 'highly affluent' group, the children are roughly on a par with the median National Center for Heath Statistics (NCHS) norm for 5-year-olds.[3]

The Indian surveys permit relatively definitive conclusions. First, well-to-do children have roughly the same height as Caucasian children at the age of five. Second, there is an enormous gap between child height within India, correlated with the economic/social status of families. These two observations suggest that (i) the genetic potential for growth in early childhood in

Indian populations is not significantly different from the norms used by WHO and UNICEF to assess child anthropometric status worldwide and (ii) consequently, the short height of the average Indian child is phenotypical rather than genotypical.

Other Asia Empirical evidence from urban China and Indonesia also suggests that 3 and 5-year-old children here have approximately the same height as children in the developed countries in the West (Table 12.1). It is notable that the children in the Chinese and Indonesian samples are not exclusively from well-to-do families: these data give averages of all urban classes. Still, they have the same height as Caucasian children at that age. Droomers *et al.* (1995) found preschool children from high socio-economic classes in Jakarta (Indonesia) to be taller (and heavier) than the NCHS reference population. Children of South-Asian ancestry living in the UK (Sikhs, Pakistani Muslims, and Indian Hindus; cf. Table 12.1) also have heights-for-age comparable to the NCHS norms. Children in Japan seem to be a little shorter, but only by a few centimetres. There is, however, some more recent evidence on the growth of Japanese children which suggests the same growth path as in the US for *males* (only) up to the age of fourteen (Table 12.2).

Americas There is no evidence from well-to-do native populations in Middle and South America. The only study of some relevance in this context is the one of Mexican Americans reported in Table 12.1. These children are marginally shorter than the NHCS norm; they do not come from well-to-do, but average, families.

12.2.4. Evidence on Genetic Potential for Final Adult Stature

The estimates presented in the previous chapter (see Fig. 11.5) suggest that the incidence of stunting among women of reproductive age in South Asia,

TABLE 12.2. Stature of male adolescents and adult males in Japan

	Boys (cm)			Adults (cm)	
	Age (years)			Centile	
	10	14	17	5	50
Japan	137	164	169	163	172
NCHS	137	163	176	171	181
Difference	0	+1	−7	−8	−9

Sources: *Asiaweek* 1988; Jürgens *et al.* 1990 (height norm for adult men = Northern European average); Stephenson *et al.* 1983 (NCHS norm).

South-East Asia, and Middle America is about *five times* as high as in SSA. These estimates have been derived on the assumption that the genetic potential for final adult stature is the same in all populations. The standard method for checking the genetic potential for final adult height in deprived populations is to sample individuals who have lived for a generation or two in places (often abroad) where there is no such deprivation.

Africa   Several studies have found that blacks living in the US and the UK have the same average adult stature as the Caucasian population of the respective countries (Eveleth and Tanner 1976). However, the blacks in the US and the UK have different mixtures of ethnic (genetic) background and cannot be taken to represent a homogeneous ethnic group. To answer the question of whether there are differences in the genetic potential for growth across ethnic groups in Africa itself, the third method outlined above has to be applied.

Using this method, Hiernaux (1964: p.287) argues that it would be 'misleading to consider "the" African as a homogeneous genetic entity'. The very tall *de facto* stature of adults in populations of Nilotic origin suggests that they have a higher average genetic potential for growth than Africans of Sudanese or Bantu stock, or for that matter, Caucasians. Many Nilotic people live in the same environment as significantly shorter Bantu groups. The best studied case is that of the Tutsis and the Hutus, the two predominant tribes in Rwanda and Burundi. The Tutsis, a Nilotic ethnic group, are 5 per cent taller as adults than the Hutus, a Bantu group (Hiernaux 1964).[4] This suggests that the Tutsis' potential for growth is greater than that of both Bantus and Caucasians, as also concluded by Roberts and Bainbridge (1963).[5]

The same seems to apply to other Nilotic populations. Fig. 12.1, suggests that the height of the average adult male in the Nilotic populations is the same as in the European countries with the tallest people (Scandinavia, The Netherlands, and the UK). In all seven Nilotic populations, the average male is taller, by 3–4 cm, than the average male in the average European country. However, the average male in the various Bantu populations, at 167 cm (ranging from 164 to 169 cm), is 5–6 cm shorter (3–4 per cent) than the average European male. The picture is roughly the same for females (but there are fewer observations than for males). The Nilotic people are found mostly in the Eastern and North-Eastern countries in SSA.[6] It is thus notable that the average adult male and female in Western Africa are somewhat shorter than in Eastern (and Southern) Africa (Table 11.4).

Asia   Greulich (1957, 1967) found that Japanese who had lived under favourable circumstances in the US for two or more generations were still somewhat shorter than Caucasians living in the same environment. More recent measures from Japan itself seem to corroborate this conclusion. At the age of 17, Japanese boys are an estimated 9 cm shorter than their US

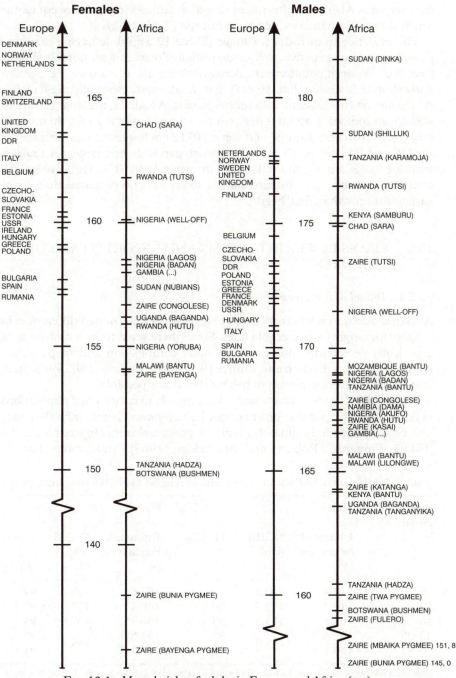

FIG. 12.1. Mean height of adults in Europe and Africa (cm)
Source: Eveleth and Tanner 1976, 1990.

counterparts. Also, as adults, males as well as females in Japan are equally as much shorter than men in Northern Europe (Table 12.2).

The evidence from India is similar (Table 12.3). While having the same growth up to the age of five, well-to-do Indian adolescents are notably shorter than their Western counterparts. Already by the age of 12 they are significantly shorter (by more than 10 cm) than Westerners, especially the females. At the age of 16, the same differences persist. As adults, the final stature in well-to-do Indians is about 9 per cent (*c*. 15 cm) lower than for their counterparts in Northern Europe and some 10–12 cm lower than the average for the US and Europe. At all ages, the growth gap is slightly larger for females than for males among the well-to-do in urban India. The tentative overall conclusion is thus that Indians have a lower genetic potential than Caucasians for growth in *final* height.

12.3. BIASES IN WEIGHT NORMS AND REPORTED AGE OF CHILDREN

12.3.1. Biased Weight Norms?

A related question is whether there are genetically determined differences in weight (for height) along ethnic lines. Since there seem to be a multitude of genetically determined differences in body composition and shape across ethnic groups (see Eveleth and Tanner 1976, 1990, Jürgens *et al.* 1990), there is at least a theoretical reason to believe that this is possible.

Empirical evidence is scarce and relates mainly to rather small populations in Africa. Niolitic populations may not be exceptionally tall only; they may also be more slenderly (linearly) built for genetic reasons. In examining the 'Nilotic Physique', Roberts and Bainbridge (1963) found more than 20

TABLE 12.3. Height of well-to-do Indians and in relation to NCHS standards, by age

Age group	Males			Females		
	Estimated height (cm) (1)	NCHS (cm) (2)	(1)/(2) (%) (3)	Estimated height (cm) (4)	NCHS (cm) (5)	(4)/(5) (%) (6)
5	110.4	110.0	100	107.6	109.0	99
12	144.2	149.5	96	140.4	152.0	92
16	164.5	173.5	95	156.2	167.0	94
22–25	166.4 }	181.0	92	154.6 }	169.0	92
40–45	166.8 }		92	153.1 }		91

Sources: Heights of well-to-do Indians are from Gopalan (1992) based on the Indian National Nutrition Monitoring Bureau. The NCHS data are from Stephenson *et al.* 1983, Charts III-6 and III-7. The height norms for adults are from Jürgens *et al.* 1990.

different body characteristics of the Niolitic peoples that make them light for their height, ranging from 'thin, fragile-boned face' to 'weak musculing of thighs'.[7]

Again, the Tutsis and the Hutus in Rwanda and Burundi make an interesting comparison. The Tutsis are not only significantly taller than the Hutus, they are also much thinner (as measured by the BMI). At least some observers have found it difficult to believe that this 'was due to nutritional factors alone' (Hiernaux 1964: p. 282; see also Roberts and Bainbridge 1963). It is notable that at the time of these observations, the Hutus 'were the serfs of the Tutsis'. The economically better-off Tutsis had 'a similar, if not slightly *better* diet than the Hutus' and the two groups lived 'in roughly similar environmental conditions' (Hiernaux 1964: pp. 279–80, my italics added). Hiernaux's (1964: p.282), conclusion is that 'for some genetic reason, the Tutsi escape adult fattening in conditions in which the Hutu do not'.[8]

However, while Nilotic people may be exceptionally thin for genetic reasons, they seem to be exceptional. There is no known reason for believing that genetic differences in 'weight potential' could constitute a serious source of bias in comparisons of weight-for-height and weight-for-age failures within Africa, or between Africa and other regions. The main weight differences in the world are most likely to be phenotypical. This is also concluded by Conwey (1995) in his analysis of ethnical differences in the predisposition for obesity.

12.3.2. Biases in the Reported Age of Children

In many places, neither officials nor parents record the birth date of children, and parents often have very imprecise recollections of when a particular child was born. Even if the errors in the reported age are randomly distributed, there will be biases in the height-and weight-for-age estimates due to non-linearities in height-and weight-for-age growth (Bairagi 1986). It may also be that parents systematically tend either to over- or to understate the age of the children, knowingly or unconsciously. Anthropologists and demographers have noticed that in societies where girls marry early and a bride-price is paid, e.g. in SSA, parents tend to overstate the girl's age (Caldwell and Caldwell 1987). In the parts of India and South Asia where a dowry is the custom, there is an incentive to understate girls' ages. Eveleth and Tanner (1990) further argue that: 'In some countries with a male-predominant culture parents knowingly increase the age of boys so as to get them as early as possible into school'. This applies mostly to India, China, and some parts of South and South-East Asia, where the women are underrepresented in the population: the 'missing women', in Sen's words (Sen 1992).

There are techniques for handling errors and biases in reported age, such as double-checking and excluding children for whom two or more independent sources do not give approximately the same birth date. But these techniques are time-consuming and costly, and in most surveys reporting height- and weight-for-age data, the problem is simply ignored (Eveleth and Tanner 1976: pp.13–14, 1990: pp.14–15).[9]

That there may be biases in the reported age of children inflicts three possible biases in the anthropometric evidence presented in Chapter 11. The first relates to the inferior anthropometric status of boys *vis-à-vis* girls in Africa. If the ages of girls are generally overestimated (but not boys'), this means that their 'true' anthropometric performance is better than actually estimated. It also means that the relatively higher incidence of anthropometric failure in males would be accentuated if the estimation bias of girls' ages were corrected for.

The second relates to the inferior anthropometric status of female children reported in a number of studies from India (especially in the Northern Hindu states) and Bangladesh, *vis-a-vis* boys.[10] If girls' ages are underreported here, this means that the anthropometric status of females is, in fact, worse than the estimates suggest. Conversely, if boys' ages are overstated, this means that their *de facto* anthropometric performance is better than hitherto thought. A correction for these biases in reported age would imply that the 'true' over-representation of anthropometric failure for females in these countries is larger than the actual observations suggest. This would also mean that the gender differences between SSA countries and South Asia in this respect are more accentuated than we have had reason to believe so far.

Finally, if the reported age for girls tends to be overstated in SSA and/or understated in South Asia, and there is no bias in the reported age of boys in Africa, while there is in Asia, this will influence the average estimated anthropometric status of children in general (average for boys and girls). In Africa, the 'true' prevalence of anthropometric failure would be lower (*cet par*); in South Asia, it would be higher. All the above biases may be large or small; we have no way of quantifying them—we can only identify their plausible directions.

12.4. REPRESENTATIVENESS OF THE ANTHROPOMETRIC EVIDENCE

There are three levels at which some of the available anthropometric surveys (reported from in the previous chapter) may not be representative, i.e. may contain selection biases. First, the estimates for the SSA region as a whole in 1990 are derived from samples from only 33 out of approximately 50 countries in the region; in other regions the coverage is more complete. Secondly, the subpopulations that have been sampled in the various countries in the world may not be nationally representative. Thirdly, the individuals examined in the respective samples may not be representative of the particular ethnic and economic group to which they belong.

12.4.1. Representative Countries?

WHO has conducted what it considers to be nationally representative, anthropometric surveys for about 70 of countries (as of the end of 1995) with some 90 per cent of the under-five population (reproduced in FAO*a* 1996: appendix 2, table 8). In Africa, data are lacking for some relatively large countries such as Angola, Mozambique, Zaïre (now the Congo), and South Africa, and also for some small countries in West Africa. South Asia is more completely covered. However, considering the high percentage coverage of the child population in both the SSA and South Asian regions, there is little reason to suspect a large representativeness bias in this dimension in the most recent WHO data. (Also, earlier UNICEF estimates for the SSA region were obtained from a much smaller number of countries, which may have induced bias in the inter-temporal comparisons; see below.)[11]

12.4.2. Representative Samples?

Many of the 50 SSA countries are highly diverse in terms of ethnic composition. According to one inventory, there are more than 1,000 ethnic groups in SSA (Oliver and Crowder 1983). Some countries, such as Nigeria and Zaïre, have more than 100 ethnic groups within their borders. As discussed above, one cannot preclude the possibility that there are differences among the ethnic groups in genetic potential for growth, even though the (incomplete) empirical evidence for pre-school-age children suggests that there is no difference.

More importantly, however, there are wide differences in living standards and access to food and health care within countries that induce regional differences in the anthropometric status of children. As we saw in Chapter 11 (Table 11.3), the intra-country differences in the incidence of anthropometric failure are as large as the inter-country differences in SSA. If samples are not nationally representative, relatively large biases can thus be induced. How well national representativeness is ensured in large and diverse SSA countries, such as Nigeria and Ethiopia, is open to question. The Nigerian estimate for 1990 is based on a sample of 5,560 children. This sample is larger than those of most other African countries (for which the average is about 2,000), but considering the size and diversity of Nigeria, one must doubt the representativeness of the sample.

There are also large inter-state differences in child anthropometric status in India, according to many sources (e.g. Millman 1992). There is also high diversity along ethnic lines: according to Eveleth and Tanner (1990), 56 ethnic groups live in India. The UNICEF estimates for India are obtained from only 10 out of 25 states, which casts serious doubt on their representativeness. Unfortunately, WHO does not publish any details that can be of help in assessing the representativeness of their samples.

12.4.3.   Representative Individuals?

Children   Some years ago, a substantial part of the children in the WHO/
UNICEF samples were not randomly selected: the sample frame often com-
prised mainly children who had been brought to a health clinic (which most
probably induced an upward bias in the estimated incidence of anthropometric failure). In recent years, anthropometric data have been obtained
from cross-sectional, national-level household surveys (UNICEF*a* 1993:
p.7), which are less likely to contain significant selection bias at the level of
individuals.

Adults   The ACC/SCN (1992), the main provider of estimates of the incidence of the underweight and stunting among women of reproductive age in
the various regions of the world, acknowledges that their data are not always
based on representative samples, but say nothing about what possible biases
their estimates may contain.

12.5.   THE TIME DIMENSION

Introducing a time dimension into the analysis opens up possibilities for additional errors and biases in the anthropometric evidence presented in the
previous chapter. One concerns the comparability between countries, the
other the estimates of trends over time.

12.5.1.   Inter- and Intra-year Fluctuations

As is well documented, there are large annual variations in weather and other
factors that influence peoples' food and health standards—and thus anthropometric status—in Africa. The years 1972/4 as well as 1984/5 were especially bad in the countries in and bordering the Sahel zone. A prolonged
drought initiated a famine that took an estimated 100,000 lives in the early
1970s and presumably left the rest of the population more wasted and
stunted than before (and after). Ethiopia, Sudan, and Somalia too were badly
affected by drought and famine in these years. In Southern Africa, Botswana,
Zimbabwe, Angola, Zambia, and Mozambique experienced drought and
impending famine during several years in the 1980s and early 1990s.

Even between less extreme years there are variations in conditions that affect food (and health) standards, and thus the anthropometric status of the
population. The surveys for the various countries reported in Chapter 11
above were conducted in different years (between 1985 and 1994). In some
of the countries, the surveys were probably conducted in a year with relatively
favourable local conditions, and in other countries in a year with below
normal conditions. This implies that the results are not strictly comparable.

There is little scope for assessing the importance of this bias, since swings in weather and related natural, as well as economic, conditions are not easily quantifiable.[12]

It is also possible that seasonality (intra-year variations) has adversely affected the comparability of the weight-for-height estimates of pre-school-age children in the different countries. The seasonal variations in anthropometric status of both children and adults have been observed to be relatively large. One study from Gambia showed 4 and 9 per cent of the children to be wasted in the most and least favourable months of 1982; in the previous year the equivalent figures were 5 and 8 per cent (Tomkins *et al.* 1986). Monthly weight-for-age observations for 5–8 year-olds in the 1980s, obtained in several countries in the Sahel as well as in Botswana and Ghana, show the incidence of underweight children to vary by more than 10 percentage points between the best and the worst months in most years (UNICEF*a* 1985: figure 3, ACC/SCN 1989). WHO does not say whether it derives its annual estimates as an average for several seasons; if not, some of the estimates are likely to be biased.[13]

12.5.2. Long-term Trends

When recent estimates of the prevalence of undernutrition are compared to earlier ones in order to monitor long-term trends, problems arise. The estimated trends in the 12 SSA countries shown in Fig. 11.1 are derived by drawing a line between two point estimates. If one of these two years (or both) is atypical, the 'trend' has little meaning.

As we also saw in Chapter 11, the ACC/SCN (1992, 1997*a*) has produced estimates of the incidence of under-weight children for the period 1975–95 by major geographical regions in the world (reproduced as Fig. 11.2 in the previous chapter). The estimates for 1975, 1980, and 1985 are based on surveys from 40 countries for one (or two) particular year(s) between 1970 and 1986, for which a nationally representative anthropometric survey was available. The regional estimates were derived with the help of a regression equation, where predicted prevalence of undernutrition in the remaining countries was estimated from data on per-capita calorie availability and infant mortality rates, and some regional dummies.

There are two main problems with this approach. One is of errors and biases in the two 'explanatory' variables. The per-capita calorie availability data for SSA countries (in international comparison) were scrutinized in Chapter 6, and need no further comment. Infant mortality rates for a large number of countries are either not available for nationally representative samples, or are interpolated by various techniques similar to that used by the ACC/SCN to estimate the prevalence of undernutrition (Chamie 1994). The second problem is that practically no nationally representative data for the SSA countries were available before 1985. Keller and Fillmore (1983)

claimed that only three surveys from this region were nationally representative in the early 1980s. This means that the data base for the estimates for the
SSA region as a whole in 1975, 1980, and 1985 (Table 11.1) is very small and
most likely non-representative. All this is not to say that the downward trends
in anthropometric failure (by the underweight indicator) in most of the world
since 1975 should be questioned: it is possible that the slopes of the downward trends from 1975 to 1990 are too steep.

12.6. SUMMARY AND CONCLUSIONS

In this chapter we have discussed potential and actual errors, and measurement and selection biases in the anthropometric measurements from WHO
that were presented in the previous chapter. One of the 'positive' findings is
that the Western height norms used to assess the anthropometric status of
children up to the age of 5 in Africa are probably applicable to most ethnic
groups of Sudanese and Bantu ethnic origin (i.e. more than three-quarters of
the total population in SSA). Also Asian pre-school-age children seem to
have roughly the same potential for age-specific growth as Caucasian children.[14] There is thus no compelling reason to expect that the estimated differences in average incidence of anthropometric failure in small children
between SSA and South Asia is to a significant extent genotypical. Phenotypical explanations, including poor nutrition and ill health, are more likely.

However, the use of the same norm for final adult height has most likely induced a bias in the comparative estimates of incidence of adult stunting in
women. The Western height norms for adults seem to be good proxies for the
average genetic potential for final growth in stature of most Africans (although they may not apply as well to people of Nilotic, Bushmen, and Pygmy
origin). However, the genetic potential for final adult stature seems to be
lower in parts of Asia (at least in India and Japan). The true difference in adult
stunting between SSA and most of Asia (and also Middle America) could
thus be significantly smaller than reported by the ACC/SCN (Fig. 11.6
above).

Another complication is that there probably is an upward bias in the reported age of female children in most of Africa. This bias tends to induce an
upward bias in the estimated prevalence of anthropometric failure in female
children when weight- or height-for-age are used as indicators. The age bias
also compromises the comparability of anthropometric performance between SSA and South Asia, both in terms of gender differentials and for children in general.

The representativeness of the anthropometric surveys available was assessed further in different dimensions. The WHO anthropometric estimates
for children from the most recent years appear to have been obtained for
reasonably representative countries, population groups, and individuals,

although sample sizes are generally too small. The main problems arise when the time dimension is introduced into the picture.

The comparability across countries is distorted by the fact that the surveys have been conducted in different years, when weather and other conditions affecting child anthropometric status have been different. The other distortion relates to inter-temporal comparability in individual countries. Only in recent years has there been reason to expect WHO (and other) data on child anthropometric status to be acceptably reliable and based on nationally representative samples. In order to estimate developments over time, the WHO compares the recent estimates with earlier ones derived with much less accurate methods and less representative samples.

Most of the issues discussed in this chapter are related to *technical* measurement and estimation problems. In the next chapter, we shall focus more on the *conceptual* problems involved in using anthropometric measurements as indicators of undernutrition.

NOTES

1. On closer scrutiny, however, the van Loon *et al.* study only provides indications that the average height of the average child in a few different African countries does differ. There is no evidence to show that the height of well-off children differs across countries (see section 12.2.2 below).

2. The main studies are: Burgess and Burgess 1964 (Kenya), Bohdal and Simmons 1969 (comparative), Cant *et al.* 1982 (Uganda), Eksmyr 1970 (Ethiopia), Janes 1970, 1974 (Nigeria), Habicht *et al.* 1974 (comparative), Alnwick 1980 (Kenya), Graitcer and Gentry 1981 (comparative), Kulin *et al.* 1982 (comparative), Stephenson *et al.* 1983 (Kenya), Macfarlane 1995 (Nigeria), and Quinn *et al.* 1995 (Malawi). Most of these studies conclude that the well-to-do children in their samples have a height comparable with their Western counterparts.

3. Similar results from other surveys in India are reported in Dasgupta (1993). It is interesting to note further that also in nineteenth century Europe there were as marked differences in the anthropometric status of children along income and class lines (Floud 1992: p.239). That the well-to-do children here, as well as in contemporary India (and also other developing countries), have such a favourable anthropometric status is somewhat surprising, considering what Floud has termed the 'peerage paradox'. That is, children from the most affluent families, one would expect, are to *some* extent also exposed to the negative consequences for growth that follow from living in an overall unhealthy environment. The answer to the 'paradox' must be that the children from the affluent homes have been efficiently protected from the health hazards in society in general.

4. Although the question of whether the very short stature of the Pygmies, Hottentots, and Bushmen is due to genotypic or phenotypic adaptation is of considerable theoretical interest, it is less important in practice. These ethnic groups, once the sole human inhabitants of most of Eastern and Southern SSA, make up only one per cent of the population in the region today.

5. These observations were made in the early 1960s, when Hutus and Tutsis were clearly distinct ethnic groups. Later, it has become more difficult to distinguish between the two (Dowler *et al.* 1980, Cant *et al.* 1982).

6. Peoples of Nilotic ethnic origin make up about one quarter of the population in contemporary SSA (Oliver and Crowder 1983). They dominate in Southern Sudan and in the northern parts of the Sahelian countries. They are also found in northern Kenya, Uganda, Tanzania, and in Burundi and Rwanda. The Nilo-Hamites in Ethiopia and Somalia are usually considered a separate race.

7. In the words of physical anthropologists, 'The Nilotic group is particularly low in endomorphy and mesomorphy and shows an extreme degree of ectomorphic dominance' (Roberts and Bainbridge 1963: p.357).

8. The Pygmies and the Bushmen fulfil 96–100 per cent of the weight for height norm used here. Whether this norm is applicable to these exceptionally short peoples is open to question on the same grounds as those regarding the Nilotic peoples.

9. The skeletal age of children can be estimated with different methods. Across a dozen such studies conducted using the Tanner-Whitehouse method, the chronological age exceeds the skeletal age more in the one African sample (from Dakar in West Africa) than in all the others, which include two black populations from Jamaica and the USA (see Eveleth and Tanner 1976: appendix table 105). The conventional interpretation would be that this shows late skeletal development of the children in Africa (supposedly because of undernutrition and poor health). An alternative interpretation is that the reported age of the African children is systematically overstated.

10. The evidence from India does not point uniformly in this direction. Millman (1992: chapter VI) reports data from the Indian National Nutrition Monitoring Board from several states in the southern part of the country, which show female children to be underweight much less frequently than males.

11. In ACC/SCN (1997a), regional estimates of the prevalence of the underweight for the years 1993 and 1995 are presented. They point to a slight decline in SSA over the 1990s, but whether the estimate for 1995 is based on a sufficient number of countries in the region to ensure representativeness is yet unclear.

12. For Ghana and Botswana, there are annual estimates for the 1980s of the prevalence of the underweight in small children brought to health clinics. The annual samples are based on some 100,000 children in each country obtained nationwide. In both countries there are significant inter-year fluctuations, by more than 10 percentage points. In none of the countries in Fig. 11.1 are the estimated 'trends' based on variations of that order of magnitude.

13. See Dasgupta (1993: p.254 and note 38) for more evidence on seasonal fluctuations in anthropometric status. There is also at least one study that has found significant seasonal differences in anthropometric status in multivariable regression tests (Kumar 1994: table 45).

14. This is counter to what is claimed by Eveleth and Tanner (1990: p.15). They argue that there are inter-ethnic differences in the growth potential for children below the age of five. This is a bit surprising, considering that much of the evidence that suggests the opposite (reported in Table 12.1 above) is taken from tables in their book. The main exception is the data from well-to-do children in India, which further strengthen the conclusion derived here. (See also references in footnote 2, above.)

13

Anthropometric Status: An Incomplete Indicator of Undernutrition

13.1. INTRODUCTION

Evidence on the anthropometric status of children and adults in the SSA countries was presented and compared internationally in Chapter 11. Actual and potential measurement errors and biases and the representativeness of the available anthropometric surveys were analysed in Chapter 12. In this chapter, the objective is to address the more conceptual question of how complete and accurate anthropometric measures are as indicators of nutritional status.

The chapter proceeds as follows. Section 13.2 deals with the question of whether failure in anthropometric status is a necessary and/or a sufficient condition for defining a person as undernourished, taking into consideration the physical activity dimension of undernutrition. In section 13.3, the extent to which the conventional height-for-age indicator captures the failure of an individual to attain his or her genetic potential growth rate is analysed. In section 13.4, it is proposed that a more disaggregated anthropometric classification system than that conventionally used (distinguishing between stunting, underweight, and wasting) could be a way of improving the predictive power of anthropometric measures of future impairments, such as mortality risk. In section 13.5, it is shown that none of the three conventional height and weight indicators fully captures all children with anthropometric failure in one or more of the three dimensions; a new index is proposed that does this. The chapter closes with a brief summary.

13.2. ANTHROPOMETRIC FAILURE: IS IT NECESSARY AND/OR SUFFICIENT FOR UNDERNUTRITION?

13.2.1. The Missing Physical Activity Dimension

The use of retarded growth in stature and/or low weight as indicators of undernutrition has a strong common-sense appeal. These measures also form the bulk of the available evidence on 'undernutrition' in Africa and elsewhere, as we have seen in previous chapters. However, the height and weight measures are often used to estimate undernutrition in individuals or in groups without clarification of how undernutrition is defined.

The simplest 'definition' is to equate undernutrition with anthropometric shortcoming in one dimension or another. This is the backbone of the so-called genetic potential approach, focusing on height. UNICEF, in some of its publications, states that 'the term malnutrition is used interchangeably with underweight' (UNICEF*a* 1993: 6). Also, the FAO*a* (1996: appendix 2, table 8) equates anthropometric failure with 'undernutrition'. This is, of course, a crude simplification. First, it means that the physical activity dimension of undernutrition is ignored.[1] Secondly, it implies than 'mal- or undernutrition' is the only cause of being underweight (ignoring the possibility that illness could be the prime reason for low weight; see Chapter 15 below).

13.2.2.   *A Simple Model*

The concern for nutrition-related physical inactivity is focused mainly on small children.[2] A child may have normal height and weight and yet be undernourished in the sense that he or she does not expend enough energy in play and other physical activities to maintain health and develop fully his or her cognitive and psychomotoric capabilities (Osmani 1984). He or she will then be 'undernourished' in the physical activity dimension.

'Acceptable' height and/or weight are thus neither necessary, nor sufficient for defining an individual as well-nourished. The point can be illustrated with the help of Fig. 13.1. On the vertical axis we measure the anthropometric status (e.g. weight for age) of children in a population. On the horizontal axis we measure the physical activity of the children. The ellipse encloses the distribution of weights (for age) and the activity levels observed (hypothetically). By the weight-for-age cut-off point ($W/A^\star$) in Fig. 13.1, the children in areas a and b fall out as 'undernourished'. If one also introduces a cut-off

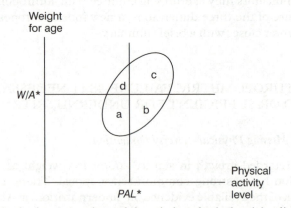

FIG. 13.1. Anthropometrics and the missing physical activity dimension

point for physical activity, at PAL^*, we see that the anthropometric indicator provides a (downward-) biased estimate of the undernourished, i.e. it misses the children in area d, who have a weight above the norm, but exert too little physical activity.

Whether the children in area d make up a small or large share of the total population depends on how children react to undernourishment. If the first line of defence is reduced physical activity below the level that is compatible with health, and mental and physical fitness and development, followed by wasting (and stunting), the anthropometric indicators will miss the inactive children with acceptable weights. On the other hand, if reduced body size is the first sign of inadequate nutrition, using anthropometrics will cause no problem, since these measures will include the inactive children too. This is to say that the number of children in area d would be small relative to the total population.

Unfortunately, there is no generally accepted theory of, and no empirical evidence on, how the young child normally adapts to nutritional stress (see Rutishauser and Whitehead 1972, Beaton and Ghassemi 1982, Martorell and Ho 1984, Rogers 1995). Martorell (1995) concludes that: 'Almost nothing is known about the role of diminished physical activity in coping with energy deficiency in children'. A related problem is that we know rather little about where to set the physical activity cut-off point (PAL^*). That is, there are no clear indications as to at what low physical activity levels children's mental development and health are impaired (see Chapter 15 below). Yet another problem is that it is inherently difficult to measure the physical activity exerted by small children (although the DLW method discussed in Chapter 7 is a possibility).

13.3. ANTHROPOMETRIC CUT-OFF POINTS AND GENETIC POTENTIAL

The adherents of the genetic potential paradigm see an individual's failure to attain his or her full genetic potential for growth in stature as the hallmark of undernutrition (or deprivation in other dimensions).[3] When the aim is to identify stunted individuals, the genetic potential height has little practical relevance, however. The simple reason is that the *biological/genetical technology available today does not allow us to measure the genetic potential for growth of an individual*. This also has the consequence that when the aim is to estimate the prevalence of stunting in a population, anthropometric cut-off points have to be established, and that will induce biases in the estimates, as we shall see.

13.3.1. The Height Cut-off Point

The *average* genetic potential for growth in a population can be estimated quite accurately by studying subsets of individuals for which food and health care pose little problem, or using a population from the rich countries as reference (as discussed in Chapter 12 above). In most of these reference populations, only about 3 per cent of the children have a height-for-age below 2 SD of the median. If the children in a study population have the same *average* genetic potential for growth in stature and the *distribution* around the mean is the same (the standard assumptions), one would expect 3 per cent of the children in the study population, in the absence of external constraints on growth, to be below the 2 SD cut-off point as well. Now, if 40 per cent of the children are found to be below the height norm (roughly the average for the African countries), it is conventionally concluded that the excess 37 per cent is explained by external (non-genetic) factors, such as chronic undernutrition. And for the individual child who belongs in the 40 per cent group, there is only a 3 per cent probability that he or she is erroneously classified as undernourished when the true reason is low genetic potential for growth.

Can one conclude that the 60 per cent of children who are above the cut-off point in the African countries are well-nourished in the growth-potential dimension, as is implicitly claimed by WHO/UNICEF and other users of the height-for-age indicator? This depends on what is meant by well-nourished. If we mean that the individual's *own genetic potential for growth* should be achieved, one cannot conclude this. When the average *de facto* height for age is substantially lower in the study than in the reference population, while the average genetic potential is the same, almost every single child in the study population may in fact be below his or her individual-specific genetic-potential growth path.

13.3.2. Underestimation of Genetic Potential Failure: A Simple Model

The underestimation of failure to attain genetic-potential growth can be illustrated with the help of Fig. 13.2. Along the vertical axis we have the actual height of children. Along the horizontal axis we have the genetic potential growth of the children (which we cannot measure). In a (reference) population, where there are no or few constraints on the children to attain their genetic-potential growth rate, actual and genetic potential growth will be approximately the same. In Fig. 13.2, this means that most of the observations for the reference population lie on the 45° line (the solid part) and a few close below it. (There are, for evident reasons, no observations above the 45° line.)

Also the height observations for the children in (hypothetical) deprived population have been depicted by dots (one for each child) in Fig. 13.2. Only a few are on or close to the 45° line (by assumption). When the standard –2 SD from the median in the reference population is taken as the cut-off point, the children in the study population who fall below the horizontal line corresponding to $H/A^\star$ will be classified as stunted (area b) and all the children above this line as non-stunted (area a).

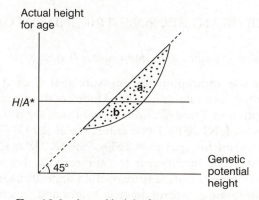

FIG. 13.2. Actual height for age and genetic-
potential height

We immediately see that there are two errors in the estimates. Some children with an actual height below the cut-off point will be classified as stunted (growth retarded), while they in fact are this short for genetic reasons. These are the children in the study population who are on the 45° line below the cut-off point. Other children will be classified as 'normal' while they in fact have not attained their genetic-potential growth. These are the children above the cut-off point but below the 45° line in area a.

Under the assumption that the average, and the distribution, of the genetic potential for growth in the study population and in the reference populations are the same, we can say something about the size of the first error. As only some 3 per cent of the children in the reference population fall below the cut-off point, no more than this should have such a small genetic potential for growth in the study population. An upper-bound estimate of the share of children erroneously classified as stunted is thus 3 per cent under the assumptions made (for which the empirical support was reported in Chapter 12).

The size of the other error, i.e. towards underestimating the incidence of stunting, is more difficult to put numbers on. Considering the small height of the average child in South Asia and, to a lesser extent, in the African countries, one would conjecture that very few children outside the most well-to-do families have attained their full genetic potential growth (see Chapter 12). All this is to say that the incidence of Type I errors (false negative) is large, and probably much larger than the offsetting Type II errors (false positive), with the own-genetic-potential norm.[4] Exact estimates are not possible to derive as long as the genetic potential for growth in an individual child cannot be measured. Considering, however, that almost two-thirds of the children in South Asia fail in height according to the conventional norm (2 SDs below the reference median), it may well be that 80–90 per cent fail according to their genetic potential (norm).

13.4. CHOICE OF ANTHROPOMETRIC INDICATOR

13.4.1. Interrelationship between Anthropometric Indicators

Weight for age is the anthropometric measure that is used by WHO and UNICEF as a composite, one-dimensional index of the overall prevalence of child undernutrition in Third-World countries (see for instance UNICEF 1985*b*: figs 1 and 2, UNICEF*a* 1989: annex tables, 1993). That is, all children who have a weight-for-age below 2 SD of the NCHS median are defined as undernourished. The intention is to capture both the stunted and the wasted; 'to contrive one global measure of child undernutrition'.

The three conventional anthropometric height and weight measures are not independent entities: in mathematical terms the weight-for-age indicator is identically the *product* of the other two:

$$\frac{W}{A} = \frac{H}{A} \times \frac{W}{H}. \tag{13.1}$$

In other words, the *W/A* indicator does not identify the *sum* of those who are stunted and/or wasted. The *W/A* indicator will in fact miss some of the children who are undernourished in the two latter dimensions. The total prevalence of anthropometric failure in a population will thus be underestimated by the weight-for-age indicator (as well as by any of the other two). This point can be more formally demonstrated with the help of Fig. 13.3.

On the vertical axis we have *deviation* from the weight-for-age norm; on the horizontal axis, *deviation* from the height-for-age norm. The diagonal line gives the combinations of weights for heights that comply with the norm. Suppose that we have a child population of a specific age with a weight and height distribution that is encompassed in the ellipse in Fig. 13.3. Six subsets of children can be identified:

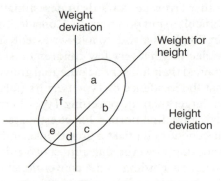

Fig. 13.3. The total prevalence of
anthropometric failure

(1) The children in area a have weights and heights above the age-specific norm, as well as a weight-for-height that is acceptable; they are thus *well-nourished* by all three indicators.

(2) The children in area b have acceptable weights and heights for age, but, being relatively tall, they have subnormal weights for their heights and are thus *wasted*.

(3) The children in area c have above-norm heights, but weights that are too low, both for their heights and for their age. They are thus both *wasted* and *underweight*.

(4) The children in area d fail on all three norms: they are *wasted*, *underweight* and *stunted*.

(5) The children in area e are *underweight* and *stunted*, but have acceptable weights for their low heights.

(6) The children in area f are *stunted*, but have above-norm weights, both for their age and for their small heights.

13.4.2. What Biological Shortcomings and Risks are Conventional Anthropometric Measures Indicating?

Failure by the *height-for-age* indicator has a clear correspondence to a well-defined biological shortcoming: that of being less tall than the genetic potential allows. It is widely agreed that being abnormally short is mainly a consequence of more or less chronic deprivation of food and/or prolonged and frequent illness (although in a few cases, it is for genetic reasons). What the H/A measure indicates is thus relatively unambiguous.

Failure by the *weight-for-age* indicator is a more ambiguous biological state. A child can have abnormally low weight either because it is short (area e in Fig. 13.3), or wasted (c), or both (d). These three 'statues' reflect different biological states with partly different outcomes in terms of health and functions (which we shall investigate in more detail in Chapter 14). Children with a low weight-for-age thus comprise both those who are *chronically* and those who are *acutely* deprived in terms of nutrition and/or health (care). We know, however, that most of the children who have a low weight-for-age have this because they are short for their age, not because they are wasted. In South Asia, about 60 and 70 per cent of children are stunted and underweight, respectively, but only some 15 per cent are wasted. In SSA, the corresponding numbers are 30, 40, and 7 per cent, respectively (Table 13.1; see Chapter 11 for further details).

That relatively few children, especially in South Asia, who have a height-for-age above the norm suggests that only a tiny share of the wasted children are neither stunted nor underweight (area b). This means that the stunted and underweight groups overlap to a large extent (i.e. that areas e + d are relatively large compared to area f and c in Fig. 13.3) *in populations with an overall high prevalence of anthropometric-failure rates*, such as those in South

TABLE 13.1. Empirical simulations of the total incidence of
undernutrition with the Composite Index of
Anthropometric Failure

	India	SSA (average)	Colombia
Conventional Indicators			
(a) Underweight (W/A)	60	30	10
(b) Stunting (H/A)	70	36	15
(c) Wasting (W/H)	15	8	5
Composite Index of			
Anthropometric Failure	75	45	20

Asia. This, in turn, suggests the hypothesis that failures by these two indicators have rather similar correlations to subsequent morbidity/mortality and other impairments (something that we will look at in Chapter 14).

Failure by the *weight-for-height* indicator is most difficult to associate with a well-defined biological state. In terms of Fig. 13.3, out of the children who fall into the 'wasted' category, those in area d are both stunted and underweight; those in area c are underweight only. However, these children are only a small part of the entire sets of stunted (d + e + f) and underweight children (c + d + e). As stunting and being underweight carry distinct (but partly different) health risks, an assessment with the weight-for-height indicator will thus exclude these children from the risk group. This, in turn, implies that the additional information contained in the wasting indicator, over and above that in the stunting and underweight indicators, is small, if not negligible. This leads to the hypothesis that the weight-for-height indicator will not be very efficient in predicting subsequent mortality or various dysfunctions (to be looked at in the next chapter).

Moreover, that the children in area b are relatively tall and thus show no signs of permanent deprivation suggests that their weight 'failure' is a temporary state reflecting acute illness or short-term food shortage. The relatively few children of above-norm height, but who are too thin, are thus not likely to constitute a high-risk group. The 'wasted' children thus comprise a highly diverse group in terms of stature: it may contain individuals at the highest tail of the distribution as well as the lowest. On the presumption that being both stunted and underweight (areas e and d), is more risky than being wasted only (area b), one is—again—inclined to expect the 'wasting' indicator to be a poor predictor of impairments.

All studies so far that have attempted to estimate mortality risk associated with anthropometric failure in small children have used the conventional indicators: stunting, being underweight, and wasting (see Chapter 14 below). Most of these show the expected association between anthropometric failure and subsequent risk of death, but the predictive power of the anthropometric indicators is generally low. It is possible that the 'fit' in such future studies could be improved by having a more disaggregated anthropometric classification system (along the lines suggested above). That would be the case if specific anthropometric failures and *combinations* of failures carried different risks. This is just a hypothesis, yet to be tested, but it would be surprising if children who are stunted, underweight, and wasted do not run a higher risk of dying within the next year or so than children who fail in 'only' one of these three dimensions.[5]

13.5. THE COMPOSITE INDEX OF ANTHROPOMETRIC FAILURE

13.5.1. Underestimation of Overall Anthropometric Failure by Conventional Indicators

Above, we have provided a case for using a more *disaggregated* classification scheme for anthropometric status when the purpose is to use anthropometrics as a device for predicting risks of various types. On the other hand, when the purpose is to estimate what proportion of a child population suffers from anthropometric failure, a more *aggregated* measure seems warranted. It is notable that all the children except those in area a in Fig. 13.3 are 'undernourished' in at least one of the dimensions captured by the three standard anthropometric indicators. If failure in each of the three indicators is of concern, that is, to be stunted, underweight, or wasted, has negative effects on a child's health and functions (which the evidence to be presented in Chapters 14 and 15 suggests is the case, but to different degrees), it follows that none of the three conventional indicators will capture all children who fail in at least one of these three dimensions.

By the *weight-for-age* indicator, the children in areas c, d, and e are classified as undernourished. The children in areas b and f are classified as well-nourished, while in fact being either wasted or stunted.

By the *height-for-age* indicator, the children in areas d, e and f fall out as undernourished (in the stunting dimension), but the children in areas b and c also are undernourished in the two weight dimensions.

By the *weight-for-height* indicator, the children in areas b, c, and d are undernourished in the wasting dimension, but the children in areas e and f also fail in other dimensions.

If one considers a child who is either stunted, wasted, or underweight by any of the three conventional anthropometric measurements to be in a non-acceptable state, the only anthropometric indicator capable of giving an all-inclusive estimate is:

$$CIAF = (1-a)/(a + b + c + d + e + f) = (1-a)/1 = 1-a, \qquad (13.2)$$

which we call the Composite Index of Anthropometric Failure.

13.5.2. Simulating Overall Prevalence of Anthropometric Failure

Without access to the hundreds of primary data sets that form the base of the WHO/UNICEF estimates of the incidence of stunting, wasting, and the underweight in different countries and regions, the incidence of total anthropometric failure (CIAF) cannot be calculated directly. We shall, however, provide an indicative simulation of the orders of magnitudes involved.

In Table 13.1, the UNICEF estimates of the percentage of children in India, and the average for the SSA countries and a third country, Colombia, who fail by the three conventional anthropometric measures, are reproduced. The three 'countries' have been chosen to represent the typical pattern in countries with a high, medium, and low-prevalence of anthropometric failure. On the fourth row in Table 13.1, a 'simulated' estimate of the total prevalence of anthropometric failure is given. This number corresponds to the areas (b + c + d + e + f) = (1–a) in Fig. 13.3. It thus encompasses the percentage of all children in the population who are either stunted, wasted, or underweight (or fail by one, two, or all three of the conventional anthropometric indicators).[6]

13.6. SUMMARY AND CONCLUSIONS

The conventional anthropometric measurements tend to lead to *underestimation* of undernutrition (*cet par*) for at least three reasons. The first is that no anthropometric indicator captures children who are undernourished in the sense of being too inactive physically, while being anthropometrically normal. The second is that a potentially large part of the children in Asia in particular, but also in Africa, who are stunted are not captured by the height-for-age indicator. This is mainly a concern from the perspective of the GP paradigm of undernutrition, in which deviation from genetic potential for growth in stature is central. The third is that neither of the traditional indicators captures all children who have anthropometric failure in at least one of the three dimensions considered. On the other hand, the anthropometric measurements tend to lead to *overestimation* of undernutrition (*cet par*) because they also capture those who are primarily ill for reasons unrelated to nutrition. The net outcome cannot be ascertained with the present estimation technology.

Furthermore, which anthropometric indicator is the most relevant depends on what purpose it is used for. If one is concerned with the distinct adverse outcomes of being stunted, wasted, or underweight, the conventional indicators are appropriate. If one is interested in knowing what *synergistic* risks are associated with anthropometric failure in more than one dimension, a more disaggregated classification scheme is needed (the six category suggested here could be a starting point).[7] This is what most adherents of the

Adjustment and Adaptation paradigm of undernutrition probably would say is the important issue. On the other hand, if the purpose of the indicator is to capture all children with anthropometric failure in at least one dimension (to obtain a 'global' measure, to use UNICEF terminology), all the conventional indicators produce estimates which are downward biased. Then a more composite index of the type suggested here is warranted.[8]

NOTES

1. In chapter 9, we saw that in the construction of its calorie cut-off points, the FAO estimates the energy required for physical activity to account for a little more than one-third of total energy expenditure requirements for people in the developing countries.
2. Little in the nutritional or medical literature suggests that physical inactivity *de facto* is an important health concern for adults in the developing countries. Most are engaged in agriculture, with little help of machines and other tools, and they get the rather limited physical exercise a person needs for cardiovascular, muscular and respiratory fitness as a by-product of work.
3. Proponents of the AA paradigm of undernutrition are primarily concerned not with the height and weight that would be realized under perfect external conditions, but rather with the height and weight that are safe for health and other primary objectives of welfare (see Chapter 14 below).
4. False positives and false negatives are usually termed Type II and Type I errors by economists and statisticians. Among nutritionists, the terms 'sensitivity' and 'specificity' are used (e.g. Habicht *et al.* 1982).
5. There is some support for this hypothesis in data on mortality risk for adults in developed countries. Re-analysing Waaler's (1984) estimates of mortality risk for adults in Norway related to body weight and stature, Fogel (1992: fig. 9.3, 1994: fig. 6) found that being both underweight and stunted carried significantly higher mortality risk than being in one of these states only (for a given value of either entity).
6. The estimated number assigned to area a is derived the following way. In all three countries, the incidence of wasting is considerably lower than the incidence of stunting. In terms of Fig. 13.3, this means that the sum of areas b, c and d is relatively small; at most 15 per cent of the total area in India (3 per cent in Columbia). On the other hand the sum of the areas a + b + c, representing those with a height for age above the cut-off-point, is comparatively large in all three countries. Assigning 'fake' numbers to the sizes of areas b + c we obtain an 'estimate' of a. The numbers presented in Table 13.1 are thus only indicative of possible orders of magnitude.
7. It may be preferable to distinguish also between 'mild-to-moderate' and 'severe' failure in the six categories. This, however, would necessitate a very large number of observations.
8. Also, when the purpose is to monitor changes in the overall nutritional situation in a given population over time, the purpose of this monitoring, of course, determines which anthropometric indicator is the most relevant.

14

Anthropometric Failure:
Morbidity and Mortality Risks

14.1. INTRODUCTION

The anthropometric norms and cut-off points used in the literature for assessing the nutritional status of children in developing countries are with few exceptions derived from what are 'statistical abnormalities' in Western reference populations (see Chapters 11 and 12). Several researchers have argued that such norms are misplaced in developing countries since they do not necessarily delineate children with some incapacity or health impairment. Children may be 'small but healthy', it has been claimed (e.g. Seckler 1982). However, proponents of this adjustment-and-adaptation paradigm also acknowledge that at some low weight and/or height for age, there is a risk of impairments of various types, most notably increased morbidity and mortality risk. Only recently has enough empirical evidence come forth to allow a tentative identification of these critical low weights and heights.

Making use of these new findings, the chief objective of this chapter is to derive some (admittedly crude) estimates of the shares of child deaths in SSA and South Asia that are associated with and attributable to anthropometric failure. The chapter is organized as follows. In section 14.2 the two-way linkages between anthropometric status and the main diseases that account for the bulk of child deaths are analysed. In section 14.3, the child mortality rates in different child populations according to anthropometric status, as estimated in surveys, are presented. In section 14.4, a simple 'accounting' method is used to estimate the shares of all child deaths in SSA and South Asia that are *related to*, and *unrelated to*, anthropometric failure. In section 14.5, the possibility that the differences in the results for SSA and South Asian countries are explained by measurement errors and biases is scrutinized. The significance of the difference is discussed in section 14.6, where a sensitivity test is also presented. In section 14.7, the most serious long-term impairments that have been found to be associated with stunting in adulthood are briefly discussed.

14.2. ANTHROPOMETRIC FAILURE AND MORBIDITY

14.2.1. Synergism

While undernutrition increases the risk of morbidity, it is also well established that many diseases have a detrimental impact on the nutritional status
of children (and other age cohorts). Unfortunately, for the observer who
wants to know what comes first—disease or inadequate access to food—it is
seldom the case that there is a clear beginning and a clear end to the spells of
illness and primary undernutrition among the children in severely deprived
populations (Chen 1983, Tomkins and Watson 1989). The children in such
populations are easily caught in a vicious circle, where infection and undernutrition are mutually reinforcing. These synergistic effects between nutrition and some diseases have been known for a long time (e.g. Scrimshaw *et al.*
1959, 1968).

Several attempts have nevertheless been made to establish causality between anthropometric status, on the one hand, and nutrition and disease on
the other, in various child populations. Most such empirical studies are
nowadays built on longitudinal data. The common way of estimating the effect of undernutrition on morbidity risk is to correlate undernutrition, as
anthropometrically measured in the base period, with the incidence/severity/
duration of one or more diseases in the following few months (prospective
studies). Investigations of the link in the other direction, i.e. the effect of disease on nutritional status, correlate observations of disease in the base period
with speed of body growth in subsequent periods.

14.2.2. Disease as Cause of Anthropometric Failure

That several widespread and fatal diseases affect the anthropometric status
of children negatively is reasonably well established. There are three main
links from illness to loss of weight and retarded growth. One is that the child's
(gross) energy intake is reduced due to the loss of appetite. A second is that
the disease reduces the amount of energy absorbed by the body (the net intake). A third is that many diseases increase the child's energy expenditure in
the form of heat generation (fevers).

The most clear-cut case is infectious disease in the gastro-intestinal tract,
such as diarrhoea. Children who suffer from prolonged or chronic diarrhoea
lose their appetite and absorb less of the food that they ingest, which entails
an increased risk of weight (and possibly height) failure. Several studies show
a great many children in Africa and other developing regions to have more
than a dozen spells of diarrhoea in a year.[1] In the case of measles, the main
problem seems to be that during the illness, the energy intake is lowered
considerably, which leads to body weight loss (Eveleth and Tanner 1990:
pp. 191–2). Also, acute respiratory infections lead to the loss of body weight

through two main channels. One is that the fever that accompanies many respiratory infections increases the energy expenditure of the child, by some 10–20 per cent. The other is that the child loses its appetite and has difficulties ingesting solid food (Waterlow and Tomkins 1992: p. 305). Other infections and fevers of all kinds, including malaria, reduce the children's appetite; intestinal worms lower the children's effective absorption of food (Chen 1983, Tomkins and Watson 1989).

The relatively extensive body of prospective studies corroborates the notion that nearly all the most prevalent diseases that affect children in Africa and Asia (diarrhoea, infections, respiratory diseases, measles, and malaria) often result in retarded growth in subsequent periods. Also, occasional and mild spells of these diseases slow down growth, although in circumstances of adequate nutrition, the slow-down is followed by a catch-up. When nutrition is inadequate and illness frequent, stunting occurs (Eveleth and Tanner 1990: chapter 9).

14.2.3. Anthropometric Failure and Immunocompetence

Waterlow and Tomkins (1992) provide a brief summary discussion of a dozen channels through which malnutrition, in the sense of both PEM and micronutrient deficiency, is theorized or actually found to be detrimental to the immune system. (They also provide references to several more thorough reviews of relevant literature.) Some of the theoretical links from malnutrition to depressed or modified immune response have been verified repeatedly, others have not. For instance, they find that 'It appears that the hormonal immune response is only affected in acute and severe PEM and is rapidly restored as the child recovers' (ibid.: p. 295). They also found that: 'it has long been recognised that cell-mediated immunity is undoubtedly impaired in malnutrition'.

In their review of the empirical evidence, Tomkins and Watson (1989: pp. 29–30) argue that the *level* of inadequacy by anthropometric measures 'below which immune response becomes impaired and risk of morbidity increased' have only recently been studied'. They report from studies which found that 'immune abnormalities were only detected in children below 60 per cent of normal weight for age'. They cite other studies, however, which 'show a gradual lowering of cellar immune functions as weight for age declines' (ibid.: 30). Thus there seems to be no consensus on what degree of anthropometric failure is indicative of an impaired immune response, or on the relative roles of PEM and various forms of micro-nutrient deficiencies.

14.2.4. Anthropometric Failure and Specific Diseases

The amount of available evidence is sufficient to permit reasonable affirmative conclusions only regarding diarrhoea and measles. Low body weight or height in the initial period of observation is usually not found to be associated with increased frequency and severity of diarrhoea in the following months, but with spells of longer duration (Tomkins and Watson 1989: table 3). In their review of the literature, which focuses on measles and their own extensive work, Aaby *et al.* (1988: p. 1227) conclude that there is no 'community study' that shows measles mortality to be correlated with nutritional status; however, this finding is contested by Scrimshaw (1989). The frequency of malaria, which WHO claims is responsible for up to one-third of all child deaths in large parts of Africa, has not been found to be intimately related to anthropometric status (Eveleth and Tanner 1990). There is no information about causal links between nutritional status and subsequent illness in diseases other than diarrhoea, measles, and malaria in the reviews consulted here. It is not stated whether this is so because there is no *a priori* reason to expect anthropometric status to have any consequences for morbidity in 'other' diseases, or whether the explanation is simply the paucity of studies.

14.2.5. Remaining Uncertainty about Causality

In most studies in which a significant correlation has been found, causality has not been established beyond doubt. In the set of studies correlating low anthropometric status in the base period with subsequent illness, it is usually *claimed* that initial anthropometric failure reflects undernutrition. As Tomkins and Watson (1989) point out, however, 'few of the studies of immune status in children with growth failure have defined the reasons why subjects were underweight or short in the first place'. If low anthropometric status in the base period is due to disease rather than undernutrition, a positive correlation with disease in later periods does not imply that undernutrition causes increased morbidity. In this case, the correct conclusion is that disease causes disease. For instance, it has been observed that measles causes growth faltering and immune suppression, which in turn leads to an increased risk of (post-measles) diarrhoea.

Most studies of disease as a cause of inadequate growth in subsequent periods are beset with similar problems. The incidence of disease is known to correlate strongly with poor sanitation and a variety of socio-economic variables that also affect child growth and weight, which have seldom been controlled for. That is, malnutrition [low anthropometric status] 'might be regarded as a marker of a disadvantaged child rather than a biologically active risk factor' (Waterlow and Tomkins 1992: p. 291).

In examining the relationship between anthropometric status and morbidity—both ways—it is usually impossible to separate effects due to energy inadequacy from those due to micronutrient deficiency. As argued by Tomkins and Watson (1989: p. 13), 'It is the exception rather than the rule to have a single nutritional deficiency'. And the consequences of this 'vary according to level of micro-nutrient deficiency, environmental exposition and social

factors' (Waterlow and Tomkins 1992: p. 291). All in all, a correlation between anthropometric failure and high mortality in a child population can
seldom be demonstrated to have a clear-cut causal order.[2] Anthropometric
failure is in most cases jointly determined by inadequate nutrition, illness,
and a variety of other 'insults' on child growth (Eveleth and Tanner 1990:
chapter 9).[3] The use of anthropometric measures as synonyms for 'undernutrition' (e.g. FAO*a* 1996 and UNICEF 1993*a*: p.6) is thus a crude
simplification that is bound to lead to the wrong policy conclusions (see
Chapters 17 and 18 below).

14.3.   ANTHROPOMETRIC FAILURE AND MORTALITY

14.3.1.   *Anthropometric Failure as a Direct versus Indirect Cause of Death*

The link from anthropometric failure to increased risk of death can be both
direct and indirect. Severe starvation for a prolonged period of time may
cause death without concomitant disease.[4] Almost all child deaths related to
anthropometric failure, however, even in famine situations, are caused by one
or more diseases. In the joint WHO and World Bank assessment of the
'Global Burden of Disease' in 1990 (IBRD*a* 1993: annex table B.8),[5] only 2
per cent of all child (0–4 years) deaths in developing countries are classified
under the label 'Nutritional and Endocrine'. Out of these deaths, roughly
half are estimated to be caused by PEM and the other half mainly by vitamin
A deficiency and anaemia.

A superficial consultation of the WHO/IBRD data base may give the impression that PEM (undernutrition in the terminology preferred here) is a
very minor—only 1 per cent—cause of child deaths in the developing countries. A considerably higher share is caused by injuries (4 per cent). This
would be the wrong conclusion, however, as nutritional status is one of the
factors behind morbidity, as discussed above, and, thus, mortality. According
to the WHO/IBRD estimates, about half of all child deaths are caused by four
communicable diseases: acute respiratory infections (22 per cent), diarrhoeal diseases (20), measles (7), and malaria (5). At least for respiratory
infections and diarrhoeal diseases, the risk of death is aggravated by poor
nutritional status. Yet another 19 per cent of the deaths are classified as
'perinatal', i.e. deaths during the first month in life (these deaths are to some
extent related to the nutritional status of the mother; see below). Non-
communicable diseases account for another estimated 9 per cent of deaths,
out of which congenital abnormalities, chronic respiratory infections, and
digestive diseases are the most serious ones. Little seems to be known about
how the nutritional status of children affects their risk of dying from this type
of disease.

14.3.2. The Relationship between Anthropometric Failure and Mortality

The simultaneity problem (reversed causality), which arises when one attempts to estimate the role of low anthropometric status in explaining morbidity, has not been adequately resolved so far, as argued above. The problem of reverse causation when it comes to the relationship between anthropometric failure and mortality 'reduces' to the possibility that both are caused by the same exogenous factors (to be tested in Chapter 15, on the basis of cross-country observations).

Three main methods have been used to estimate the correlation between anthropometric status and child mortality in samples of children. One set of studies examine the effect of *interventions*, i.e. the child mortality rate in a population is estimated before and after some type of intervention (e.g. nutrition, health, and/or education) is made.[6] Another set of studies is *retrospective*, i.e. children dying or surviving in a population are related to their previous anthropometric status. Most such studies have been based on children admitted to hospitals or health clinics, which has induced serious selection bias. The third type of study is *prospective*. As a first step, the anthropometric performance of (hopefully randomly selected) children in a population is assessed. The same children are then observed at one or more later point(s) in time, and the incidence of death and survival in different groups according to previously assessed anthropometric status are recorded.

In the following, the main focus will be on results from prospective studies. There are two main reasons for this. One is that this method is normally beset with less severe simultaneity and selection biases than the retrospective method. The second is that prospective studies provide data that can be used for providing a first, tentative, estimate of the overall role of anthropometric failure as a cofactor in explaining the high mortality in SSA and South Asia (in section 14.4 below).

14.3.3. Estimated Relationship

There have been about two dozen prospective sample studies conducted aimed at estimating the correlation between anthropometric status and subsequent mortality in child populations, all of them from SSA and various parts of Asia (there seems to be no study from Latin America). The available studies have been thoroughly reviewed and synthesized by ACC/SCN (1992: pp. 69–74), Pelletier (1994), and Pelletier *et al.* (1994*a*).

In all but a few of the sample studies, there is a positive association between degree of anthropometric failure and elevated mortality risk in the under-fives age group. By two of the four anthropometric indicators used in these studies, weight for age and arm circumference,[7] there is a more-than-proportional increase in the mortality risk with linear anthropometric failure. For the weight-for-height indicator, the relationship is more or less linear in most

samples. For the height-for-age indicator, the results are frequently in-
conclusive (Pelletier 1994). In the majority of the studies, there is also an
elevated mortality risk in the range of anthropometric failure that conventionally is called 'mild to moderate'. This is contrary to what was found in one
of the early studies (Chen *et al.* 1980), which reported an abrupt and
significant increase in mortality risk (a 'kink' in the function) only at the degree of anthropometric failure that traditionally is taken to indicate 'severe
undernutrition'. Since this early study has been widely cited, its results have
erroneously become 'conventional wisdom' according to Pelletier (1994).

14.3.4. Inter-regional Differences at Face Value

The estimated average child mortality rate (CMR) for three groups of children with different anthropometric status in terms of weight for age, derived
from prospective studies from SSA and South Asia, are presented in Fig.
14.1.[8] The data bars represent the average for the SSA and South Asian
samples, but since there are only a few observations, there is a problem with
representativeness. Moreover, the studies from which the base data are taken
are not totally comparable (discussed in section 14.5).

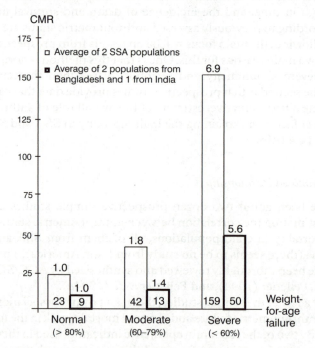

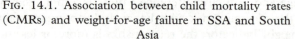

FIG. 14.1. Association between child mortality rates
(CMRs) and weight-for-age failure in SSA and South
Asia

At face value, Fig. 14.1 shows large differences between the observation sets from SSA and South Asia (the estimated child mortality rate is given at the bottom of respective bars). In fact, the mortality risk in all three categories of child anthropometric status, 'normal', as well as 'mild-to-moderate', and 'severe' failure, is almost *three times* as high in the African samples as in the South Asian ones.[9] However, in relative terms, which is what matters for our subsequent deliberations, the *increase* in the death rate with anthropometric deterioration is quite similar in the African and Asian samples.[10] The number on top of each bar gives the relative mortality risk in the 'failed' groups (expressed as a ratio of that in the 'normal' group).

14.4. ESTIMATED SHARE OF CHILD DEATHS ATTRIBUTED TO ANTHROPOMETRIC FAILURE

In the following we shall construct a simple 'accounting model' that makes it possible to use the existing sample estimates on 'excess' mortality related to anthropometric failure of different degrees so as to obtain rough indications of the role of 'anthropometric failure' in explaining high child mortality in SSA and South Asia at large. As we have argued above, there is no reliable method that can be used to estimate the relative role played by inadequate nutrition and illness in explaining anthropometric failure. However, by estimating the share of child deaths that are attributable to anthropometric failure, we will be able to derive a crude 'upper-bound' estimate of the share of child deaths that is caused by undernutrition.

14.4.1. Method

The three anthropometric categories considered are 'normal', 'mild-to-moderate' failure, and 'severe' failure. We start out with the following identity:

$$X_a \equiv \theta_n X_n + \theta_m X_m + \theta_s X_s, \quad \Sigma\theta_i = 1 \qquad (14.1)$$

where the X_a is the average mortality rate in the population, X_n is the mortality rate in the group with normal anthropometric status, and X_m and X_s are the mortality rates for the mild-to-moderate and severe failure categories, respectively. The θs are the shares of the respective anthropometric categories in the population.

We further have that:

$$X_m = X_n (1 + ER_m) \text{ and} \qquad (14.2a)$$

$$X_s = X_n (1 + ER_s), \qquad (14.2b)$$

where ER_m and ER_s are the excess mortality ratios in the mild-to-moderate and the severe anthropometric failure categories, respectively ($ER_n = 0$). In order to keep the formulae reasonably clean, no (sub-)indices are inserted for region or anthropometric indicator.

Solving for X_n and substituting (14.2a and 14.2b) into identity (14.1), we have that:

$$X_n \equiv X_a [\theta_n + \theta_m (1 + ER_m) + \theta_s (1 + ER_s)]^{-1}. \qquad (14.3)$$

The distribution of all deaths according to anthropometric category is:

$$\omega_i = \theta_i X_i [X_a]^{-1} \text{ for } i = n, m, \text{ and } s, \Sigma \omega_i = 1, \qquad (14.4)$$

where the ω_i is the percentage of all deaths occurring in anthropometric category i.

Finally, the share of all deaths that are attributable to anthropometric failure, i.e. the deaths that take place in each category of anthropometric failure over and above the mortality rate in the category with normal anthropometric status, is given by:

$$\Omega_m = \theta_m (X_m - X_n) [X_a]^{-1}. \qquad (14.5a)$$

$$\Omega_s = \theta_s (X_s - X_n) [X_a]^{-1}. \qquad (14.5b)$$

Ω_m and Ω_s are thus the percentages of all deaths that are attributable to 'mild-to-moderate' and 'severe' anthropometric failure, respectively. The sum of the two gives the total share of all deaths that are linked to anthropometric failure. The share of deaths associated with normal anthropometric status is:

$$\Omega_n = 1 - (\Omega_m + \Omega_s) \qquad (14.5c)$$

14.4.2. Data

The base data are presented in Table 14.1. In the top panel (A), we have the distribution of children according to anthropometric status (the θs) in SSA and South Asia, respectively, by each of the three standard anthropometric indicators. These estimates purport that the prevalence of (total) anthropometric failure in SSA is between half and two-thirds of that found in South Asia.[11] In panel (B), the estimated child mortality risks, the $(1 + ERs)$, for each anthropometric category and indicator are given. These base data are obtained from the sample studies covered in the previous section. The values of the X_a (the national average under-fives mortality rates) for SSA (177/1000) and South Asia (124/1000) are from UNICEFa (1996).

14.4.3. Results

From the data provided in panels (A) and (B) in Table 14.1, we first estimate the mortality rates in the 'normal' category (X_n) with the help of equation (14.3). Inserting the estimated values for X_n into equations 14.2a and b, we obtain mortality rates for the children with 'mild-to-moderate' and

TABLE 14.1. Percentage distribution of children according to anthropometric status, relative mortality risk, and death rates, by anthropometric category

Anthropometric indicator	SSA						South Asia					
	Total	Normal	Failure				Total	Normal	Failure			
			Total	Mild-to-Moderate	Severe				Total	Mild-to-Moderate	Severe	
(A) Estimated distribution of child population by anthropometric status (%)												
W/A	100	70	30	22	8		100	42	58	36	22	
H/A	100	62	38	20	18		100	40	60	26	34	
W/H	100	93	7	6	1		100	83	17	14	3	
(B) Estimated relative mortality risk $(1 + ER_i)$												
W/A	–	1.0	–	1.8	6.9		–	1.0	–	1.4	5.6	
H/A	–	1.0	–	1.3	2.3		–	1.0	–	1.3	3.7	
W/H	–	1.0	–	2.0	3.8		–	1.0	–	1.0	1.8	
(C) Estimated death rates by anthropometric category (per 1,000)												
W/A	177	107	–	193	738		124	58	–	81	325	
H/A	177	137	–	178	315		124	62	–	81	229	
W/H	177	163	–	326	619		124	121	–	121	218	

Sources: (A) The shares of children with normal and 'failed' anthropometric status in the respective regions are from the FAO*a* (1996: Table 21), based on WHO's global anthropometric database. The distribution between 'mild-to-moderate' and 'severe' anthropometric failure is estimated from national data, mainly from Demography and Health Surveys (DHSs), collected by UNICEF (1993*b*). The estimates for South Asia are weighted averages for 16 countries in the region, representing 75 per cent of the total population. The estimates for SSA as a whole are derived from national estimates for four countries with 97 per cent of the population in this region. (B) The relative mortality risks are derived from the sample studies listed in the sources to Table 14.2. (C) The estimates of death rates for different anthropometric categories are derived with the help of equations 14.2a,b and 14.3 in the text. The regional average mortality rates for the under-fives for SSA and South Asia, 177 and 124 (per 1,000 children), respectively, are from UNICEF*a* (1996).

'severe' anthropometric failure. These estimates are presented in panel (C) in Table 14.1.

The next step is to estimate the share of all deaths by anthropometric category with the help of equation 14.4. The estimates, presented in the top panel of Appendix Table 14.1, suggest that by the weight- and height-for-age indicators, slightly fewer than half the deaths in SSA affect children with normal anthropometric status. In South Asia, only about 20 per cent of all child deaths affect children with normal status in terms of weight and height for age. This result is not very surprising, considering that the prevalence of anthropometric failure of children in general is almost twice as high in South Asia as in SSA, while the under-fives mortality rate (U5MR) is considerably lower. Such a result cannot come about unless a significantly larger share of all child deaths in Africa are unrelated to poor anthropometric status than in Asia.[12]

Finally, the share of all deaths that are *attributable* to anthropometric failure in Africa and Asia, respectively, is estimated with the help of equation 14.5. The estimates are presented in Fig. 14.2 (and also in the lower panel of Appendix Table 14.1). The estimates suggest that there is a notable interregional difference. With the weight-for-age indicator, an estimated 39 per cent (11 plus 28) of the deaths in SSA are 'attributable' to anthropometric failure in this dimension (the shaded areas). The equivalent figure for South Asia is 53 per cent (7 plus 47). (With the height-for-age indicator, the figures are slightly lower.) All in all, roughly two-thirds of all child deaths in SSA are *unrelated* to anthropometric failure. In South Asia the figure is around 50 per cent. It is of further note that about 80 per cent of all the excess deaths in both South Asia and SSA that are attributable to anthropometric failure are estimated to be in the *severely* failed category.

14.5. CAVEATS

All the data used in the above section to estimate the share of child deaths attributable to anthropometric failure are of more or less dubious quality. As we have seen in a previous chapter (12), most data on anthropometric status and mortality of children in individual countries in the African and Asian regions are questionable in terms of representativeness and reliability. This applies to data obtained in the sample studies, as discussed in the previous section, as well as the data collected by the UN agencies in order to derive 'national' estimates. However, the weakest link in the previous estimation exercise is the data on 'excess death risk' by anthropometric category. In this section, an attempt is therefore made to scrutinize these data in more detail. We will also examine whether the relatively limited number of observations are reasonably representative for respective regions.

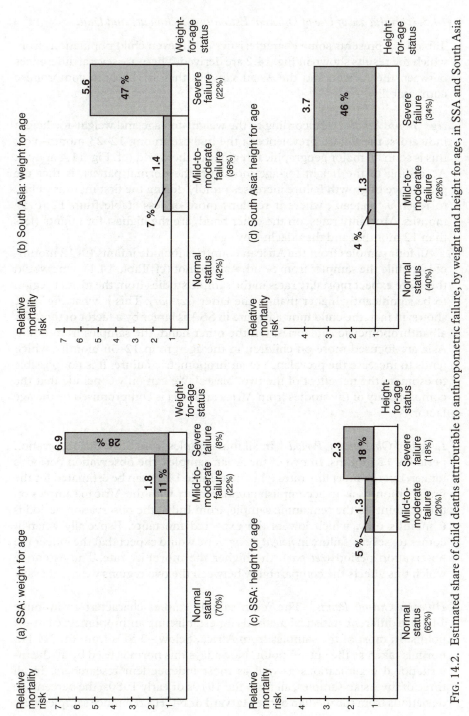

Fig. 14.2. Estimated share of child deaths attributable to anthropometric failure, by weight and height for age, in SSA and South Asia

14.5.1. Influence of Use of Different Estimation Techniques and Data

Table 14.2 presents some characteristics of all seven child populations from which the results shown in Fig. 14.2 are derived. There are several differences between the African and the Asian samples that are likely to compromise comparability.[13]

Age Groups Studied   According to the weight-for-age and weight-for-height indicators, the failure prevalence is the highest among 12–23 month-olds; this is so in all major geographical regions of the world (cf. Fig. 11.4 above). According to the height-for-age indicator, the normal pattern is that the prevalence of growth failure increases rapidly during the first months of life, to reach a 'plateau', where it remains more or less stable from 12 to 59 months. Mortality rates, on the other hand, are the highest for infants (less than 12 months) and then decline by age.

All four samples from the African countries include infants (0–12 month-olds), while the samples from South Asia do not (cf. Table 14.1). One would therefore expect mortality rates in the sample studies from the former region to be significantly higher than in the latter (*cet par*). This is what Fig. 14.1 shows; in fact, the child mortality rate in SSA is larger by a factor of three for all anthropometric categories. On the other hand, the samples from South Asia are focused more on children in the age group 12–36 months, which tends to increase the prevalence of anthropometric failure. It is not possible to estimate the net effect of the two 'biases'. We can only conclude that the comparability of the studies from Africa and Asia is compromised by the age factor.

Length of Observation Period   In all four samples from SSA, the observation period is 12 months. In two of the Asian samples, the observation period is longer, but the mortality rates (shown in Table 14.1) can be estimated for the first 12 months as to accomplish comparability with the African samples on this account. In the remaining sample, from India, the observation period is 6 months only, which lowers the expected mortality. Especially when it comes to 'severe' failure in *height for age*, one would expect that the longer the observation period (*cet par*), the higher the mortality rate. The extent to which this affects the comparability between the two regions we cannot say.

Different Cut-off Points   The seven sample studies characterized in Table 14.1 use different statistical methods for establishing anthropometric cut-off points. In most of the samples from Africa, below –2 SDs from the NCHS norm is taken as the cut-off point. Nowadays this norm is used by all the international organizations as well as most independent researchers. In all three of the Asian samples, all from the 1970s or early 1980s, the percentage deviations from the median of the Harvard or NCHS reference samples were

TABLE 14.2. Selected characteristics of sample studies of associations between anthropometric status and mortality from SSA and South Asia

Country (years)	Indicators (cut-off points)	Sample size (age group)	Length of observation period	Mortality rate (%) (number of deaths)	Supplementary Information			
					Socio-economic data	Cause of death	Mortality trend (by Age)	Se/Sp (RR)
(1)	(2)	(3)	(4)	(5)	(6)	(7)	(8)	(9)
Tanzania (1985/7)	WA,HA,WH (% NCHS)	2452 (6–36)	12	36 (88)	no	yes	yes (yes)	no (yes)
Malawi (1986/90)	WA,HA,WH,ACA (<–2 SDs)	3519 (6–59)	36	28[a] (253)	yes	no	yes (yes)	yes (yes)
S Uganda (1988/9)	WA,HA,WH,AC (<–2 SDs)	3814 (0–59)	12	25 (96)	yes	yes	no ( )	yes (yes)
N Uganda (1987/8)	WA,HA,WH (<–2 SDs)	1066 (0–59)	12	35 (37)	yes	yes	no (yes)	yes ( )
Bangladesh Matlab1 (1975/6)	WA,HA,WH,AC (% Harvard)	2019 (12–23)	24	30[a] (112)	yes	yes	yes (yes)	yes (yes)
Teknaf (1981/5)	WA,HA,WH,AC (% NCHS)	2625 (12–59)	6	5 (60)	no	no	yes (yes)	yes
India (1968/73)	WA (% Harvard)	2808 (12–36)	12	53 (148)	no	no	yes (yes)	yes (yes)

[a] Mortality rate for the first 12 months only.

Sources: Yambi *et al.* 1991 (Tanzania); Pelletier *et al.* 1994b (Malawi); Vella *et al.* 1992, 1994 (Uganda); Chen *et al.* 1980 (Matlab1); Alam *et al.* 1989 (Teknaf); Kielman and McCord 1978 (India, Punjab).

used as cut-off points. There is no general 'conversion key' that can be used to translate one cut-off point to the other. It is also verified that the choice of cut-off point can have a large impact on the estimates.[14] Again, we can only conclude that comparability between the African and Asian samples is compromised.

Underreporting of Deaths   The gross mortality rates in most of the sample studies are considerably lower than one would expect from national mortality rates, as noticed by Pelletier (1994). In none of the studies from which results are reported in Table 14.1 is there a description of how the research team has attempted to check the reliability of reported deaths and survivals.

14.5.2. *Representative Countries?*

The observations from Africa are from three countries only—Malawi, Uganda, and Tanzania—with a joint population of barely 11 per cent of the total in the region. These three small countries, all located in South-East Africa, may be atypical for SSA as a whole. With India and Bangladesh holding 90 per cent of the population of South Asia, there is no problem with representativeness of countries, although there can be for the samples therefrom (see next subsection).

In Table 14.3, mortality rates and incidence of anthropometric failure in Malawi, Uganda, and Tanzania are contrasted with SSA averages. The estimated weighted-average child mortality rate for the three countries deviates by only 5 per cent from the SSA average. Also, in terms of anthropometric failure, the average for the three countries is reasonably close to the SSA average,

TABLE 14.3. Mortality rates and prevalence of anthropometric failure among children under the age of 5 years in Malawi, Uganda, and Tanzania (1990's) compared with the averages for SSA as a whole

Indicator	Malawi	Uganda	Tanzania	Weighted average for 3 countries[a]	Weighted average SSA	(4)/(5)
	(1)	(2)	(3)	(4)	(5)	(6)
Mortality of						
the under-5s	221	185	159	168	177	0.95
Anthropometric failure						
W/A	27	23	29	27	30	0.90
H/A	49	45	43	45	38	1.18
W/H	5	2	6	5	7	0.71

[a] Weighted by child population under five.

Sources: UNICEF*a* 1996: tables 1 and 10 (mortality rates) and the FAO*a* 1996: table 21, and table 8 in appendix 2 (anthropometric failure).

considering the large variations that are seen when one looks at all countries in the region.[15] Malawi, Uganda, and Tanzania are definitely not outliers among the SSA countries in terms of mortality and anthropometric status of children—one may even conclude that they are fairly representative.

14.5.3. Representative Samples?

None of the authors of the studies reported in Table 14.1 claim that their samples are representative of the country in question. As revealed by Table 14.4, two of the three African samples, which apply the same cut-off points as those used in the national estimates (Tanzania being the exception), show a somewhat lower incidence of underweight and stunting compared with the national averages for the same time period. Also, the Asian samples show mostly lower incidences of underweight and stunted children than the national averages from approximately the same time. It thus seems that the samples are not fully representative in terms of anthropometric status, but there is no systematic difference between the samples from Africa and Asia, respectively.[16]

14.6.   SIGNIFICANCE AND SENSITIVITY TEST

14.6.1. Significance of Difference

The mortality rate in the group with 'severe' anthropometric failure in Africa is surprisingly high compared with South Asia. The estimates suggest that two-thirds of all children with severe underweight and/or stunting die before the age of five. Although this is not entirely implausible, considering that an estimated one-fifth of all children never reach that age, one cannot exclude the possibility that the relative mortality risk in the severely failed group is inflated.

However, the estimated child mortality rate (among the under fives) in SSA is significantly higher than in South Asia also at the *national level*. At the same time, the prevalence of anthropometric failure, both moderate and severe, is considerably higher in South Asia than in Africa (Table 14.1). By implication, it is most likely that the mortality rates for children in Africa in all anthropometric 'categories' are notably higher than in South Asia.

Moreover, the *inter-regional* variability in the observations is larger than the *intra-regional* variations. In the total 12 observation sets (3 times 4) that allow comparisons between the two regions, there are only two cases in which a study from South Asia shows a higher mortality rate than the lowest reported for an African sample (children with normal weight for height and children with severe stunting (height for age)). Concerning the remaining 10 observation 'pairs', the lowest mortality rate among the African populations exceeds that in the South-Asian populations with the highest mortality rate.

TABLE 14.4. Incidence of anthropometric failure of children in SSA and
South Asian samples compared with national averages

Region/ Country/ (Norm)/ (Years)	Indicator	Percentage of children below norm		
		Sample (1)	National[a] (2)	(1)/(2) (3)
Sub-Saharan Africa				
Tanzania	W/A	23[b]	29	0.79
(% NCHS)	H/A	27	43	0.63
(1985/7)	W/H	4	6	0.67
Malawi	W/A	14	27	0.52
(<−2SDs)	H/A	42	49	0.86
(1986/90)	W/H	23	5	4.60
Uganda (sw)	W/A	18	23	0.78
(<−2SDs)	H/A	32	45	0.71
(1988/9)	W/H	4	2	0.50
Uganda (nw)	W/A	25	23	1.09
(<−2SDs)	H/A	42	45	0.93
(1987/8)	W/H	3	2	1.50
South Asia				
Bangladesh[c]	W/A	73[b]	77	0.94
(% Harvard)	H/A	58	73	0.79
(1975/6)	W/H	31	28	1.11
Bangladesh[d]	W/A	75	71	1.06
(NCHS)	H/A	58	68	0.85
(1981–5)	W/H	47	15	3.13
India[e]	W/A	65	72	0.90
(% Harvard)				
(1968–73)				

[a] All cut-off points are <−2 SDs from the median NCHS. Data for the SSA
countries are from the early 1990s or late 1980s. National estimtates for the Asian
countries are from an earlier year closer to the sample study period and when
available, for the specific age groups in the sample.
[b] <75 per cent of norm.
[c] Matlab district.
[d] Teknaf district.
[e] Punjab state.

Sources: See Table 14.2 (sample studies). National averages are from the FAO*a*
1996: table 8 in appendix 2 and UNICEF 1993*a*.

14.6.2. Sensitivity Test

As a final check on the reliability of the estimated share of deaths attributed
to anthropometric failure, the estimations were recalculated, using alternative values of the relative mortality risks (from those presented in Table
14.1, panel B). The alternative estimates were derived on the assumption that
the relative excess mortality rates in Africa are some 25 per cent lower than

previously postulated and 25 per cent higher in South Asia (an assumption that means that the relative mortality rates in the two regions become almost identical in most anthropometric status groups). This simple test reveals that the sensitivity of the estimates to changes in the relative mortality risks between the two regions is small (Appendix Table 14.2). It is notable that under the 'alternative' assumptions concerning relative mortality risks, the difference between Africa and Asia in the incidence of deaths attributed to anthropometric failure widens.

14.7. CHILD ANTHROPOMETRIC FAILURE AND IMPAIRMENTS IN ADULTHOOD

So far, this chapter has been chiefly concerned with the link between anthropometric failure in children and subsequent *child* mortality, 'the most definitive and serious consequence of malnutrition' (Chen *et al.* 1980). However, as we have seen, a non-negligible share of the children observed to be 'severely' short or underweight for their age at one or more points in time do survive. The main impairments that at least some of these children carry with them into adolescence and adulthood are briefly discussed in this section: (i) cognitive and psychomotoric handicaps, (ii) increased adult morbidity and mortality risk, (iii) impaired reproductive health, and (iv) lower work capacity/productivity.[17]

14.7.1. Cognitive and Psychomotoric Capability

Undernutrition has been postulated to impair the cognitive and psychomotoric development of children in two main ways. One is that undernutrition damages the brain and the central nervous system. The other is that undernutrition leads to physical inactivity, both directly and indirectly through increased morbidity (see above) and mental apathy, which hampers the training that is necessary for cognitive and psychomotoric development.

Waterlow (1992: chapter 3) cites a few studies in which it was found that the brain is the body organ that is the least affected by severe undernutrition (i.e. 50 per cent of normal body weight for age) in terms of weight loss. 'Even in children dying from malnutrition the weight of the brain . . . was relatively well preserved' (about 90 per cent of normal). In such children even the skeleton was slightly more reduced in terms of weight. Also, DeLong (1993: p. 286) asserts that: 'Brain development in humans is remarkably resistant to permanent damage from protein–energy malnutrition'. However, impairments of the brain have been related to various forms of malnutrition, such as insufficient intake/absorption of various minerals, vitamins, etc. (ibid).

Very few attempts seem to have been made to investigate the possibility that exceptionally short adults in countries with widespread undernutrition have cognitive and/or phsycomotoric handicaps (see Waterlow 1992:

pp. 74–5). There is a fair amount of empirical support for the notion that very short people in developed countries are less apt in various ways than people with normal stature,[18] but this is most likely related to chronic illness rather than primary undernutrition.

Most studies of interrelationships between undernutrition and impaired cognitive and motoric capacities in developing countries focus on the intermediate variables of physical and mental activity. In his review of the main findings in this literature, Grantham-McGregor (1992) finds that most studies are not designed and carried out with sufficient rigour to render the results trustworthy. The studies are often based on small samples, differences are not subjected to significance testing, non-nutritional adverse influences on child development are not controlled, and the follow-up period is usually short. Moreover, the tests that the undernourished children in developing countries have been subjected to are designed to fit conditions prevailing in developed countries, which may be of little relevance in highly different cultural contexts.

Grantham-McGregor's (1992: p. 352) overall conclusion from his review of the few 'studies which used carefully matched controls and reported sufficient detail to allow evaluation' is that: 'None of the studies have provided evidence that severe malnutrition leads to poor mental development' (ibid: p. 348).[19] McGuire and Austin (1987: p. 10), in their review article, conclude that 'there is almost a total lack of empirically based longitudinal studies examining adult competence as a function of early childhood undernutrition'. Colombo et al. (1988: p. 208) further argue that: 'Our data seem to indicate that stunting and impaired development have no causal link but are both associated effects of poverty and deprivation'.

14.7.2. Adult Stature and Morbidity/Mortality

From the presumptions that chronic undernutrition in childhood leads to (i) adult stunting and (ii) impaired lifelong immunocompetence (broadly defined) in a synergistic manner, one expects short adults in nutritionally constrained populations to have especially poor health and high mortality.

In recent years, clinical and experimental results have come forth which indicate that there may be causal links between foetal and infant growth and chronic diseases in later life, such as diabetes, cardiovascular disease, and hypertension (see Eveleth and Tanner 1990: chapter 11, Scrimshaw 1996, Beaton 1997, Hoet 1997, and the references therein).[20] The mechanisms are yet not fully understood and most of the evidence is from animal experiments. It nonetheless seems as if the health impairments (as for brain damage; cf. above) are more closely related to deficiencies of certain proteins, fats, and mircronutrients than to low energy intakes. However, an insufficient energy intake often carries with it inadequate supplies of some other nutrients, indicating that calorie deficiency may be part of the explanation.[21]

The evidence on links between adult stature and longevity is relatively scant and almost exclusively from the contemporary developed countries. Perhaps the best-known study is from Norway (Waaler 1984), which found shortness to be linked to higher mortality, both for men and women. In this observation set, however, shortness is not likely to be related to poor nutrition in childhood, but rather to high morbidity and an unfavourable social environment earlier in life (Thuluvath and Triger 1994).[22]

14.7.3. Anthropometric Status and Reproduction

There are at least four areas in which links from anthropometric status of women and their 'reproductive health' have been studied: (i) fecundity, (ii) fertility, (iii) maternity, and (iv) infant health/mortality. Most of the evidence concerns the effects of wasting in adult women (reflecting current nutritional status) rather than stunting, the variable of prime interest here. Moreover, the focus will be solely on women for the simple reason that studies of the effect of undernutrition on the reproductive capability of men seem to be non-existent.

Fecundity The reproductive capacity of a woman depends first and foremost on her not being permanently (primarily) sterile and, secondly, on the number of years during which she ovulates. The second factor is determined by her age at menarche and at menopause. There seems to be no medical evidence which indicates that low height (or weight) causes primary sterility. The age at which menarche begins, however, is clearly related to nutritional status. Evidence from many parts of the world shows that menarche starts at the age of 12–13 in well-nourished populations, and 2–3 years later in many undernourished groups (Eveleth and Tanner 1990: pp. 161–72 and table 10; whether the menopausal age is related to anthropometric status is not discussed here).

Fertility Rate Fertility—the number of children women give birth to—depends on a large number of cultural, economic, social, and, it is widely thought, nutritional factors. On a cross-sectional basis, fertility is normally *negatively* correlated to nutritional status: the better fed, who tend to be those with higher incomes and better education, have fewer children than the undernourished. This may not always be the most relevant observation, however. One non-trivial question is whether undernutrition lowers women's fertility in the poorest population strata, where many children may be an asset for the household (although not necessarily so for society at large).

There are practically no studies of the relationship between women's stature and fertility, however, only of the relationship between being underweight and fertility. The most studied links between being underweight and fertility in developing countries are the following. First, there is the question of whether undernutrition can cause *temporary* (secondary) sterility. The empirical evidence suggests that ovulation and menstruation cease only in situations of extreme undernutrition and weight loss, such as in famine, or in connection with anorexia nervosa. Secondly, there is the link between undernutrition and lactational amenorrhoea (the temporary infertility during breast-feeding). Undernutrition has been observed to shorten the period of breast-feeding, thereby *increasing* fertility (*cet par*). Thirdly, there is the relationship between spontaneous abortion or miscarriage and undernutrition. The evidence on early foetal death is—for rather obvious reasons—almost non-existent in the poorest countries, but stillbirths have been observed to be more frequent in women under great nutritional stress.[23]

Maternal Morbidity/Mortality   The incidence of death during childbirth is more than a hundred times higher in SSA and South Asia than in the developed countries (Table 16.6 below). The chief reason must be that a large share of the births take place in the absence of qualified health personnel (or none at all) under highly unhygenic conditions (UNICEF*a* 1997). However, that a large share of the women giving birth in these regions are stunted entails increased obestric risks that add to the risk of the mother not surviving. In fact, this risk is the very reason why the ACC/SCN (1992) chooses to use a height below 145 cm as the cut-off point for delineating 'stunting' in adult women in the developing countries (Fig. 11.5 above). Also, current undernutrition, taken as a weight below 45 kg, is associated with increased obstetric risk.

Infant Morbidity/Mortality   It has frequently been observed that stunted (and also underweight) women give birth to less healthy infants and children. The main concern is that maternal 'undernutrition' leads to premature births and/or low-birth-weight babies. One study from India showed that among women with a BMI below 16.0, 50 per cent of their children had an LBW (James 1994: p. 7). It is also well established that LBW is associated with increased infant and child mortality risk (Tomkins and Watson 1989: pp. 41, 87) as well as short stature in adulthood (Martorell 1995). Stunting in women thus tends to carry over from one generation to the next in deprived populations (also see ACC/SCN 1992, 1994, Osmani 1997, Ramakrishnan *et al.* 1999). There are also findings regarding nutritional status of mothers and breast-feeding, as well as the role of breast-feeding in infant and child development (see Waterlow 1992: chapter 16).

14.7.4. Adult Stature and Physical Work Capacity and Productivity

If short stature can cause retarded cognitive and psychomotoric capabilities and poorer health, as discussed above, this would imply reduced work capacity. Short stature *as such* may also impair work capacity and productivity.

The evidence on the link between undernutrition in childhood, as measured by stature, and physical work capacity in adulthood is rather difficult to interpret. It has been shown that shortness is associated with low maximum physical work capacity, as measured by VO_2 max (Spurr 1988 and references therein), but only in those who are considerably below the norm (Seckler 1982, Osmani 1990). Tallness and a high maximum work capacity are important in activities that 'need the use of the body mass to exert part of the force required to accomplish the work' (Durnin 1994: p. 42). Typical such activities in the developing country context are sugar and timber cutting, carrying heavy loads, digging or shovelling earth, pulling or cycling a rickshaw, splitting stones, and clearing land. In such activities, tall men have been found to be more productive than short men (Thomas and Strauss 1992, Kennedy and Garcia 1994).

In many other work activities in which large shares of the population in developing countries, not least women, are engaged, tallness and maximum strength are not what matter the most.[24] Such activities include most forms of household tasks and most light agricultural work (planting and weeding). In most of these activities endurance is more important and, in some, also small size, quickness, flexibility, and mobility. The work output at a submaximal work level in such work situations has been found to be not significantly related to height in India (Satanarayana et al. 1977, 1989) or BMI in some other developing countries (Kennedy and Garcia 1994).

There are several studies which show that moderately underweight adults (taken to reflect recent undernutrition) have almost the same maximum physical work capacity as persons of normal weight, but that being severely underweight impairs the work capacity. On the basis of a review of the existing empirical evidence, as well as on some theoretical inferences, Durnin (1994: p. 43) concludes that negative effects on work capacity 'would not appear until BMI reached 17 or less'. All in all, there is simply no combination of height and weight that is optimal for performance in all types of manual work activities; 'the nature of the work task is crucial' as put by Durnin.

14.7.5. Caveat: Low Stature has Many Explanations Besides Undernutrition

The major problem in assessing links between undernutrition in early life to long-lasting impairments in adulthood is that, in the developing country context, the only available indicator of an adult's nutritional 'history' is his or her stature. Short stature, however, reflects not only energy intake/expenditure earlier in life, but also malnutrition (inadequate intake of several minerals, vitamins, proteins, and fats), illness, inadequate psychosocial environment and a large number of other 'insults' on body growth (Keller 1988, Nabarro et al. 1988, Eveleth and Tanner 1990: chapter 10, Waterlow 1992: chapter 13). Adult stature must thus be considered a marker of the totality of these various 'insults' rather than of undernutrition alone. Again, we cannot distinguish

the negative consequences of undernutrition from those of other manifestations of poverty.

14.8.   SUMMARY AND CONCLUSIONS

That significantly increased mortality risk is 'the most definitive and serious
consequence of malnutrition' is widely agreed. The main contribution of this
chapter has been to provide estimates of the shares of all child deaths in SSA
and in South Asia, respectively, that are attributed to anthropometric failure
of differing severity. These estimates suggest that about one-third of all child
deaths in Africa are attributed to anthropometric failure, and in South Asia,
roughly half. Out of all these deaths, about 80 per cent were found to belong
to the 'severely failed' category in both South Asia and SSA. All these results
should of course be considered as rough indicators of orders of magnitude
rather than being taken literally.

Irrespective of the exact degree of reliability, however, the results point to
an important fact. A substantial share of all child deaths, be it 40 per cent or
60 per cent, affect children who do not suffer from anthropometric failure.
These deaths can thus not easily be attributed to undernutrition, but rather
low income, illiteracy, poor sanitation, poor health care, and several other
manifestations of general poverty (a notion to be explored in Chapters 15
and 16). Moreover, that about one-third of child deaths in SSA are attributed
to anthropometric failure is not to say that primary undernutrition is *the*
cause in all these cases. In some, illness may well be the primary reason for
weight and/or height failure. The one-third figure should thus be interpreted

APPENDIX TABLE 14.1. Estimated distribution of all child deaths by anthropometric
status and estimated distribution of all child deaths attributable to anthropometric
failure

Anthropometric indicator	SSA				South Asia			
	Normal	Failure			Normal	Failure		
		Total	Mild-to-moderate	Severe		Total	Mild-to-moderate	Severe
(A) Estimated distribution of child deaths according to anthropometric status (%)								
W/A	42	58	24	34	19	81	24	57
H/A	48	52	20	32	20	80	17	63
W/H	85	15	11	4	81	19	14	5
(B) Estimated share of deaths attributable to anthropometric failure (%)								
W/A	61	39	11	28	46	54	7	47
H/A	77	23	5	18	50	50	4	46
W/H	92	8	5	3	97	3	0	3

Source: Estimated on the basis of data from Table 14.4 with the help of equations 14.4 and 14.5.*a–c* in the
text.

APPENDIX TABLE 14.2. Estimated share of all child deaths attributable to anthropometric failure (per cent): sensitivity test

	SSA			South Asia		
	Total	Mild-to-moderate	Severe	Total	Mild-to-moderate	Severe
(a) Base estimate						
W/A	39	11	28	54	7	47
H/A	23	5	18	50	4	46
(b) Alternative estimate[a]						
W/A	31	9	24	61	8	53
H/A	18	3	15	56	5	51

[a] Estimated on the assumption that the ERs are 25 per cent lower in SSA Africa and 25 per cent higher in South Asia than the values presented in Table 14.1 (panel B).

as a rough upper-bound estimate of the share of the deaths that are related to undernutrition in the African countries.

NOTES

1. Lipton (1983: p. 19) cites a study which suggests that 'moderate diarrhoea may result in an increased loss of calories in the stools of 500 to 600 per day.' Martorell and Ho (1984) report on studies that have found gross intake to be reduced by 20 per cent or more during spells of diarrhoea. Considering that the normal (required) calorie intake of 2–6-year-olds is estimated to be in the range 1000–1500, prolonged illness must have a significant impact on current weight. (For a review of the literature, see Tomkins and Watson 1989: pp. 51–4.) It has further been estimated that an increase in body temperature of 1°C above the normal increases energy expenditure by 10–15 per cent (ibid: p. 20). Somewhat surprisingly, in most of the eight studies covered in the Tomkin and Watson review (1989: table 3), there is little or no correlation between anthropometric status and incidence of diarrhoea, although, its duration is increased by anthropometric shortcomings in some of the studies covered. As one would expect, there is a much weaker link between height for age and diarrhoea than between the two weight indicators.
2. The difficulties of interpreting causality is brought out clearly by the fact that the very same anthropometric measures have been used both as indicators both of health and of nutritional status. That is, in some studies, weight for age (or height) is used as an indicator of current health (the dependent variable) and is correlated to dietary data. In other studies, weight for age is used as a proxy for nutritional status (the independent variable) and correlated to the frequency of specific diseases, such as diarrhoea and tuberculosis (see Beaton and Ghassemi 1982).
3. The above brief attempt to summarize a large literature has for obvious reasons remained incomplete and unnuanced. The reader who wants more detailed and knowledgeable reviews of the literature should consult the main studies cited

here. These reviews highlight what is known, what is not known, and what is controversial. For a brief summary and comments on 20 studies of the effect of poor growth on the immune system, see ACC/SCN (1992: pp. 82–7) and Scrimshaw (1989). Also see Murray and Lopez (1998).

4. Clinical examinations find that the critical low weight for height at which death occurs in adolescents and adults corresponds to a BMI of 11 for males and 13 for females (James *et al.* 1988). For small children, it appears that no corresponding limits for low weight are available.

5. See ACC/SCN (1997*a*) and Murray and Lopez (1998).

6. See, for instance, Gillespie and Mason (1991) and Gillespie *et al.* (1996, 1997) for surveys of results from such studies.

7. On the basis of his assessment of the empirical literature, Palletier concludes that the most accurate predictor of mortality risk is simple arm circumference; that is, arm circumference *non-adjusted* for age and height. It is therefore unfortunate that arm circumference, which used to be commonly applied, is no longer used by the large international organizations that today are the sole providers of anthropometric measures that are, with many reservations (see Chapters 11–13), comparable across countries and over time. Simple arm circumference also has the advantage of being independent of age, which is important in the many situations and places where children's age are not registered properly.

8. Similar graphs of height for age and weight for height could be derived, but these would look rather the same as Fig. 14.1. The estimated average mortality rates for these two indicators are given in Table 14.4.

9. Also Pelletier (1994: p. 2054) notices 'that (over the entire range of weight for age) mortality in the three African studies appears to be elevated relative to the South Asian rates'.

10. Pelletier's (1994) review of studies from other parts of Asia show the same general 'pattern', as do the retrospective studies (Pelletier 1991).

11. There are no national estimates of the prevalence of failure with the arm-circumference indicator.

12. With the weight-for-height indicator, which is a dubious predictor of subsequent mortality (see Chapter 13 above), more than 80 per cent of all child deaths in both regions are in the 'normal' category'.

13. There are also other differences that make inter-study comparisons difficult, i.e. accidental deaths are included in some while not in others, and different cut-off points are used in different studies. There seem also to be some studies in which the number of deaths has been severely underreported; these studies are not included here.

14. Vella *et al.* (1992: table 1), for instance, provide estimates of the prevalence of anthropometric failure by both methods, and for some categories the results differ notably. The prevalence of stunting in their sample is 42 per cent with the <–2 SDs cut-off point, while only 28 per cent with the <90 per cent of median cut-off point. When it comes to the underweight, the difference is in the other direction (although considerably smaller). Similar discrepancies are reported by Mora (1984).

15. As discussed at length in Chapter 12, there is reason to doubt the representativeness of estimates of prevalence of anthropometric failure in any one country from a particular year, since there are large inter-year fluctuations in factors affecting

child weight and height. The small sizes of most of the national samples are also worth remembering.

16. As noted earlier, the 'gross mortality rates' reported from the various studies are not derived in a way that permits comparison with conventionally estimated national under-five mortality rates.

17. The brief treatment of these issues here is intended only as a remainder of the possible existence of long-term impairments related to undernutrition in early life. The reader who wants more detailed and knowledgeable analyses would do better to consult the works cited here and other expert assessments.

18. For an entertaining but not highly scientific account of the various ways being 'too small, or too tall' have been claimed to be a disadvantage, see Gillis (1990).

19. For similar conclusions regarding psychomotoric development, see Connolly (1984), and Greisel (1984). Again, it appears that there is an almost complete lack of longitudinal studies of the correlation between anthropometric status and psychomotoric performance.

20. According to the WHO/IBRD, chronic and non-communicable diseases account for about one-third and three-quarters of the total 'burden of disease' in young adults (15–44) and mature and old adults (above 45), respectively, in developing countries (IBRD*a* 1993: table B.7).

21. Garcia and Kennedy (1994) claims furthermore that concerning adults in developing countries, 'no systematic study on the relationship between low BMI and ill health is available'. In their own investigation they found 'a small but statistically significant effect of BMI (after controlling simultaneity) on proneness to morbidity in Pakistan and Kenya but none in the Philippines and Ghana', but also that 'the threshold at which morbidity begins to rise is not consistent with the suggested cut-off of BMI 18.5'.

22. There are a few studies, however, that report contrary results, e.g. Samaras and Storms (1992). In addition, there is evidence from historical records in the present developed countries, which suggests that relative shortness has been associated with poorer health and higher mortality in certain diseases (Floud 1992, Fogel 1992, 1994). It is further notable that over the past three centuries, especially the last, people have become notably taller while life expectancy has increased dramatically in the present developed countries. In the 18th and 19th centuries, the average height of adult males in Europe and the US was roughly on a par with men in contemporary India (Fogel 1994: pp. 372–3, also see Steckel 1995).

23. The literature on nutrition and fecundity is surveyed in Bongaarts (1980) and that on nutrition and fertility in Menken *et al.* (1981). They reach approximately the same conclusion: 'Moderate chronic malnutrition has only a minor effect on fecundity and the resulting effect on fertility is very small' (Bongaarts 1980: p. 564, Menken *et al.* 1981: p. 425).

24. Several studies have demonstrated 'that the maximum relative work load that can be sustained for an 8-hour work day usually does not exceed about 35–40 per cent [of] VO_2 max' (Spurr 1988: p. 222).

PART V

15

On Reasons for Child Mortality and Anthropometric Failure

15.1. INTRODUCTION

In the previous chapter, anthropometric failure as a cause of child mortality was assessed and found to be a contributing, but far from complete explanation. An estimated two-thirds and half of the child deaths in the SSA and the South Asian countries, respectively, are unrelated to anthropometric failure. However, behind both anthropometric failure and excessive child mortality lie common factors which can be arranged under the label 'poverty', the focus of this chapter.

The more specific objectives are fivefold. The first is to test how much of the inter-country variances in child-mortality and anthropometric-failure rates are explained by differences in (i) per-capita income, (ii) income distribution, and (iii) parental literacy. The second objective is to derive estimates of the relative role of per-capita real income and public provision of services in explaining child mortality and anthropometric failure. A third objective is to test the extent to which child mortality and anthropometric failure are explained by the same basic manifestations of poverty and—consequently—what differences there may be. The fourth objective is to check whether weight-for-age failure is a significant determinant of child mortality. The final objective is to investigate whether there are systematic differences between countries in SSA and in South Asia, respectively. The method used is multiple regression analysis on the basis of cross-sectional observations for up to 117 countries, using data from the 1990s.

The plan of the chapter is as follows. In section 15.2, the main hypotheses to be tested, the proxy variables, and the data are presented. The econometric model and the first round of results are provided in section 15.3. Further results are presented in section 15.4. The results are discussed and qualified in section 15.5. Differences between SSA and South Asian countries are highlighted, and individual outlier countries are identified in section 15.6. Section 15.7 closes the chapter with a brief summary and conclusions.

15.2. ECONOMIC CAUSES OF CHILD DEPRIVATION

15.2.1. Hypotheses and Models Tested

The hypothesis that mortality and anthropometric failure rates are negatively correlated to per-capita income across countries is too evident to need detailed elaboration. There is also plenty of earlier evidence demonstrating these obvious relationships (e.g. Preston 1975, Rodgers 1979, Haaga *et al.* 1985).[1] However, simple correlations between national income and mortality/ anthropometric failure do not tell us through what channels higher income tends to improve child health. Is it mainly because higher national per-capita income ensures that a larger proportion of households can afford more and better food, housing, sanitation and other private goods? Or is it that higher per-capita income at the national level means more adequate public provision of health and education services? Or are variations in public spending on health-related facilities and basic education across countries, after income is controlled, important variables in explaining child mortality and anthropometric status? Is the internal distribution of income in the various countries important for children's well-being? These are among the questions to be addressed in the following.

The 'mortality' and the 'anthropometric-failure' (AF) models to be tested can be written as:

$$U5MR = f(Y/c, \theta, \boldsymbol{\Phi}, \boldsymbol{D}) \text{ and} \tag{15.1}$$
$$AF = g(Y/c, \theta, \boldsymbol{\Phi}, \boldsymbol{D}), \tag{15.2}$$

where Y/c is national per-capita real income, θ is the income distribution parameter, $\boldsymbol{\Phi}$ is a vector of public services, and $\boldsymbol{D}$ is the vector of geographical dummy variables. The starting hypothesis is thus that child mortality and anthropometric failure are determined (simultaneously) by the same basal macro-variables, although the functional form of the relationships may differ ($f \neq g$).

15.2.2. Dependent Variables and Data

The measure of mortality to be used is the under-fives mortality rate (U5MR). The U5MR represents cumulative mortality over the years during which mortality is considerably higher than later in life (up to about 60) in deprived populations; it is therefore a particularly sensitive indicator (Hill and Pebley 1989). Moreover, this mortality statistic is available for almost all countries in the world. In an initial round of regressions, the infant mortality rate (IMR) was also used as an alternative dependent variable, but it showed itself to be highly correlated to U5MR (0.99), thus providing no additional information. The U5MR was used rather than IMR because it covers the same age group (0–5 years) as the data on anthropometric failure, which facilitates comparison of results.

The indicator of anthropometric failure used subsequently is weight-for-age failure (WAF). There are two main reasons for this choice. First, this is the anthropometric indicator that is the most closely related to subsequent death among children, as shown by the sample evidence analysed in the previous chapter. Secondly, estimates of WAF are available for more countries than either weight for height and height for age, the main alternative indicators.[2]

15.2.3. Explanatory Proxy Variables and Data

Real Per-Capita Income   This variable is proxied by estimates of the Gross National Product per capita (GNPc) measured in internationally comparable US dollars (purchasing power parity). This proxy was preferred to conventional national gross national product per capita (GNPc) estimates, which are converted through official exchange rates (often in disequilibrium) and do not reflect differences in the prices of non-traded goods and services.[3]

Income Distribution   For any given level of real income per capita, the hypothesis is that the more unequal the distribution of income is in a country, the higher the proportion of poor people and, thus, the higher the mortality—and the anthropometric-failure rates in the child population. The choice of proxy variable(s) was determined solely by data availability. Deininger and Squire (1996a) provide GINI coefficients and quintile distributions for some 80 countries, taken from surveys of 'acceptable quality' (according to three main criteria) that are (reasonably) comparable for a year in the late 1980s or the early 1990s. These GINI coefficients, and the ratio of the fourth and the first quintiles ($Q4/Q1$), are the two alternative proxies for income distribution used in the tests below.[4]

Education   Basic education is fundamentally a public rather than a private good and is typically provided by the state. Several different proxies for the level of education (or human capital) have been used in various strands of empirical literature. In this chapter, the adult literacy rate (ALR) is used on the assumption that it is the literacy of parents (adults) that is important for the well-being of the children in the same period. As an alternative proxy for education, we use the adult female literacy rate (FLR) on the basis of the hypothesis that women are the chief caretakers of children worldwide and that their education is more important than that of adult males in this special context.

Disease Prevention and Health Care   In choosing proxy variables for public provision of services that supposedly affect child health and, thus, mortality, the availability of data has been the main guiding principle, although some theoretical considerations have been made. Government spending on 'health' has not been considered a good proxy variable, both for conceptual and data reasons. Aggregate data on public spending on the health sector (or the education sector) say nothing about what kinds of health services (education) are provided. Here we are interested in health services benefiting small children specifically, but no sufficiently disaggregated public expenditure data are available. Moreover, health expenditure data, when available, are usually not comparable across countries.[5]

Data on (public) provision of certain more specific facilities, i.e. safe water, basic sanitation, and a health service, are available for most countries. *A priori*, one would expect that the share of the population that has access to such facilities should have a bearing on child morbidity and anthropometric status, and, in the end, child mortality. In the tests below, we have included an index based on these estimated shares as an explanatory variable (ACC). Also, the frequency of the use of oral rehydration therapy (ORT) in treating diarrhoea is used as an explanatory variable. We also use the percentage of 1-year olds who are immunized against TB, diphtheria, typhoid, polio, and measles as an alternative proxy variable (IMM) for public health intervention directed (directly) towards small children. Finally, as yet another alternative variable, we use the number of people per medical doctor (DOC) as a proxy for public health-service provision more generally.

Demographic Characteristics   High fertility (FERT) can be expected to have a negative influence on child health through several channels, e.g. the more children per household, the lower the per-person income, the less time for parental care of the individual child, the younger the mother at the birth of her first child, and the easier the transmission of infectious disease.

Rural/Urban Differences   The base data on the prevalence of anthropometric failure reveal large and significant differences between rural and urban samples in almost all countries (see Chapter 11). We therefore hypothesize that the degree of urbanization (URB) has an influence on child mortality and the prevalence of anthropometric failure across countries, other things being equal. To some extent, 'urbanization' is likely to reflect higher income, literacy, and better access to public services *within* countries, variables already taken into consideration at the *national* level.

Dummy Variables   A quick glance at the basic data set reveals that there are regional traits in the pattern of child mortality and anthropometric failure. The SSA countries have higher child mortality rates than almost all other countries with similar per-capita incomes. The South Asian countries stand out in terms of high prevalence of anthropometric failure. The tests below are (partly) aimed at explaining these disparities by differences in public health services and other variables discussed above. However, there may be additional explanations, which would then be reflected in dummy variables for the SSA and South Asian countries, respectively. The entire set of variables entered into the tests is described in Appendix Table 15.1, together with information on data sources and minimum/maximum values of the variables.

15.3. CROSS-COUNTRY REGRESSIONS

15.3.1. *Econometric Specifications*

The tests are based on reduced form equations. In order to be able to identify exactly through what intermediate factors per-capita income affects the mortality and anthropometric status of children, we would require a much more complex structural model and considerably more disaggregated data than are available at present. All explanatory variables are assumed to have an additive effect on the dependent variables, a standard assumption in the related literature. The tests are carried out on data on *levels* (1990s) rather than *changes* between different points in time. The latter approach would in some respects be preferred, but no sufficient data are available for many of the variables.

No explicit theory will be advanced for justifying the special functional (reduced) forms tested below. Following the related literature, however, the relationship between the dependent variables and per-capita income will be assumed to be concave. That is, the decline in mortality (and anthropometric failure) is assumed to diminish as income goes up and to 'approximate' a plateau when income approaches the levels of the richest countries. Many specific functional forms have been used in the related literature in order to capture the non-linearity and the asymptotic maximum values that variables can assume (e.g. Preston 1975, Rodgers 1979, Sen 1981*b*, Kakwani 1993, Schultz 1993). Some of these were tested here in an initial round, and the one that provided the best fit, lnGNPc, was chosen.

Two estimation techniques will be used: the ordinary least square (OLS) and two-stage least square (2SLS). The 2SLS is used mainly to handle multi-colinearity; almost all the proxy variables for the provision of public services are correlated to national income per capita. Simple OLS estimations will therefore produce biased coefficients for lnGNPc, necessitating a two-stage estimation procedure. First we obtain OLS estimations for the U5MR (alternatively WAF):

$$\text{U5MR} = \beta_0 + \text{lnGNPc}\,\beta_1 + \theta\,\beta_2 + [\boldsymbol{\Phi}_i][\boldsymbol{\beta}_i] + \varepsilon \qquad (15.3)$$

where $[\boldsymbol{\Phi}_i]$ is the row vector of the $n{-}2$ explanatory variables, in addition to lnGNPc and θ, the income distribution variable. $[\boldsymbol{\beta}_i]$ is the column vector of coefficients to be estimated ($i = 3 \ldots n$) and ε is the residual error term.

In the second stage we regress each element in Φ_i on lnGNPc:

$$\Phi_i = a_{0i} + \text{lnGNPc}\, a_{1i} + \mu_i \qquad (15.4)$$

For all μ_i, the residual for each observation (country) is calculated and used as a new explanatory variable set (indicated by ®).

Substituting (15.4) into (15.3) gives:

$$\text{U5MR} = \beta_0 + \text{lnGNPc}\,\beta_1 + \theta\,\beta_2 + [\alpha_{0i} + \text{lnGNPc}\,\alpha_{1i} + \mu_i]\,[\beta_i] + \varepsilon.$$

Defining $\beta_{00} = (\beta_0 + [\alpha_{0i}]\,[\beta_i])$ and rearranging, we obtain:

$$\text{U5MR} = \beta_{00} + \text{lnGNPc}\,(\beta_1 + [\alpha_{1i}]\,[\beta_i]) + \theta\,\beta_2 + [\mu_i]\,[\beta_i] + \varepsilon. \quad (15.5)$$

Comparing (15.3) and (15.5), we see that the estimated regression slopes for the GNPc variable are expected to differ unless the vector product $[\alpha_{1i}]\,[\beta_i]$ is zero, which will not be the case when most of the explanatory variables are correlated to lnGNPc. The estimation of the correlation slope for lnGNPc based on (15.5), $(\beta_1 + [\alpha_{1i}]\,[\beta_i])$, will thus give the total impact of income on the dependent variable(s), i.e. both the direct effect and the indirect effects *via* the better education and public health provisions that follow from higher income. We also see that the estimated coefficients for Φ_i and μ_i will be identical.

15.3.2. Results

Income and Income Distribution   The results of the first round of regressions are reported in Table 15.1. Regression (1) shows the expected high (negative) correlation between U5MR and lnGNPc. The latter variable alone explains 69 per cent of the inter-country variance in child mortality and the estimated

TABLE 15.1. Regression results; dependent variables: U5MR and WAF, White-corr

Dependent variable: estimation technique	(1) U5MR OLS	(2) U5MR OLS	(3) U5MR 2SLS	(4) WAF OLS	(5) WAF OLS	(6) WAF 2SLS
Explanatory variable(s)						
lnGNPc	−128.8	−120.1	−122.2	−21.8	−22.8	−22.6
	(13.8)★	(10.0)★	(11.7)★	(5.8)★	(4.5)★	(4.8)★
Q4/Q1	—	0.1	0.4	—	1.0	0.9
		(0.0)	(0.4)		(1.6)	(1.5)
ALR®	—	—	−1.3	—	—	−0.2
			(3.8)★			(1.6)
No. of observations	117	84	81	65	48	48
R^2-adjusted	0.69	0.65	0.76	0.28	0.29	0.33

Absolute values of t-statistic are given in parentheses;★ significant at 0.05.

coefficient is significant at the 0.0000 level. Adding the income distribution proxy variable (*Q4/Q1* in regression 2) does nothing to improve the fit. (The alternative proxy for income distribution, the GINI coefficient, did not come out as significant either.) The results for weight-for-age failure (WAF), regressed on the same income variables, are reported in columns 4–5. The lnGNPc variable is highly significant, but explains only 28 per cent of the variance in WAF. The income distribution variable is not significant (but close to).

Adult Literacy   As an additional explanatory variable, the (residual) adult literacy rate (ALR®) was included in the 2SLS tests. Also this variable turns out highly significant in the U5MR tests, and the explanatory power increases to 76 per cent (regression 3 in Table 15.1). Also in the WAF tests, lnGNPc is highly significant, while the coefficient for ALR® is insignificant. It is notable that the R^2-adjusted is notably lower in the WAF test compared with that for U5MR.[6]

Public Health Services   Four different proxy variables for public provision of health-related services were used alternatively. In combination with the lnGNPc and ALR® variables, ACC® came out as significant and explains some 80 per cent of the variance in U5MR (Table 15.2). The variables IMM®, DOC®, and ORT® were not significant. In the WAF regressions, all

TABLE 15.2. Regression results; dependent variable: U5MR; 2SLS, White-corr

Explanatory variables	(1)	(2)	(3)	(4)	(5)	(6)
lnGNPc	−174.9	−183.4	−173.7	−146.1	−142.8	−143.2
	(13.7)*	(8.9)*	(8.2)*	(9.3)*	(8.0)*	(7.9)*
ALR®	−0.8	−0.6	−0.4	−0.7	−0.6	−0.6
	(3.3)*	(1.7)#	(1.2)	(2.6)*	(1.7)#	(1.6)
ACC®	−1.0	−1.2	−1.0	−0.8	−0.9	−0.9
	(4.1)*	(3.5)*	(3.0)*	(3.5)*	(3.0)*	(2.8)*
WAF	—	−0.2	0.1	—	0.7	0.7
		(0.3)	(0.2)		(1.5)	(1.5)
FERT®	—	—	10.1	—	—	2.8
			(2.3)*			(0.6)
SSA	—	—	—	32.8	28.2	25.1
				(3.1)*	(2.7)*	(2.1)*
SA	—	—	—	−15.1	−41.4	−42.5
				(0.8)	(1.2)	(1.3)
No. of observations	73	53	53	73	53	53
R^2-adjusted	0.80	0.75	0.76	0.83	0.79	0.79

Absolute values of *t*-statistic are given in parentheses;* significant at 0.05; # significant at 0.10.

'health proxies' turned out to be statistically insignificant (Table 15.3). However, the percentage of the population living in urban areas (URB®) was found to be a highly significant explanatory variable for WAF (while not for U5MR). In combination with lnGNPc, URB® explains some 40 per cent of the variation in WAF.

Fertility The total fertility rate (FERT®) came out as significant in the U5MR tests (Table 15.2), but not in the WAF regressions (Table 15.3).

Weight-for-Age Failure It is widely hypothesized that undernutrition is the main factor behind anthropometric failure and that undernutrition, in turn, is an important determinant of child mortality. This hypothesis was tested by including WAF among the explanatory variables in the U5MR tests. Across the 53 countries for which sufficient data are available, there is no significant correlation between U5MR and WAF net of other influences (Table 15.2).

15.4. SEPARATING INCOME AND PUBLIC INTERVENTION EFFECTS

In this section we shall make a bold attempt to quantify the relative effect on child mortality of higher income as such, on the one hand, and the more adequate provision of public services that higher income enables, on the other. We shall also estimate the 'independent' (from income) influence that access to public services (ACC) have on child mortality.

TABLE 15.3. Regression results; dependent variable: WAF; 2SLS, White-corr

Explanatory variables	(1)	(2)	(3)	(4)	(5)	(6)
lnGNPc	−22.5	−19.0	−22.5	−19.2	−17.1	−19.4
	(4.6)*	(5.9)*	(5.6)*	(4.8)*	(6.5)*	(6.4)*
ALR®	−0.2	−0.2	−0.1	0.0	0.1	0.0
	(1.4)	(1.8)#	(1.1)	(0.1)	(1.1)	(0.3)
ACC®	−0.1	—	−0.1	−0.1	—	−0.1
	(1.0)		(1.0)	(1.4)		(1.5)
URB®	—	−0.3	−0.3	—	−0.2	−0.2
		(3.7)*	(3.3)*		(2.2)*	(2.6)*
SA	—	—	—	36.6	30.1	34.4
				(6.1)*	(5.2)*	(5.8)*
No. of observations	53	64	53	53	64	53
R^2-adjusted	0.25	0.41	0.34	0.62	0.66	0.66

Absolute values of t-statistic are given in parentheses;* significant at 0.05; # significant at 0.10.

15.4.1. Direct versus Indirect Effects of lnGNPc on Dependent Variables

As can be seen from equation 15.5 above, the 2SLS estimates produce co-efficients for lnGNPc that incorporate the sum of the direct effect of income on the dependent variable (β_1) and the indirect effects through the positive effects that income has on literacy and the provision of health-related public services ($[\alpha_{1i}][\beta_i]$). In order to get an idea of the relative size of the direct and indirect effects, respectively, we re-estimated all regressions reported in Table 15.2 using simple OLS. The latter estimations provide the estimated size of the β_1 coefficient. Subtracting β_1 from the total effect, $(\beta_1 + [\alpha_{1i}][\beta_i])$, gives the indirect effect ($[\alpha_{1i}][\beta_i]$). The quotient ($[\alpha_{1i}][\beta_i]$) $(\beta_1 + [\alpha_{1i}][\beta_i])^{-1}$ is thus the share of the total effect of lnGNPc that is indirect, working through literacy and access to the public services.

The findings are presented in Table 15.4 for three regressions, with ALR and ACC as the explanatory variables in addition to lnGNPc.[7] Column (4) suggests that about 40 per cent of the total impact of lnGNPc on U5MR comes from the indirect effects, i.e. *via* the higher literacy and better access to public services that follow from higher income. Consequently, about 60 per cent of the total effect of lnGNPc on U5MR is direct, i.e. independent of literacy and the provision of public services. The size of this estimate is plausible, but great caution should nevertheless be exercised in interpreting the exact figures. They are probably rather crude, as it was not possible to estimate any synergistic, interactive effects. However, it is a first shot at delineating the relative orders of magnitude of the 'private income' and the 'public-service provision' effects, respectively, of higher national per-capita income on child mortality.

15.4.2. Excluding and Including the Income Variable

A further (equally crude) test of the relative size of the 'income-dependent' and the 'own' effects of adult literacy and the provision of public services on child mortality can be made by regressing U5MR on the explanatory variable set with and without the lnGNPc variable. The estimated size of the

TABLE 15.4. Separation of direct and indirect effects of lnGNPc on U5MR

Indirect effects of lnGNPc through variable(s):	2SLS Total effect $\beta_1 + [\alpha_{1i}][\beta_i])$	OLS Direct effect β_1	Indirect effect $[\alpha_{1i}][\beta_i]$ (1)–(2)	Share of in-direct effect (3)/(1)
	(1)	(2)	(3)	(4)
Regression (1): ALR	−128.3	−79.0	−49.3	0.38
Regression (2): ACC	−180.2	−118.4	−61.8	0.34
Regression (3): ALR, ACC	−174.9	−104.9	−70.0	0.40

coefficient for the ALR and ACC variables, with lnGNPc included among the explanatory variables, reflects their effects net of income. The regressions without lnGNPc, gives an estimate of the total effect, i.e. 'own' effect plus that going through the income variable. The difference between the two will thus constitute a rough estimate of the 'own' effect.

The results are presented in Table 15.5. In the fourth column, we have the estimated 'own' effect of ALR and ACC on U5MR. The 'own' effect of ALR is 45 per cent of the total effect and slightly higher for ACC. Although the method is crude, it is comforting that these estimates are consistent with those obtained with the previous test (as reported in Table 15.4 above).[8]

15.5.   REGIONAL DIFFERENCES AND OUTLIERS

15.5.1. Regional Dummy Variables

The base data show the U5MRs to be exceptionally high in most SSA countries, while the incidence of anthropometric failure is much higher in the South Asian countries than elsewhere. Introducing regional dummy variables into the multivariable tests provides an opportunity to check whether these regional differences persist when other explanatory variables are controlled for.

The results for U5MR are shown in Table 15.2 (regressions 4–6). The dummy for the SSA countries is highly significant. In the tests without this dummy, FERT® comes out as significant, but when the SSA dummy is included in the tests, it loses significance. (This is not surprising, since extremely high fertility rates—above 6—are exclusively an African phenomenon.) The dummy for the South Asian countries comes out as insignificant throughout. Overall, introducing the regional dummy variables increases the explanatory power of the model by about 3 percentage points on average.

TABLE 15.5. Estimated coefficients for ALR and ACC, in (OLS) regressions of U5MR, with and without including the lnGNPc variable

Explanatory variable(s)	Without lnGNPc		With lnGNPc		Differ- ence (1) − (2)	Ratio (3)/(1)
	(1)		(2)		(3)	(4)
Regression (1): ALR	−2.54	(15.1)*	−1.41	(6.2)*	−1.13	0.45
Regression (2) ACC	−2.73	(13.5)*	−1.46	(5.3)*	−1.27	0.47
Regression (3): ALR,	−1.24	(5.6)*	−0.78	(3.3)*	−0.46	0.37
ACC	−1.75	(7.0)*	−1.01	(4.1)*	−0.74	0.42

Absolute values of t-statistic are given in parentheses;* significant at 0.05.

The parallel results for WAF are presented in Table 15.3 (regressions 4–6). In all the regressions, the SSA dummy is insignificant (not shown), while the SA dummy comes out as highly significant throughout. No major change in significance is obtained by introducing the dummies: lnGNPc and URB® remain highly significant, while ALR® and ACC® remain insignificant. The explanatory power of the model increases notably though: the R^2-adjusted almost doubles and goes above 0.60. The SA dummy is by far the most significant variable, and the results demonstrate that the especially poor anthropometric status of children in South Asia prevails even after differences in various other aspects between these and other poor countries are controlled for.

15.5.2. Identification of Outliers

As indicated by the significant dummy variable in the above tests, *en masse* the SSA countries are outliers in terms of high U5MRs and the South Asian countries when it comes to the high incidence of WAF. Some countries in both regions have worse scores than others, though. In order to identify the countries that are statistically significant outliers, a Student's *t*-test was applied on the basis of regressions (3) reported in Tables 15.2 and 15.3. The outliers are thus the countries that have statistically significantly higher or lower U5MRs and WAFs than expected, given their *GNPc*.

Six African countries came out as having exceptionally high U5MRs: Sierra Leone, Mozambique, Niger, Guinea-Bissau, Gambia, and Mauritania. Only two countries in the entire country set (112) have exceptionally (statistically significant) low U5MRs: Georgia and Armenia (Fig. 15.1), but Sri Lanka and Jamaica come close.

When it comes to WAF scores, no country has a statistically (significant) better performance than predicted by the model. The three South Asian countries India, Nepal, and Bangladesh also have exceptionally high WAF rates by this test (confirming what was found earlier). Close to being exceptional in terms of high WAF are Mauritania, Indonesia, the Philippines, and, perhaps surprisingly, Sri Lanka (Fig. 15.2).

15.6.   DISCUSSION AND INTERPRETATION OF RESULTS

15.6.1. Data Inaccuracies?

As noted by Hill and Pebley (1989: p.658): 'Any study of child mortality in the developing world is hindered by shortcomings in availability, accuracy, and timeliness of appropriate data'. It is well known that the child mortalities for some countries have been estimated with methods which are dubious due to the small samples taken (Hill and Pebley 1989, Chamie 1994, Deaton

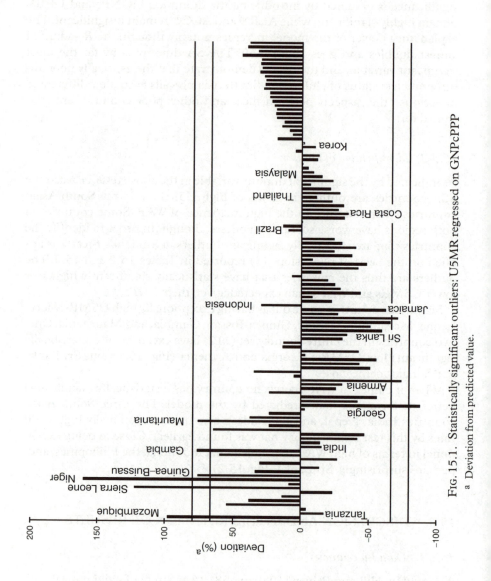

FIG. 15.1. Statistically significant outliers: U5MR regressed on GNPcPPP

[a] Deviation from predicted value.

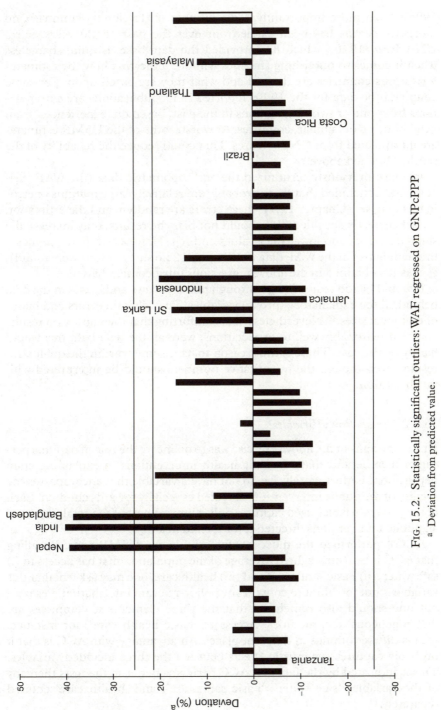

FIG. 15.2. Statistically significant outliers: WAF regressed on GNPcPPP

[a] Deviation from predicted value.

1995). Even more importantly, for a number of developing countries, no mortality census has been carried out over the past 15–20 years or so. UNICEF*a* (1996), which has provided the data base, is quite shameless when it comes to publishing statistics without indicating how the estimates for various countries are derived and what they are based upon. For some countries the data for the 1990s reported in its publications are extrapolations from one or two observations in the past, based on 'experiences' from neighbouring or 'similar' countries. At worst, some of the U5MR estimates are intrapolated from GNPc figures. That could reduce the reliability of the results obtained above.[9]

We have previously scrutinized the anthropometric data (the WAF variable) and concluded that there probably are relatively large margins of error in this data set (Chapter 12). If these errors are random, and the estimation model correctly specified, this should not bias the results, only increase the standard errors and lower the *t*-values and R^2s. However, if there are measurement biases in the WAF data (in Chapter 12 no such reasons were found), the results obtained in the above regressions must contain biases.

It would be too tedious to go through possible flaws and biases in the data behind all the explanatory (proxy) variables. They contain errors and biases of unknown sizes.[10] Nevertheless, it is comforting that the regression results conform reasonably well to expectations; were all the data bad, this would hardly be the case. There is thus reason to have some trust in the qualitative results, even though the quantitative numbers should be interpreted with much caution.

15.6.2. Crude Proxy Variables?

One of the aims of the above exercise was to delineate the role of national per-capita income and that of public health interventions in explaining child deprivation. Unfortunately, we do not have a variable that encompasses the totality of the public interventions directed especially towards children. Each of the proxy variables used captures only a limited part of the total impact of all public interventions directed toward child health.

ACC® performed the most satisfactorily in the U5MR tests. Recalling that ACC is the (unweighted) average of the population that has access to (i) safe water, (ii) basic sanitation and (iii) health care, one may ask whether this variable is not too blunt to contain any policy-relevant information. Perhaps, but one should also remember that the three elements it comprises are 'heterogeneous' commodities. Access to 'basic health care', for instance, means different things in different places. An advantage with ACC is that it probably captures synergistic effects between the three included variables. This is indicated by the fact that ACC performs better in the tests than any of the variables 'safe water', 'basic sanitation', and 'health care' entered separately.[11]

In the WAF regressions, all four proxy variables for public provision of health-related facilities came out as insignificant throughout. The degree of urbanization, on the other hand, proved to be a highly significant and robust explanation for anthropometric performance. What exactly URB® captures is not possible to tell, but an informed guess is that it is the combined effect of the higher income, literacy rates, and more adequate provision of public facilities in urban than in rural areas, which seems to be a worldwide phenomena (Lipton 1983, Lipton and Ravallion 1995).

15.6.3. Selection Bias?

In trying to answer the question of whether U5MR and WAF are explained by the same 'basal' variables, a problem is that the number of observations for these two (dependent) variables differs. The WAF results are derived on the basis of about 50 countries, while some of the results for U5MR are based on up to 117 observations. Moreover, some of the latter results are derived on a national sample spanning the entire income range, while the WAF results are derived from countries at the lower income tail (since no anthropometric data are available for other countries). This could be a reason why U5MR shows much stronger correlations with lnGNPc and ALR® than does WAF (Table 15.1). However, comparing, for instance, regressions (1) and (2) in Table 15.2, reveals that nothing dramatic changes in terms of significance and explanatory power when the U5MR estimates are based on the same subset of countries (53) that were used for the WAF tests.

15.6.4. Omitted Variable Bias?

In addition to per-capita income, one earlier study incorporated the estimated relative price of basic food as an explanatory variable for life expectancy at birth (LEB) in a cross-country regression (Horton et al. 1988). These authors found this price variable significant and also that the relative price of food facing consumers differs substantially between countries, i.e. by a factor of four between the countries with the highest and lowest relative food prices. Indeed, the latter result suggests that there may be an omitted-variable bias of unknown size in the results derived above.[12] There are, however, no recent data available on relative food prices that are comparable across countries.[13]

15.6.5. Reverse Causality?

To the extent possible, heteroskedasticity and multicolinearity have been handled by White (1980) corrections and the use of 2SLS regressions. A problem that we have not been able to resolve (due to the difficulty of finding good instrument variables) is that of reverse causality. For most of the explanatory variables, this does not seem to be a serious problem. It is difficult to envisage that the child mortality rate in a particular year should have a strong influence on lnGDPc or the literacy rate of the adult population.

The problem with reverse causation is the most obvious with fertility as an explanatory variable for child mortality. That is, while there are many reasons to expect high fertility to produce high mortality (see p. 232 above), high child mortality is likely to lead to high fertility through the replacement effect. In practice, however, this turns out to be a minor problem since FERT does not come out as significant.

There are also problems with the ORT and IMM variables, which may explain their lack of significance. As noted by Hill and Pebley (1989: p. 676): 'A major criticism of international child survival programs is their focus on elimination and control of a specific set of infectious disease through immunisation or palliative measures (especially the use of oral dehydration therapy) instead of provision of comprehensive primary health care. Critics of this approach assert that rather than preventing infant and child deaths, these programs merely postpone deaths of children who will die from other causes later in childhood'. That is, if IMM and ORT are used especially frequently in the poorest countries, with the highest mortality rates, but where the provision of basic public services, such as clean water, sanitation, and primary health care, are grossly inadequate, it is of little surprise that these variables turn out to be insignificant.

15.7. SUMMARY AND CONCLUSIONS

As stated in the introduction, the aim of this chapter has been to answer, on the basis of cross-country data, five questions. The first was the extent to which a rather limited number of macro-aggregates can explain inter-country differences in child mortality and anthropometric failure rates: national per-capita income, income distribution, and parental literacy. Together these three variables explained about three-quarters of the variability in the U5MR and one-third of the WAF variability. The strongest effect comes from per-capita income, but adult literacy also comes out as significant in the mortality tests. The results turned out to be reasonably robust to changes in the observation set, the choice of conditioning variables, and the econometric specification.

Over the years, several studies also using cross-sectional regression analysis, have found a relative close (concave) bivariable association between *levels* of real income per-capita and mortality, as measured by IMR, U5MR, or life expectancy (e.g. Preston 1975, Sen 1981b, Isenman 1980, Schultz 1993). Relatively close associations between *changes* in mortality indicators and changes in real income have been demonstrated by Kakwani (1993). It has also been shown that the prevalence of anthropometric failure among developing countries is highly correlated to levels and changes in per-capita real income (Haaga *et al.* 1985, ACC/SCN 1994). These results were, to little surprise, replicated in the present study.

There seems to be only one earlier study that has incorporated income distribution among the explanatory variables (Rodgers 1979). He found income distribution, as proxied by the GINI coefficient, to have a significant association with life expectancy, but a non-robust association with IMR, when per-capita income was controlled for, among a sample of 56 developing countries. The latter finding was also found in the above tests.[14] Parental literacy has not been included in the cross-country tests that I have seen, but various proxies for adult education have been shown to be correlated to child mortality risk and anthropometric failure in several studies based on inter-household observations.[15]

The second question addressed was that of the relative importance of real per-capita income and the provision of public services in explaining child mortality (and also anthropometric failure, but it was not possible to conduct a test for the latter). An estimated 40 per cent of the total impact of higher incomes on child-mortality reduction take the route via the higher literacy and more adequate public provision of health services that go hand in hand with higher income. Another test suggested that about half of the beneficial effect of education and health services are unrelated to income differentials.

The third question was whether child mortality and anthropometric failure are explained by the same 'basal' explanatory variables. The perhaps surprising answer is no. Only three variables came out as highly significant and robust in the WAF regressions: per-capita income, 'urbanization', and the South Asia dummy variable. Together these three variables explain about two-thirds of the variance in WAF across countries. The URB variable probably picks up the advantaged position of the urban population *vis à vis* the rural population in most countries. Literacy and the provision of health services were all insignificant in the WAF tests.

The fourth question concerned anthropometric failure as a reason for child mortality. However, when the WAF variable was entered as an explanatory variable in the U5MR tests, it came out as insignificant throughout.[16]

The fifth and final question was whether there are notable differences between the countries in SSA and those in South Asia, countries that belong to roughly comparable low income groups. The answer is 'yes indeed'. In the African countries, U5MR is exceptionally high—vindicated by a highly significant dummy variable as well as identification of outliers. Some of the regression results suggest that the reason is especially inadequate public-health facilities compared with South Asia, and with the rest of the world for that matter (also see Appendix Table 15.4). That the African countries do not have exceptionally high WAF scores indicates *indirectly* that undernutrition is not the main cause of child deaths (which the results in the previous chapter corroborate).[17] In the South Asian countries, quite the opposite holds, i.e. the mortality rate is significantly lower and the anthropometric performance of children far worse (highly significant) than expected considering income per capita, adult literacy, and the provision of services. The most likely explanation is poor nutrition, both for children and their mothers (cf. the anthropometric evidence in Chapter 11). No other explanation seems entirely plausible.[18]

APPENDIX TABLE 15.1. Variable definitions and data sources

Variable abbreviation	Variable definition (Year)	Min/max value
Dependent Variables		
U5MR	Under-fives mortality rate (‰), 1994	5/320
IMR★	Infant mortality rate (‰), 1994	4/191
WAF	Weight-for-age failure (%), 1990–4	1/66
Explanatory Variables		
lnGNPc	Log of gross national product per capita, 1993 (purchasing power parity-adjusted USD)	520/23,660
GINI★	GINI-coefficient for income distribution (0, 100), 1988–94	.22/.62
Q4/Q1	Ratio of income share of 4th to 1st quintile (ratio), 1988–94	6/35
ALR	Adult literary rate (%), 1990	12/99
FLR★	Adult female literacy rate (%), 1990	5/99
ACC	Unweighted average of the following three shares:	
ASW★	Share of population with access of safe water (%), 1990–5	12/100
ASA★	Share of population with access to sanitation (%), 1990–5	3/100
AHS★	Share of population with access to health service (%), 1985–95	18/100
IMM★	Share of 1-year-old children fully immunized against TB, DPT, Polio, and Measles, average (%), 1990–4	23/99
ORT★	Oral dehyderation therapy use rate (%), 1990–4	6/96
DOC★	Population per medical doctor (1,000s), 1984	0.2/57
URB	Share of population urbanized (%), 1994	6/100
FERT	Total fertility rate (No. of children per woman), 1993	1/8
SSA	Dummy variable for SSA countries	0/1
SA	Dummy variable for South Asian countries	0/1

★ Indicates that results for this variable are not reported in the text tables because it came out as insignificant or not robust throughout.

Sources: UNICEF*a* 1996: end tables 1, 3, 4, and 5; FAO*a* 1996: appendix 2, table 8; IBRD*a*: 1995: end table 30; Deininger and Squire 1996*b*; UNDP 1996*a*: end table 33.

NOTES

1. Also, in the historical data from Western Europe during the nineteenth and twentieth centuries, 'height growth is highly correlated to movements in GDP

APPENDIX TABLE 15.2. Simple correlation matrix

Variable	U5MR	GNPcPPP	Q4Q1	ALR	WAF	DOC	IMM	URB
U5MR	1	−0.6*	0	−0.7*	0.5	0.7*	−0.7*	−0.6*
GNPcPPP	−0.6*	1	0.1	0.5*	−0.4	−0.5*	0.4	0.6*
Q4Q1	0	0.1	1	0.2	−0.3	−0.3	0	0.2
ALR	−0.7*	0.5*	0.2	1	−0.5	−0.6*	0.6	0.5
WAF	0.5	−0.4	−0.3	−0.5	1	0.4	−0.3	−0.6
DOC	0.7*	−0.5*	−0.3	−0.6*	0.4	1	−0.7	−0.6
IMM	−0.7*	0.4	0	0.6	−0.3	−0.7	1	0.4
URB	−0.6*	0.6*	0.2	0.5	−0.6	−0.6	0.4	1

* Indicates that in the simple regression between the two variables, the coefficient is significant at the 0.05 level and R^2-adjusted is higher than 0.5.

per capita' (Floud 1992: p. 236). In some countries, however, most notably England and the US, there have been periods when economic growth has coincided with a fall in the stature of adult males. The most common explanations are deteriorating diets and increased frequency and severity of illness associated with early industrialization and concomitant urbanization (ibid: pp. 235–40; Steckel 1995: pp. 1926–31). Conversely, in England, improvements in anthropometric status of adults have been negatively correlated with economic growth during the first six decades of the twentieth century. The main reason seems to be that during wartime, when growth was low, diets improved and food entitlements were more equitably distributed (Sen 1998).

2. Arm circumference is even more closely related to subsequent death in many of the sample studies, but no *national* estimates on arm-circumference failure are available.

3. The correlation between conventional and Purchasing Power Parity (PPP) GNPc estimates is very high (0.99), signifying that the results to be derived are not influenced by the choice between the two.

4. Ideally, one would also like to have data on relative prices of basic food and other essential goods for each country in the regressions. No such recent data are readily available, however (see note 13 below).

5. A major problem is that only data on central government spending on the health sector are available. In many countries, local governments have the main responsibility for health care, which make data incomplete and non-comparable. In a related study, Anand and Ravallion (1993), derived comparable estimates of public per-capita expenditure on health, but were able to do this for 22 countries only.

6. As an alternative proxy for literacy, the female literacy rate (FLR) was used. The results derived were practically identical to those reported in Table 15.1. The reason is the high correlation between ALR and FLR (0.99), which also makes it impossible to say whether and, if so, to what extent literacy of adult females is more important than that of males.

7. The reason for reporting only these regressions is that none of the other explanatory variables came out as significant and/or robust, which makes this type of exercise meaningless in those cases. The same applies to all tests of WAF, in which only URB comes out as significant throughout.

8. No equivalent estimates can be derived for WAF because of low significance and/or inrobust results for the proxy variables for the provision of public health services in these regressions.

9. The same problem, i.e. uneven quality of the data from different countries, applies to all the variables used in the tests. Only for the income distribution variable has there been a possibility of using only the observations which are of 'acceptable' quality (according to Deininger and Squire (1996a), who collected these data. In the future, it should be desirable, as noted by Srinivasan (1994b), that all international organizations provide indications of the quality of individual observations in their statistical publications.

10. The population data have been examined recently by Chamie (1994) and Deaton (1995); Barro and Lee (1993) and Behrman and Rosenzweig (1994) have looked at the education data; and Heston (1994) at national account data. Also see Srinivasan (1992, 1994a,b).

11. The problem here is very close to one encountered in the vast empirical literature aimed at identifying determinants of economic growth on the basis of cross-country regressions. While most economists believe that countries' fiscal and monetary policies affect growth, cross-country regressions largely fail to produce such a result. The similarity is that there is no good proxy variable that in one measure captures the totality of countries' fiscal and monetary policies and that countries that do well in one area tend also to do well in the others (see Levine and Renelt 1992, Mankiw 1995, Caselli et al. 1996).

12. For references to empirical studies of relationships between mortality and food supply/prices in historical data from countries which are now developed, see Fogel (1992: pp. 244–5). In most of these studies, no significant correlation was obtained.

13. Horton and her two co-authors from the FAO constructed their price data themselves on the basis of information available to the FAO. These data are for the mid-1970s and considered too dated to be used in the above regressions for the 1990s. The construction of new data was too complicated to be undertaken here.

14. Rodgers (1979) used data on income distribution for 56 countries taken from Paukert (1973). In their detailed assessment of income distribution data, Deininger and Squire (1996a) did not find the data from Paukert to be of 'acceptable' quality.

15. For a survey and assessment of such studies published up to the late 1980s, see Behrman and Deolalikar (1988). More recent studies include Thomas et al. (1990, 1991), Strauss and Thomas (1990), Thomas and Strauss (1991, 1992), Desai (1992), Kennedy and Haddad (1994), Kassouf and Senauer (1996), and Sahn and Alderman (1997).

16. Unfortunately, we have not been able to find a reliable proxy variable for *national* nutritional standards that could *directly* provide us with an estimate of the role of undernutrition in explaining child death and weight-for-age failure across all countries. We have previously deemed the per-capita calorie availability estimates, provided by the FAO, to be too unreliable and, in the case of the African countries, also biased, to be of use here.

17. That undernutrition should be more prevalent in Africa than in South Asia—as argued by the FAO (see Chapter 5 above)—and that this should be the main

explanation of the exceptionally high mortality rates in the former region, is not corroborated by either anthropometric data or the results obtained in this or the previous chapter.

18. The hypothesis that the genetic potential for growth during the first 5 years of life is lower for South Asian children than for children from other parts of the world was tested in Chapter 12 (section 12.2.2). This hypothesis was rejected on the basis of evidence from several child populations from well-to-do households in India, which showed these children to have the same average height and weight for age as the Western/Caucasian reference child populations. It may be that within India (and possibly other SA countries), different subpopulations have different genetic potentials for growth in stature during early childhood. The poorest sections may have a lower potential in the wake of negative selection over many centuries, a selection that has been enforced through the strict barriers to marriage along caste lines. This seems a long shot, however, as Sri Lanka, where no similar barriers exist, also has unexpectedly high anthropometric failure rates.

16

Excess Mortality, Economic Growth, and Public Action in Sub-Saharan Africa

16.1. INTRODUCTION

The child mortality rate is widely agreed to be the most sensitive indicator of the totality of deprivation in the form of inadequate health care, education, and nutrition in a population. That the SSA countries stand out in terms of high child mortality has been demonstrated by several econometric tests, including the one reported in Chapter 15, based on both level and change-over-time data. These tests suggest that economic poverty is the chief reason for differences in mortality worldwide, along with underprovision of basic public services in the health and education sectors. The latter is partly determined by the former since absolute government per-capita expenditure in the social sectors is closely correlated to gross domestic product per capita (GDPc). However, over and above income-normal provision, public-health-spending on related services and education tends to be significantly and negatively correlated to child mortality (and thus to life expectancy with the opposite sign).

On the basis of the evidence presented in earlier chapters, primary undernutrition does not seem to be *the* major cause of the exceptionally high child mortality in Africa. First, the anthropometric status—the least inappropriate proxy variable for undernutrition—of children in Africa is far better than in most parts of South Asia and on a par with what is found in South-East and East Asia, while the child mortality rates are considerably higher.[1] Secondly, 'only' about one-third of all child deaths in SSA are *attributable* to anthropometric failure (Chapter 14). Since not all children suffering from anthropometric failure are primarily undernourished (some are primarily ill), the 'one-third' constitutes an upper-bound estimate of the share of children dying primarily because they are undernourished; the 'true' share may be significantly lower. The remaining two-thirds, or more, die primarily because they are not treated for preventable and curable disease(s). Thirdly, when weight-for-age failure was included in the cross-country tests of mortality determinants in Chapter 15, it turned out insignificant once income, parent education, and access to public services were controlled for. These observations tentatively suggest—the data are unreliable—that the chief cause of high mortality in the SSA region is uncared-for morbidity related to poverty rather than to primary undernutrition.

The results derived in previous chapters are too 'aggregate' to tell us much about *how* public interventions in the health, but also the education and nutrition sectors, affect mortality (and human well-being in other dimensions). Accordingly, the objective of this chapter is to examine why mortality is exceptionally high in almost all the African countries given their per-capita real income levels. We shall try to discriminate between the hypotheses that this is mainly because of (i) government under-investment in the social sectors, (ii) low quality of the public services provided, or (iii) that public services are ill targeted.

16.2.   PUBLIC ACTION AND HUMAN WELL-BEING

16.2.1.   *Public Intervention: Objectives and Instruments*

The objective of public interventions is to change the allocation of resources.[2] The rationales for this can be severalfold. First there are efficiency considerations. Intervention is called for when a good or service is collective, i.e. there is no or too little incentive for private agents to undertake socially profitable investment and production. Another reason is that there are externalities in an activity, i.e. benefits over and above those accruing to the individual(s) undertaking the activity.[3] Secondly, public intervention can be normatively warranted (as a second-best method) in order to change the distribution of assets and/or income in a country. Thirdly, some government interventions are made for political-economy reasons, i.e. public funds are allocated with the intention to gain political favours for the government and its backers.

Public activities in the social spheres often have elements of all three objectives. There is certainly an efficiency case for the public provision of *primary* education and *basic* health services, not least in the poorest countries, where failure in the credit and insurance markets is common (Appleton *et al.* 1996: p. 322). Education and health are important for labour productivity, but the infrastructure needed to provide such services is characterized by significant economies of scale that render private investment unattractive. A good health status of individual people has positive externalities, which is the most evident for communicable diseases.[4] By targeting specific health and education services to specific groups and locations, governments also affect the distribution of income and assets, sometimes intentionally, sometimes not.

When it comes to nutrition, food is essentially a private good for which there is no equally clear efficiency or distribution justification for public intervention (see Behrman 1993 for a discussion). Many interventions in food markets, e.g. urban food subsidies, seem to be primarily motivated by political-economy considerations, since the anthropometric status of children is much more favourable in urban than in rural areas (Chapter 11).

In the poorest developing countries, the *instruments* available for government to reallocate resources and redistribute incomes and assets are typically considerably fewer and blunter than in more advanced economies. Income taxes are only paid by a minor share of the population. Even in a country such as India, with a 'middle class' comprising two to three hundred million people, only 5 per cent of the population fill in income tax reports (Ahluvalia 1993). Moreover, the administrative system is usually incapable of identifying the households that may be eligible to receive income transfers. There are simply no data on incomes of specific households, especially not the poorest ones (Lipton and Ravallion 1995: p. 2573). Direct income transfers are for these reasons not used extensively in most developing countries.

The redistribution that takes place—in whatever direction—is mainly through the public expenditure side (van de Walle 1995*b*: p. 1). Public provision of basic health care and primary (and secondary) education can be seen as asset redistribution. That is, tax (or foreign-aid) financed public activities in these sectors, in so far as they benefit poor people who would otherwise go without, are a form of redistribution of human capital. At best, such capital improves the private earning potential, as well as enhancing other functions that are important for the quality of life (Dreze and Sen 1995: pp. 14–15).

16.2.2. *What Public Actions Influence Human Well-being?*

Some types of public interventions may seem to be linked *directly* to human well-being objectives: public provision of primary schooling to foster literacy and numeracy; public provision of basic health care to improve peoples' health status; and public food subsidies to improve nutritional status. However, on closer scrutiny, it is not easy to draw an unambiguous line between public interventions that do have a favourable impact on human well-being in a particular dimension and those that do not.

Usually there are complicated general-equilibrium effects that are sometimes difficult to assess. Government actions and policies in many spheres, that on first sight may not be expected to affect 'well-being', do this, directly or indirectly, intentionally or unintentionally. For instance, a country's trade and foreign exchange-rate policy regime may have a more profound effect on food prices and, consequently, poor peoples' effective demand of food, and thus their nutritional-cum-health status, than food subsidies and other interventions in the food sector proper. Moreover, public interventions in the social sectors may have consequences that cannot be observed by looking at a narrow set of social objective variables only. If the public services are provided at a low price, for instance, it may affect labour supply and/or crowd out private provision of the service in question.

Sometimes there are also strong synergistic effects between different kinds of public interventions. Interventions in the educational spheres may have a stronger impact on health outcomes than the provision of health services as such. This is a case of positive complementarity. There are other cases in which the interdependence is competitive rather than complementary. For example, urban food subsidies, while helpful for the nutrition of the urban population, may, at the same time, have an adverse effect on the nutrition of non-urban people (including the rural poor who are often the *poorest* people in a developing country). This is because the urban food subsidies have to be financed through resources that would have been put to other uses. Consider a few alternative possibilities. First, if urban food subsidies are 'paid for' by cutting other public expenditure, we have to see in which fields public expenditure would be curbed to meet the budgetary needs of these subsidies and what the effects might be on the non-urban population. If, for example, educational expenditure was cut, this might have an adverse effect not only on education but also on nutrition (for reasons that we have already discussed).

Secondly, if the urban food subsidies were financed through increased taxes, this would tend to curtail private expenditure of those sections of the community who directly or indirectly bear the burden of the taxes. There could also be adverse incentive effects, particularly in food production. Thirdly, if those urban subsidies were financed through manipulated low procurement prices (as they often are), rural food-producing households would have to bear the burden of the cheapening of food prices for the urban population who are often substantially richer than the rural food producers. This too could have negative incentive effects on food production. The overall result could easily be a deteriorating nutritional status of the population at large—comprising the rural as well as the urban population. Sensible choice of public action requires that we take into account the indirect as well as the direct effects.

It is also usually difficult to identify constraints on the demand side, as opposed to the supply side. Ideally, evaluations of public interventions should consider all these general-equilibrium effects; in practice, however, this is often too complicated and the required data are not available. Most evaluations from SSA are more partial, i.e. assessments are confined to bivariate associations between two variables, mainly owing to a lack of more sophisticated data.[5]

16.2.3. *Quality and Targeting of Public Interventions*

Most public interventions in the social sectors in the African countries (as well as in most other places) are targeted in one or more dimensions, intentionally or unintentionally. First, typically not all individuals in a local population will be given access to basic health care and other public services.

Secondly, provision is often geographically targeted, in many instances mainly to urban areas. Thirdly, in some countries, there is also gender targeting (implicit or explicit). Fourthly, the relative priority given to primary, secondary, and tertiary education, and to basic health clinics versus big hospitals also entails targeting certain population groups, mainly along the rural/urban divide. There are also several quality aspects that differ across population groups which indicate that those who will enjoy the better services should be targeted. All these differences have a bearing on the efficiency of, and above all, the incidence impact on the relative poor and rich, respectively, of public interventions in the health and education spheres.

The public interventions in the nutrition sphere are mostly indirect in the SSA countries. Except for urban food subsidies on basic staple foods, it is uncommon that these countries have comprehensive national food-subsidy schemes of the type found in Egypt and Sri Lanka.[6] Food price manipulation, however, through government regulation of food distribution and internal trade, has been, and still is, a common intervention at the macro level. Food prices have also been affected by governments' external-trade and the foreign-exchange-rate policies. Unfortunately, there are no data that can be used to assess these effects.

16.3. MORTALITY, EDUCATIONAL ATTAINMENT, AND GROWTH: RECENT DEVELOPMENTS IN OUTPUT INDICATORS

The analysis of the correlation between child mortality and economic standards in the previous chapter was based on data at the cross-country *level* (the main reason being that for child mortality, but also for many of the explanatory variables, no reliable time-series data are available). In this section, we shall nevertheless look at recent changes in 'output' data—with due reservations for their dubious quality—on child mortality, education attainment, and economic growth in the African countries. In subsequent sections, we shall examine whether there have been changes in public expenditures on health and education (i.e. quantitative 'input' data) and in the quality and targeting of these 'inputs'.

16.3.1. Child Mortality

Since the early 1960s, there have been improvements in the mortality indicators, including the under-fives mortality rate (U5MR) throughout SSA, but considerably less so than in other parts of the world (Table 16.1). During the period 1980–94, however, the earlier slow improvements in the U5MR indicator continued to decelerate in SSA, while U5MR fell at an accelerating rate in all other regions except East Asia, where the decline in the period 1960–80

TABLE 16.1. Tentative estimates of changes over time in child mortality, school enrolment, and per-capita GDP growth rates, by major geographical regions

Indicator	Period/ year	SSA	SA	ME/NA	EA/P	LA/C
U5MR. Annual reduction	1960–80	1.1	1.4	2.6	4.6	3.0
rate (per cent)	1980–90	1.0	2.6	5.9	2.5	4.4
School enrolment	1980	79	76	86	110	107
rate. Primary (gross)	1993	72	99	97	118	—
School enrolment	1980	15	27	42	43	41
rate. Secondary (gross)	1993	25	47	58	56	—
School enrolment	1980	39	37	48	51	59
rate. All levels	1990	36	45	55	49	62
(percentage aged 6–23)						
Growth of real GDP	1960–70	1.7	1.5	3.7	—	2.5
per capita (percentage	1970–80	0.1	1.1	2.6	5.7	3.2
per year)	1980–90	–0.8	3.3	1.4	6.3	–0.3
	1990–94	–2.7	1.7	–1.1	8.1	1.4

Sources: UNICEF*a* 1996: end table 10 (U5MR); IBRD*a* 1997: table 7 (primary and secondary school enrolment rates); UNDP*a* 1996: table 47 (total school enrolment rate); UNCTAD*a* 1984: table 6.2, 1995: table 6.2 (growth of GDP per capita).

was exceptional. Although the availability of data is not yet sufficient to allow definite conclusions, it seems that the decline in the child mortality rate has come to a halt, or even increased in some countries, mainly in Eastern Africa (Appleton *et al.* 1996: figs 1 and 2, Brockerhoff and Derose 1996: table 1). Yet unpublished estimates from the UN population division suggest that mortality rates have increased and, thus, that life expectancy at birth has fallen by 2–10 years in Botswana, Kenya, Malawi, Uganda, Zambia, and Zimbabwe over the 1990s (*The Economist* 1998). Here it seems that the spread of AIDS is the main reason (WHO*a* 1996, Ntozi *et al.* 1997). The data available for most SSA countries are too dated and unreliable, however, to permit a definite assessment of changes over the most recent years.

16.3.2. Educational Attainments

The most commonly used indicators of educational standards are the *gross* school enrolment data, usually originating from UNESCO. By these estimates, the share of children aged 6–11 who are enrolled in primary school has declined significantly since 1980 in SSA as a whole (Table 16.1) and in about half of the SSA countries (Brockerhoff and Derose 1996: Table 3, UNICEF*a* 1996). This decline is in sharp contrast to the other developing regions. The secondary-school gross enrolment rate, on the other hand, has increased notably. The overall school enrolment rate (covering the entire 6–23-year-old population) is estimated to have declined by three percentage points over the 1980s in SSA, while it has increased in South Asia and most other places (Table 16.1).

The school enrolment rates are *flow* estimates (i.e. estimates of the inflow of education to the *stock* of education), which we sometimes refer to as the 'human-capital'. Barro and Lee (1996) have provided such stock estimates for the population at or above the age of fifteen by country since 1960. Summaries of these estimates for the years 1970 and 1990, aggregated to major geographical region, are reproduced in Table 16.2.

First we see that about half the population in SSA at or over the age of 15 in 1990 had not received any formal education whatsoever. In South Asia the percentage was even higher, while in East Asia and Latin America, about 15 and 17 per cent of the population, respectively, had no formal education in that year. The second pair of rows suggests that 85 per cent of the population in SSA had no or incomplete primary education in 1990, down from 90 per cent in 1970. Also, in the other developing regions, the share is relatively high, above two-thirds. This is a revealing indicator of the smallness of the human capital stock in the developing countries in general as compared with the OECD countries in which the share is a little more than one-third (in 1990).

In the third pair of rows in Table 16.2, the estimated shares of the population (above the age of 15) that have completed primary education in the respective regions are presented. In SSA, as well as in South Asia, the Middle East, and the North African regions, the share was below 10 per cent in 1990. Only in East Asia was the share notably higher, above that in the OECD countries. When it comes to the share of the population that has completed

TABLE 16.2. Output indicators of educational attainments for members of the population at or above the age of 15, by major geographical regions, 1970 and 1990 (per cent)

Educational level attained		SSA	SA	ME/NA	EA/P	LA/C	OECD
No formal education	1970	63.8	69.3	69.8	35.4	31.2	5.0
	1990	48.3	55.2	41.0	15.4	17.3	4.5
None or incomplete	1970	90.6	92.9	87.8	84.3	83.3	55.3
primary education	1990	85.4	76.4	69.6	67.6	70.3	37.1
Completed primary	1970	6.1	8.9	6.5	20.1	18.4	32.4
education	1990	7.6	7.5	9.8	26.1	13.2	16.0
Completed secondary	1970	1.8	1.1	3.2	4.1	5.0	11.6
education	1990	1.8	6.4	8.5	11.5	7.4	15.3
Completed higher	1970	0.6	0.2	0.6	1.2	1.0	4.0
education	1990	0.5	1.7	2.4	3.5	3.7	10.2
Mean No. of school	1970	2.1	2.0	2.1	3.8	3.8	7.6
years completed	1990	2.9	3.9	4.5	6.1	5.2	9.0

Source: Barro and Lee 1996.

secondary school, the SSA countries stand out even more. Fewer than 2 per cent in this region had attained that level in 1990, which is about one-quarter of the percentage in South Asia and even an ever lower proportion compared with the other developing regions. The same applies to the share that had completed higher education in SSA (the fifth pair of rows). Finally, also measured in terms of mean number of school years completed, the SSA countries had exceptionally low achievement, only 2.9 years, compared with South Asia's 3.9 years.

Almost every attainment share has improved in all major regions since 1970, but not very rapidly. This reflects the fact that there have also been relatively large short-term changes in educational *flows*, i.e. school enrolment and completion rates, which affect the stock variables only slowly. Even in the East Asian countries, where primary school enrolment has been close to (or at) 100 per cent for quite some time, about two-thirds of the population had no or only rudimentary education in 1990 (because many of the older generations had never received or completed primary education). The improvement in SSA is confined, however, to a slight increase in the share of those who have completed primary education. The share of the population that has completed secondary has remained unaltered, while there has been a decline in the share that has completed higher education. Both the latter observations are in sharp contrast to all other regions, not the least South Asia. Unfortunately, the available education-stock estimates are rather dated (1990), but the recent decline in the (flow) primary-enrolment estimates in SSA points to a decline in the stock estimates over the 1990s that may continue into the new millennium.

16.3.3. Economic Growth

Economic growth in the SSA countries was (on average) positive in the 1960s. Since then there has been a steady decline. In the 1970s, real per-capita income growth was about nil and then in the negative during the 1980s and 1990s (Table 16.1). Fewer than half the SSA countries had positive per-capita growth during the period 1985–95. Only two countries have 'outstanding' long-term and stable growth records: Botswana and Mauritius. Uganda has had impressive growth in the 1990s (IBRD*a* 1997: tables 1 and 11). For SSA as a whole, the dismal growth record is in sharp contrast to all other regions in each and every decade.

If one is inclined to think that the cross-country results obtained earlier (Chapter 15) carry over to changes over time, the economic decline in most of Africa is both a cause and a consequence of the relative deterioration in mortality and educational attainment that have taken place since the early 1980s.[7] In the following sections we shall make an attempt to assess the extents to which poor health and education records (outputs) are due to (i) quantity and (ii) quality, as well as (iii) targeting failures on the input side in these sectors; and we shall also investigate what relationship these failures have on the overall growth failure in the African economies.

16.4. THE PUBLIC HEALTH SECTOR

16.4.1. Public Health Provision: Quantitative Input Indicators

The share of the budget spent on health (and education) is the first variable usually looked for in trying to answer the question of governments' priorities for the 'social' sectors. There are such data (which will be displayed below), but unfortunately, the reliability, comparability, and completeness of these data leave much to be desired. The IMF's *Government Finance Statistics* is by far the least unreliable source for such data, but the country tables therein contain too many blanks for any truly meaningful comparisons over time and space to be made (also see IBRD*a*, various issues). The data from other sources (e.g. UNDP) are extrapolated from a few countries to broad regional aggregates, even though the individual country estimates (when they are at all available) are usually not comparable. Thus, all the statistical data to be presented below must be interpreted with much caution.

The available estimates suggest that central government spending on health as a percentage of GDP (or total expenditures) is not lower in the African countries than in most other developing regions and that there was a notable increase between 1960 and 1990 (Table 16.3). What has happened in the 1980s and 1990s has only been estimated for a limited number of SSA countries; the World Bank has provided estimates for the 1980s which show huge variation across the ten countries examined, from a 50 per cent decline in Tanzania to a 38 per cent increase in Zimbabwe, and little change on average (IBRD*a* 1994: table 6.2). The most extensive source of information on total, not only central government but also private health, expenditures, is

TABLE 16.3. Estimated central government expenditure on health and education as a percentage of GDP, by major geographical regions, various years

	Year	SSA	SA	ME/NA	EA/ China	SEA/ P[a]	LA/ C
Expenditure on	1960	0.7	0.6	0.9	0.9	0.5	1.2
health/GDP	1990	2.4	1.4	2.9	2.2	1.0	2.4
Expenditure on	1980	5.1	4.3	4.1	2.9	2.8	3.7
education/GDP	1992	5.7	3.8	6.4	2.8	3.4	4.2

[a] In almost all other tables, what is labelled East Asia includes China and what in many sources is labelled South-East Asia. The distinction between East and South-East Asia made in this table is due to more disaggregated data presentation in the source table.

Source: UNDP*a* 1996: table 47.

Murray *et al.* (1994), for the single year 1990 (Table 16.4). These estimates suggest that public health expenditures as a ratio to GDP is higher in SSA than in India and Bangladesh, but that the total is lower (including private health expenditures).

Murray *et al.* (1994) also provide estimates of real per-capita absolute expenditures on health in 1990 for almost all developing countries (although half the country estimates are derived through extrapolation). Such estimates are more informative than are shares of government expenditures going to health when one is trying to understand developments in health outcomes (e.g. mortality rates). The estimates suggest that total absolute per-capita expenditure on health in the SSA countries is on a par with that in India, but double that in China (Table 16.4). Considering the enormously better health outcomes in China, this result can only be interpreted in either of two ways (that are not mutually exclusive). The first is that one or both estimates are seriously biased. The other is that the health services in Africa are of utterly poor quality and/or heavily concentrated to those who need them the least in a medical sense (to be analysed below).

Yet another indicator is the number of people per medical doctor. By this indicator, the SSA countries stand out even more; in this region, the estimated number is 18,500 people per doctor. This is about five times higher than in South Asia and even more so compared with other developing regions (Table 16.5).

TABLE 16.4. Estimated health expenditures as a share of GDP (per cent), by source and major geographical regions, 1990

Region/country	Public expend/ GDP	Private expend/ GDP	Aid expend/ GDP	Total expend/ GDP	Public/ total expend	Total expend (US $) per capita
				$(1+2+3)$	$(1)/(4)$	
	(1)	(2)	(3)	$(=4)$	$(=5)$	(6)
SSA	1.85	1.97	0.39	4.23	43.8	22
China	2.05	1.44	0.02	3.51	58.5	11
India	1.20	4.70	0.10	6.00	20.0	21
Bangladesh	0.79	1.81	0.59	3.19	24.8	6
Other Asia	1.71	2.73	0.07	4.50	38.0	61
Middle-East/N. Africa	2.05	1.51	0.02	3.53	57.6	97
Latin America and Caribbean	2.37	1.54	0.05	3.98	59.8	103
Developed market economies	5.67	3.61	0.00	9.29	61.1	1,958

Source: Murray *et al.* 1994: annex table.

TABLE 16.5. Percentage of population with access to health-related public services, urban/rural, by major geographical regions, 1990–5

Access to service	SSA	South Asia	North Africa/ Middle East	East Asia	Latin America/ Caribbean
Primary health service					
Total	57	77[a]	85	89	73
Urban	79	100	97	98	81
Rural	50	80	72	—	51
Rural/Urban ratio	0.63	0.80	0.74	—	0.63
Safe water					
Total	45	80	76	66	80
Urban	63	87	93	92	87
Rural	34	78	58	56	51
Rural/Urban ratio	0.54	0.90	0.62	0.61	0.59
Adequate sanitation					
Total	37	30	62	34	68
Urban	56	69	87	75	71
Rural	29	17	35	17	36
Rural/Urban Ratio	0.52	0.25	0.40	0.23	0.51
Population per medical doctor (1,000s)	18.5	3.8	1.5	1.2[b]	1.0
Memo item: urbanization	31	26	55	32	74

[a] India only (see also footnote 12)
[b] Excluding South-East Asia, for which the equivalent estimate is 6.2.
Sources: UNICEF*a* 1996: table 10; UNDP*a* 1996: table 47.

16.4.2. Public Health Provision: Qualitative Input Indicators

In their assessment of 'the state of the art' of using economic techniques for evaluating quality and efficiency in the health sector, Evans and Hurley (1995) discuss the relative merits and demerits of the four main methods used: the cost-minimization, the cost-effectiveness, the cost-utility, and the cost–benefit approaches. Their collection of empirical evidence on the actual use of these techniques in the African countries reveals that they are occasionally applied to the answering of questions such as which is the most efficient way of preventing malaria (nets versus drugs) in a specific location. Important as such studies are, it appears that strict economic evaluations of the health sector at large have not been undertaken in the African countries. The assessment below must therefore be based on admittedly much cruder indicators than one would ideally apply.

Objective Assessments   The closest to objective assessment of the health sector in the SSA countries is to be found in studies that have started by setting up 'technical' norms for what is 'good practice' in various areas and subsequently contrasted these to actual practice. Not many such studies seem to have been undertaken, but one example is the investigation of Tanzania by Mogedal *et al.* (1995: p. 364). These authors concluded that: 'The current quality of services delivered in rural Tanzania has been found to be far below what is considered a minimum acceptable level'.

Subjective Assessments   Almost all assessments that have been undertaken in Africa provide subjective indications of quality only; statistics, whatever their quality, are seldom reported. Leighton (1996) has conducted a broad such investigation of the public health sector in some 20 countries in West as well as East/South Africa. While highlighting many differences across countries, Leighton finds several problems that are strikingly similar throughout Africa. These include:

'Insufficient funding, ineffective use of available resources, inadequate allocation of resources to cost-effective health services (especially for primary health care in favour of support of hospitals), lack of incentives for health workers to provide quality care, inadequate regulation of inappropriate barriers to private sector provision of health care, inequitable distribution of resources between urban and rural areas and between poor and better-off populations, and high household health expenditures even in the midst of 'free care' systems' (ibid: p.1511).

Much the same conclusions are reported by the World Bank (IBRD*a* 1993, IBRD 1994, 1995), Gilson *et al.* (1995), Mogedal *et al.* (1995), Zwi and Mills (1995), Appleton *et al.* (1996), Brockerhoff and Derose (1996) and several others who have examined the health sector in the African countries. That all these predominantly 'subjective' assessments arrive at broadly the same conclusions is reassuring, considering that hard facts are largely missing.

16.4.3. Recent Reforms

During the past 5–10 years, at least 30 SSA countries have initiated reforms in the health sector. The most common (and controversial), but far from only ingredient (see, Zwi and Mills 1995, Cassels 1995, Mogedal *et al.* 1995) in these reforms is the introduction of, or raise in, user fees for public health services. This reform has been pressed for by the World Bank as part of the standard structural-adjustment package (IBRD 1993). The aims are to enhance efficiency and to recover costs in tight-budget times. In the zero-growth situation of most African economies, government revenues have stagnated or declined. At the same time foreign aid has been reduced (since 1992).[8] The introduction of user fees may therefore seem necessary for improving, or even maintaining, present public health provisions (but there are alternative ways to be discussed in Chapter 17).

The main concern about the increased application of user fees in large parts of Africa is that they conflict with equality considerations, i.e. the objective that 'all people should have access to primary health care, free of charge', a frequent claim in African government rhetoric. User fees will most certainly hurt a *proportion* of the poorest in the African countries. However, half the rural population in Africa as a whole does not have *de facto* access to any health service at all (Table 16.5). For them, the introduction of user fees makes little difference. It has also been observed that in some countries where the provision of basic health services is officially 'free of charge', in practice, patients do not receive any care unless they pay (Leighton 1996: p. 1517, Mogedal *et al.* 1995: p.358).

If the introduction of user fees for those who have access to health services (mainly in urban areas), which presumably are not the poorest, leads to better government finances *and* an expansion of the provision of basic health services in rural areas, the net benefit for the poor as an aggregate may be positive. But this is a big 'if', and the few empirical observations that have been made so far indicate that the increased use of user fees has not led to any detectable extension of primary health care in rural Africa (IBRD 1994, 1997, Gilson *et al.* 1995, Zwi and Mills 1995).

The user fees that most governments have been able to collect, however, are not large. In a sample of 16 SSA countries for which data are available, user fees account for only 5–6 per cent of recurrent government expenditures on health services (Gilson *et al.* 1995: table 1). In no single country is the share above 12 per cent. This suggests that user fees are generally not sufficient to improve and extend the health sector in a significant way, even *if* directed towards this end. The reasons for the small revenues are not known in any detail, but exemptions are common (in some countries for the poorest, but also for other groups such as civil servants). Demand has also gone down as fees have increased (Gilson *et al.* 1995: pp.378, 387).

16.4.4. Targeting of Health Services

User fees are one way of targeting health services—to those who can pay— but there are many other ways in which health services are targeted in the African countries. The allocation of resources between primary and more advanced health care, between preventive and curative care, between clinic and hospital health care, and between rural and urban areas, entails targeting different population segments.

Primary and Preventive versus Advanced and Curative   Detailed statistics on the allocation of public resources in the health sector is indeed uncommon in the African countries (IBRD*a* 1993). Despite these and other measurement problems, it seems widely agreed that the African health systems are *not* targeted to primary and preventive health care. According to Mill's (1990) somewhat dated data, more than 50 per cent of government recurrent health expenditure typically goes to hospitals and most of this to one or two central

hospitals. In their review of the evidence, Zwi and Mills (1995: p.309), conclude that 'health systems in most countries remain biased towards hospitals
and curative medicine'. The World Bank (IBRD 1994: p.173) concludes:
'Many SSA countries have a strong bias towards secondary and tertiary care
(in district and capital hospitals), and there is little discernible movement towards primary health care or basic health services.' It is also interesting to
note that in a selection of five African countries, most financial funding for
primary health care has been provided by donors, while the governments'
own resources (priorities) have been heavily directed to main hospitals
(Lafond 1994).

That primary and preventive health care is pro-poor biased is shown by
several benefit–incidence studies from other parts of the world, while more
advanced curative health care is usually pro-rich biased (van de Walle 1995c
(Indonesia), Deolalikar 1995 (Indonesia), Hammer et al. 1995 (Malaysia),
Grosh 1995 (several Latin American countries)). Similar investigations do
not seem to be available for African countries, but there is no compelling
reason to expect a completely different incidence of benefits in this region.

Urban/Rural Targeting   The concentration on urban hospital-based curative
health care in cities in the African countries means that large shares of the
rural populations are deprived of all forms of health service. The data from
WHO/UNICEF (which contain large margins of error), suggest that only
half the population in rural Africa at large has access to basic health services,
while 79 per cent of the urban population has. The rural:urban ratio is thus
0.63 in SSA, which could be compared with 0.80 in India,[9] where 100 per
cent of the urban population has access to health services (Table 16.5). The
overall access to health services is thus not only lower in Africa than in any
other region, but also more concentrated to the urban areas.

Turning to individual SSA countries, the estimated share of the urban
population with health-service access is 80 per cent or more in 15 out of the
19 countries for which there are separate data for rural and urban areas.[10] In
eight of the 19 countries, the rural access is less than half that of the urban.
Only in Botswana and Mauritius is access in urban areas 100 per cent. In the
latter country, this applies to rural areas as well, while in Botswana it is 85 per
cent (UNICEFa 1996: table 3).

Also, when it comes to access to other health-related public services, most
notably safe water, the discrepancy between rural and urban areas is larger in
SSA than in other regions (Table 16.5). Only in terms of estimated access
to sanitation, does SSA have an overall score on a par with the other regions,
and the relative positions of rural areas are in fact better than in some other
regions.

The low priority given to rural primary health care is bound to stifle mortality reduction. Evidence from many parts of the world suggests that the
cost-effectiveness in saving lives is larger in population groups deprived of

basic preventive health care earlier (e.g. vaccination) than for marginal improvements in population groups which already have access to both preventive and curative health care (Brockerhoff and Derose 1996).

Gender Targeting   The most useful indicators of possible targeting of one sex
or the other in terms of (public) health care (and nutrition) are relative mortality rates (Svedberg 1990), life expectancy at birth (Table 16.6), the female:
male ratio in the population (Sen 1992, Klasen 1994) and various indicators
of anthropometric status (Svedberg 1996). All these indicators suggest that
there are no major 'abnormal' differences between females and males in the
SSA region. Compared with women in South Asia, in particular, those in
Africa have an advantaged position *vis-à-vis* men.

However, when it comes to some women-specific indicators, women in
Africa are at a disadvantage compared with women elsewhere (Table 16.6).
The maternal mortality rate in SSA is about 25 per cent higher than in South
Asia. Whether this should be interpreted as more discrimination of women in
SSA terms of health-care provision is difficult to say. First, overall mortality
rates are higher in SSA than in South Asia. Secondly, the provision of health
care in general is lower in Africa than in other parts of the world, especially

TABLE 16.6. Demographic indicators of female/male differences and selected female-
specific indicators of health-service provision, by major geographical regions, 1990s

Indicators	SSA	South Asia	North Africa/ Middle East	East Asia	Latin America/ Caribbean
Female/male ratios					
Life expectancy at birth	1.07	1.01	1.04	1.05	1.08
DALYs lost (per 1,000)[g]	0.89	1.09[d]	0.99	0.87[e]	0.79
Female-specific indicators[a]					
Maternal death rate[b]	597	482	200	165	178
Total fertility rate[c]	6.2	4.0	4.4	2.3	3.0
Contraceptive use rate	13	40	44	74	59
Share of pregnant women immunized against tetanus	35	71	49	29	48
Births attended by health personnel (per cent)	39	33	46	94[f]	83

   [a] For the incidence of anthropometric failure of women in different regions, see Chapter 11
above.
   [b] Per 100,000 women.
   [c] Number of births per woman.
   [d] India only.
   [e] Excluding China, for which the equivalent estimate is 1.01.
   [f] Excluding South-East Asia and the Pacific, for which the equivalent estimate is 56.
   [g] Disability-adjusted life years (see IBRDa 1993).
Sources: UNICEFa 1996: table 10; IBRDa 1993: table B. 1; UNDPa 1996: table 47.

in rural areas (cf. above). Thirdly, and most importantly, the total fertility rate in Africa is far above that in any other region. That the average African woman gives birth six times, while her South Asian counterpart gives birth 'only' four times, increases the maternal mortality risk in Africa considerably.

16.5.   THE PUBLIC EDUCATION SECTOR

16.5.1. *Public Education Services: Quantitative Input Indicators*

Given their low income levels, Schultz (1988: p. 546) found the Africa countries, together with East Asian ones, to be 'over-achievers' in the education sector in quantitative terms in the early 1980s. As suggested by Table 16.3, the average African government spent more on education as a share of GDP in 1992 than it did a decade earlier. In some countries, though, not the least in East Africa, there has been a significant drop (IBRD 1994: table 6.2, Brockerhoff and Derose 1996). However, the average for the SSA countries compares favourably with all other regions except the Middle East and North Africa.

Barro and Lee (1996) provide alternative estimates of government inputs in the education sectors, i.e. government expenditure *per pupil* at the primary and secondary levels, expressed as shares of GDPc (Table 16.7). Such estimates provide information that also take into consideration that the share of school-age children in the population varies across countries and regions (being the highest in SSA). Also these estimates corroborate Schulz's notion that once the African countries were 'over-achievers'. In 1970, the expenditure-per-pupil/GDPc ratio for both primary and secondary schooling was higher in the SSA countries than in all other regions. In fact, for the secondary level, the ratio was more than twice as high in SSA as it was anywhere else. By 1990, however, there had been significant drops in the ratios for SSA, although it was still higher for secondary schooling than elsewhere (no more recent data are available yet).

Comparing per pupil-expenditure ratios across regions over time fails to account for the fact that the denominator in these ratios, i.e. GDPc, has developed very differently in different places between 1970 and 1990 (Table 16.1). In the lower part of Table 16.7, the Barro–Lee estimates have been transformed to real 1990 US dollars per pupil. The emerging picture is different from the earlier one in two main dimensions. First, the SSA countries' status of 'over-achievers' becomes questionable for 1990.[11] In that year, per-pupil expenditure in primary school was lower than in all other regions, including South Asia. Per-pupil spending in secondary schools in SSA is still much higher than in South Asia and even in East Asia and Latin America, but not by as much as in earlier periods. Secondly, comparing absolute spending

TABLE 16.7. Input indicators of government provision of education, by major
geographical regions, 1970 and 1990

Indicator		SSA	SA	ME/NA	EA/P	LA/C	OECD
Primary school:	1970	0.18	0.09	0.14	0.09	0.09	0.13
spending per pupil/	1990	0.10	0.09	0.11	0.11	0.09	0.20
GDP per capita							
Secondary school	1970	1.28	0.28	0.55	0.22	0.21	0.18
spending per pupil/	1990	0.39	0.12	0.25	0.16	0.13	0.20
GDP per capita							
Primary school	1970	266	105	631	77	388	1,312
spending per pupil	1990	129	140	496	296	518	3,028
(1990 US dollars; PPP)							
Ratio	1990/1970	0.48	1.33	0.79	3.84	1.33	2.50
Secondary school	1970	1,888	328	2,481	187	906	1,876
spending per pupil	1990	503	187	1,128	430	479	3,028
(1990 US dollars; PPP)							
Ratio	1990/1970	0.27	0.57	0.49	2.30	0.53	1.61

Sources: Barro and Lee 1996: table 1; Appendix Table 16.1 below.

per pupil in 1970 and 1990 reveals that by far the largest decline has taken place in SSA, both for primary and secondary schooling. There has also been a decline in some of the other regions, though not as large, while in East Asia (inclusive China) there has been a dramatic improvement.[12]

Without more sophisticated estimations (which would require data which are not available) we cannot say for certain, but it seems that overall economic decline (GDPc) in SSA during the past 20 years is one major reason why real spending per pupil in the school system has fallen drastically. This, in turn, is consistent with lower demand for education (see section 16.6 below) and the fall in the enrolment rates observed earlier. However, related to this is the possibility that the quality of the schooling provided has also dropped.

16.5.2. Public Education Services: Qualitative Input Indicators

It is difficult to envisage that a decline in government spending on education per pupil by half or more in absolute terms in the SSA countries between 1970 and 1990 could have taken place without a concomitant deterioration in quality. However, the assessment of quality of education is a complex and difficult endeavour even in the most developed countries (Weale 1993). In the least developed countries, including the African ones, it is even more so (Schultz 1988). The brief assessment in this section is based on a few indicators of quality, admittedly crude and incomplete, for which there are some (although generally unreliable) data.

Teachers' Salaries   Teachers' salaries in primary schools, expressed as a percentage of GDP per capita, have been estimated to be higher in SSA than in other regions in both 1970 and 1990 (Table 16.8) and only declined marginally over time. Also, in most other regions, the relative salary for primary school teachers has fallen. However, since GDP per capita has declined since 1970, the drop in teachers' salaries in Africa in real terms has been relatively large. Absolute salaries have also dropped in South Asia and the Middle East/ North African regions. Nevertheless, teachers' salaries in SSA compared favourably with those in South Asia as late as 1990 (Table 16.8).

Pupil/Teacher Ratio   The estimates presented in Table 16.8 suggest that this ratio remained unaltered at 43 between 1970 and 1990 in primary schools in the average SSA country. The ratio increased in South Asia (from a lower

TABLE 16.8.   Quality indicators of government provision of education, by major geographical regions, 1970 and 1990 (ratios and percentages)

Indicator		SSA	SA	ME/ NA	EA/P	LA/C	OECD
Primary school	1970	6.7	3.6	4.7	2.7	2.9	2.3
teacher salary ratio[a]	1990	5.1	2.5	3.1	2.9	2.6	2.2
Teacher salary	1970	9.7	4.2	21.2	2.3	12.5	23.2
(1,000 US 1990	1990	6.6	3.9	14.0	7.8	15.0	33.3
dollars PPP)							
Primary school	1970	43	38	31	32	36	25
pupil/teacher ratio	1990	43	44	24	26	28	16
Secondary school	1970	20	24	20	22	19	17
pupil/teacher ratio	1990	24	23	16	21	19	13
Primary school	1970	17.4	21.3	13.0	4.4[b]	14.7	5.3
repeat fraction	1990	20.4	9.0	8.6	3.9	10.5	3.3
Secondary school	1970	10.5	22.5	13.1	6.7[b]	7.7	8.4
repeat fraction	1990	16.5	8.7	12.3	1.0	7.8	12.0
Primary school drop-out rate	1994	34	41	9	13	26	—
Primary school completion rate (percentage of all 6–11-year-olds)	1994	46	54	87	87	74	—
Share of higher education in total government expend- iture on education	1992	15	15	25	16	23	22

[a] Expressed as a ratio of GDP per capita.
[b] 1980.

Sources: Barro and Lee 1996; and UNICEF*a* 1996: table 10, based on data from UNESCO; Appendix Table 16.1 below.

level), while it declined in the other regions. The ratio increased (deteriorated) in secondary schools in SSA during this period; elsewhere it declined somewhat.

Repeat Fractions   SSA is the only region in which the share of pupils repeating classes at both primary and secondary school increased between 1970 and 1990 (Table 16.8). In some of the other regions, most notably South Asia, the shares declined significantly. By 1990, the estimated share of the pupils repeating classes at primary school was more than twice as high in SSA as in any other region. Also in secondary schools, the repeat fraction in SSA was notably higher in 1990 than elsewhere, especially compared with East Asia.

Drop-out Rates   That children get enrolled at a primary school, but do not finish, indicates that parents, after having experienced the quality of the education, do not expect the returns of schooling to exceed the opportunity cost of the children's (and their own) time in other pursuits. The estimated drop-out rate from primary school in SSA as a whole is about one-third (Table 16.8). The rate ranges from 80 per cent to close to nil in the individual countries (UNICEF*a* 1996: table 4).[13] That only two-thirds of the children enrol in primary education, and that one-third of these, or more in some countries, never complete grade five implies that more than half of the present African child population will end up illiterate or semi-illiterate as adults.[14] These failures indicate that the quality of education is poor and/or that expected returns—and thus demand—are low (to be analysed in section 16.6 below).

16.5.3. Targeting of Education Services

Primary and Secondary versus Higher   Primary education is of especial importance for the poorest population segments, while government-financed secondary and, especially, higher education benefit mostly the relatively well off. This is suggested mainly by the fact that in Africa, as well as elsewhere, the share of children who enrol in secondary school increases sharply with higher income deciles (IBRD 1997: fig. 1.5).

A good indicator of targeting along income lines would thus be relative government spending on primary, secondary, and higher education. As expected, the available data on how the education budget in the African countries is allocated to different educational levels are meagre. Data for 22 SSA countries show the primary level to receive about half, secondary education about 30 per cent, and higher (university) education the remaining 20 per cent of the budget (IBRD 1994: table A.28). There are large variations across the SSA countries in allocation between primary and secondary education, but a relatively consistent pattern is the high priority given to higher education. The SSA countries spend a larger share of the education budget on higher education than the East Asian countries, according to the World Bank (ibid: p.173), which considers this to be 'too much'. However, the UNICEF estimates by major region (Table 16.8) gives a slightly different picture: here SSA spending is comparable with that in South Asia, and below that of other regions.

That the number of pupils engaged in primary education is much larger than in secondary and higher education, suggests that money goes to primary education to a disproportionally low extent in SSA. This hypothesis is corroborated by the Barro and Lee estimates of government spending per pupil in primary and secondary schools, respectively (Table 16.7). The secondary to primary spending ratio is about 4 in SSA, while it is below 1.5 in most other developing regions, although somewhat higher than that in the Middle East and North Africa. (In the Organisation for Economic Co-operation and Development (OECD) countries, the ratio is unity, signifying equal spending on primary and secondary schooling per pupil.) If correct—the data are unreliable—this is a strong indication of the extent to which African governments give priority to education for the not-so-poor population segments.

Rural/Urban   There are few disaggregated data on *enrolment* in, and/or *completion* of, primary and secondary education in rural and urban areas, respectively. The World Bank reports data from Niger which show the urban enrolment rate in primary education to be about three times higher than the rural rate for all income deciles (IBRD 1997: fig. 1.6). That the secondary school enrolment rate in SSA as a whole is only 23 per cent, roughly half of that in South Asia, may be revealing. There are at least a dozen countries in SSA where fewer than 10 per cent of the children are enrolled in secondary education. (Only in four countries, Zimbabwe, Namibia, Botswana, and Mauritius, are about half the children enrolled in secondary school (UNICEF*a* 1996).) Typically, secondary schools are found in cities or big towns only, which provide (an admittedly) weak indication of targeting secondary schooling to the not-so-poor urban populations.

Gender   The enrolment rates for both primary and secondary schools are lower for females than for males in SSA as a whole; the ratios of female to male enrolments are 0.83 and 0.87, respectively (Table 16.9). The figure for primary education is higher than in South Asia,[15] but lower than in other regions, where total primary school enrolment is close to 100 per cent. When it comes to secondary schools, the enrolment ratio in Africa compares well with most other regions. (In Africa the problem is the overall low enrolment.) A comparison of enrolment ratios from 1960 with data from around 1990, reveals that there has been a worldwide trend towards declining gender differences in primary school enrolment and that this decline has been the largest in SSA.

The educational attainment estimates (Table 16.9) suggest that the female:male ratio in terms of mean number of school years completed in 1990

TABLE 16.9. Indicators of education achievements, by major geographical regions, 1994; female:male ratios

Indicators	SSA	South Asia	North Africa/ Middle East	East Asia	Latin America and Caribbean
Primary school enrolment					
Total (gross)	70	91	96	116	104
Male	76	102	103	119	105
Female	63	80	89	112	103
Female/Male Ratio	0.83	0.78	0.86	0.94	0.98
Secondary school enrolment					
Total (gross)	23	42	54	52	48
Male	24	52	61	56	46
Female	21	32	46	48	49
Female/Male ratio	0.87	0.61	0.76	0.85	1.08
Mean school years 1970	0.59	0.37	0.50	0.68	0.85
Female/Male ratio 1990	0.61	0.52	0.66	0.84	0.96
Adult literacy rate	52	46	58	80	85
Female/Male ratio	0.68	0.54	0.66	0.81	0.97

Sources: UNICEF*a* 1996: table 10, based on data from UNESCO, and Barro and Lee 1996.

is 0.61 in SSA, while 0.52 in South Asia. In the other main regions, the ratio is higher, especially in Latin America. However, compared with 1970, the slowest relative improvement in the female:male ratio has taken place in SSA and the fastest in South Asia (where it was by far the lowest in 1970). There is thus an (unexplained) discrepancy in the UNESCO estimates, which suggests a rapid closing of the female/male education 'flow' gap and the Barro–Lee findings of a largely unaltered 'stock' gap.

16.6. ECONOMIC GROWTH AND DEMAND FOR EDUCATION

In the next chapter ample evidence showing education to be beneficial for economic growth will be presented. As we have seen above, however, economic growth is at the same time important for providing financial means to invest in the *supply* of education, public as well as private. There is also a link between economic growth and *demand* for education, the focus of this section.

16.6.1. Estimated Returns on Education

Social and private returns on education at different levels are indicators of the quality of education (as well as quantity). Higher than 'normal' social returns on education in general are an indication of (relative) underprovision; higher *social* returns on education at one level than an other signal that reallocation of resources towards the subsector with the highest returns is socially motivated. High *private* returns indicate constraints on the demand side (for privately financed education). Ideally, from an efficiency point of view, each unit of public funding provided to the education sector should be allocated to different levels (primary, secondary, and higher) so that the marginal social returns are reasonably equal (Weale 1993: p.729) and the same across different types of education and in different locations.

In a recent review of the empirical evidence, Evans and Hurley (1995: p.519) concluded that: 'We could find no published information on the extent to which economic appraisals have influenced decision making in developing countries.' Perhaps this is because no economic evaluation is normally undertaken, with the allocation of public resources being determined by other criteria (political priorities). From a policy perspective it is nevertheless important to know what the returns on education are at different levels in the African countries.

Over the 1970s and 1980s, some 20 studies have suggested that returns on formal education in the SSA countries are exceptionally high. The results of these studies have been compiled and 'averaged' by Psacharopoulos at regular intervals. In his latest 'update' Psacharopoulos (1994: table 1) reported the following:

- Private returns to primary, secondary, and higher education in the SSA countries are on average 41, 27, and 28 per cent, respectively.
- Social returns, at 24, 18, and 11 per cent, are lower, but still much higher than returns on capital investment (which seem to be close to nil in most places, judging from the overall growth achieved in SSA).
- Private, as well as social, returns on education at all levels are higher in SSA than in any other region of the world.

The World Bank, where Psacharopoulos has been a senior officer since the 1970s, reproduced his findings unfettered in 1990 *World Development Report* (IBRD*a* 1990: box 5.2). The main evidence on returns on education presented in the chapter on education in developing countries (Schultz 1988) in the *Handbook of Development Economics* was taken directly from one of Psacharopoulos' earlier compilations. Because of their prominent publication and frequent citation, these estimates have been the conventional wisdom for quite some time.

With such extraordinary high returns to education in SSA—social as well as private—the obvious question is why governments do not invest more in education and why people do not demand education more vigorously. One possible explanation is government and/or market failures. Governments may not realize how high social returns are, or is it that they are constrained for political reasons to divert public funds from other uses? Households may be constrained, by low incomes and credit-market failures, from asserting efficient demand for education despite high private returns. This may well be so, but there is another possible answer to the apparent puzzle: the returns on education in SSA have been seriously overestimated.

Bennell (1996) has undertaken a painstaking and thorough job in scrutinizing the individual studies from which Psacharopoulos derived his 'averages' for the SSA countries. Among Bennell's findings are:

- The data used in about half the studies are obtained with methods that do not stand up to minimal scientific standards.
- The small sample populations are not representative: they are confined to employees in the public sector, or in the 'formal' sector, which in the SSA countries is almost equivalent to the public sector (where wages are not set competitively).
- The returns on education in the agricultural sector, in which some 70 per cent of the population earns its living, are not estimated in any of the studies.
- The estimation methods are flawed in most cases; perhaps the most serious problem in all the studies is that the opportunity cost for the time spent in education has been set to nil or a very low amount.

Bennell provides no alternative estimates (as also pointed out by Psacharopoulos (1996)), but his analysis convincingly supports his conclusion that the 'average' results provided by Psacharopoulos and the World Bank[16] have 'very seriously overestimated returns to education in Africa'. He also claims that the existing empirical evidence does not permit a ranking of returns across education levels. As for the policy implications, Bennell (1996: p. 195) argues that 'the results are so flawed that they should be discarded altogether in any serious discussion on education investment priorities both for the continent as a whole and for individual countries'.

Several recent studies corroborate Bennell's claim that returns to education have previously been overestimated. A dozen studies from the 1990s, summarized in Appleton *et al.* (1996), suggest relatively low returns to education in general and to primary education in particular in the African countries.

16.6.2. Declining Returns on Education?

Since there are no reliable estimates of returns on education in Africa before 1990, no trends can be estimated. There is *a priori* reason, however, to expect that returns have declined generally over the past decades. The main reason is that the increase in the supply of adult people with education (as measured by literacy rates)[17] has outstripped growth of demand. Demand for (and returns on) formal education in subsistence and non-mechanized agriculture, which employs the great majority of the African work force, is most probably low or even non-existent.[18] The demand for educated labour stems mainly from the formal sectors, where returns can be expected to be positive (even though not as high as argued by Psacharopoulos). However, the formal sector in the African countries is small; only 5–15 per cent of the workforce are wage-earners in most of the countries (Bennell 1996: table 5).

Moreover, as reflected in the negative overall growth rates in all but a few of the African economies, there has been no expansion of the formal sectors. The share of the workforce in industry in the stagnant SSA economies has remained below 10 per cent since 1980 (UNCTAD*a* 1995, IBRD*a* 1996). The demand for educated labour has probably declined in the public sector of many African countries in the wake of the structural adjustment programs. According to the World Bank, there was some reduction of civil-service personnel between 1985 and 1991 in a few SSA countries, but in about equally as many countries, there was an increase (IBRD 1994: fig. 4.1, IBRD*a* 1997: p. 95). In some countries there have been cuts in public sector salaries/wages, but there are about equally as many SSA countries in which there has been an increase, both in relation to total government expenditures and to GNP (IBRD 1994, 1997). Thus, on the whole, public sector employment seems to have remained largely unchanged, but since no major expansion has taken place, the demand for new employees must increase only very slowly, if at all.

In short, if the expected private returns on education are small in agriculture, which the scant evidence suggests, and the job market in other (formal) sectors is more or less stagnant, demand for education is bound to be low and non-increasing.[19] That the share of children aged 6–11 years attending primary school has declined since the early 1980s is fully consistent with this hypothesis.

16.7. SUMMARY AND CONCLUSIONS

Some of the conclusions arrived at in this chapter cannot but be somewhat hesitant, given the limitations of the data that are available. But, given the data that we have, the following inferences seems to be the best we can draw.

A first finding is that the excess mortality rate in the African region (and that the decline has come to a halt in some of the countries) is not primarily caused by low priority of the public social sectors in general. The *share* of government expenditure going to health is roughly on a par with that in other parts of the world and the share going to education is higher. Due to low and declining per-capita income and, consequently, low government revenues/expenditures, however, the *absolute* amount spent on a per-capita basis is lower and has dropped more than it has in most other countries.

The quality of the health services provided in the African countries has not been systematically evaluated in the works consulted in this chapter. The assessments that have been made are mainly subjective, as few statistical data are available. However, almost all the dozen or so 'subjective' recent assessments arrive at roughly the same conclusion: quality is deteriorating and improvements in the health sector are badly needed. This broad agreement is reassuring in the absence of hard facts.

Another reason for the exceedingly high mortality rate in SSA is the uneven distribution of the health (and education) services. Only half the rural population in SSA as a whole has access to primary health care, and less than one-third to safe water and sanitation. Only half the children are immunized against the four most common communicable fatal diseases. This combination of lack of health care, lack of safe water/sanitation, and incomplete immunization coverage for large sections of the population is most probably the chief direct explanation for the excess child mortality. All these 'explanations' are to a large extent manifestations of the same underlying problems, i.e. economic poverty and misdirected government policies.

Primary school enrolment is declining while secondary school enrolment is increasing in SSA. This is most probably a reflection of an increased concentration of decline in government expenditure on education to priority areas (urban). Government spending per pupil in secondary schools is four times higher than the spending in primary schools in SSA, a ratio far higher than elsewhere. The high priority given to secondary schooling is consistent with efficiency objectives if one is to trust recent assessment of relative social returns on education at different levels (Appleton *et al.* 1996: appendix). From an equity and poverty-reducing perspective, however, other priorities would probably be preferable.

The high drop-out rates (80 per cent in some countries) and the high repeat fractions are more likely to be an outcome of the low quality of schooling rather than non-availability. However, the declining school enrolment rates and drop-out rates are most probably also related to declining demand in the wake of falling expected economic returns on education in the stagnant African economies.

The crucial question is what the African governments can do to speed up the decline in mortality and reverse the deteriorating educational achievements,

APPENDIX TABLE 16.1. Estimated per-capita growth rates of real GDP 1970–90 and GDP per capita, by major geographical regions, 1970 and 1990

	SSA	SA	ME/ NA	EA/ PA	LA/ CA	OECD
Growth of per-capita real GDP 1970–90. Percentage per year	–0.6	2.2	0.0	5.9	1.1	2.1
Per-capita GDP 1970	1,475	1,170	4,510	850	4,310	10,090
real 1990 US 1990 dollars (PPP)	1,290	1,560	4,510	2,690	5,760	15,140

Sources: IBRD*a* 1993: table 1 (per-capita GDP in 1990); UNCTAD*a* 1995: table 6.2 (growth of per-capita GDP 1970–90); per-capita GDP in 1970 is calculated from the other two entities.

especially at the primary level. Can anything be done in the absence of growth and if so, what? This is the main question to be addressed in the next chapter, where we will also discuss what lessons African countries can learn from other, more successful countries.

NOTES

1. Also, the anthropometric status of adult women in Africa is far better than in any other part of the so-called Third World, except for China (see Chapter 11).
2. The terms public action and intervention are used interchangeably in the following and refer to government activities whenever not otherwise explicitly stated.
3. Some government interventions are primarily aimed at macro-stabilization of the economy, which could also be considered an efficiency objective.
4. It has been argued that the main reason why the colonial powers already provided some health care in the colonies was that 'protecting the health of expatriates required addressing health needs among the colonialized subjects' (Zwi and Mills 1995: p. 302). Sen (1995: p. 21) puts the argument well: 'I sometimes wonder whether there is any way of making poverty terribly infectious. If that were to happen, its general elimination would be, I am certain, remarkably rapid.'
5. Studies of countries from other parts of the world have been based on more sophisticated methods, e.g. Shan and Alderman 1995 (Sri Lanka), Deolalikar 1995, Pitt et al. 1995 (Indonesia), and Hammer et al. 1995 (Malaysia).
6. For recent evaluations, the distributional impact, and costs in these two cases, see Ali and Adams 1996 (Egypt), and Shan and Alderman 1995 (Sri Lanka). See also ACC/SNC (1996: p. 63) for some other countries.
7. This is not to say that declining real income is the only, or even most important explanation of the stagnating or even increasing mortality rates in the African countries. Another explanation may be increased morbidity related to re-emergence of 'old' diseases and the appearance of 'new' ones, most notably HIV/AIDS. (For a large number of articles on HIV/AIDS in Africa and India, see Ntozi et al. (1997).) Old diseases that appear to have come back increasingly include (resistant) malaria and tuberculosis (Zwi and Mills 1995: p. 307, also see Mogedal et al. 1995: p. 351, Brockerhof and Derose 1996: p.1844, WHOa 1996). Most of these diseases, however, have a connection with economic variables (see Behrman and Deolalikar 1988: pp. 666–7). Moreover, these diseases are not confined to Africa, but are prevalent also in Asia, where no similar effect on child mortality is discernible (AsDB 1997: p. 39).
8. Foreign aid accounted for 'only' 10 per cent of estimated total health expenditure in the SSA as a whole in 1990. This weighted average, however, is partly misleading, since it includes Nigeria and South Africa, which receive little aid in general and to health in particular, but weigh heavily on the average. In more than one-third of the other SSA countries, aid accounts for more than one-third of total health expenditure (IBRDa 1993: table A.9).
9. There are no rural/urban data on access to health services for Bangladesh and Sri Lanka, where the national figures are 45 and 93 per cent, respectively. In Pakistan, the rural/urban difference is even larger than for most African countries (35 versus 99 per cent).

10. That rural/urban data are available for only 19 countries means that the averages for SSA as a whole presented by UNICEF are crude estimates. There are also other complications that make inter-country comparisons difficult, such as varying definitions of rural/urban, 'access', and how this is measured.

11. The estimates suggest that in 1970, the SSA countries spent more per pupil in secondary school in absolute dollars than did the OECD countries. To what extent this finding reflects reality is uncertain, considering the quality of the data.

12. Great caution must always be taken in comparing health and education spending across countries. In some countries the central government accounts for almost all expenditures, which are in the data reported by the IMF*b* (1996). Local government expenditures (large in India and Brazil for instance), and private expenditures, which are large especially in the East Asian countries, are not included in the official statistics for most countries. Also, changes over time must be interpreted with care since in many countries, changes in the statistical reporting have taken place (indicated in the IMF publications). For discussions of biases and errors in the standard statistics on education in developing countries, see Barro and Lee (1993) and Behrman and Rosenzweig (1994).

13. My only personal experience of evaluating education in Africa is from Guinea–Bissau. In the early 1990s, this country had a drop-out rate from primary school of 80 per cent. We identified several confounding reasons for this, the most basic being that all teaching was in Portuguese, a language that fewer than one per cent of the rural population master (Svedberg *et al.* 1994).

14. It also provides a 'leading indicator' of stagnant or declining 'stock' of educational attainment, or human capital, in years to come.

15. See Drèze and Sen (1995) for an assessment of the education sector in India. They claim that official enrolment rates for India are grossly overstated. This seems to be the case in most developing countries (see Barro and Lee 1993, Behrman and Rosenzweig 1994).

16. In the 1995 *World Development Report* (IBRD*a* 1995), the World Bank is more cautious in claiming high returns to education in the least developed countries. Moreover, the data on returns presented here show the highest returns on upper secondary education, not primary as claimed earlier (IBRD*a* 1990).

17. The adult literacy rates increased from an estimated 29 to 52 per cent between 1970 and 1990 in the SSA as a whole (UNICEF*a* 1996), reflecting the increase in school enrolment that took place up to the early 1980s. The more recent decline in the share of children attending school will show up in declines in literacy in the near future.

18. Appleton *et al.* (1996: p. 328) cite a few studies from *rural* Africa which found no positive returns on education for non-wage earners. Evidence from other countries is more mixed.

19. There could be demand for education in households from this sector for reasons other than expected private returns; Appleton *et al.* (1996: pp. 316–17) provide a discussion of such reasons. Moreover, education is important for many reasons other than income-earning potential; see Drèze and Sen (1995: pp. 14–15) for a discussion.

17

Growth, Public Action, and Well-being: What Can Sub-Saharan Africa Learn from Others?

17.1. INTRODUCTION

The decline in child mortality in SSA as a whole slowed down in the 1980s and came to a halt in some of the countries; in still others mortality has increased during the 1990s. Also, primary school enrolment has deteriorated in the region at large since 1980 and in about half the countries. The latter development implies falling parental literacy in years to come, which may further impede future child-mortality reduction. Although not possible to quantify in detail (mainly due to lack of reliable time-series mortality data), the main reason for the dismal developments in the social sectors seems to be overall economic decline. Over the period 1985–95, per-capita real income fell by about 1 per cent per year in the region as a whole. Declining incomes and, consequently, falling government revenue, have probably affected health and education standards adversely from both the supply and demand sides.

The main aim of the present chapter is to investigate the possibilities for the SSA countries of improving the utterly dismal performance in the social sectors. In this endeavour, we start by discussing what lessons can be learnt from the experiences of more successful countries elsewhere. These experiences are both from individual countries that have outstanding achievements in the social sectors even in the absence of rapid economic growth, and countries that have accomplished both impressive social development and high growth (section 17.2). We shall also discuss the lessons that can be drawn from findings concerning complementarities and trade-offs between public intervention in social sectors and long-term economic growth, as suggested by recent cross-country regression analyses (section 17.3). On the basis of these experiences, we shall try to identify reforms that are needed in the African countries if they are to emulate—both in terms of growth and social development—more successful countries elsewhere (section 17.4). In section 17.5, the prospects for these reforms to be undertaken are assessed in the light of the prevailing political and economic situation in the SSA countries.

17.2. WHAT AFRICAN COUNTRIES COULD LEARN FROM OTHERS

17.2.1. The Growth-cum-Equity-Oriented Countries as Models

The East Asian countries' development over the past three decades must have been the envy of most governments in the rest of the world, not the least in SSA, where the contrast is the sharpest. Rapid economic growth in South Korea, Taiwan, Hong Kong, and Singapore has raised per-capita real income in about one generation to levels comparable with most European countries. These economic achievements have gone hand-in-hand with equally remarkable (but less frequently observed) improvements in all social-development indicators. During the first half of the 1990s, the four Asian countries have surpassed Costa Rica, Sri Lanka, and Jamaica in terms of low child mortality rates, life expectancy at birth, and literacy. (At the time, they also had a four to eight times higher per-capita real income.) By 1994, South Korea, Hong Kong, Singapore, and Taiwan also had lower child morality rates than the US and several other developed OECD countries (UNICEF*a* 1996).

Hundreds of articles and books have been written with the aim to explain the East Asian growth 'miracle' (IBRD 1993, Romer 1993, Birdsall *et al.* 1994, Rodrik 1994, Ranis 1995, to cite just a few). A convincing and systematic empirical study has been provided by Young (1995). Using a refined growth-accounting model, he finds that between 80 and 100 per cent of the growth in South Korea, Taiwan, Hong Kong, and Singapore is accounted for by standard variables in growth theory: high savings and capital investments, reallocation of resources from low to high productivity sectors (mainly the export manufacturing sector), and skill improvements in the labour force. The unexplained part of growth, conventionally referred to as total factor productivity (*TFP*), accounts for 0–20 per cent only in these four countries. Young's results thus suggest that there is no *economic* miracle behind the extraordinary growth: simple text-book explanations are sufficient.[1]

There is growing consensus that government policy has been important in explaining the success of South Korea, Taiwan, and Singapore (and, perhaps, the minimal but apt government intervention in Hong Kong). The miracle thus lies more with the persistent government policies that have provided incentives for the high savings/investment rates, the upgrading (education) of the labour force and the reallocation of resources to the export sectors. The successive governments in these countries have followed up on old traditions of favouring education. Considerably less has been spent on public health services (see Murray *et al.* 1994), which are commonly provided by employers and financed through private insurance. Judging from health-outcome indicators, this system must have been efficient. It thus seems as if the remarkable growth and social developments (human capital creation) have been two mutually reinforcing factors in the East Asian countries. Without high investments in education, the growth of the skill-intensive industries would not have been feasible. Without rapid growth, the finances for both the public and private health and education provision would not have come forth.

Many observers further stress that the favourable policies have been facilitated by the fact that the populations in these countries are relatively homogenous and that inequality has been low traditionally. The latter is mainly attributed to early land reforms in Korea (1905) and Taiwan (1949) and the fact that primary education became universal at an early stage. However, that relatively high inequality has not been an *absolute* hindrance to growth and rapid improvement in social indicators is exemplified by Malaysia and Thailand. Both countries have Gini coefficients of around 0.55 (compared with around 0.32 in South Korea and Taiwan), and in the case of Thailand, it has increased trendwise by 10 points over the past 30 years (Deininger and Squire 1996a). Malaysia also shows that ethnical division is not an absolute hindrance for economic and social progress.

There is the possibility that *some* of the East and South-East Asian countries—notably South Korea, Indonesia, and Thailand—may experience grave set-backs in terms of growth and social development in the wake of the financial crises that erupted in mid-1997. This remains to be seen. In the 1980s and 1990s, similar financial turmoil in Mexico, as well as in several other Latin American and OECD countries, was followed by poor overall economic performance for some time, but there was a return to rather normal growth a few years later in almost all the cases.[2] There is no guarantee that there will be a quick return to normality in the Asian countries with the most severe financial problems in 1997–9. However, whatever happens in these countries during the next few years, it should not distract from the fact that they have had a remarkable development along almost all dimensions for the past 30–40 years (as have Hong Kong, Singapore, and Taiwan, which had been only moderately affected by the financial crises in the region as of early 1999). And there are several valuable lessons to be learnt from this; the present crisis and its aftermath, whatever happens, will also offer others the possibility of learning from them.

17.2.2. The Equity-Oriented Countries as Models

Given the present pessimism for per-capita economic growth in the great majority of the SSA countries in the foreseeable future (see section 17.4.1 below) it is tempting to look at as 'models' the few countries that have accomplished drastic improvements in social indicators in the absence of rapid growth. Three such countries are Costa Rica, Jamaica, and Sri Lanka. These countries, and a few more, have accomplished enormous improvements in life expectancy and literacy, mainly through huge public-sector investments in health care, education, and, to some extent, nutrition support. What are the main explanations behind *these* 'miracles'?

(1) *Long-term Political Commitment*   What has been achieved in Costa Rica, Jamaica, and Sri Lanka has taken a long time to accomplish. At the end of the nineteenth century universal primary education had already been introduced in Costa Rica and Jamaica, and in Sri Lanka in the 1930s. Maternity and obstetric health care in the two American countries dates equally far back in history. The infant mortality rate began to decline in Jamaica as early as 1895 (Caldwell 1987). In Sri Lanka, the IMR declined from around 200 in the 1920s to 75 in the early 1950s (Anand and Kanbur 1991, Langford 1996). The infrastructure (both hard- and software) needed for efficient and large-scale provision of public health and education services has thus been built up during a long period.

(2) *Democratic Governments*   Costa Rica has been an independent country for almost two centuries and a democracy since the late nineteenth century (Caldwell 1987). Sri Lanka gained its independence in 1948, but, in practice, Ceylon had self-rule from the mid-1930s. Jamaica has been independent and democratic for half a century and had self-rule long before that. All three countries have been dominated by elected left-leaning governments, but also other political parties have by and large accepted that the state should provide at least basic services to the entire population.[3]

(3) *Homogenous and Educated Populations*   As stressed by Caldwell (1987) and several other observers, the fact that large percentages of the population in the 'model' countries were already literate at the beginning of this century induced high demand for public services, which democratic governments supplied. There are many (mainly subjective) assessments on record that many reforms have been 'bottom-up', i.e. initiated by organized popular movements with strong political clout.[4] Moreover, the population in Costa Rica, in particular, but also the two other countries, is relatively homogeneous by the standards of most other developing countries. This has probably been a contributing factor to the relatively modest political splits on public-sector issues (which the cross-country evidence also suggests; see below). The fact that public health and education provision were close to universal from the start may also have reduced political conflict and obstruction by groups otherwise paying for the services but not directly benefiting from them (see Caldwell 1987 for further discussion and details).

(4) *High Levels of Investment in Social Sectors*   In the 1960s and 1970s, public health and education expenditures as a share of GDP were exceptionally high in Costa Rica, Jamaica, and Sri Lanka. However, by 1990, these countries have no longer been topping the list. In Sri Lanka, public health expenditures as a percentage of GDP are only slightly larger than in India and slightly lower than in South Korea and Taiwan. Total health expenditure (including private and aid-financed) is lower than in India as a ratio to GDP and

also lower than the average for developing Asia (Murray *et al.* 1994). In absolute dollars per capita, health expenditure in Sri Lanka is on a par with that in India, in Jamaica it is on a par with Mexico; and in Costa Rica it is on a par with Brazil. Despite roughly the same absolute per-capita expenditures, the U5MR in the three 'equity-oriented' countries is between half and one-fifth of that in the respective country of comparison. The tentative lessons to be learnt are, first, that in order to 'lift' the health status of an impoverished population, it takes substantial government finance for a long period of time, but also, secondly, once the lift is assured, adequate health standards can be maintained with relatively lower expenditures. What matters seems to be quality, not only quantity, and also that expenditures are targeted to the poorest population segments.

(5) *Growth Achieved* Taking a 45-year perspective, the rate of economic growth in Costa Rica and Sri Lanka has been low by East Asian standards, but impressive by African ones. For most of the period, these two countries have had growth roughly on a par with the developing-countries average (Table 17.1) In Jamaica, real GNPc has been stagnant since the early 1970s, while it grew by more than 5 per cent annually during the 1950s and 1960s. That Sri Lanka and Costa Rica have had positive per-capita growth rates for every decade since 1950 indicates that substantive public intervention in the social sectors has been consistent with at least 'average' growth.

17.2.3. *Conflict Between Public Action and Rapid Growth?*

There are indications that the high public spending on the social sectors induced macroeconomic instability that reduced growth, at least temporarily, in both Costa Rica and Sri Lanka. In the mid-1970s, Costa Rica began financing rapidly growing public expenditures and a widening budget deficit by foreign borrowing. By 1980, social public expenditures reached 23 per cent of GDP. By 1981 the foreign debt situation became untenable and as the first country to do so in modern times, Costa Rica cancelled its foreign debt

TABLE 17.1. Growth of real per-capita GDP in selected 'equity-oriented' countries, 1950–94, percentage per year

Country	1950–60	1960–70	1970–80	1980–90	1990–94
Costa Rica	1.1	2.9	3.7	0.1	3.0
Sri Lanka	1.0	2.5	3.1	2.6	3.8
Jamaica	6.3	4.1	−2.6	0.9	0.3
Developing country average	2.4	2.9	3.0	1.0	2.2

Sources: UNCTAD*a* 1972, 1984, and 1995: table 6.2 in all editions.

service (one year before Mexico). The structural adjustment that took place in the 1980s entailed curbing social expenditures, but no growth was achieved until the early 1990s. It thus seems that the economic crisis of Costa Rica in the 1980s was partly induced by 'too much' government spending on social sectors, but there were also other reasons (such as an inability to enhance export growth and foreign-exchange earnings sufficiently).

There has been a long and intensive debate on the question of whether or not the large public expenditures in social sectors in Sri Lanka have stifled (relatively favourable) growth (for short summaries see Kakwani 1993, and Anand and Ravallion 1993). No totally conclusive evidence for either position has been presented, but the economic crisis Sri Lanka experienced in the early and mid-1970s induced the government to undertake drastic cuts in the social expenditure budget (in 1977). This indicates that, at the time, the government itself saw previous expenditures on social services excessive and not consistent with macroeconomic stability and growth.

The previous high growth in Jamaica and the stagnation since the early 1970s is usually attributed to the collapse of the world market price for bauxite, Jamaica's dominant export product. 'Excessive' public spending on social sectors may have contributed, but no convincing study that quantifies the relative role of this and other adverse internal policies and external factors seems to have been undertaken.

17.3. GROWTH, PUBLIC ACTION, AND POVERTY ALLEVIATION: CROSS-COUNTRY EVIDENCE

The study of individual 'successful' countries is one way of learning lessons that could be of relevance to the African countries; inter-country comparisons, based on regression analysis and similar methods, are another.

17.3.1. Growth and Income Distribution

Until quite recently, the predominant view was that growth in the *least* developed countries inevitably led to a worsening of the income distribution (*à la* Kuznets 1955) and that growth was stimulated by an uneven distribution of income; 'only the relatively rich save and invest' (*à la* Kaldor 1956). These two conventional truths have been challenged lately.

Deininger and Squire (1996*a*) found no inverted U-curve relationship in their vastly extended and improved data set on income distribution, neither on a cross-country nor on a time series basis. This data set suggests that for 21 of the 32 developing countries for which there are reasonably comparable observations at different points in time, there has been no significant change in the income distribution (as measured by GINI). In four countries, GINI has increased by more than 5 points, indicating a significant worsening of income distribution (in Brazil, Chile, China, and Thailand). In the remaining seven countries GINI has fallen significantly. Investigating the whole spectrum of countries, Li *et al.* (1998) found income distribution to be a very stable entity over time in all but a few countries.

Alesina and Rodrik (1994), Persson and Tabellini (1994), Clarke (1995), and Perotti (1996) found an even initial distribution of income to be conducive to subsequent growth over cross-sections of countries (both developing and developed). The basic underlying hypothesis is that an uneven distribution of income leads to political claims for redistribution through high progressive taxes, which induce inefficiencies in the economy. There thus seems to be little justification in expecting a negative trade-off between growth and distribution over a considerable range (while this is not to say that *enforced redistribution* of income or assets is conducive for growth).

17.3.2. Growth and Poverty Reduction

A widely accepted definition of poverty is provided by Lipton and Ravallion (1995: p. 2553): 'Poverty exists when one or more persons fall short of a level of *economic* welfare deemed to constitute a reasonable minimum, either in some absolute sense or by the standards of a specific society'. For any given poverty line, the incidence of poverty must decline in the wake of growth—*unless growth is accompanied by a worsening of the distribution of income*. Of course, poverty decline can also follow from income-distribution improvements in the absence of economic growth.

Evidence on growth and poverty alleviation from country-specific studies have been reviewed and summarized by Lipton and Ravallion (1995: p. 2603). They found that 'on average, a 2 per cent growth of consumption per person at all consumption levels will result in a 3–8 per cent rate of decline in the poverty gap'. However, during the period of investigation, the 1980s, many countries in Latin America and Africa experienced negative growth and, consequently, increased poverty, while positive growth and poverty alleviation continued in most of Asia. Overall, Chen *et al.* (1994) tentatively concluded that worldwide poverty therefore fell only slightly during the 1980s.[5]

Since the SSA countries as a group had an annual decline in per-capita real income of one per cent in the period 1985–95, and only modest growth in *total* GDP, there is a large risk that the incidence of poverty in many countries in this region increased notably (also see section 17.4.1 below). The lack of observations on the distribution of income at more than 1 year in almost all SSA countries (Deininger and Squire 1996*a*) makes it impossible to test thoroughly the increase-in-poverty hypothesis. There is, however, another set of data, collected by the World Bank and derived on the basis of household survey information, which shows the incidence of poverty in SSA to have increased, but only marginally, between the years 1987 and 1993 (IBRD 1997: p.142).

17.3.3. Poverty Reduction and Mortality Decline

That rapid growth in the absence of a simultaneous deterioration of the income distribution leads to poverty reduction is almost tautological and, conversely, that real per-capita income decline is followed by poverty increase (Ravallion 1997*b*). That *economic* poverty reduction is important for improvements in health and other functions that determine human well-being in a broader sense is perhaps non-controversial (although the cross-country empirical evidence seems to be limited to one study by Anand and Ravallion (1993)).

17.3.4. Human Capital and Growth

Improved and extended provision of education and health services in a population (human capital) are important for growth according to much recent empirical study, stimulated by the emergence of the so-called new growth theory. Barro (1991) found that over a cross-section of some 100 countries, growth was significantly and positively related to the initial stock of human capital (approximated by secondary and primary school enrolment at the beginning of the period). This finding has been corroborated by several subsequent studies. Levine and Renelt (1992), for instance, in their robustness test, found that 'education' was one of a very few theoretical determinants of growth that came out as significant irrespective of what other conditioning explanatory variables were included on the right-hand side. Gemmel (1996), Sala-i-Martin (1997), Easterley and Levine (1997), and Baffes and Shah (1998) corroborate this finding.

While most tests of 'new' growth theory have focused on education as a proxy for 'human capital', there are at least three studies that have taken 'health status' into consideration. Barro and Sala-i-Martin (1995: chapter 12), Sala-i-Martin (1997) and Radelet *et al.* (1997) obtained high significance for LEB at the initial point in time as an explanatory variable for subsequent growth. Barro and Sala-i-Martin (1995: p. 432) conclude that 'It is likely that life expectancy has such a strong, positive relationship with growth because it proxies for features *other* than good health that reflect good performance of a society. For example, higher life expectancy may go along with better work habits and a higher level of skills.'

17.4. GROWTH AND/OR EQUITY-ORIENTED DEVELOPMENT IN SSA: REQUIRED POLICY CHANGES[6]

As a brief summing up of the above section, cross-country empirical evidence shows no general tendency for growth to be followed by more unequal distribution of income: the distribution tends to be largely unaltered. Therefore, growth, with few exceptions, leads to poverty alleviation which, in turn, is followed by mortality decline and improvements in other forms of human well-being. Moreover, government 'consumption', in the form of expenditures for education and health, are important not only for their intrinsic values, but are also conducive for growth over a considerable range. What then is there to be learnt from these lessons for the SSA countries' policy priorities?

17.4.1. Required Policy Changes for Growth

Almost as many articles and books have been written on the failure of the African countries to accomplish growth and social development as there have about the favourable developments in East Asia. The main explanations for the growth failure in Africa that have been offered are too well-known to be repeated here in detail (i.e. excessive state involvement in the production and internal trade of private goods, overvalued exchange rates, excessive protection of industry, discrimination of agriculture, lack of property rights and functioning financial markets, inadequate infrastructure, dependence on inefficient foreign aid, and a few other factors).[7]

The overall aim of the structural adjustment programs that some 30 SSA countries have been struggling with over the past 5–15 years—whether appropriately designed or not—is to reverse these policies and thereby establish the necessary preconditions for growth. At present, it seems that about one-third of these 30 countries are making some progress. Only Uganda, however, has achieved notable growth for several years in a row (IBRDa 1997: table 11).[8] (At the other extreme—in terms of establishing preconditions for growth—are the dozen SSA countries where ongoing civil war has destroyed all possibilities for economic development for years to come.) Even the sometimes over-optimistic World Bank sees little prospect for a significant improvement in the preconditions for growth in most of SSA. Its prediction is that average growth in the region will be 3.8 per cent per year in the coming decade, implying per-capita growth of about 1 per cent annually (IBRD 1997: p. 9). The same World Bank study estimates that in order for the incidence of poverty to be reduced, substantially higher growth rates are required, on average above 5 per cent. In the SSA countries with the most unequal initial distribution of income and the most rapid population growth, the required growth rate is estimated to be 6–8 per cent if poverty is to decline (Lensink and White 1999: appendix 4.1).

The World Bank study does not reveal what its pessimistic growth forecast is based on. However, a quick consultation of recent results from empirical growth studies may give some clues. Mauro (1995), Burnside and Dollar (1997), Easterly and Levine (1997), Edwards (1998), and Sala-i-Martin (1997) have undertaken some of the most ambitious such studies conducted so far. In most instances, these studies confirm, first, the results obtained several times earlier, i.e. that high growth is dependent on high domestic savings/investment, rapid human capital formation and a stable and outward-oriented trade regime. What is interesting in the present context, however, is that they further find a large variety of less traditional variables to have a significant and robust correlation with growth.

Sala-i-Martin (1997) found 25 variables to have a *significant and robust* association with growth (out of 62 variables that had been significant, but not necessarily robust, in previous studies). In order to get an idea of what it takes to change a growth-detrimental political and economical environment into a growth-friendly one, the 25 'positive' variables can be classified in terms of the time-frame in which they are subject to policy change.

(1) *Short and Medium Terms*   Among the variables that have repeatedly been found to be significant and robustly correlated to growth, only three are amenable to relatively quick changes through policy alterations. These are trade and foreign exchange-rate policies and central government budget policy. These are also the variables that have been 'improved' recently in the wake of the structural adjustment programs that have been undertaken in the African countries (IBRD 1994, 1997).

(2) *Long Term*   Most of the variables that correlate significantly with growth—and are robust—in cross-country tests, are either institutional or demographic characteristics of countries that can only be altered in the long term, more than a decade, through policy reorientation. Such variables include various proxies for 'rule of law', 'political rights', 'civil liberties', 'revolutions and coups', a 'war dummy' (Sala-i-Martin 1997), and also 'instability' in neighbouring countries (Ades and Chua 1998).[9] They also include several proxy variables for bureaucratic (in)efficiency, institutional (in)efficiency, and level of corruption, which all correlate significantly, and with the expected sign, with growth, mainly through investment (Mauro 1995, Barro 1995).

Furthermore, the fact that most SSA countries are much more heavily dependent on foreign aid than other countries seems to be of no help for growth. Boone (1995, 1996) and also Burnside and Dollar (1997) found that investment financed by aid does not increase overall investment. Through reallocation of resources (fungibility) almost all aid ends up as public consumption, mainly in the form of expansion of the public work force. To reduce aid dependency is also a long-term prospect.

(3) *Unchangable?*   Easterly and Levine (1997) investigated the reasons why so many countries, especially in SSA, pursue growth-detrimental policies. They found that high ethnic fragmentation explains a significant part of why there is low schooling, political instability, underdeveloped financial systems, distorted foreign-exchange markets, high government deficits, and insufficient infrastructure. These variables, in turn, account for about two-fifths of

the growth differential between the countries of SSA and fast-growing East Asia. They conjecture that: 'Ethnic diversity may increase polarisation and thereby impede agreement about the provisions of public goods and create positive incentives for growth-reducing policies . . . . that create rents for the groups in power at the expense of society at large.' (ibid: p. 1206). Ethnic fragmentation is exceptionally high in most of SSA; among the 15 countries with the highest scores, 14 are in this region (India is the remaining country). According to one estimate there are more than 1,000 ethnic groups in SSA (Oliver and Crowder 1983).

Sachs and Werner (1995, 1997) and Radelet *et al.* (1997) have identified additional factors that are not amenable through policy, but negatively correlated with growth. These variables include being land-locked, being located far away from main markets and being located near the equator, other characteristics that are given for most SSA countries.[10]

In short, if one is to believe the recent regression results, the prospects for most African countries for accomplishing significant growth in the near future seem bleak. On almost all 'variables' that can be altered significantly in the long term only, the African countries score relatively worse than most other developing countries (IBRD*a* 1997: p. 112, Radelet *et al.* 1997). This is not to say that modest per-capita growth is impossible in the medium term, say 5–10 years, but that for accomplishing this, policy changes in a large number of areas, as discussed above, are required.

17.4.2. Required Policy Change for Equity-Oriented Development

Postulating that the pessimistic, or perhaps realistic, prediction for growth will hold for the foreseeable future, can the SSA countries reduce child mortality and improve human well-being in other dimensions in alternative ways? Is there an 'equity-oriented' policy alternative for *short-term* improvements in the social areas?

As the examples of Costa Rica, Jamaica, and Sri Lanka suggest, it takes political will and ability, as well as very high public spending on health and education over a long period of time, to accomplish what they have done. Leaving the political constraints aside for the moment, a crucial question is how the African countries should be able—if at all—to mobilize the government finances required to bring the public expenditures up to the levels of the equity-oriented 'model' countries—in a situation with very low initial per-capita GDP and no or minuscule growth. There are basically five 'technical' possibilities (in addition to what has already been tried, i.e. increased use of user fees in the health sector (see Chapter 16)).

(1) *Raise Government Domestic Revenue*   In order to increase spending on health and education, one option for the African governments is to raise more internal revenue. This has been advocated by the International Financial

Institutions (IFIs) for a long time, and is part and parcel of almost all current structural-adjustment packages. The IFIs' advice has not been to raise tax rates, but to broaden tax bases, eliminate tax loop-holes, strengthen the tax-collection effort, and stifle tax evasion. Some success in this endeavour has been observed (IBRD 1994). However, the simultaneous strive to liberalize foreign trade so as to improve the allocation of resources and to accomplish export growth, has led to lower taxes (and tariffs) on foreign-traded goods, traditionally the most important source of tax revenue in the African countries. The net impact on government revenue has therefore been negligible (IMF*b* 1997).

(2) *Foreign Aid, Debt Relief, and Foreign Private Borrowing*   In the early 1990s, foreign aid began to fall in absolute terms and since then the share going to the SSA countries has declined (OECD/DAC 1996). The prospects for a reversal are bleak: aid fatigue in general, and aid to non-performing African countries in particular, seems to spread. The new multilateral (but conditional) debt-relief scheme for the most highly indebted countries (the majority of which are African) may lead to improvement in African government finances in a more distant future in two ways. First, to qualify for multilateral debt relief, governments must undertake (among other things) public-sector reforms, e.g. reduce non-essential expenditures, that are sustained for a number of years. Secondly, to the extent to which this is accomplished, the debt-service burden will ease, adding strength to government finances that could be used for improving and extending public health and education services. By early 1999, however, Uganda and Mozombique were the only SSA countries that had qualified for multilateral debt relief.

Foreign private direct investment in SSA, another potential tax base, is minuscule and confined to mineral exploitation projects, such as the Ashanti gold fields in Ghana, the largest foreign direct investment project in recent times. In order to attract more foreign private investment that could bring increased tax revenues, the (general) investment climate has to be improved, as judged by the revealed preferences of foreign investors, who have so far largely abstained from entering Africa. This is still another so far unfulfilled aim with the structural-adjustment programs.

(3) *Government Expenditure Reallocation*   A further alternative is to increase the health and education budgets at the expense of other public expenditures. These other expenditures include infrastructure of various kinds, public sectors that are underprovided according to the World Bank (IBRD*a* 1995). The best scope for government reallocation seems to be to cut down on subsidies—financed either directly from the budget or indirectly via a state-controlled bank system—to loss-making public enterprises, and/or to sell these to private agents, yet another ingredient of most structural-adjustment packages. There are no precise data on the size of these subsidies, but

there are several indications that they are very substantial indeed (IBRD 1994).

The World Bank is guardedly optimistic about the progress made in some areas of structural reform, e.g. trade liberalization, exchange rate management, and price deregulation in selected sectors. The Bank concludes, however, that 'Privatisation and reforming state-owned enterprises and creating sound financial systems have proved to be among the most difficult adjustment reforms' (IBRD 1994). It finds evidence that a few countries have privatized and reformed, but that equally as many countries have increased the number of state enterprises. All in all, at least up to 1994, there were no signs of overall improvement in this area.

In most recent years there has been an increase in the number of privatization schemes according to Bennell (1997). He also finds that the World Bank has systematically underestimated the extent of privatization that has actually taken place. Bennell acknowledges that the data do not permit a good estimate of the share of public enterprise value that so far has been privatized in the region, 'But even in a country like Nigeria which, by African standards, has had a large privatisation program, this figure was still less than 5 per cent' as of early 1995 (ibid: p. 1791). It thus seems as if the process, even if not as slow as purported by the World Bank, has hardly begun.

Another potentially promising alternative is to reduce 'wasteful' expenditures by cutting down on the excess employment often found in African public sectors. Public wages and salaries account for between 18 and 80 per cent of current government expenditures (excluding interest payments) in the SSA countries for which there are data (IBRD 1994). In half a dozen of the 29 SSA countries undergoing structural adjustment, the number of public employees declined by more than 5 per cent between 1985 and 1992. However, in about equally as many countries, the number increased by more than 5 per cent (ibid: table 4.8). Somewhat more recently, the World Bank maintained that: 'In many a [SSA] country, public employment has not merely been maintained, it has actually risen' (IBRD*a* 1997: p. 95).

A revealing aspect is the huge inter-country differences in the public sector wage bill. Uganda, one of the economically most successful SSA countries in the 1990s, has the lowest public wage/salary bill (1 per cent of GDP); Zimbabwe has the largest, estimated at 16 per cent of GNP. Moreover, Zimbabwe increased the public wage sector bill by an amount corresponding to 3–4 per cent of GDP between 1985 and 1992. This increase is the equivalent of the country's entire expenditure on health.[11] Most countries are in the 5–10 per cent range. The large differences suggest that there is ample scope for reduction in the countries with the highest percentages. The reluctance most SSA governments have shown for such reforms apparently bears on a long tradition, where public employment is part and parcel of the welfare system (IBRD 1994), or the patron–client network that characterizes African political life (Ndulu 1997: p. 627, IBRD*a* 1997: p. 95).

To cut down on defence expenditure, which accounts for 8–35 per cent of the budget in the dozen SSA countries for which there are data (incomplete and unreliable), is a favourite suggestion by many outsiders (e.g. UNDP*a* 1996).[12] In this context, it has to be recalled that over the past 10–15 years, there has been more-or-less fierce civil war in at least a dozen SSA countries. Moreover, all but a handful of the 50 countries in the region do share at least one border with a country in strife during this period. In addition, nearly half the number of refugees, returnees, and internally displaced persons in the world, estimated at 27 million, are found in Africa (IBRD 1997*a*: fig. 8.2). It may thus seem unrealistic to expect significant disarmament until Africa has become a more peaceful place.

(4) *Reallocation of Expenditures within the Health and Education Budgets*   As noted by Leighton (1996), the World Bank (IBRD*a* 1993), Knight *et al.* (1993), and several other observers, the provision of government health services in the African countries is highly pro-urban biased (and thus anti-poor). The standard advice that the African governments get is to spend less on curative health in big hospitals in the cities and more on primary, preventive health care in rural clinics (IBRD*a* 1993, 1994: p. 104). The expectation is that if such a reallocation were to take place, mortality would decline. However, as noted by the World Bank (IBRD 1994: p. 173): 'there is little discernible movement towards primary health care or basic health services'.

(5) *Efficiency*   Finally, there is the option of getting more out of the resources that are devoted to public health and education by improving efficiency. (As the evidence presented in Chapter 16 reveals, the outcome–input ratios in the health and education sectors are drastically low in the SSA countries in international comparison.) This includes questions of which subsectors to target and what kind of interventions should be given priority, e.g. immunization, health infrastructure, etc. To what extent should decisions on health care and education be decentralized? Should children be targeted especially? What role should the private sector have for health-care insurance and for higher education? Should vocational training, as stressed by the World Bank, be a priority sector? These, and related questions, are highly controversial (political) and the number of stakeholders with different interests is large. This is so not only within respective countries—the foreign lender/donor community is not in agreement either. WHO and the UNDP favour public primary health and basic education in general, UNICEF wants resources to be allocated to children, the World Bank wants more private incentives and efficiency (growth), and all bilateral donors have their own priorities. All this suggests that it will not be easy to reach a consensus on what would be the best strategies for efficiency improvements (see also Appleton *et al.* 1996: p. 330, Leighton 1996: p. 1517).

17.5. PROSPECTS FOR REFORM

From a purely technical point of view, there is considerable 'room' for more and better public education and health-care provision in the African countries. Even with a present per-capita income in the average SSA country of a little above 1,000 US dollars in purchasing power parity, significant increases in per-capita expenditures on health and education can be attained through budget reallocations (especially by cutting government finance to loss-making public enterprises and a reduction of 'excess' employment in the public sector). Most SSA countries have public expenditures corresponding to 25–30 per cent of GNP. If half of these expenditures were allocated to the health, education, and nutrition sectors (as in Costa Rica in the 1970s), this would mean a per-capita expenditure of 150 dollars, a sevenfold increase compared to the actual situation (see Table 16.4). Moreover, observations from other countries suggest that *if* increased expenditures—even of lower magnitudes—could be used more efficiently and be better targeted to the most vulnerable in the respective population, mortality and deprivations of functions could be reduced.

17.5.1. Preconditions for Change in Political Priorities

The wasting of huge resources in most African countries on loss-making state enterprises and an oversized public bureaucracy may seem totally irrational from an efficiency point of view. But efficiency is one thing; distribution and political priorities are other concerns. The pro-urban bias in public health and education provision is not a random outcome, but a reflection of political priorities. The urban population, relatively well-off compared to the rural, exerts strong political pressure for hospital-based services and higher education that few African governments so far have not complied with. As the World Bank (under)states the problem: 'A strong focus by governments on poverty reduction is not evident' (IBRD 1997*b*: p.17).

The prospects for radical political change in the great majority of the African countries in the near future may seem bleak. That some 30 countries in the region have held some form of election since the late 1980s does not mean that they have become truly 'democratic'. As *The Economist* (1996) notices, the cynical view of democracy in Africa is that it is mostly 'donor democracy', i.e. 'just enough to keep aid-givers happy'. There are no indications that the rural vote has become more influential in decisions of where and how to allocate public expenditure. Whatever reforms some countries have made in the public sector, there are few signs yet of higher priority of rural basic health care and education (IBRD 1994, 1997), although Zambia in the 1990s is a possible exception.[13]

Whether the political priorities are likely to change in the future one may speculate about, but, presumably, a reallocation of existing resources from urban hospitals and schools to rural facilities would necessitate different types of governments in most of Africa, with a much stronger rural base and concern for equity at the country level. One can envisage such a change—if the present feeble democratization process in the African countries gains momentum—and the rural vote becomes important, but that is yet to be realized and may take considerable time.

Some of the basic preconditions for more long-term radical and *concensual* political change are not the best. First of all, almost all African countries are considerably more heterogeneous in terms of ethnicity, religion, and traditions than are Costa Rica, Jamaica, Sri Lanka, and most, but not all, other developing countries. Two of the largest, and potentially most explosive SSA countries, Nigeria and the Congo (formerly Zaïre), both contain some 200 ethnic groups. Even a small country like Guinea–Bissau, with one million people, has 23 ethnic groups within its borders. Only Swaziland, also with one million people, is ethnically homogeneous. Moreover, the most dominant private-sector economic groups are often non-indigenous, such as the Lebanese in West Africa and the Asians in East Africa.[14]

Furthermore, practically none of the present African countries has a history of being a national state. The colonial powers—no doubt—carved up Africa with little or no regard for the ethnic geography at the Berlin conferences in the 1880s. But the colonial powers did not break up what were earlier national states. Most of pre-colonial Africa was without formal borders, and huge waves of migration over several hundreds of years changed the ethnic map constantly. Few of the more than 1,000 ethnic groups in Africa can claim long-term historical rights to a well-specified territory. In many places several ethnic groups have lived side-by-side for generations, sometimes in harmony, sometimes in conflict. The absence of a tradition of their being national states seems to be reflected in present day political life in these countries, where frequent internal wars are much along ethical lines and where the group in power 'takes all' (see also Easterly and Levine 1997).

Power sharing and consensus building do not seem to be part of the political realities in Africa yet. At the same time, as stressed by Leighton (1996), ACC/SCN (1996), and many others, including the World Bank (IBRD 1994), building consensus on public priorities is a crucial and necessary precondition for more favourable development in most of the African countries.

17.5.2. Why Growth is Necessary (but not Sufficient) for Enhancing Well-being

Experience from the past 30 years, together with an (admittedly subjective) assessment of the present political realities in most African countries, suggests that for them to emulate the 'equity-oriented countries' is not a realistic political prospect in the short term. The political will is not there, as manifested in the reluctance to comply with the structural-adjustment reforms that are primarily aimed at redefining the role of the government and to undertake public sector changes that could improve the conditions for the rural poor (making up the great majority of most African countries). However, even if there were to be an unexpected radical change in the political priorities in some African countries in the not-so-distant future, there are several reasons why African governments would be wise not to concentrate all their efforts on directly equity-enhancing policies, but also growth.

(1) *The Long-term Perspective*   To rely on economic growth may seem too long-term a method to accomplish improvements in human well-being in the presently poorest countries, most of which are found in SSA. However, as argued above, the experience from the equity-oriented countries suggests that it has taken them many decades to accomplish what they have done. To expect that the African countries should be able to achieve similar results in a significantly shorter period is wishful thinking. The reliance on public-sector interventions as the chief instrument for enhancing human well-being more profoundly is probably as long-term a policy as is reasonably rapid growth.

(2) *Limits to Improvements*   Reallocation of expenditures in the government budget is a technically feasible way of expanding expenditures on basic education and primary health care in rural areas. If conducted, one would expect some improvements in health outcomes also in the not-so-long term. However, whatever the size of these improvements, they would be *once-and-for-all gains* (even though the reforms might take decades to implement). Present real-income levels are too low in SSA to generate enough government revenue to improve *substantially* and extend public health care. Incomes are also too low for the ordinary citizen to be able to afford sufficient health services in a system based on user fees or paid for through the tax system. Without growth of real per-capita income, neither supply nor demand for services will be enough to ensure sufficiently large improvements in health outcomes in SSA over the longer term.

(3) *Demand Side*   There is a widespread tendency to see the solution to the problem with education as one of expanding supply only. The World Bank, most bilateral donors, and most non-governmental organizations (NGOs) have pressed for an 'education-for-all' policy in the African countries. Such a policy may sound warranted from an equity point of view, but a failure to realize that demand for education may be very low in large sections of the population (see Chapter 16) can lead to serious policy mistakes. In order to create demand, returns on education must be relatively high. It is difficult to see how that would come about in totally stagnant or declining economies. If growth is not restored, demand for education is apt to remain low, which in turn has a negative impact on growth and a vicious circle is established.

There are also demand constraints in the health sector, although not as clear as for education. Several studies have shown that demand for health services, even when provided 'for free', depends on the opportunity cost (of the time it takes to consult the medical service), the distance to the clinic, the cost of transportation, and many other things related to personal income. Also, lack of education has been shown to affect demand for health services negatively. Low quality of public health services and long waiting times are also reported to reduce demand (for more detailed discussions of demand-side constraints in the health sector, see Appleton *et al.* 1996, Brockerhoff and Derose 1995, Gilson *et al.* 1995).

(4) *Private-Good Constraints*   A development strategy focused on enhancing human well-being solely through a quantitative expansion and quality improvement of public provision of health and education services is to disregard the importance of 'private' goods. Private goods are not only providing material welfare in the traditional 'utilitarian' sense (which most people probably regard as essential). Many private goods are also important for health and other capabilities. Housing and sanitation are the most evident examples; others include means of transportation to schools and health clinics, and radio and television receivers that (at best) are important channels for information and education. Without growth, there will be no increase in the real purchasing power of the population and, thus, no possibility of consuming more essential private goods. The old saying that 'man cannot live on bread alone' is no more true than 'man cannot live on health care alone'.

(5) *Political Will*   Finally, there is the question of political will to undertake redistribution. In a totally stagnant (or declining) economy all forms of redistribution towards the poorest population segments inevitably entail reduced absolute standards for the not-so poor—relatively speaking. The tolerance for redistribution from these groups is likely to be at least somewhat higher in a growing economy, where this could take place without *absolute* losses for those paying.

17.6.   SUMMARY AND CONCLUSIONS

Recent findings in the empirical growth literature lend new support to the long-standing claim that the optimal development path is 'growth with equity'. Growth without equity and/or ill-targeted public interventions—as exemplified by Brazil and Indonesia[15]—generate suboptimal amounts of human capital, which tends to slow down future growth. 'Excessive' focus on public-sector action with disregard to growth will leave many important material needs unsatisfied and hinder future expansion of public-sector activities. It is not a question of putting all efforts on 'growth' or 'equity'. Balanced growth, not in terms of simultaneous expansion of all (private) sectors, as advocated by Nurkse (1953) and argued against by Hirschman (1958) some 45 years ago, but balanced between private sector and public sector, seems to be the most promising route ahead. What this optimal balance is in a particular country is, of course, not possible to tell, and it varies according to many country-specific circumstances that have to be assessed.

Many of the required reforms in the African countries are likely to be beneficial for both growth and equity, or at least they could be. The public-sector reforms that are needed to enhance efficiency and growth can free substantial government revenue that can partly be used to improve and extend public provision of basic health and educational services. Trade liberalization and the move towards equilibrium exchange rates will induce shifts in relative prices that are likely to favour net-producers of food and agricultural products, i.e. the rural poor.

A further conclusion is that there seems to be no quick way of improving living conditions in Africa. Public sector interventions to bring about lower mortality and better education cannot be implemented efficiently overnight. The achievements of Costa Rica, Jamaica, and Sri Lanka, as well as South Korea and Taiwan, have long traditions. Some of the equity-oriented reforms in these countries were initiated about a 100 years ago.

Although both political and economic prospects for changes that would stimulate growth as well as social development may look bleak—for roughly the same reasons—in Africa at present, one should recall that 'history' has played tricks with economic forecasting before. In the early 1960s, most economists, to the extent that they even noticed South Korea, considered the country a basket case and no one really anticipated the remarkable development that started a few years later (and continued at least up to 1997). It should be remembered that in 1965, Korea and Ghana had about the same GNPc and child mortality rates (IBRD 1994, UNICEFa 1996). Only 30 years later, Korea had a GNPc about five times larger, and a child mortality rate one-eighth of that of Ghana. Who predicted in the late 1970s, that China would take off as one of the fastest growing countries 1980–97? China, with a state-regulated macroeconomy, a vast and highly inefficient state enterprise sector, and hundreds of million peasants working in low-productivity agriculture, seemed to be doomed to economic stagnation. There is still no comprehensive and widely shared explanation of the Chinese growth record (Borensztein and Ostry 1996), but it is not entirely unlikely that part of the answer lies in the fact that almost the entire population was literate when the economic reforms were initiated and that health standards were comparatively good (Drèze and Sen 1995), as judged by life expectancy at birth. This is not, however, the case in the African countries of today.

NOTES

1. Young's results and conclusions have been debated: see, for instance, Ranis (1995) and Krugman (1994).

2. A recent World Bank study has identified over 100 major episodes of bank insolvency in ninety countries since the late 1970s (IBRDa 1997: p.68). Some of these bank crises carried fiscal costs that corresponded to an estimated 30 per cent of GDP, but in most cases considerably less.

3. Many examples suggest that that a government is formally democratic is no guarantee for public provision of adequate health and education services, e.g. India (Drèze and Sen 1995) and Brazil.

4. For accounts of why such movements have largely failed to get political influence in two other formal democracies, India and Brazil (since 1987), see Drèze and Sen (1995) and Weyland (1996).

5. See Lipton and Ravallion (1995: pp.2602–20) for more details. Also see IBRDa (1990, 1994) as well as Chen et al. (1994) and AsDB (1997: pp.285–6).

6. The following sections of this chapter are focused mainly on SSA. For a policy-oriented analysis of India, the dominant country in South Asia, see Drèze and Sen (1995).

7. See Easterly and Levine (1997: footnote 2) for references to a large set of studies aimed at explaining the 'African Growth Tragedy' by various methods.

8. See Sharer et al. (1995) for an assessment of development and growth in Uganda.

9. Sala-i-Martin (1997) also finds a dummy variable for the SSA countries significantly negative and robust. This indicates that there are additional (omitted) variables in his tests that also affect growth adversely in the SSA countries.

10. The parameters discussed in this section are not amenable to normal and internationally accepted policy alterations. If wars and ethnic cleansing are considered policy tools, of which we have seen plenty in Africa, the picture becomes different.

11. In 1996 an additional increase took place, which induced the IMF to cancel loans.

12. According to the highly uncertain data provided by the UNDPa (1996: table 19), defence spendings in SSA increased from 2.1 per cent of GDP in 1985 to 2.9 per cent in 1994. According to the World Bank, there has been a slight decline over the past 10 years (IBRDa 1997: box 8.5).

13. Zambia increased the share of government expenditure going to social sectors to 59 per cent in 1995, up from 23 per cent in 1980 (IBRDa 1997: end table 14).

14. That ethnical diversity is not an *absolute* hindrance to economic growth and public provision of basic services of good quality to most of the populations is exemplified by Malaysia.

15. For assessments of this in Indonesia, see Deolalikar (1995), and van de Walle (1995c) and Weyland (1996) for Brazil. Tendler and Freedhaim (1994) contains an interesting story of how a local government in north-eastern Brazil managed to reduce child mortality drastically in a few years through efficiency reforms in the public sector.

18

Synthesis and Conclusions

18.1. INTRODUCTION

Chronic undernutrition is one of the most deplorable manifestations of the poverty and deprivation that still plague millions of people in the world at the beginning of the twenty-first century. There is wide agreement on this: in November 1996, representatives of 186 countries signed a declaration at the World Food Summit in Rome with the aim of halving the number of the undernourished before the year 2015. Subsequently, various working groups within the FAO, other international organizations, and national agencies with a mandate in the world nutrition sphere, have begun to design strategies on how to implement this resolution.

In order for any strategy to stand a possibility of accomplishing the objective of halving undernutrition, a number of preconditions have to be fulfilled. First, there has to be an agreement on *what* constitutes undernutrition and how undernutrition should be defined and measured. In the absence of such concretization, the objective of 'halving' the number of undernourished people becomes inoperational and meaningless. Secondly, in order to direct policy, the undernourished (as defined) have to be identified: *who* are they and how many are they? We also have to know *where* they are, globally, nationally, regionally, and by type of location (such as urban versus rural areas) and *when* they are undernourished. We also have to understand *why* they are undernourished. These are all necessary (although not sufficient; see below) preconditions for improvement of the nutritional situation in the developing countries through new policy initiatives.

Much of this book has been devoted to scrutinizing existing methods for answering the questions posed above. In the following section (18.2) we shall summarize the reasons why the FAO measurement approach is incapable of providing appropriate answers to these questions. In section 18.3, the merits and demerits of the only alternative approach—anthropometrics—are summarized, and ways of improving on this method are discussed. In section 18.4, the focus is on findings concerning the role of (primary) undernutrition relative to other forms of deprivation (such as illness) in explaining premature deaths and functional impairments. The main contrasts between SSA and South Asia are the focal point in section 18.5. In section 18.6, the main policy strategies for reducing poverty and undernutrition are summarized.

The chapter closes with some reflections on what it would take in resources and political priorities, at the international as well as national levels, to 'reduce hunger by half before 2015', the bold and well-intended chief resolution adopted at the World Food Summit.

18.2. WHY THE FAO MEASUREMENT APPROACH FAILS

The FAO is the only provider of estimates of the prevalence of overall undernutrition in the world that are purportedly comparable across countries and over time. This is perhaps the chief reason why these estimates are so widely cited and, also, why the FAO was honoured with the role as convenor of the World Food Summit. The FAO estimation model is seemingly quite simple and easy to comprehend at a superficial level. It contains only three parameters: national per-capita availability of calories, the distribution (function) of calories across households, and a calorie requirement norm (a cut-off point). On closer scrutiny, however, which was undertaken in Chapters 5–10 above, the FAO estimation model is not reliable and robust enough to provide policy-relevant information on any of the questions to which we need answers.

18.2.1. The What Question

The general broad definition used by the FAO, and also WHO and the UNU, is not subject to much controversy. Few would disagree with the notion that an habitual calorie *intake* below the calorie *expenditures* required to work enough to earn a (minimum) income and to maintain a body weight that is consistent with health and mental and physical capabilities—the essence of the FAO/WHO/UNU definition (see p. 21 above)—is inadequate. The problems arise when this general definition is to be operationalized. First, there are several scientific issues concerning minimum energy requirements that are unresolved and highly controversial, e.g. whether there is costless intra-individual adaptation to low energy intake, what is the health-consistent minimum body weight, and how large are inter-racial differences in metabolism, all of which the FAO has not resolved satisfactory. Secondly, minimum energy expenditure requirement differs between individuals and households. For individuals, it differs owing to differences in stature, body build and, above all, in the kind of work they pursue in order to earn a living (as more formally demonstrated in Chapter 3). Across households, which is the unit of measurement in the FAO model, the per-capita calorie requirement also differs, because of differences in age and sex composition. The FAO calorie cut-off points, used to determine *what* undernutrition is, fail to take such differences into proper consideration.

18.2.2. *The* Who *Question*

The FAO does not purport that its aggregate estimation method can be used to identify the individuals and/or households that are undernourished. The method thus cannot be used as a screening device for targeted intervention, which is one of the purposes for which we need indicators of undernutrition. The method can only be used—at best—to obtain estimates of the share of a large population that falls below what FAO considers to be an 'acceptable' minimum calorie intake. Inherent in the method is that some households are erroneously classified as undernourished when they are not, while other households are classified as well-nourished when in fact they are not. This is because the FAO uses a single calorie cut-off point for all households, when, in reality, minimum requirements vary across households for reasons stated above (Chapter 9). The FAO freely admits this, but the organization claims that the two errors tend to cancel out so that unbiased estimates of the share of a population that is undernourished are obtained. If so, we are provided with national estimates that could be used for targeting countries for intervention, a worthwhile purpose for which nutrition indicators are needed.

In Chapter 5, a simple test was conducted that showed the FAO estimates of the prevalence of undernutrition to be highly sensitive to relatively small variations in the values (plus or minus 10 per cent) of the three parameters that comprise the model. The test was conducted for the SSA countries, for which the estimated parameter values contain the largest margin of uncertainty. The test revealed that anything between 21 and 61 per cent of the population in SSA falls out as undernourished, depending on the combination of parameter values. In subsequent Chapters (6–9) the empirical support for the plus/minus range of uncertainty was presented. The unambiguous conclusion is that, given the uncertainty of the appropriate parameter values, the FAO method is not capable of producing estimates of the prevalence of undernutrition in the African countries that are reliable enough to have any policy relevance. The method is simply not robust enough; this conclusion definitely holds for SSA, but is valid also for most other parts of the world, including South Asia.

18.2.3. *The* Where *Question*

In order for targeted intervention to be feasible, the location of the under-nourished has to be identified. In which parts of the world are they predominantly found: in which countries, in which districts, in rural or urban areas? Up until quite recently, the FAO had published only estimates of the prevalence of undernutrition for five large geographical areas; this was the case in the main document produced for the *World Food Summit* (FAO*a* 1996). Estimates for such large aggregates of countries could have policy relevance for some questions, such as whether the international organizations and the bilateral donors concerned with undernutrition should concentrate their efforts mainly on SSA or South Asia. This is provided, of course, that the FAO estimates give an accurate indication of where the undernutrition problems are the most pressing, which is not the case (see section 18.5.2 below).

As late as in 1996, the FAO considered its estimates of the prevalence of undernutrition in individual countries too uncertain to be published—that only broad aggregates in which the country errors (if random) tend to be offsetting, were reliable enough. At the World Food Summit, it was widely, and rightfully, claimed that more disaggregated estimates of incidence of undernutrition are needed to direct policy. In response to these demands, the FAO published its estimates for individual countries shortly after the Summit in the form of a poster (FAO 1997a). The FAO also expressed a readiness to provide subnational estimates, if provided with a mandate and the required funding (FAO 1997c).

As hopefully convincingly demonstrated in Chapters 5 to 10, the FAO method is not reliable enough to provide policy-relevant estimates of the prevalence of undernutrition, even at the broad regional level. There are several conceptual and theoretical issues to be resolved, and data collection has to be extended and improved, before anything ressembling reliable estimates at this high level of aggregation, or for individual countries, can be obtained. *Some* of these issues could be resolved if enough time and money were invested, others probably not (Chapter 10). Moreover, there is also remaining doubt as to whether the effort would be worthwhile, considering that alternative estimation methods are more reliable. To apply the present, or a slightly modified, version of the FAO model to estimate prevalence of undernutrition at the subcountry level would be a waste of resources and time. The data needs are simply enormous: not only would the inter-household distribution of intakes in each and every district have to be estimated, but also the relation of these distributions to the distributions of requirements.

18.2.4. *The* When *Question*

The *when* question can be divided into several subquestions to which one needs answers in order to target interventions efficiently. One such question is of when in life the risk of undernutrition is the highest. This question cannot be answered with the FAO method, which is aimed at estimating the availability of calories at the level of households, or rather large (income) groups of households. The extent to which young children and women are the main victims of undernutrition, which is a central question for many concerned with nutrition, thus cannot be answered with the FAO measurement approach (while it can with the anthropometric approach; see below). In fact, the whole question of intra-household distribution of food is beyond the reach of the FAO method.

For policy purposes, information is also needed on inter- and intra-year variations in the prevalence of undernutrition in specific locations. These are yet more *when* questions that cannot be answered by the FAO methodology, which is designed to allow for annual variations in aggregate food supplies only. Changes over time in energy requirements and in the level and distribution of effective demand over food cannot be handled with the FAO method.

18.2.5. The Why Question

In short, the FAO answer to the *why* question is that aggregate food supplies are too low. With the FAO model about 90 per cent of the inter-country variation in the prevalence of undernutrition is explained by differences in estimated per-capita availability of calories. The remaining 10 per cent are due to (FAO) estimated differences in requirements following from differences across countries in demographic composition and (slight) differences in the distribution of calories across households within countries.

In various other tests, up to two-thirds of the variation in weight-for-age failure for under-5-years-olds is explained by variables such as differences in per-capita income, the degree of urbanization and a South-Asian dummy variable (Chapter 14). Similar results have been obtained in several cross-household investigations, where parental (adult) literacy and various public services also turn out significant (see section 18.3.5). This type of explanatory variable does not enter the FAO model; here aggregate food supply is the only variable of significance.

The FAO further estimates that the total food availability failure in the developing countries corresponds to some 2–3 per cent of world food supplies. This is roughly equal to the annual variations in the long-term trend of global food production. Had global food availability—trade in main staple food products is relatively free—been the predominant explanation for undernutrition, we would thus have seen little undernutrition in years of global plenty and severe undernutrition in years of global shortage. No such swings can be observed. To focus mainly on food availability, global or national, is to ignore the nowadays widely shared view in almost all quarters—except for the FAO—that poverty, or insufficient food entitlements (Sen 1981*a*), in large sections of the population in many countries is the chief cause of undernutrition and other forms of human deprivation. To apply the availability-biased model for estimation of prevalence of undernutrition is to start on the wrong foot and proceed in the wrong (policy) direction.

18.3. WHY ANTHROPOMETRICS ARE PREFERABLE

The only alternative to the FAO (and related) approach(es) of estimating the prevalence of undernutrition is the use of anthropometric indicators.[1] With some modifications and extensions, to be suggested below, anthropometric indicators do provide more accurate and meaningful answers to all the questions raised above.

18.3.1. The What Question

The basic advantages of the anthropometric approach are simplicity and accuracy. The FAO method relies on estimates of energy intakes, requirements, and the distribution of the two in large populations (countries), which are impossible to obtain with accuracy, as discussed at length in Chapters 8 and 9. The anthropometric approach is based on the notion that when a person's intake is below his/her calorie minimum expenditure requirement, this shows up in body deformation, i.e. in low weight (for age or height) and growth retardation (in children and adolescents). These deformations are easy and inexpensive to measure at the level of individuals.

All this is not to say that the anthropometric method is devoid of problems when it comes to answering the question of *what* undernutrition is. If one adheres to the genetic-potential-for-growth paradigm of defining undernutrition, the individual's height is the theoretically appropriate indicator of habitual nutritional status before adulthood and a marker of the nutritional history of adults. The problem is that the genetic potential for growth cannot be observed at the level of individuals. The method thus cannot be used to identify all those who have failed to reach their own potential for growth. Within this paradigm, anthropometrics can only be used to estimate the share of a population that fails, but much more accurately so than the FAO approach.

If one adheres to the adjustment-and-adaptation paradigm, the anthropometric approach is also relatively accurate for identifying undernutrition in individuals. Within this paradigm, it is not height in relation to the individual's genetic potential that is the hallmark of undernutrition, but rather the height (for age) below which there are measurable impairments in terms of increased morbidity and mortality risk and functional incapability. If a certain individual is below the critical low height (or weight), there is only a few per cent probability that this low height is attributed to undernutrition/illness when the true explanation is low individual genetic potential for growth (Chapters 11 and 13).

A common problem with all anthropometric measurements is that they do not capture undernutrition in the sense of an unduly low level of physical activity. As observed by Martortell (1995), we do not know much about how people (especially children) react to an insufficient calorie intake. Do they start by losing weight and slowing-down growth, followed by reduced physical activity? Or is the first line of defence reduced activity followed by anthropometric failure? In the first case, anthropometrics capture also those who are undernourished in the activity dimension, while this is not so in the second case (Chapter 13). Here there seems to be an urgent need for research to determine in what sequence people react to low calorie intakes.

Yet another problem with anthropometrics is where to set the cut-off points for 'non-acceptable' deviations from norm heights and weights. If one accepts the AA paradigm, and sees increased mortality risk as the most serious outcome of undernutrition, the conventional cut-off points (2 SD below the reference mean for children) seem relevant. Several sample studies (reviewed and summarized by Pelletier 1994) demonstrate significantly elevated mortality risk below these cut-off points, and that the risk increases with additional failure. (It should further be recalled that the problems of defining the weight for age, or height, that delineate undernutrition, are the same for the FAO and the anthropometric approaches.) With the AA paradigm, undernutrition is simply a weight or height below which there is discernible increased risk of premature mortality and/or health and functional impairments.

18.3.2. The Who Question

Until recently, the anthropometric approach was used almost exclusively to estimate undernutrition among children under the age of five. Only during the 1990s, have a few more systematic attempts been made to collect anthropometric observations also for women of reproductive age and, to a very small extent, adolescents. These new data sets are far too few and non-representative, however, for allowing comparisons with children at the country or district levels. Moreover, there are no anthropometric data for adult males and old people of either sex. The anthropometric evidence available today thus does not have sufficiently broad coverage to allow us to answer the question of who the undernourished are. A number of extensions and refinements are required.

First, and most obvious, the collection by the international organizations of anthropometric data has to be extended to all age categories. This would not only increase our knowledge of in what age/sex categories anthropometric failure is the most prevalent. Today, it is often claimed that small children and women are the chief victims of undernutrition. It may well be so, but this is merely assumed rather than known (adolescents are a sensitive group not sufficiently studied). In the endeavour to derive anthropometric norms for adults, it is important that these are reasonably comparable with those applied to small children. A related point is that it would be preferable if the anthropometric status of all members of (randomly) selected households were estimated at the same point in time. Such measurements would provide valuable information on the allocation of resources within households as well as the reasons for anthropometric failure of individuals (as suggested by Payne 1992).

Secondly, in order to increase our knowledge of who the undernourished are and their number, sample sizes will have to be increased in many countries with large and diverse populations; the existing samples are often too small to be representative. It also seems that more has to be done to ensure that the reported age bias in the child populations is reduced in future collection of anthropometric measures.[2]

Thirdly, on the question of how many or how large a share of a specific population are undernourished, each of the three most commonly used anthropometrics indicators provides downward-biased figures. That is, none of these indicators delineate all children who fail by one or more of the three norms for stunting, underweight, and wasting. If each of these three failures carries risks of impairment, which seems to be the case (Pelletier 1994), we need an indicator that captures all children with at least one such failure. The Composite Index of Anthropometric Failure (CIAF) proposed in Chapter 13, is such an indicator.

18.3.3. The Where Question

The anthropometric approach, focusing on individuals, allows a much more detailed identification of where the undernourished are found than the aggregate food-supply-based FAO approach. This is so especially if the anthropometric coverage is extended to include all age categories, as discussed above. As of now we have estimates almost exclusively for children below the age of five. For this age group we have a fairly good picture of where they are found in terms of major geographical region (South Asia) and in what countries (India, Bangladesh, and some SSA countries). We also have fairly extensive evidence, showing that they are found predominantly in rural rather than urban areas. There are also indications from some countries that there are large variations in the prevalence of anthropometric failure across districts within countries.

In order to allow more precise geographical identification, and targeting when required, more detailed anthropometric observations are needed. At present there are no anthropometric data by main districts in most countries. If the detailed 'hunger maps' that were demanded at the World Food Summit are to become reality, anthropometric observation must be extended to the district level in all developing countries.

18.3.4. The When Question

The question of *when* in life people are at the greatest risk of becoming undernourished can only be answered if, again, the anthropometric measurement coverage is extended to all age categories. As of now we only know that, by the weight-for-age indicator for under-5-year-olds, there is a peak between 24 and 36 months of age. However, not only are we in need of anthropometric assessment of all age categories, we also need longitudinal observations of the same individuals. Such observations are needed to answer the question of to what extent anthropometric failure early in life (below the age of three or five) is the explanation for short stature in adulthood, with the negative consequences for health and functions that this entails. As of now, only a few such studies have been undertaken (Martorell 1995: p.19).

In order to monitor trends in prevalence of undernutrition in individual countries, more frequent anthropometric assessment is required. As we saw in Chapter 11, 'time-trends' for countries are estimated by the WHO/UNICEF by interpolation between estimates for 2 (occasionally 3) years. Since there are large annual fluctuations, experience for a few countries with more frequent observations suggests that such 'interpolated trends' are highly unreliable. There is also evidence from a few countries that suggests large intra-year (seasonal) fluctuations in the incidence of anthropometric failure. Again, to answer the question of when people are the most prone to undernourishment, more frequent observation has to be undertaken in the great majority of countries so as to facilitate efficient targeting in the time dimension.

18.3.5. The Why Question

Despite the many attempts that have been made to isolate food inadequacy and illness as the prime *direct* cause of anthropometric failure, little is known. In the most deprived populations, the interaction between illness and food inadequacy is simply too complex and entangled to allow reliable estimation of what comes first.

The basal causes for undernutrition, as manifested in anthropometric failure, we know more about. There are two main sources of evidence. The first is the cross-country investigations. The one reported in Chapter 14 above found per-capita real income, the share of the population living in urban areas, and a dummy variable for South Asian countries to explain almost two-thirds of the inter-country variation in weight-for-age failure in young children. This investigation did not find parental literacy and above-normal provision of public services to be significantly correlated to prevalence of anthropometric failure. The latter result does not, of course, prove that education and public health services are unimportant for child health. Unfortunately, the national data at hand are far too crude and unreliable for allowing strong conclusions either way. However, that parents' education and public provision of basic services, as well as household income, are important for child anthropometric performance is suggested by a large number of inter-household investigations from several individual countries. More such studies based on refined data are required in order to obtain quantitatively more precise knowledge on the relative importance of different 'explanatory' parameters in different parts of the world.

18.4. UNDERNUTRITION VERSUS OTHER REASONS FOR MORTALITY

Anthropometric failure *as such*, especially growth failure, in the wake of primary undernutrition (inadequate access to food) or secondary undernutrition (initiated by illness), is considered by many as a non-acceptable state of human deprivation. This is the position taken by adherents of the so-called Genetic Potential paradigm of undernutrition. Others tend not to see growth failure in itself as the (most) serious manifestation of undernutrition, primary or secondary, but rather the increased risk of health and functional impairments that are associated with anthropometric failure below certain levels. Among these risks, the elevated mortality risk is the best-studied one and also the normatively most serious consequence of undernutrition according to many observers.

18.4.1. Anthropometric Failure and Mortality Risk

There are by now more than a dozen sample studies from Africa and Asia that show mortality risk to increase with the degree of anthropometric failure in child populations. Some of these studies, but not all, find mortality risk to increase more than proportionally with linear anthropometric failure. The studies that have been undertaken so far have all used one or more of the four indicators: being underweight, stunting, wasting, and arm circumference. The best predictors for subsequent death have been being underweight and arm circumference, while results for stunting and wasting are usually weak or, in some studies, even non-existent. Overall, however, the results, including those that are statistically significant, suggest relatively low prediction power of all conventional anthropometric indicators. That is, each of the four anthropometric indicators applied leads to large type I and type II errors (i.e. a large share of the anthropometrically failed children do survive and many of the children with normal anthropometric status do die). This implies that the currently applied anthropometric indicators are relatively imprecise targeting tools.

There are many possible explanations for this, but one likely reason is that the conventional height and weight indicators are too 'aggregated' to allow more precise prediction. For instance, children who are classified as 'wasted' by the conventional standards comprise three anthropometrical subsets: (i) those who are wasted, but have normal height and weight for age, (ii) those who are wasted and stunted and (iii) those who are wasted and stunted as well as underweight. *A priori*, it seems plausible that the children in the third category, with three anthropometric handicaps, face a higher mortality risk than children in the first category, who are thin for their (above) normal height 'only'. Also, the conventional height-for-age and weight-for-age classification groups contain three subsets of failed children (see Chapter 13 for details).

There is thus the possibility that a more disaggregated classification of children according to anthropometric status would lead to smaller errors of both types and, thus, that the screening power would increase and targeting would become more efficient. The simplest possible test of this would be to recalculate the results obtained in some previous studies, using a more disaggregated anthropometric classification of the children (into at least six groups).

18.4.2. Estimated Share of Deaths Attributable to Undernutrition

That undernutrition leads to anthropometric failures and that these failures are associated with elevated mortality risk is not to say that all 'excess' child deaths are caused by undernutrition. The tentative estimates derived in Chapter 14 suggest that 'only' about one-third of all child deaths in SSA can be attributed to anthropometric failure (by the conventional indicators); and one-half in South Asia. These estimates thus suggest that two-thirds and half of all child deaths in SSA and South Asia, respectively, are attributable to other causes, mainly untreated but preventable and curable disease.

Moreover, that one-third of deaths in SSA are attributable to anthropometric failure is not the same as saying that primary undernutrition is the cause in all these cases. An unknown proportion of the anthropometrically failed children are in this state because of illness rather than lack of access to a sufficient amount of food. The one-third figure should thus be interpreted as an upper-bound estimate of the share of children dying primarily because of undernutrition. This observation is not intended to neglect the role of undernutrition as opposed to disease as a cause of excessive child mortality in SSA and South Asia. It is important, however, that, being primarily concerned with nutrition, we do not lose sight of the fact that ill health, unrelated to primary undernutrition, is also a major contributing factor to the human deprivation manifested in the death of millions of children each year in the developing countries.

18.5. CONTRASTING SUB-SAHARAN AFRICA AND SOUTH ASIA

According to all available assessments, a larger proportion of the populations in SSA and South Asia suffer from undernutrition, illness, increased mortality risk, and most other forms of human deprivation than those elsewhere. Also, in terms of absolute numbers of destitute people, these two regions stand out. There are, however, marked differences between these two regions along at least two dimensions, which may seem puzzling.

18.5.1. Puzzle One: Extent of Undernutrition, the FAO versus WHO

According to the FAO, the prevalence of undernutrition is by far the highest in SSA (43 per cent), almost twice as high as in South Asia (22 per cent).

According to the anthropometric indicators provided by WHO, the opposite situation holds. The estimated rate of weight-for-age failure for young children is 58 per cent in South Asia while 'only' 30 per cent in SSA (see Fig. 1.1). Three possible explanations to this puzzle have been examined in previous chapters. One was that the norms used to delineate the undernourished in the respective age categories are in some way distorted. The second was that children fare much worse in relation to adults in South Asia than in SSA. The third was that there are estimation biases in one or both data sets.

The first and second explanations were discharged. Although it has been claimed by authoritative authors (Eveleth and Tanner 1990) that the potential for growth in children differs across ethnic groups, this is not the reason why the prevalence of anthropometric failure for the under-fives is so much higher in (most of) South Asia than in SSA. A very extensive data set, based on observations of children in the most well-to-do Indian households, show them to have approximately the same average potential for growth as African as well as Caucasian children (Chapter 12). The hypothesis that children should fare worse in comparison to adults in South Asia than children in SSA was also found inconsistent with the data. The ratio of anthropometric-failure prevalence in children to that in adult women is several times higher in SSA than in South Asia (see Fig. 11.4). This implies that children in Africa are worse off relative to adults than are children in South Asia, rather than the other way around.

18.5.2. Answer to Puzzle One: The FAO Estimates for Africa are Biased

Having discharged two possible explanations for the 'reversal puzzle' when it comes to conflicting FAO and WHO estimates of relative prevalence of undernutrition in SSA and South Asia, respectively, a third explanation remains. That is, the prevalence of undernutrition in SSA is overestimated with the FAO method. The first reason we found for expecting this was that calorie availability in this region is systematically underestimated by the FAO. The acreage cultivated under major crops is underestimated, and most minor food items are incompletely covered. The primitive average estimation techniques used throughout Africa have previously been shown (in India and Pakistan) to produce estimates that are on average about 25 per cent on the low side (Chapter 6).

Secondly, a vast collection of calorie-consumption estimates obtained in various types of household surveys of African populations that were identified to have *abnormally* low intakes (this being the reason for the survey) come up with per-capita calorie intake estimates that are on a par with the FAO per-capita calorie availability estimates, which are claimed to represent the *normal* state in the population (Chapter 7). Moreover, evidence from admittedly few and unreliable food-consumption surveys suggests that the cost-efficiency of the calorie consumption in SSA is considerably lower than in South Asia. If, as claimed by the FAO, per-capita calorie consumption in Africa is markedly lower than in South Asia, one would expect that the African diet to be more concentrated on cheap calorie sources than in India; the data suggest the opposite.

Thirdly, the anthropometric performance, not only of young children but also for other age categories, is considerably better in Africa than in South Asia. Especially women of reproductive age in Africa are less frequently underweight and exceptionally short than are their South Asian counter-parts. Moreover, the average adult stature, not only of women, but also of men, is somewhat higher in Africa compared with South Asia (but this could be for genetical reasons). The larger body mass of the average African person is only consistent with a lower calorie intake if Africans spend less energy in physical activity than South Asians. There is no conclusive evidence on relative levels of physical activity. All in all, however, the overwhelming evidence suggests that the 'reversal puzzle' is explained by overestimation of the prevalence of undernutrition in SSA by the FAO.[3]

18.5.3. Puzzle Two: Anthropometric Failure and Mortality Reversals

The estimated under-fives mortality rate in SSA is 177 compared with 124 in South Asia. At the same time, the estimated anthropometric failure rates are notably lower in Africa than in South Asia. By the most frequently used indic-ator, weight-for-age, the failure incidence in Africa is only about half that in South Asia (Chapter 11). There are several hypothetical explanations for this 'puzzle'. One is that there are biases and errors in the estimates for the African region, where all statistics are of especially dubious quality. Another is that the disease environment is worse in SSA than in South Asia, while nutrition is better. A third is that whatever the relative prevalence of disease vectors in the two regions, primary-health care provision is less adequate in Africa than in South Asia, leading to a higher mortality/morbidity ratio in the former.

There are no doubt errors in the estimated mortality rates for the African region, and in addition, the estimated anthropometric failure rates are un-reliable. This cannot be the main reason for the reversal puzzle, however. The average mortality and anthropometric failure estimates for the African region are obtained by weighting individual country estimates. Since the latter are obtained independently of each other, and almost every single individual SSA country has an estimated higher mortality rate and a lower anthropometric-failure rate than India and Bangladesh, the two dominant countries in South Asia, there is reason to expect that the 'average' figures do reflect reasonably correct relative orders of magnitude. There are no data on the relative pre-valence of fatal diseases in the two regions, which makes it impossible to in-vestigate this hypothesis at present. (Hopefully, the updated and revised forthcoming WHO/IBRD estimates of the global burden of disease will throw new light on this issue.)

18.5.4. Answer to Puzzle Two: Inadequate Health-care in SSA

Although not perhaps the whole answer, much of the excess mortality in SSA as compared with South Asia must be the relatively less adequate provision of primary health care and other public services that has been shown in many studies to have a bearing on child-survival chances. The African countries do not spend less on health care (and education) than the South Asian countries, and not less than China, which has an excellent health record for its low income (Chapter 16). The main problems in the African region seem to be the uneven allocation of the public health services within the countries and the low quality of the services provided.

By almost every statistic on the populations' access to various (public) services, the share is smaller in Africa than in South Asia. Moreover, the disparity between rural and urban areas is especially large in the African countries. The poor quality of the services is indicated by two sets of observations. One is the (admittedly somewhat subjective) assessments made by various experts in the field. The other is that in the cross-country regressions used to estimate determinants of U5MR, the dummy variable for SSA countries, comes out as significant when other influences are controlled for (including access to public services). Also, all the individual countries that fell out as significant outliers were African (Chapter 15). Inadequate health-care facilities thus seem to be the prime suspect for the exceptionally high child mortality rates in SSA, while undernutrition is a relatively smaller problem than in South Asia.

18.6.   THE POLICY ROUTES AHEAD

To understand *what* undernutrition is and, consequently, most appropriately measured, to know *who* and how many the undernourished are, *where* they are found and *when* undernutrition is the most severe, and *why* there is undernutrition, are necessary preconditions for remedying the problem. This knowledge is by no means sufficient. We also need insight into which policy routes are the most promising, and a political will to pursue these policies.

With some simplification, one may argue that there are two main policy strategies for alleviating undernutrition and other related forms of human deprivation in the two regions where these are the most pressing, SSA and South Asia. One is to rely more heavily on broad-based public actions in the nutrition, health and education spheres.[4] The other is to focus on policies primarily aimed at enhancing overall economic growth.

18.6.1. Public Action: Policy Requirements and Prospects

There is a fair amount of evidence suggesting that significant reductions in child mortality and anthropometric failure can be accomplished through public provision of basic health care and education also in relatively poor countries. This is shown by the experiences of several individual countries, such as Costa Rica, Jamaica, and Sri Lanka (and the State of Kerala in India). Also, cross-country regressions (Chapter 15) demonstrate statistically significant correlations between provision of public services, over and above what is normal for the respective country's income level, and low child mortality rates. There is also a highly significant negative correlation between urbanization and prevalence of anthropometric failure, most likely reflecting the fact that in most developing countries, public-health and education facilities are heavily concentrated in urban areas. These correlations thus corroborate the rather obvious, i.e. that if more resources are spent on primary health care and education, this leads to better health and a lower mortality risk—unless of course, these resources are totally inefficiently used.

In most African countries, there is no lack of opportunity—in the purely technical sense—for reallocating a substantially larger share of current government expenditures to health and education. Large shares of these expenditures are now 'wasted' on subsidies to loss-making government enterprises, and wages and salaries to a bloated public labour force engaged in nonessential activities, or, at worst, ghost workers. There is little doubt that improvements in terms of health and nutrition could be accomplished with existing means, but this would require a fundamental change in political priorities that we so far have seen little of in most African countries.

18.6.2. Economic Growth: Policy Requirements and Prospects

Whatever improvement in social indicators could be accomplished through budget reallocations alone, these would be once-and-for-all gains, of a magnitude far short of what would be acceptable in the long term. If truly substantial improvements are to be accomplished, economic growth has to be restored throughout Africa. Only with much higher per-capita real incomes can the resources for the finance of sufficiently large provision of health and education services be mobilized on the supply side and sufficient demand be generated in the population (Chapter 17). Moreover, in order for economic poverty to decline, growth of total GDP has to be in the 5–6 per cent range in the SSA countries (for present population growth rates and distributions of incomes).

The prospects for substantial growth in the African countries in the near future seem bleak if judged by the findings on determinants of growth in recent empirical research. Of all the growth-enhancing factors identified, only a few can be altered in the short term, such as the real exchange rate and the government budget deficit. Most crucial constraints on growth can be lifted in the long term only, such as inadequate property rights and their enforcement, widespread corruption, inadequate infrastructure, dependence on (inefficient) foreign aid and primary-product exports, low levels of education (human capital), and a small and misallocated physical capital stock. Still other significant factors contributing to low growth are impossible to change at all, e.g. high ethnic diversity, being land-locked, and having a long distance to main markets, or through very drastic action (redrawing borders and ethnic cleansing). In terms of all these medium- and long-term constraints on growth, as well as the irrevocable ones, most African countries have inherently low potential for growth.

The World Bank's projection for only minuscule per-capita growth in SSA for the next decade is unfortunately realistic in the light of the findings in recent quantitative growth research. This, however, in no way invalidates the fact that only through rapid growth is there a possibility of improving substantially the quality of life for the great majority of Africans. Moreover, that the growth potential is low, does not mean that no growth can be achieved. To accomplish relatively high growth is a long-term prospect, but if this is ever to be realized, the process has to start at some point, and the sooner the better. Otherwise, there is a high risk that poverty and undernutrition will become endemic forever in Africa. It is also noteworthy that there seems to be no major trade-off between public action in the 'social' spheres and growth-enhancing policies over a considerable range. Improved health and education have repeatedly been demonstrated to create human capital that is a crucial positive determinant for growth.

18.7.   THE FAO PLAN FOR ACTION: A CRITICAL ASSESSMENT

Declarations and resolutions, even when signed by high-level representatives of 186 countries at the World Food Summit, do not themselves resolve the nutrition problems in the developing countries.[5] They are none the less important for focusing attention—worldwide—on a grave problem and, at best, they may strengthen the political forces in some countries that take the situation of the most deprived population segments seriously. At the very best, the 'Plan of Action' adopted on this occasion may help direct policy in the right direction. We shall therefore end this chapter, and the book, by scrutinizing the objectives and means agreed upon in Rome.

The chief objective in the Rome *Declaration of World Food Security*, adopted at the Summit, is to reduce 'the number of undernourished people to half the present level no later than 2015' (FAO 1997*b*: p.83). From the perspective of developments over the *past* 20 years, this could be a tall order, if one is to judge by the FAO estimates of the scope and location of the undernutrition problem. As we have argued at length in previous chapters, these estimates are fictions, but let us nevertheless take the estimated 841 million undernourished as the starting point for an explorative discussion of what is required to meet the 2015 objective. The 841 million make up 20 per cent of the population in the 'developing' countries, at about 4.1 billion (FAO*a*

1996: table 14). To reduce the number of 'undernourished' to 420 million in the year 2015, taking a projected annual population growth rate of approximately 1.5 per cent into account,[6] implies that the *share* of undernourished people has to drop to about 7 per cent. This, in turn, entails a decline by two-thirds from the present 20 per cent. The FAO estimates suggest that between 1969/71 and 1990/2, the share of undernourished people declined from 34 to 20 per cent. The ambition is thus to speed up the reduction rate substantially. This raises two questions: (i) where is the reduction to take place and (ii) by what means.

18.7.1. *Reduction of Undernutrition: Where?*

The main documents from the World Food Summit, the *6th World Food Survey* (FAO*a* 1996), the *Declaration of World Food Security* and the *Plan of Action* (FAO 1997*b*), are all silent on the question of where the main reductions in undernutrition are supposed to take place. If there are no restrictions on 'where', the objective is much more easily attained than if, for instance, the objective is to reduce the share of undernourished people by half in all major regions (such as SSA and South Asia), or in all individual developing countries.

With no restrictions on 'where', the 2015 objective stands a fair chance of being reached, even in the absence of any new or more forceful policies directed to the poverty-cum-undernutrition problem. What is required, then, is basically that past trends in, first and foremost, China, East, and South-East Asia continue for another decade and a half. By the FAO estimates, the share of the population that went undernourished in this large region, with a present population of approximately 1.7 billion, dropped from 41 per cent in 1969/71 to 16 per cent in 1990/2 (FAO*a* 1996: table 14). In terms of absolute numbers of people, this corresponds to a decline from approximately 480 million undernourished to 270 million over this 22-year period, or a reduction by more than 200 million.

By simply extrapolating this downward trend, estimated undernutrition in this large region will be, if not eliminated, down to relatively low numbers by the year 2015. Postulating some reductions also in the Middle East, North Africa, and Latin America, the objective would be more or less accomplished. As suggested by Fig. 18.1, a halving of the number of undernourished people in China, East, and South-East Asia, the Middle East, North Africa, and Latin America (labelled 'other developing regions' in the figure), from an estimated 370 million in 1990/2 to 185 million in 2015, 'only' requires that past trends continue for another 15 years. One big 'if' in this scenario is, of course, whether the financial turmoil in parts of Asia in 1997–9 turns out to be a temporary phenomenon, or marks a downward shift in long-term economic growth rates. This remains to be seen.

However, even if the optimistic scenario painted above comes true, the objective to reduce the number of 'undernourished' by 420 million must

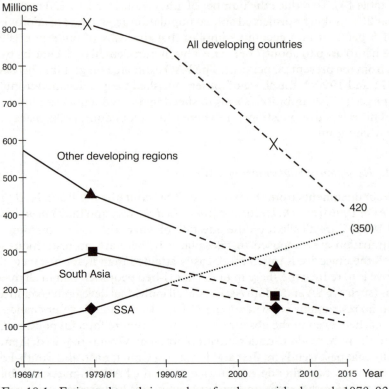

FIG. 18.1. Estimated trends in number of undernourished people 1970–92 and
required reduction if halving by 2015 is to be accomplished

Source: FAO*a* 1996: table 14.

substantially involve both SSA and South Asia. The 'historical' trends for
these two regions do not point at easy, 'business-as-usual' solutions. In South
Asia, the share of the population that were undernourished declined from an
estimated 34 to 22 per cent, while the absolute number fell from about 300
million in 1979/81 to 255 million in 1990/2, according to the FAO. If this
trend continues for another 20 years, the number of undernourished in the
region will be reduced by half by 2015.

In South Asia, it should be noted, there has not been a consistent downward trend in the number of undernourished as estimated by the FAO; between 1969/71 and 1979/81, there was an increase (Fig. 18.1). What will
happen up to 2015 is open to speculation, but hinges a lot on future developments in India, by far the biggest country in the region. If the economic reforms initiated in 1991 are continued and extended, there is a good chance
that economic growth will accelerate (which has as yet not happened) and the
number of undernourished (however measured) substantially reduced. But
whether the latter will happen also depends on the content of growth. If not,

more will be done in the future to involve the poorest population segments through public provision of education and basic health care (see Drèze and Sen 1995), even high growth may not be enough to alleviate poverty and undernutrition (however defined and measured) in this region.

However, whatever happens in South Asia, the biggest challenge is found in SSA, if one is inclined to believe in the FAO estimates. According to these estimates, the *share* of the population that went undernourished in SSA has increased from 38 to 43 per cent during the past 20 years.[7] In *absolute* terms, which is what matters the most here, the estimated number of under-nourished people doubled, to above 200 million. A straight extrapolation of this trend up to 2015 gives a number of undernourished of about 350 million (Fig. 18.1). The order of magnitude of this number clearly indicates that the past trend in this region has to be reversed if the 420 million reduction glob-ally is to be realized. This, in turn, requires new policies, and a crucial ques-tion is—consequently—what 'new' policy actions the FAO recommends in general and for SSA in particular.

If, alternatively, the objective of the Rome Declaration is to reduce the number of undernourished by half—as measured by the number of children who are underweight—the main 'action' has to be in South India rather than in SSA.[8] As revealed by Fig. 18.2, more than half the underweight children in the world are found in South Asia and 'only' some 18 per cent in SSA (in 1995). Moreover, if a decline in the numbers has taken place in South Asia during the past 20 years, it is minuscule. In SSA the number has increased over this period. These numbers point to the fact that if the 2015 objective is to be reached in terms of reduction of underweight children, past trends have to be significantly altered, which require new policies. Again, it becomes interesting as to what new policy alternatives are advanced in the FAO *Plan of Action*.

18.7.2. Reduction of Undernutrition: How?

The brief *Declaration of World Food Security*, the main official summary ana-lysis of the undernutrition problem and the proposed solutions, was pre-pared by the FAO and underwritten by the delegations at the *Summit* in Rome. In this document, one finds many general statements that are not at odds with the policy analysis conducted in Part V of this study. It is rightfully argued that 'Attaining food security is a complex task for which the primary responsibility rests with individual governments' . . . and that 'continued in-adequacy of household and national income to purchase food' is a main reason for undernutrition and that 'poverty eradication is critical to improve access to food'. The document also mentions 'equitable distribution of in-come' and 'access to health care and education' as being important for allevi-ating undernutrition. Quite obviously, the *Declaration* (after all, it is a FAO document) also stresses that increased food production 'must be undertaken'.

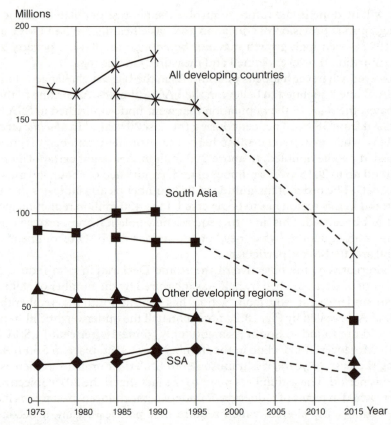

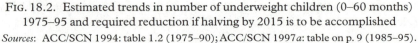

FIG. 18.2. Estimated trends in number of underweight children (0–60 months)
1975–95 and required reduction if halving by 2015 is to be accomplished
Sources: ACC/SCN 1994: table 1.2 (1975–90); ACC/SCN 1997*a*: table on p. 9 (1985–95).

All in all, however, this short document (three pages) gives a balanced and
non-controversial view—although very general—of what are reasons for and,
consequently, solutions to undernutrition (or food insecurity).

The *Plan of Action* is much more detailed: it lists 27 specific objectives and
some 250 one-to-two line proposals for 'action'. This document is also more
amenable to objections. A first critique is that the recommendations are either at a very high level of abstraction or concern details in the poverty-cum-
undernutrition complex, and not much in between. On the highly general
level, the *Plan* stresses the need for peace, human rights, democracy, equal
opportunity, and stable economic conditions. It also sets as one objective to
eradicate, not only poverty, but also *inequality* (the latter objective must be the
boldest and most far-reaching claim for a new world order stated so far in an
international-organization policy document). Most of these are fine objectives, or visions; the problem is that the *Plan* is silent on how all this should be

accomplished. As noted in the *Declaration*, the responsibility for the accomplishment of these objectives rests with individual governments, and many of these (who have also signed the *Plan*) have in the past revealed completely other preferences.

Secondly, when it comes to the more specific objectives and recommendations for action, most of these are more or less directly focused on how to increase food production. The *Plan* is thus heavily biased towards seeing the world nutrition problems as 'food availability failures' rather than income or 'entitlement failures' (although the latter aspects are not totally ignored). The FAO view has thus been allowed to dominate the *Plan*, although it was negotiated with several other 'stakeholders', for whom food production has a less dominate role in explaining nutrition. Moreover, the 'availability' approach favoured in the document is not substantiated with analysis. Increased food production by those who are undernourished could be one way to reduce undernutrition, but the questions of how to reach these, by what means, and to what extent that would be sufficient are not discussed in the *Plan*.

A third (related) objection to the *Plan* is that there is no mention, let alone analysis, of how poverty is to be alleviated and the need for (i) higher incomes (growth) and (ii) more concern for the most deprived population segments in the allocation of government expenditures in the most afflicted countries (in SSA and South Asia). Such an analysis (see Chapters 14–17) would have to address the question why more than half the 186 governments who signed the *Plan* in fact pursue growth-detrimental economic policies and allocate only minuscule shares of the budget to basic health care, primary education, and other public services in rural areas. The question of how substantial poverty reduction and nutrition improvement are to come about without growth, especially in SSA, where the FAO's own estimates suggest undernutrition is the most rampant, is simply ignored. The terms economic growth, real income, and political priorities are not even mentioned. The FAO is obviously not prepared to express even the slightest critique of specific governments or policies, in the way the World Bank and the IMF constantly do.[9]

Fourthly, there is no reflection of an awareness of the possibility that the fundamental reasons for 'undernutrition' are different in different parts of the world and also across countries. For instance, the analysis in Chapters 14–16 above at least tentatively suggests that in SSA, the chief human problem is not low supply of food and primary undernutrition, but rather grossly inadequate health care for large sections of the population. In South Asia, where the anthropometric status of the population is far worse than in Africa, while mortality is considerably lower, primary undernutrition is a chief suspect for the overall deprivation. Any 'plan of action' that fails to recognize such differences over space (and time) is doomed to fail.

In sum, the *Plan* is a non-analytical, highly political document. Airy abstract 'visions' are listed next to one or two-sentence proposals for the need of better food storage, etc. Almost every short proposal is a claim for 'better' and 'more', but there is no analysis of the ways in which all these big and small issues are related and what policy reorientations are needed to accomplish the objectives. Similarly, there is no discussion of political priorities: what kind of macroeconomic environment is required to make all the items on the 'shopping list' feasible to implement? Of course, the *Plan* is the result of a long and tedious political negotiation process involving representatives of 186 highly diverse governments and countries. A 'plan of action' that could be agreed to, without too many reservations,[10] has to be rather general and sweeping. This document, however, has gone so far in this direction that it has become close to empty.

18.7.3. Final Remark

Undernutrition, excessive morbidity, mortality, and illiteracy, are all mani-festations of widespread poverty in large parts of the developing world. There are therefore no partial, sector- or problem-specific final solutions. Under-nutrition cannot be resolved through increases in food supply only; fatal ill-ness cannot be eliminated through vaccination and primary health-care provision; literacy alone is not sufficient to ensure good nutrition and health. The nutritional status of a household is affected by access to food, but also by health care and education. Health status is affected by provision of medical services, but also by nutrition and education. Educationability, in turn, depends on nutrition and health status. In short, all the major markers of human deprivation are part and parcel of the same overall problems: low income and government misallocation of scarce public resources. This has been said before and is accepted in most quarters, although not in the FAO *Plan of Action*. This is why the 'policy strategy' contained in this *Plan* is non-sensical. Any strategy that should stand a chance of becoming successful has to be directed towards the roots of the poverty problem, not at the symptoms.

NOTES

1. By related approaches we mean estimations based on food consumption estimates in the sample population related to estimated requirements (see Chapter 7).
2. There is no known method for coming to grips with the bias in reported age. A common practice is to exclude observations for children for which no verifiable birth certificate is available. This, however, carries the risk that there will be a se-lection bias in that children from the poorest and least-educated households will be over-represented in the excluded group. If these children are more frequently failed, there will also be selection bias in the anthropometric estimates.
3. It is also possible that the FAO has underestimated the prevalence of under-nutrition in South Asia, at 22 per cent, in relation to that in China and South-East

Asia (at 16 per cent). Other indicators suggest a larger discrepancy, but a detailed answer to this 'puzzle' has to await further investigation.

4. It may be argued that there is a third policy route: interventions through *narrowly* targeted programs in order to help the most seriously affected people in specific locations. There are two main reasons why this alternative has not been considered seriously in previous chapters. The first is that the scope of the health and nutrition problems, as judged by the incidence of anthropometric failure among children in most African countries, and even more so in India and Bangladesh, is too large for narrow targeting programs to be meaningful on a national scale. When half the population, or more, is the target group, broad-based interventions are warranted. The other reason is that few fully-fledged nutrition programs have been carried out in SSA and even fewer have been properly evaluated. (See Jennings *et al.* 1991, Gillespie *et al.* 1996, Gillespie and Manson 1991, ACC/SCN 1997*b* for summaries and brief evaluations.)

5. At the World Summit for Children in 1990, the participating governments called for halving the prevalence of underweight children by the year 2000. This ambitious goal was re-endorsed at the International Conference on Nutrition in 1992. It is difficult to detect any explicit actions undertaken by most of the signatory governments to reach the objective. On the contrary, a preliminary assessment of the prevalence of underweight children suggests that during the first half of the 1990s; (i) the worldwide rate of decline has been notably lower than in the 1980s, (ii) in some major regions, the decline has stopped, and (iii) something extraordinary must have happened during 1998 and 1999 if the objective is to be reached (ACC/SCN 1997*a*: p.8).

6. This is the most recent UN (1996) estimate.

7. The FAO estimate, suggesting that there has been no significant *change* in the share of the population in SSA going undernourished, was not contested in previous chapters. What was contested was the level of the prevalence of undernutrition, absolutely, and compared with South Asia.

8. Oddly enough, in none of the main documents from the World Food Summit is there a clear statement regarding which indicator of undernutrition the objective is related to. This could be deliberate since a clarification would undoubtedly lead to difficulties in coming to an agreement between the FAO, which favours its own food-supply based estimates, and WHO/UNICEF, which uses anthropometric measures.

9. It is also noteworthy that signing the *Plan* does not involve any commitment whatsoever of individual governments to undertake any form of *concrete* measure so as to 'reduce undernutrition', as for instance the Rio declaration on the environment did, concerning, above all, reducing the emission of 'greenhouse gases'.

10. About a dozen countries filed reservations, or 'interpretative statements'. Most of these were made by Islamic countries and referred to paragraphs which mentioned 'family planning, population policies and reproductive health'. Also the US made several reservations, e.g. to the end that it saw no legal commitment to be implied in the *Resolution* or in the *Plan of Action*.

REFERENCES

AABY, P. *et al.* (1988), 'Decline in Measles Mortality: Nutrition, Age at Infection, or Exposure?', *British Medical Journal*, 296.

ACC/SCN (1987), *First Report on the World Nutrition Situation*, New York, United Nations.

—— (1988), *Supplement on Methods and Statistics to the First Report on the World Nutrition Situation*, Geneva, WHO.

—— (1989), *Update on the Nutrition Situation*, New York, United Nations.

—— (1992), *Second Report on the World Nutrition Situation, Vol. 1, Global and Regional Results*, Geneva.

—— (1994), *Update on the Nutrition Situation, 1994*, Geneva.

—— (1996), *Update on the Nutrition Situation 1996*, Geneva.

—— (1997*a*), *SCN News*, 14, Geneva.

—— (1997*b*), *SCN News*, 15, Geneva.

—— (1997*c*), *Third Report on the World Nutrition Situation*, Geneva.

ADAMU, S. O. (1989), 'Trends and Prospects for Cassava in Nigeria', Working Paper 5, International Food Policy Research Institute, Washington DC.

ADES, A. and CHUA, H. B. (1997), 'The Neighbor's Curse: Regional Instability and Economic Growth', *Journal of Economic Growth*, 2.

AHLUVALIA, D. (1993), 'Public Distribution of Food in India: Coverage, Targeting and Leakages', *Food Policy*, 18.

AHRIN, K. (1985), *Marketing Boards in Tropical Africa*, London, KPI Limited.

ALAM, N. *et al.* (1989), 'Anthropometric Indicators and Risk of Death', *American Journal of Clinical Nutrition*, 49.

ALESINA, A. and RODRIK, D. (1994), 'Distributive Politics and Economic Growth', *Quarterly Journal of Economics*, 109.

ALI, S. M. and ADAMS, R. H. (Jr) (1996), 'The Egyptian Food Subsidy System: Operation and Effects on Income Distribution', *World Development*, 24.

ALNWICK, D. (1980), 'The Weight, Length and Mid-Upper Arm Circumference of Kenyan Children in Nairobi Nursery Schools', *UNICEF Social Statistics Bulletin*, 1.

ANAND. S and HARRIS, J. C. (1992), 'Issues in the Measurement of Undernutrition', in Osmani (1992*a*).

ANAND, S. and KANBUR, R. S. M. (1991), 'Public Policy and Basic Needs Provision: Intervention and Achievements in Sri Lanka', in Drèze and Sen (1991).

ANAND, S. and RAVALLION, M. (1993), 'Human Development in Poor Countries: On the Role of Private Incomes and Public Services', *Journal of Economic Perspectives*, 7.

APPLETON, S. *et al.* (1996), 'Education and Health in Sub-Saharan Africa', *Journal of International Development*, 8.

AsDB (Asian Development Bank) (1997), *Emerging Asia: Changes and Challenges*, Manila: The Philippines.

ASKEW, E. W. (1995), 'Environmental and Physical Stress and Nutritional Requirements', *American Journal of Clinical Nutrition*, 61.

Asiaweek (1988), 'Growing Up and Up and Up', Tokyo.

ÅSTRAND, P.-O. and RODAHL, K. (1986), *Textbook of Work Physiology*, New York, McGraw-Hill.

ATWATER, W. O. and BENEDICT, F. G. (1899), 'Experiments on the Metabolism of Matter and Energy in the Human Body', *Bulletin*, 69, Washington DC, US Department of Agriculture.

ATWOOD, D. (1990), 'Land Registration in Africa', *World Development*, 18.

BAFFES, J. and SHAH, A. (1998), 'Productivity of Public Spending, Sectoral Allocation Choices, and Economic Growth', *Economic Development and Cultural Change*, 46.

BAIRAGI, R. (1986), 'Effects of Bias and Random Error in Anthropometry and in Age on Estimation of Malnutrition', *American Journal of Epidemiology*, 123.

BARAD, R. (1988), 'Unrecorded Transborder Trade in Sub-Saharan Africa and its Implications for Regional Economic Integration', Mimeo, Washington DC, World Bank.

BARDHAN, P. K. (1979), 'Wages and Unemployment in a Poor Agrarian Economy: A Theoretical and Empirical Analysis', *Journal of Political Economy*, 87.

BARRO, R. J. (1991), 'Economic Growth in a Cross-section of Countries', *Quarterly Journal of Economics*, 106.

—— (1995), 'Democracy and Growth', *Journal of Economic Growth*, 1.

—— and J. W. LEE (1993), 'International Comparison of Educational Attainment', *Journal of Monetary Economics*, 32.

—— —— (1996), 'International Measures of Schooling Years and Schooling Quality', *American Economic Review*, 86.

—— and X. Sala-i-Martin (1995), *Economic Growth*, New York, McGraw-Hill.

BARROWS, K. and SNOOK, J. T. (1987), 'Effects of High-protein, Very-low-calorie Diet on Resting Metabolism and Energy Expenditure on Obese Middle-aged Women', *American Journal of Clinical Nutrition*, 45.

BATES, R. H. (1981), *Markets and States in Tropical Africa: The Political Basis of Agricultural Policies*, Berkeley, University of California Press.

BEATON, G. H. (1983a), 'Energy in Human Nutrition', *Nutrition Today*, September–October issue.

—— (1983b), 'Energy in Human Nutrition: Perspectives and Problems', *Nutrition Reviews*, 41.

—— (1989), 'Small but Healthy? Are We Asking the Right Question?', *Human Organisation*, 48.

—— (1997), 'Prevention and the Role of Nutrition', *SCN News*, 14, Geneva

—— and GHASSEMI, H. (1982), 'Supplementary Feeding Programs for Young Children in Developing Countries', *American Journal of Clinical Nutrition*, 35.

—— et al. (1993), 'Effects of Vitamin A Supplementation of Young Child Morbidity and Mortality in Developing Countries', ACC/SCN, *SOA Papers*, 13.

BEHRMAN, J. R. (1992), 'Intra-household Allocation of Nutrients', in Osmani (1992a).

—— (1993), 'The Economic Rationale for Investing in Nutrition in Developing Countries', *World Development*, 21.

—— (1995), 'Household Behavior and Micronutrients: What We Know and What We don't Know', Agricultural Strategies for Micronutrients Working Paper, 2, International Food Policy Research Institute.

BEHRMAN, J. R. and DEOLALIKAR, A. B. (1987), 'Will Developing Country Nutrition Improve with Income? A Case Study of Rural South India', *Journal of Political Economy*, 95.

—— —— (1988), 'Health and Nutrition', in H. Chenery and T. N. Srinivasan (eds), *Handbook of Development Economics*, Amsterdam, North-Holland.

—— —— (1990), 'The Intrahousehold Demand for Nutrients in Rural South India: Individual Estimates, Fixed Effects and Permanent Income', *Journal of Human Resources*, 25.

—— and ROSENZWEIG, M. R. (1994), 'Caveat Emptor: Cross-country Data on Education and the Labor Force', *Journal of Development Economics*, 44.

BENEFICE, E. *et al.* (1981), 'Surveys on Nutritional Status in Semi-Arid Tropical Areas (Sahel 1976–79): Methods and Results', in IDRC (1981).

BENNELL, P. (1996), 'Rates of Return to Education: Does the Conventional Pattern Prevail in Sub-Saharan Africa?', *World Development*, 24.

—— (1997), 'Privatization in Sub-Saharan Africa: Progress and Prospects During the 1990s', *World Development*, 25.

BERG, E. J. *et al.* (1985), *Intra-African Trade and Economic Integration*, Mimeo, Vols I and II, Alexandria, Virginia.

BESSARD, T. *et al.* (1983), 'Energy Expenditure and Postprandial Thermogenesis in Obese Women Before and After Weight Loss', *American Journal of Clinical Nutrition*, 38.

BHARGAVA, A. (1991), 'Identification and Panel Data Models with Endogenous Regressors', *Review of Economic Studies*, 95.

BIANCA, P. D. *et al.* (1994), 'Lack of Metabolic and Behavioural Adaptation in Rural Gambian Men with Low Body Mass Index', *American Journal of Clinical Nutrition*, 60.

BIRDSALL, N. *et al.* (1994), 'Inequality and Growth Reconsidered: Lessons from East Asia', *World Bank Economic Review*, 9.

BLACK, A. E. *et al.* (1996), 'Human Energy Expenditures in Affluent Societies: An Analysis of 574 Doubly Labelled Water Measurements', *European Journal of Clinical Nutrition*, 50.

BLADES, D. W. (1980), 'What do We Know About Levels and Growth of Output in Developing Countries? A Critical Analysis with Special Reference to Africa', in R.C.O. Matthews (ed.), *Economic Growth and Resources*, Vol. 2, *Trends and Flows*, London, Macmillan.

BLAXTER, K. and WATERLOW, J. C. (eds.) (1985), *Nutritional Adaptation in Man*, London, John Libbey.

BLISS, C. and STERN, N. (1978a), 'Productivity, Wages and Nutrition, Part 1: The Theory', *Journal of Development Economics*, 5.

—— —— (1978b), 'Productivity, Wages and Nutrition, Part 2: Some Observations', *Journal of Development Economics*, 5.

BOHDAL, M. and SIMMONS, W. K. (1969), 'A Comparison of the Nutritional Indices of Healthy African, Asian and European Children', *WHO Bulletin*, 40.

BONGAARTS, J. (1980), 'Does Malnutrition Affect Fecundity? A Summary of Evidence', *Science*, 208.

BOONE, P. (1995), 'The Impact of Foreign Aid on Savings and Growth', Mimeo, London School of Economics.

—— (1996), 'Politics and the Effectiveness of Foreign Aid', *European Economic Review*, 40.

BORENSZTEIN, E. and OSTRY, J. D. (1996), 'Accounting for China's Growth Performance', *American Economic Review*, 86.

BOUIS, H. E. (1994), 'The Effect of Income on Demand for Food in Poor Countries: Are Our Databases Giving Us Reliable Estimates?', *Journal of Development Economics*, 44.

—— and HADDAD, L. J. (1992), 'Are Estimates of Calorie-Income Elasticities too High?', *Journal of Development Economics*, 39.

—— *et al.* (1992), 'Does it Matter How We Survey Demand for Food? Evidence from Kenya and the Philippines', *Food Policy*, 17.

von BRAUN, J. (1988), 'Effects of Technological Change in Cereals Production for Household Level Food Security: Rice in a West African Setting', *World Development*, 16.

—— and PUETZ, D. (1993), (eds.) *Data Needs for Food Policy in Developing Countries: New Directions for Household Surveys*, Washington D.C., International Food Policy Research Institute.

BROCKERHOFF, M. and DEROSE, L. F. (1996), 'Child Survival in East Africa: the Impact of Preventive Health Care', *World Development*, 24.

BURFISHER, M. E. and MISSANEN, M. B. (1987), *Intraregional Trade in West Africa*, Washington DC, USDA, Agriculture and Trade Analysis Division.

BURGESS, A. P. and BURGESS, J. L. (1964), 'The Growth Pattern of East African School Girls', *Human Biology*, 36.

BURNSIDE, B. and DOLLAR, D. (1997), 'Aid Policies and Growth', *World Bank Policy Research Working Paper*, 1777.

BUTTE, N. F. *et al.* (1995), 'Energy Requirements from Infancy to Adulthood', *American Journal of Clinical Nutrition*, 62.

CALDWELL, J. C. (1987), 'Routes to Low Mortality in Poor Countries', *Population and Development Review*, 12.

CALDWELL, P. and CALDWELL, J. (1987), 'Where There is a Narrower Gap Between Female and Male Situations', Canberra, Australian National University, Mimeo.

CALLOWAY, D. H. (1995), 'Human Nutrition: Food and Micronutrient Relationships', *Agricultural Strategies for Micronutrients Working Paper*, 1, Washington DC, International Food Policy Research Institute.

CANDLER, W. and and LELE, U. (1981), 'Food Security: Some East African Considerations', in A. Valdes (ed.), *Food Security for Developing Countries*, Boulder, Colorado, Westview Press.

CANT, A. *et al.* (1982), 'A Nutritional Study of Under-fives in Eastern Uganda', *Journal of Tropical Pediatrics*, 28.

CARLSON, B. A. and WARDLAW, T. M. (1990), 'A Global, Regional and Country Assessment of Child Malnutrition', *UNICEF Staff Working Papers*, 7, New York.

CASELLI, F. *et al.* (1996), 'Reopening the Convergence Debate: A New Look at Cross-Country Growth Empirics', *Journal of Economic Growth*, 1.

CASLEY, D. J. and LURY, D. A. (1987), *Data Collection in Developing Countries*, Oxford, Clarendon Press.

CASSELS, A. (1995), 'Health Sector Reform: Key Issues in Less Developed Countries', *Journal of International Development*, 7.

CHAMBERS, R. *et al.* (1981), *Seasonal Dimensions to Rural Poverty*, Exeter, C. Frances Pinter Publishers Limited.

CHAMIE, J. (1994), 'Population Databases in Development Analysis', *Journal of Development Economics*, 44.

CHANDER, R. (1990), 'Information Systems and Basic Statistics in Sub-Saharan Africa: A Review and Strategy for Improvement', *World Bank Discussion Paper* 73, Washington DC.

CHAUDHRI, R. and TIMMER, C. P. (1986), 'The Impact of Changing Affluence on Diet and Demand Patterns for Agricultural Commodities', *World Bank Staff Working Paper*, 785, Washington DC, World Bank.

CHEN, L. C. (1983), 'Introduction', in L. C. Chen and N. S. Scrimshaw (eds), *Diarrhea and Malnutrition—Interactions, Mechanisms and Interventions*. New York, Plenum Press.

—— *et al.* (1980), 'Anthropometric Assessment of Energy-Protein Malnutrition and Subsequent Risk of Mortality among Pre-school Aged Children', *American Journal of Clinical Nutrition*, 33.

CHEN, S. *et al.* (1994), 'Is Poverty Increasing in the Developing World?', *Review of Income and Wealth*, 40.

CLARKE, G. R. G. (1995), 'More Evidence on Income Distribution and Growth', *Journal of Development Economics*, 47.

COLOMBO, M. *et al.* (1988), 'Mental Development and Stunting', in Waterlow (1988*a*).

CONNOLLY, K. J. (1984), 'Assessment in Children', in J. Brozek and B. Schürch (eds), *Malnutrion and Behavior: Critical Assessment of Key Issues*, Lausanne, Nestlé Foundation.

CONWAY, J. M. (1995), 'Ethnicity and Energy Stores', *American Journal of Clinical Nutrition*, 62 (supplement).

CUTLER, P. and PAYNE, P. (1984), 'Measuring Malnutrition. Technical Problems and Ideological Perspectives', *Economic and Political Weekly*.

DASGUPTA, P. (1993), *An Inquiry into Well-being and Destitution*, Oxford, Clarendon Press.

—— and RAY, D. (1986), 'Inequality as a Determinant of Malnutrition and Unemployment: Theory', *Economic Journal*, 96.

—— —— (1987), 'Inequality as a Determinant of Malnutrition and Unemployment: Policy', *Economic Journal*, 97.

—— —— (1990), 'Adapting to Undernutrition: The Biological Evidence and its Implications', in Drèze and Sen (1990*a*).

DAVIES, H. J. A. *et al.* (1989), 'Metabolic Response to Low- and Very-Low-Calorie Diets', *American Journal of Clinical Nutrition*, 49.

DAVIES, P. S. W. *et al.* (1995), 'Energy Expenditure in Children Aged 1.5 to 4.5 Years: A Comparison with Current Recommendations for Energy Intake', *European Journal of Clinical Nutrition*, 49.

DEATON, A. (1995), 'Data and Economic Tools for Development Analysis', in J. R. Behrman and T. N. Srinivasan (eds.), *Handbook of Development Economics*, Vol. 3A, Amsterdam, North Holland.

—— and CASE, A. (1988), 'Analysis of Household Expenditures', LSMS Working Paper, 28, World Bank.

DEININGER, K. and SQUIRE, L. (1996*a*), 'A New Data Set Measuring Income Inequality', *World Bank Economic Review*, 10.

—— —— (1996*b*), 'Explanations concerning the data-base file' on the Bank's Web Server as given in Deininger and Squire (1996*a*: footnote 2).

DeLONG, G. R. (1993), 'Effects of Nutrition on Brain Development in Humans', *American Journal of Clinical Nutrition*, 57.

DEOLALIKAR, A. B. (1988), 'Nutrition and Labour Productivity in Agriculture: Estimates for Rural South India', *Review of Economics and Statistics*, 70.

—— (1995), 'Government Health Spending in Indonesia: Impact on Children in Different Income Groups', in van de Walle (1995*a*).

DESAI, S. (1992), 'Children at Risk: The Role of Family Structure in Latin America and West Africa', *Population and Development Review*, 18.

DILLON, J. C. and LAJOIE, N. (1981), 'Report on Surveys of the Nutritional Status of the Rural Population in the Sahel from 1960 to 1979', in IDRC (1981).

DOWLER, E. A. and SEO, Y. O. (1985), 'Assessment of Energy Intake: Estimates of Food Supply v Measurements of Food Consumption', *Food Policy*, 10.

—— *et al.* (1980), 'An Anthropometric Survey of 1,074 Pre-school Children in Southern Rwanda, Central Equatorial Africa', *Journal of Tropical Pediatrics*, 26.

DRÈZE, J. (1990*a*), 'Famine Prevention in India', in Drèze and Sen (1990*b*).

—— (1990*b*), 'Famine Prevention in Africa', in Drèze and Sen (1990*b*).

—— and SEN, A. (1989), *Hunger and Public Action*, Oxford, Clarendon Press.

—— —— (1990*a*), (eds) *The Political Economy of Hunger, Vol. 1: Entitlements and Well-being*, Oxford, Clarendon Press.

—— —— (1990*b*), (eds) *The Political Economy of Hunger, Vol. 2: Famine Prevention*, Oxford, Clarendon Press.

—— —— (1991), (eds) *The Political Economy of Hunger, Vol. 3: Endemic Hunger*, Oxford, Clarendon Press.

—— —— (1995), *India: Economic Development and Social Opportunity*, Oxford, Clarendon Press.

DROOMERS, M. *et al.* (1995), 'Higher Socioeconomic Class Pre-school Children from Jakarta, Indonesia, are Taller and Heavier than NCHS Reference Population', *European Journal of Clinical Nutrition*, 49.

DUGDALE, A. E. and PAYNE, P. R. (1977), 'Pattern of Lean and Fat Deposition in Adults', *Nature*, 266.

DURNIN, J. V. G. A. (1994), 'Low Body Mass Index, Physical Work Capacity and Physical Activity Levels', *European Journal of Clinical Nutrition*, 48.

EASTERLEY, W. and LEVINE, R. (1997), 'Africa's Growth Tragedy: Policies and Ethnic Divisions', *Quarterly Journal of Economics*, 112.

Economist, The, (1996), 'Polls to Nowhere', 23 November, 1996.

—— (1998), 'AIDS in Kenya', 7 February, 1998.

EDWARDS, S. (1998), 'Openness, Productivity, and Growth: What do We Really Know?', *Economic Journal*, 108.

EICHER, C. K. and BAKER, D. C. (1982), 'Research on Agricultural Development in Sub-Saharan Africa: A Critical Survey'. *International Development Paper*, 1, East Lancing, Michigan State University.

EKSMYR, R. (1970), 'Anthropometry in Privileged Ethiopian Preschool Children', *Acta Paediatrica Scandinavica*, 59.

European Economic Commission (EEC) (1986), 'Conference Proceedings: Statistics in Support of African Food Strategies and Policies', Mimeo, Brussels, 13–16 May.

EVANS, D. B. and HURLEY, S. F. (1995), 'The Application of Evaluation Techniques in the Health Sector: The State of the Art', *Journal of International Development*, 7.

EVELETH, P. B. and TANNER, J. M. (1976), *Worldwide Variations in Human Growth*, 1st edn, Cambridge, Cambridge University Press.

—— —— (1990), *Worldwide Variations in Human Growth*, 2nd edn, Cambridge, Cambridge University Press.

EVENSON, R. E. and PREY, C. E. (1994), 'Measuring Food Production (with Reference to South Asia)', *Journal of Development Economics*, 44.

FAO*a* (occasional) *World Food Survey*, Rome, FAO.

FAO*b* (annual) *Food Production Yearbook*, Rome, FAO.

FAO*c* (annual) *Food Trade Yearbook*, Rome, FAO.

FAO*d* (occasional) *Review of Food Consumption Surveys*, Rome, FAO.

FAO*e* (occasional) *Food Balance Sheets*, Rome, FAO.

FAO (1975), *National Methods of Collecting Agricultural Statistics*, Vol. II, Rome, FAO.

—— (1983), *A Comparative Study of Food Consumption Data from Food Balance Sheets and Household Surveys*, FAO Economic and Social Development Paper, 34, Rome, FAO.

—— (1987*a*), *Expert Consultation on Production Statistics of Subsistence Food Crops in Africa*, Harare, FAO.

—— (1987*b*), *Per Capita Calorie Availability*, Computer printout, Rome, FAO.

—— (*1992*), 'World Food Supplies and Prevalence of Chronic Undernutrition in Developing Regions as Assessed in 1992', Mimeo, Rome, FAO.

—— (1997*a*), *Poster with Data*, World Food Summit, Rome: FAO.

—— (1997*b*), *Declaration of World Food Security and Plan of Action*, World Food Summit, Rome, FAO.

—— (1997*c*), *Synthesis of the Technical Background Documents*, World Food Summit, Rome, FAO.

FAO/ESN (1987–97), *Nutrition Country Profiles. Individual Countries*, Rome.

FAO/WHO (1973), *Energy and Protein Requirements*, Technical Report Series, 522, Geneva, WHO.

FAO/WHO/UNU (1985), *Energy and Protein Requirements*, Technical Report Series, 724, Geneva, WHO.

FARMER, A. and TIEFENTHALER, J. (1995), 'Fairness Concepts and the Intrahousehold Allocation of Resources', *Journal of Development Economics*, 47.

FLOUD, R. (1992), 'Anthropometric Measures of Nutritional Status in Industrialised Societies: Europe and North America since 1750', in Osmani (1992*a*).

FOGEL, R. W. (1992), 'Second Thoughts on the European Escape from Hunger: Famines, Chronic Malnutrition and Mortality Rates', in Osmani (1992*a*).

—— (1994), 'The Bearing of Long-Term Processes and the Making of Economic Policy', *American Economic Review*, 84.

FUSO, A. K. (1992), 'Political Instability and Economic Growth: Evidence from Sub-Saharan Africa', *Economic Development and Cultural Change*, 40.

GARCIA, M. and KENNEDY, E. (1994), 'Assessing the Linkages Between Body Mass Index and Mortality in Adults: Evidence from Four Developing Countries', *European Journal of Clinical Nutrition*, 48.

GEMMELL, N. (1996), 'Evaluating the Impacts of Human Capital Stocks and Accumulation on Economic Growth: Some New Evidence', *Oxford Bulletin of Economics and Statistics*, 58.

GILLESPIE, S. and MASON, J. (1991), 'Nutrition Relevant Actions: Some Experiences from the 1980s and Lessons for the 1990s', ACC/SCN, SOA Paper 10.

—— —— (1994), 'Controlling Vitamin A Deficiency', ACC/SCN, SOA Paper 14.

—— et al. (1991), 'Controlling Iron Deficiency', ACC/SCN, SOA Paper 9.

—— —— (1996), 'How Nutrition Improves', ACC/SCN, SOA Paper 15.

—— —— (1997), 'Nutrition and Poverty', ACC/SCN, SOA Paper 16.

GILLIS, J. S. (1990), *Too Small, Too Tall*, Champaign, Illinois, Institute for Personality and Ability Testing, Inc.

GILSON, L. (1995), 'Management and Health Care Reform in Sub-Saharan Africa', *Social Science and Medicine*, 40.

—— et al. (1995), 'The Political Economy of User Fees with Targeting: Developing Equitable Health Financing Policy', *Journal of International Development*, 7.

GOPALAN, C. (1983), ' "Small is Healthy?" For the Poor, Not for the Rich!', *Bulletin of the Nutritional Foundation of India*, October.

—— (1992), 'Undernutrition: Measurement and Implications', in Osmani (1992a).

GORSTEIN, J. and AKRE, J. (1988), 'The Use of Anthropometry to Assess Nutritional Status', *World Health Statistical Quarterly*, 41.

GRAITCER, P. L. and GENTRY, E. M. (1981), 'Measuring Children: One Reference for All?', *Lancet*, 8 August.

GrANTHAM-McGREGOR, S. M. (1992), 'The Effects of Malnutrition on Mental Development', in Waterlow (1992a).

GREULICH, W.W. (1957), 'A Comparison of the Physical Growth and Development of American-born and Native Japanese Children', *American Journal of Physical Anthropology*, 15.

—— (1967), 'Some Secular Changes in Growth of American-born and Native Japanese Children', *American Journal of Physical Anthropology*, 45.

GRIESEL, R. D. (1984), 'Psychomotor Sequelae of Malnutrition', in J. Brosek and B. Schürch (eds), *Malnutrition and Behavior: Critical Assessment of Key Issues*, Lausanne, Nestlé Foundation.

GROOTAERT, C. and CHEUNG, K. F. (1985), 'Household Expenditure Surveys: Some Methodological Issues', LSMS Working Paper, 22, World Bank.

GROSH, M. E. (1995), 'Towards Quantifying the Trade-off: Administration Costs and Incidence in Targeted Programs in Latin America', in van de Walle (1995a).

HAAGA, J. et al. (1985), 'An Estimate of the Prevalence of Child Malnutrition in Developing Countries', *World Health and Statistics Quarterly*, 38.

HABICHT, J-P. et al. (1974), 'Height and Weight Standards for Preschool Children—How Relevant are Ethnic Differences in Growth Potential?', *Lancet*, 6 April.

—— et al. (1982), 'Indicators for Identifying and Counting the Improperly Nourished', *American Journal of Clinical Nutrition*, 35.

HADDAD, L. J. (1997), (ed.) *Achieving Food Security in Southern Africa: New Challenges and New Opportunities*, Washington DC, IFPRI.

—— and Bouis, H. E. (1991), 'The Impact of Nutritional Status on Agricultural Productivity: Wage Evidence from the Philippines', *Oxford Bulletin of Economics and Statistics*, 53.

—— and KANBUR, R. S. M. (1990), 'How Serious is the Neglect of Intrahousehold Inequality?', *Economic Journal*, 100.

HADDAD, L. J. and KANBUR, R. S. M. (1995), 'Towards Understanding the Value of Intra-household Survey Data for Aged-Based Food Targeting', *Food and Nutrition Bulletin*, 16.

—— *et al.* (1995), 'Intra-household Inequalities at Different Welfare Levels: Energy Intake and Energy Expanditure Data from the Philippines', *Oxford Bulletin of Economics and Statistics*, 57.

—— *et al.* (1997), *Intrahousehold Resource Allocation in Developing Countries: Models, Methods, Policy*, Washington DC, Johns Hopkins University Press.

HAMMER, J. S. *et al.* (1995), 'Distributional Effects of Social Sector Expenditures in Malaysia', in van de Walle (1995a).

HARPER, A. E. (1985), 'Origin of Recommended Dietary Allowances—an Historic Overview', *American Journal of Clinical Nutrition*, 41.

HARRISS, B. (1990), 'The Intra-Family Distribution of Hunger in South Asia', in Drèze and Sen (1990a).

HAYTER, J. E. and HENRY, C. J. K. (1993), 'Basal Metabolic Rate in Human Subjects Migrating Between Tropical and Temperate Regions: A Longitudinal Study and Review of Previous Work', *European Journal of Clinical Nutrition*, 47.

—— —— (1994), 'A Re-examination of Basal Metabolic Rate Predictive Equations: the Importance of Geographical Origin of Subjects in Sample Selection', *European Journal of Clinical Nutrition*, 48.

HEALY, M. J. R. (1989), 'Comments on Adaptation', *European Journal of Clinical Nutrition*, 43.

—— and REES, D. G. (1991), 'New Predictive Equations for the Estimation of Basal Metabolic Rate in Tropical Peoples', *European Journal of Clinical Nutrition*, 45.

HESTON, A. (1994), 'A Brief Review of Some Problems in Using National Accounts Data in Level of Output Comparisons of Growth Studies', *Journal of Development Economics*, 44.

HEYMSFIELD, S. B. *et al.* (1995), 'The Calorie: Myth, Measurement, and Reality', *American Journal of Clinical Nutrition*, 62.

HIERNAUX, J. (1964), 'Weight/Height Relationship During Growth in Africans and Europeans', *Human Biology*, 36.

HILL, K. and PEBLEY, A. R. (1989), 'Child Mortality in the Developing World', *Population and Development Review*, 15.

HIRSCHMAN, A. O. (1958), *The Strategy of Economic Development*, New Haven and London, Yale University Press.

HOET, J. J. (1997), 'Poor Nutrition and Chronic Disease', *SCN News*, 14, Geneva, WHO.

HORTON, S. *et al.* (1988), 'The Social Cost of Higher Food Prices: Some Cross-Country Evidence', *World Development*, 16.

HULSE, J. H. and PEARSON, O. (1981), 'The Nutritional Status of the Population of the Semi-Arid Tropical Countries', in IDRC (1981).

IBRDa (annual) *World Development Report*, Washington DC, World Bank.

—— (1986), *Poverty and Hunger*, Washington DC, World Bank.

—— (1989), *Sub-Saharan Africa: From Crisis to Sustainable Growth*, Washington DC, World Bank.

—— (1993), *The East Asian Miracle: Economic Growth and Public Action*, Oxford, Oxford University Press.

—— (1994), *Adjustment in Africa: Reforms, Results and the Road Ahead*, Oxford, Oxford University Press.

—— (1995), *A Continent in Transition: Sub-Saharan Africa in the mid-1990s*, Mimeo, Washington DC, World Bank.

—— (1997), *Taking Action to Reduce Poverty in Sub-Saharan Africa*, Washington DC, World Bank.

IDRC (International Development Research Centre) (1981), *Nutrition Status of the Rural Population of the Sahel*, Ottawa, IDRC.

IMF*a* (monthly) *International Finance Statistics*, Washington DC, IMF.

IMF*b* (annual) *Government Finance Statistics Yearbook*, Washington DC, IMF.

IMF (1993), *Structural Adjustment in Sub-Saharan Africa*, Occasional Paper, 87, Washington DC, IMF.

ISENMAN, P. (1980), 'Basic Needs: The Case of Sri Lanka', *World Development*, 8.

JAMES, W. P. T. (1989), 'Comment on Adaptation', *European Journal of Clinical Nutrition*, 43.

—— (1994), 'Introduction: The Challenge of Adult Chronic Energy Deficiency', *European Journal of Clinical Nutrition*, 48.

—— and SCHOFIELD, E. C. (1990), *Human Energy Requirements*, Oxford, Oxford University Press.

—— *et al.* (1988), 'Definition of Chronic Energy Deficiency in Adults', *European Journal of Clinical Nutrition*, 42.

JANES, M. D. (1970), 'The Effect of Social Class on the Physical Growth of Nigerian Yoruba Children', *Bulletin of the International Epidemiological Association*, 20.

—— (1974), 'Physical Growth of Nigerian Yoruba Children', *Tropical and Geographical Medicine*, 26.

JENNINGS, J. *et al.* (1991), 'Managing Successful Nutrition Programs', ACC/ SCN, SOA Paper, 8.

JÜRGENS, H. W. *et al.* (1990), *International Data on Anthropometry*, Occupational Safety and Health Series, 65, Geneva, International Labour Office.

KAKWANI, N. C. (1992), 'Measuring Undernutrition with Variable Calorie Requirements', in Osmani (1992*a*).

—— (1993), 'Performance in Living Standards: An International Comparison', *Journal of Development Economics*, 41.

KALDOR, N. (1956), 'Alternative Theories of Distribution', *Review of Economic Studies*, 2.

KANBUR, R. S. M. (1995), 'Children and Intrahousehold Inequality: A Theoretical Analysis', in K. Basu *et al.* (1995), *Choice, Welfare and Development: A Festschrift in Honour of Amartya Sen*, Oxford, Clarendon Press.

—— and HADDAD, L. J. (1995), 'Are Better Off Households More Equal or Less Unequal?', *Oxford Economic Papers*, 46.

KASSOUF, A. L. and SENAUER, B. (1996), 'Direct and Indirect Effects of Parental Education on Malnutrition Among Children in Brazil: A Full Income Approach', *Economic Development and Cultural Change*, 44.

KELLER, W. (1988), 'The Epidemiology of Stunting', in Waterlow (1988*a*).

—— and FILLMORE, C. M. (1983), 'Prevalence of Protein–Energy Malnutrition', *World Health Statistics Quarterly*, 36.

KENNEDY, E. and GARCIA, M. (1994), 'Body Mass Index and Economic Productivity', *European Journal of Clinical Nutrition*, 48.

KENNEDY, E. and HADDAD, L. E. (1994), 'Are Pre-schoolers from Female-Headed Households Less Malnourished? A Comparative Analysis of Results from Ghana and Kenya', *Journal of Development Studies*, 30.

KIELMANN, A. and McCORD, C. (1978), 'Weight-for-Age as an Index of Risk of Death in Children', *Lancet*, 10 June.

KILLICK, T. (1992*a*) (ed.) *The IMF and Stabilisation: Developing Country Experiences*, London, Gower.

—— (1992*b*), (ed.) *The Quest for Economic Stabilisation: The IMF and the Third World*, London, Gower.

KLASEN, S. (1994), ' "Missing Women" Reconsidered', *World Development*, 22.

—— (1996), 'Nutrition, Health and Mortality in Sub-Saharan Africa: Is There a Gender Bias?', *Journal of Development Studies*, 32.

KNIGHT, J. *et al*. (1993), 'Is the Rate of Return to Primary Schooling Really 26 Per Cent?', *Journal of African Economics*, 1.

KOMLOS, J. (1990), 'Stature and Nutrition in the Habsburg Monarchy', *American Historical Review*, 90.

KRUGMAN, P. (1994), 'The Myth of Asia's Miracle', *Foreign Affairs*, 73.

KULIN, H. E. *et al*. (1982), 'The Effect of Chronic Childhood Malnutrition on Pubertal Growth and Development', *American Journal of Clinical Nutrition*, 36.

KUMAR, S. K. (1987), 'The Nutrition Situation and Its Food Policy Links', in J. Mellor, *et al*. (eds.), *Accelerating Food Production in Sub-Saharan Africa*, London, Johns Hopkins Press Ltd.

—— (1994), 'Adaptation of Hybrid Maize in Zambia: Effects on Gender Roles, Food Consumption and Nutrition', Research Report 100, Washington DC, IFPRI.

KUZNETS, S. (1955), 'Economic Growth and Income Inequality', *American Economic Review*, 45.

LA FOND, A. K. (1994), 'Sustainability and Health Sector Development, A Review and Analysis of 5 Country Case Studies', Save The Children Working Paper, 9.

LANGFORD, C. M. (1996), 'Reasons for the Decline in Mortality in Sri Lanka Immediately After the Second World War: A Re-examination', *Health Transition Review*, 6.

LAWRENCE, M. *et al*. (1985), 'The Energy Cost of Daily Activities in African Women: Increased Expenditure in Pregnancy', *American Journal of Clinical Nutrition*, 42.

LEIBENSTEIN, H. (1957), *Economic Backwardness and Economic Growth*, New York, Whiely.

LEIGHTON, C. (1996), 'Strategies for Achieving Health Finance Reform in Africa', *World Development*, 24.

LENSINK, R. and WHITE, H. (1999), 'Aid Dependence: Issues and Indicators', Expert Group on Development Issues, Swedish Ministry of Foreign Affairs, Report 1999: 2.

LEVINE, R. and RENELT, D. (1992), 'A Sensitivity Analysis of Cross-country Growth Regressions', *American Economic Review*, 82.

LI, H. *et al*. (1998), 'Explaining International and Intertemporal Variations in Income Distribution', *Economic Journal*, 108.

LIPTON, M. (1983), 'Poverty, Undernutrition and Hunger', World Bank Staff Working Paper, 597.

—— (1985*a*), 'Report of the FAO Expert Consultation on Production Statistics of Subsistence Food Crops in Africa', Harare, FAO.

—— (1985*b*), 'African Food Output Statistics: A Role for the World Bank?', Mimeo, World Bank.

—— (1986), 'Statistics in Support of African Food Strategies and Policies', Mimeo, presented to European Community Conference held in Brussels, 13–16 May 1986.

—— (1987), 'Review and Summary of Discussions', in *Expert Consultation on Data Needs for Food and Agricultural Analysis and Planning in Developing Countries*, Rome, FAO.

—— and RAVALLION, M. (1995), 'Poverty and Policy' in J. R. Behrman, and T. N. Srinivasan (eds), *Handbook of Development Economics*, Vol. IIIB, Amsterdam, North-Holland.

VAN LOON, H. *et al.* (1986), 'Local *vs.* Universal Growth Standards: The Effect of Using NCHS as Universal Reference', *Annals of Human Biology*, 13.

MACFARLANE, S. B. J. (1995), 'A Universal Growth Reference or Fool's Gold', *European Journal of Clinical Nutrition*, 49.

MANKIW, N. G. (1995), 'The Growth of Nations', *Brookings Papers of Economic Activity*, 1.

MARGEN, S. (1984), 'Prologue', in J. Brozek and B. Schürch (eds), *Malnutrition and Behaviour: Critical Assessment and Key Issues*, Lausanne, Nestlé Foundation Publication Services.

MARTIN, L. J. *et al.* (1996), 'Comparison of Energy Intakes Determined by Food Records and DLW in Women Participating in a Dietary Intervention Trial', *American Journal of Clinical Nutrition*, 63.

MARTORELL, R. (1995), 'Promoting Health Growth: Rationale and Benefits', in Pinstrup-Andersen (1995).

—— and HO, T. J. (1984), 'Malnutrition, Morbidity, and Mortality', *Population and Development Review*, 10.

—— *et al.* (1988), 'Poverty and Stature in Children', in Waterlow (1988*a*).

MAURO, P. (1995), 'Corruption and Growth', *Quarterly Journal of Economics*, 110.

MAXWELL, S. (1990), 'Food Security in Developing Countries: Issues and Options', *IDS Bulletin*, 21.

MCGLOTHLEN, M. E. *et al.* (1986), 'Undomesticated Animals and Plants', in A. Hansen and D. E. McMillan (eds), *Food in Sub-Saharan Africa*, Boulder, Colorado, Lynne Rienner Publishers Inc.

MCGUIRE, J. S. and AUSTIN, J. E. (1987), *Beyond Survival: Children's Growth for National Development*, Geneva, UNICEF.

MCLAREN, D. S. (1974), 'The Great Protein Fiasco', *Lancet*, 2 November.

MCNEILL, G. (1986), 'Energy Nutrition in Adults in Rural India', cited in Harriss (1990).

MENKEN, J. *et al.* (1981), 'The Nutrition–Fertility Link: An Evaluation of the Evidence', *Journal of Interdisciplinary History*, 11.

MILLER, D. and VORIS, L. (1969), 'Chronologic Changes in the Recommended Dietary Allowances', *Journal of American Dietetic Association*, 54.

MILLMAN, S. (1992), 'Who's Hungry? And How do We Know?', Mimeo, Brown University.

MILLS, A. (1990), 'The Economics of Hospitals in Developing Countries: Part I—Expenditure Patterns', *Health, Policy, and Planning*, 5.

MINHAS, B. S. (1986), 'Evaluating Food Crop Acreages and Yields: Indian Experience and its Relevance in Africa', in EEC (1986).

MIRRLEES, J. A. (1975), 'A Pure Theory of Underdeveloped Economies', in L. Reynolds (ed.), *Agriculture in Development Theory*, New Haven, Yale University Press.

MOGEDAL, S. *et al.* (1995), 'Health Sector Reform and Organizational Issues at the Local Level: Lessons from Selected African Countries', *Journal of International Development*, 7.

MORA, J. O. (1984), 'Anthropometry in Prevalence Studies', in J. Brosek and B. Schürch (eds), *Malnutrition and Behavior: Critical Assessment of Key Issues*, Lausanne, Nestlé Foundation.

MURPHY, J. *et al.* (1991), 'Farmers' Estimations as a Source of Production Data', *World Bank Technical Paper*, 132.

MURRAY, C. J. L. *et al.* (1994), 'National Health Expenditures: A Global Analysis', *Bulletin of theWorld Health Organization*, 72.

—— and LOPEZ, A. D. (eds) (1998), 'Malnutrition and the Burden of Disease', Vol. 8, *The Global Burden of Disease and Injury Series*, Geneva, WHO.

NABARRO, D. *et al.* (1988), 'The Importance of Infections and Environmental Factors as Possible Determinants of Growth Retardation in Children', in Waterlow (1988*a*).

NDULU, B. J. (1997), 'Editorial: Capacity for Changing Policy Environment and Research Agenda in Africa', *World Development*, 25.

NEIKEN, L. (1988), 'Comparison of the FAO and World Bank Methodology for Estimating the Incidence of Undernutrition', *FAO Quarterly Bulletin of Statistics*, 1.

NELSON, M. *et al.* (1989), 'Between- and Within-Subject Variation in Nutrient Intake From Infancy to Old Age: Estimating the Number of Days Required to Rank Dietary Intakes with Desired Precision', *American Journal of Clinical Nutrition*, 50.

NTOZI, J. P. M. *et al.* (eds) (1997), *Vulnerability to HIV Infection and Effects of AIDS in Africa and Asia/India*, Supplement to *Health Transition Review*, 7.

NURKSE, R. (1953), *Problems of Capital Formation in Underdeveloped Countries*, Oxford, Basil Blackwell.

OECD/DAC (annual), *Development Co-operation*, Paris, OECD/DAC.

OLIVER, R. and CROWDER, M. (1983), *The Cambridge Encyclopedia of Africa*, Cambridge, Cambridge University Press.

OSMANI, S. R. (1984), 'Food and the Nutrition Problem—Methodology of Global Estimation', paper presented at the Informal Gathering on Methodology of the Fifth World Food Survey, Rome, 12–14 March.

—— (1987), 'Poverty and Nutrition in South Asia', ACC/SCN *Nutrition Policy Paper*, 16.

—— (1990), 'Nutrition and the Economics of Food: Implications of Some Recent Controversies', in Drèze and Sen (1990).

—— (1992*a*), *Nutrition and Poverty* (ed.), Oxford, Clarendon Press.

—— (1992*b*), 'On Some Controversies in the Measurement of Undernutrition', in Osmani (1992*a*).

PASSMORE, R. and DURNING, J. (1955), 'Human Energy Expenditure', *Physiological Review*, 35.

PAUKERT, F. (1973), 'Income Distribution at Different Levels of Development: A Survey of Evidence', *International Labour Review*, 108.

PAULINO, L. A. and SARMA, J. S. (1986), 'A Report on the Analysis of Trend and Projections of Food Production and Consumption in Two Selected Developing Countries', Mimeo, Washington DC, International Food Policy Research Institute.

—— and TSENG, S. S. (1980), 'A Comparative Study of FAO and USDA Data on Production, Area, and Trade of Major Food Staples', *International Food Policy Research Institute Research Report*, 19, Washington DC.

—— and YOUNG, P. (1981), 'The Food Situation in Sub-Saharan Africa: A Preliminary Assessment', Mimeo, presented to the conference 'Food Policy Issues and Concerns in Sub-Saharan Africa' held in Ibadan, 9–11 February 1981.

PAYNE, P. (1992), 'Assessing Undernutrition: The Need for a Reconceptualisation', in Osmani (1992*a*).

PELLETIER, D. L. (1991), *The Relationship Between Child Anthropometry and Mortality in Developing Countries: Implications for Policy, Programs and Future Research*, Food and Nutrition Policy Program monograph 12, Ithaca, NY, Cornell University.

—— (1994), 'The Relationship Between Child Anthropometry and Mortality in Developing Countries: Implications for Policy, Programs and Future Research', *The Journal of Nutrition* 124, (Supplement).

—— *et al.* (1994*a*), 'A Methodology for Estimating the Contribution of Malnutrition to Child Mortality in Developing Countries', *The Journal of Nutrition*, 124 (supplement).

—— *et al.* (1994*b*), 'Child Anthropometry and Mortality in Malawi: Testing for Effect Modification by Age and Length of Follow up and Confounding by Social Factors', *The Journal of Nutrition*, 124 (supplement).

PEROTTI, R. (1996), 'Growth, Income Distribution and Democracy', *Journal of Economic Growth*, 1.

PERSSON, T. and TABELLINI, G. (1994), 'Is Inequality Harmful for Growth?', *American Economic Review*, 84.

PINSTRUP-ANDERSEN, P. *et al.* (eds) (1995), *Child Growth and Nutrition in Developing Countries: Priorities for Action*, Ithaca and London, Cornell University Press.

PITT, M. M. (1983), 'Food Preferences and Nutrition in Rural Bangladesh', *Review of Economics and Statistics*, 65.

—— *et al.* (1990), 'Productivity, Health, and Inequality in the Intrahousehold Distribution of Food in Low-Income Countries', *American Economic Review*, 80.

—— *et al.* (1995), 'The Determinants and Consequences of the Placement of Government Programs in Indonesia', in van de Walle (1995*a*).

POLEMAN, T. T. (1975), 'World Food: A Perspective', *Science*, 188.

—— (1977), 'World Food: Myth and Reality', *World Development*, 5.

PRESTON, S. H. (1975), 'The Changing Relationship Between Mortality and Economic Development', *Population Studies*, 29.

PSACHAROPOULOS, G. (1994), 'Returns to Investment in Education: A Global Update', *World Development*, 22.

—— (1996), 'A Reply to Bennell', *World Development*, 24.

QUINN, V. J. *et al.* (1995), 'The Growth of Malawian Pre-school Children from Different Socioeconomic Groups', *European Journal of Clinical Nutrition*, 49.

RADELET, S. *et al.* (1997), 'Economic Growth in Asia', in AsDB (1997).

RAMAKRISHNAN, U. *et al.* (1999), 'Role of Inter-generational Effects on Linear Growth', *Journal of Nutrition*, 129.

RANIS, G. (1995), 'Another Look at the East Asian Miracle', *World Bank Economic Review*, 9.

RAVALLION, M. (1988), *Markets and Famine*, Oxford, Clarendon Press.

RAVALLION, M. (1990), 'Income Effects on Undernutrition', *Development and Cultural Change*, 38.

—— (1997a), 'Famines and Economics', *Journal of Economic Literature*, 35.

—— (1997b), 'Good and Bad Growth: The Human Development Reports', *World Development*, 25.

—— et al. (1991), 'Quantifying Absolute Poverty in the Developing World', *Review of Income and Wealth*, 37.

RAVUSSIN, E. et al. (1985), 'Energy Expenditure Before and During Energy Restriction in Obese Patients', *American Journal of Clinical Nutrition*, 41.

ROBERTS, D. F. (1985), 'Genetics and Nutritional Adaptation', in Blaxter and Waterlow (1985).

—— and BAINBRIDGE, D. R. (1963), 'Nilotic Physique', *American Journal of Physical Anthropology*, 21.

ROBINSON, S. (1968), 'Physiology of Muscular Exercise', in V. Mountcastle (ed.), *Medical Physiology*, Vol. I, Saint Louis, Mosby Company.

RODGERS, G. B. (1979), 'Income and Inequality as Determinants of Mortality: An International Cross-section Analysis', *Population Studies*, 33.

RODRIK, D. (1994), 'King Kong Meets Godzilla: The World Bank and The East Asian Miracle', *CEPR Discussion Paper*, 944.

ROGERS, B. L. (1995), 'Feeding Programs and Food Related Income Transfers', in Pinstrup-Andersen et al. (1995).

ROMER, P. (1993), 'Two Strategies for Economic Development: Using Ideas and Producing Ideas', *World Bank Economic Review*, 7 (supplement).

ROSENZWEIG, M. R. and SCHULTZ, T. P. (1982), 'Market Opportunities, Genetic Endowments, and Intrafamily Resource Distribution', *American Economic Review*, 72.

ROSETTA, L. (1986), 'Sex Differences in Seasonal Variations in the Nutritional Status of Serere Adults in Senegal', *Ecology of Food and Nutrition*, 18.

ROZANSKI, J. and YEATS, A. (1994), 'On the (in)Accuracy of Economic Observations: An Assessment of Trends in the Reliability of International Trade Statistics', *Journal of Development Economics*, 44.

RUTISHAUSER, I. H. E. and WHITEHEAD, R. G. (1972), 'Energy Intake and Expenditure in 1–3 Year Old Ugandan Children Living in a Rural Environment', *British Journal of Nutrition*, 28.

SACHS, J. D. and WERNER, A. M. (1995), 'Economic Reform and the Process of Global Integration', *Brookings Papers on Economic Activity*, 1.

—— —— (1997), 'Fundamental Sources of Long-Term Growth', *American Economic Review*, 87.

SAHN, D. E. (ed.) (1989), *Seasonal Variability in Third World Agriculture*, Baltimore, Maryland, Johns Hopkins University Press.

—— (1990), 'The Impact of Export Crop Production on Nutritional Status in Côte d'Ivoire', *World Development*, 18.

—— and ALDERMAN, H. (1988), 'The Effects of Human Capital on Wages, and the Determinants of Labour Supply in a Developing Country', *Journal of Development Economics*, 29.

—— —— (1995), 'Incentive Effects on Labor Supply of Sri Lanka's Rice Subsidy', in van de Walle (1995a).

—— —— (1997), 'On the Determinants of Nutrition in Mozambique: The Importance of the Age-specific Effects', *World Development*, 25.

SALA-i-MARTIN, X. (1997), 'I Just Ran Two Million Regressions', *American Economic Review*, 87.

SAMARAS, T. T. and STORMS, L. H. (1992), 'Impact of Height and Weight on Life Span', *Bulletin of the World Health Organization*, 70.

SARMA, J. S. (1986), 'Improvements in Basic Agricultural Statistics in Support of African Food Strategies and Policies and the Role of the Donor Agencies', Mimeo, presented to the European Community Conference held in Brussels, 13–16 May 1986.

SATANARAYANA, K. *et al.* (1977), 'Body Size and Work Output', *American Journal of Clinical Nutrition*, 30.

—— (1989), 'Nutrition and Work Performance: Studies Carried Out in India', *International Congress on Nutrition: Proceedings XIV*, Seoul.

SCHOELLER, D. A. *et al.* (1990), 'How Accurate is Self-Reported Dietary Energy Intake?', *Nutrition Review*, 48.

SCHOFIELD, S. (1979), *Development and the Problems of Village Nutrition*, London, Croom Helm.

SCHOFIELD, W. M. (1985), 'Predicting Basal Metabolic Rate: New Standards and Review of Previous Work', *Human Nutrition, Clinical Nutrition*, 39C (supplement).

SCHULTEN, G. G. M. (1982), 'Post-Harvest Losses in Tropical Africa and their Prevention', *Food and Nutrition Bulletin*, 4.

SCHULTZ, T. P. (1988), 'Education Investments and Returns', in H. Chenery and T. N. Srinivasan (eds), *Handbook of Development Economics*, Vol. 1, Amsterdam, North Holland.

—— (1993), 'Mortality Decline in the Low-Income World', *American Economic Review*, 83.

SCRIMSHAW, N. (1989), 'Nutrition and Infection Re-examined: A Retrospective Comment', in Tomkins and Watson (1989).

—— (1996), 'Nutrition and Health from Womb to Tomb', *Nutrition Today*, 31.

—— *et al.* (1959), 'Interaction of Nutrition and Infection', *American Journal of Medical Science*, 237.

—— *et al.* (1968), *Interaction of Nutrition and Infection*, Geneva, WHO.

SECKLER, D. (1982), 'Small but Healthy: A Basic Hypothesis in the Theory, Measurement and Policy of Malnutrition', in P. V. Sukhatme (ed.), *Newer Concepts in Nutrition and Their Implications for Policy*, Pune, Maharashtra Association for the Cultivation of Science.

—— (1984), 'The "Small but Healthy" Hypothesis: A Reply to Critics', *Economic and Political Weekly*, 19.

SEN, A. (1981*a*), *Poverty and Famines*, Oxford, Clarendon Press.

—— (1981*b*), 'Public Action and the Quality of Life in Developing Countries', *Oxford Bulletin of Economics and Statistics*, 43.

—— (1992), 'Missing Woman', *British Medical Journal*, 304.

—— (1995), 'The Political Economy of Targeting', in van de Walle (1995*a*).

—— (1998), 'Mortality as an Indicator of Economic Success and Failure', *Economic Journal*, 108.

SEROG, P. *et al.* (1982), 'Effects of Slimming and Composition of Diets on VO2 and Thyroid Hormones in Healthy Subjects', *American Journal of Clinical Nutrition*, 35.

SHAH, C. H. (1983), 'Food Preference, Poverty, and the Nutrition Gap', *Economic Development and Cultural Change*, 32.

SHARER, R. L. *et al.* (1995), 'Uganda: Adjustment and Growth, 1987–94', *IMF Occasional Papers*, 121.

SHETTY, P. S. *et al.* (1994), 'Body Mass Index: Its Relationship to Basal Metabolic Rates and Energy Requirements', *European Journal of Clinical Nutrition*, 48.

SINGH, J. *et al.* (1989), 'Energy Expenditure of Gambian Women During Peak Agricultural Activity Measured by DLW Method', *British Journal of Nutrition*, 62.

SOARES, M. J. and SHETTY, P. S. (1991), 'Basal Metabolic Rate and Metabolic Economy in Chronic Undernutrition', *European Journal of Clinical Nutrition*, 45.

SPURR, G. B. (1983), 'Nutritional Status and Work Capacity', *Yearbook of Physical Anthropology*, 26.

—— (1988), 'Body Size, Physical Work Capacity and Productivity in Hard Work: Is Bigger Better?', in Waterlow (1988).

SRINIVASAN, T. N. (1981), 'Malnutrition: Measurement and Policy Issues', *Journal of Development Economics*, 8.

—— (1983), 'Malnutrition in Developing Countries: The State of Knowledge of the Extent of Its Prevalence, Its Causes and Consequences', Mimeo, background paper for FAO*a* (1985).

—— (1992), 'Undernutrition: Concepts, Measurement and Policy Implications', in Osmani (1992*a*).

—— (1994*a*), 'Data Base for Development: An Overview', *Journal of Development Economics*, 44.

—— (1994*b*), 'Human Development: A New Paradigm or Reinventing the Wheel?', *American Economic Review*, 84.

STECKEL, R. H. (1995), 'Stature and the Standard of Living', *Journal of Economic Literature*, 33.

STEPHENSON, L. S. *et al.* (1983), *A Comparison of Growth Standards: Similarities Between NCHS, Harvard, Denver and Privileged African Children and Differences with Kenyan Rural Children*, Program in International Nutrition, Monograph Series, 12, Cornell University, Ithaca, N.Y.

STIGLITZ, J. E. (1976), 'The Efficiency Wage Hypothesis, Surplus Labor, and the Distribution of Incomes in LDCs', *Oxford Economic Papers*, 28.

STRAUSS, J. (1986), 'Does Better Nutrition Raise Farm Productivity?', *Journal of Political Economy*, 94.

—— and THOMAS, D. (1990), 'Households, Communities and Preschool Children's Nutrition: Evidence from Rural Cote d'Ivoire', *Economic Development and Cultural Change*, 38.

—— —— (1995), 'Human Resources: Empirical Modeling of Household and Family Decisions', in J. Behrman and T. N. Srinivasan (eds), *Handbook of Development Economics*, Vol. 3A, Amsterdam, North Holland.

SUBRAMANIAN, S. and DEATON, A. (1996), 'The Demand for Food and Calories', *Journal of Political Economy*, 104.

SUKHATME, P. V. (1978), 'Assessment of Adequacy of Diets at Different Income Levels', *Economic and Political Weekly*, Special Number.

—— and MARGEN, S. (1982), 'Autoregulatory Homeostatic Nature of Energy Balance', *American Journal of Clinical Nutrition*, 35.

SVEDBERG, P. (1987), 'A Note on Famine in Sub-Saharan Africa from a Historical Perspective', Mimeo, Institute for International Economics Studies, Stockholm.

—— (1990), 'Undernutrition in Sub-Saharan Africa: Is There a Gender Bias?', *Journal of Development Studies*, 26.

—— (1991a), 'Undernutrition in Sub-Saharan Africa: A Critical Assessment of the Evidence', in Drèze and Sen (1991).

—— (1991b), 'The Export Performance of Sub-Saharan Africa', *Economic Development and Cultural Change*, 39.

—— (1993), 'Trade Compression and Economic Decline in Sub-Saharan Africa', in M. Blomström and M. Lundahl (eds), *Economic Crisis in Africa*, London and New York, Routledge.

—— (1996), 'Gender Biases in Sub-Saharan Africa: Reply and Further Evidence', *Journal of Development Studies*, 32.

—— (1999a), '841 Million Undernourished?', *World Development*, 27.

—— (1999b), 'Estimating Undernutrition: On the (Mis)use of Calorie Norms', IIES Seminar Paper, Stockholm University.

—— (1999c), 'One-dimensional Calorie Norms; Two-dimensional Undernutrition', Mimeo, IIES, Stockholm University.

—— *et al.* (1994), *Evaluation of Swedish Development Co-operation with Guinea-Bissau*, Stockholm, Nordsteds.

TANNER, J. M. (1976), 'Population Differences in Body Size, Shape, and Growth Rate: a 1976 View', *Archives in Disease in Childhood*, 51.

TENDLER, J. and FREEDHAIM, S. (1994), 'Trust in a Rent-Seeking World: Health and Government Transformed in Northeast Brazil', *World Development*, 22.

TEST, K. *et al.* (1987), 'Trends in Prevalence of Malnutrition in Five African Countries from Clinical Data: 1982 to 1985', *Ecology of Food and Nutrition*, 20.

THOMAS, D. and STRAUSS, J. (1992), 'Price, Infrastructure, Household Characteristics and Child Height', *Journal of Development Economics*, 39.

—— *et al.* (1990), 'Child Survival, Height for Age and Mother's Characteristics in Brazil', *Journal of Development Economics*, 33.

—— *et al.* (1991), 'How does Mother's Education Affect Child Height?', *Journal of Human Resources*, 26.

THULUVATH, P. J. and TRIGER, D. R. (1994), 'Evaluation of Nutritional Status by Using Anthropology on Adults with Alcoholic and Nonalcoholic Liver Disease', *American Journal of Clinical Nutrition*, 60.

TOMKINS, A. M. *et al.* (1986), 'Seasonal Variations in the Nutritional Status of Urban Gambian Children', *British Journal of Nutrition*, 56.

—— and F. WATSON (1989), *Malnutrition and Infection: A Review*, Nutrition Policy Discussion Paper No 5, ACC/SCN State of the Art Series.

UN (1992), *Child Mortality Since the 1960s*, New York, UN.

—— (1996), *World Population Prospects*, New York, UN.

UNCTADa (annual), *Handbook of International Trade and Development Statistics*, Geneva.

UNDPa (annual), *Human Development Report*, Vienna.

UNICEFa (annual), *The State of the World's Children*, Oxford, Oxford University Press.

UNICEF (1985b), *Within Human Reach: A Future for Africa's Children*.

—— (1993a), *Child Malnutrition: Progress Towards the World Summit for Children Goal*, New York, UNICEF.

—— (1993b), *Child Malnutrition: Country Profiles*, New York, UNICEF.

USDA*a* (occasional), *Agricultural Statistics*, Washington, DC, USDA.

VELLA, V. *et al.* (1992), 'Determinants of Child Nutrition and Mortality in North-West Uganda', *Bulletin of the World Health Organisation*, 70.

—— (1994), 'Anthropometry as a Predictor for Mortality among Ugandan Children, Allowing for Socio-Economic Variables', *European Journal of Clinical Nutrition*, 48.

WHO*a* (annual), *The World Health Report*, Geneva, WHO.

—— (1986), 'Use and Interpretation of Anthropometric Indicators of Nutritional Status', *Bulletin of the World Health Organization*, 64.

WHO (1995), Global Database on Child Growth, Geneva, WHO.

WAALER, H. T. (1984), 'Height, Weight and Mortality: The Norwegian Experience', *Acta Medica Scandinavica*, Suppl. 679.

WADDEN, J. A. *et al.* (1987), 'Less Food, Less Hunger: Reports of Appetite and Symptoms in a Controlled Study of a Protein-sparing Modified Fast', *International Journal of Obesity*, 11.

VAN DE WALLE, D. (ed.) (1995*a*), *Public Spending and the Poor*, Baltimore, Johns Hopkins University Press.

—— (1995*b*), 'Introduction' in van de Walle (1995*a*).

—— (1995*c*), 'The Distribution of Subsidies through Public Health Services in Indonesia, 1978–87', in van de Walle (1995*a*).

WATERLOW, J. C. (1972), 'Classification and Definition of Protein-Calorie Malnutrition', *British Medical Journal*, 3.

—— (1976), 'Classification and Definition of Protein-Energy Malnutrition', in G. H. Beaton and J. M. Bengoa (eds), *Nutrition in Preventive Medicine*, Geneva, WHO.

—— (1984), 'Current Issues in Nutritional Assessment by Anthropometry', in J. Brozek and B. Schürch (eds), *Malnutrition and Behavior: Critical Assessment of Key Issues*, Lausanne, Nestlé Foundation.

—— (ed.) (1988), *Linear Growth Retardation in Less Developed Countries*, Nestlé Nutrition Workshop Series, Vol. 14, New York, Raven Press.

—— (1989*a*), 'Observations on the FAO's Methodology for Estimating the Incidence of Undernutrition', *Food and Nutrition Bulletin*, 11.

—— (1989*b*), 'Nutritional Adaptation and Variability: Three Comments on the Paper by Professor P. V. Sukhatme', *European Journal of Clinical Nutrition*, 43.

—— (1990*a*), 'Mechanisms of Adaptation to Low Energy Intakes', in G. A. Harrison and Waterlow, J. C. (eds), *Diet and Disease in Transitional and Developing Societies*, Cambridge, Cambridge University Press.

—— (1990*b*), 'Nutritional Adaptation in Man: General Introduction and Concepts', *American Journal of Clinical Nutrition*, 51.

—— (1992), *Protein Energy Malnutrition*, London, Edward Arnold.

—— and Tomkins, A. M. (1992), 'Nutrition and Infection', in Waterlow (1992).

WEALE, M. (1993), 'A Critical Evaluation of the Rate of Return Analysis', *Economic Journal*, 103.

WEYLAND, K. (1996), 'Social Movements and the State: The Politics of Health Reform in Brazil', *World Development*, 23.

WHITE, H. (1980), 'A Heteroskedasticity Consistent Covariance Matrix Estimator and a Direct Test of Heteroskedasticity', *Econometrica*, 48.

YAMBI, O. *et al.* (1991), 'Nutrition Status and the Risk of Mortality in children 6–36 Months Old in Tanzania', *Food and Nutrition Bulletin*, 13.

YEATS, A. J. (1990), 'On the Accuracy of Economic Observation', *World Bank Economic Review*, 4.

YOUNG, A. (1995), 'The Tyranny of Numbers: Confronting the Statistical Realities of the East Asian Growth Experience', *Quarterly Journal of Economics*, 110.

ZARKOVICH, S. R. (1975), 'Agricultural Statistics and Multisubject Household Surveys', in FAO, *Studies in Agricultural Economics and Statistics. 1952–77*, Rome, FAO.

ZWI, A. B. and MILLS, A. (1995), 'Health Sector Reforms: Key Issues in Less Developed Countries', *Journal of International Development*, 7.

INDEX OF NAMES

GENERAL INDEX